PROFILES
IN
ETHNOLOGY

PROFILES IN ETHNOLOGY

REVISED EDITION

ELMAN R. SERVICE
UNIVERSITY OF CALIFORNIA AT SANTA BARBARA

HARPER & ROW, PUBLISHERS
NEW YORK, EVANSTON, SAN FRANCISCO, LONDON

The part-opening photographs are from the following sources: *frontispiece*, Australian News & Information Bureau; *page 1*, Canadian Consulate General; *pages 89, 205, 291*, The American Museum of Natural History; *page 387*, United Nations.

This book was originally published under the title
A Profile of Primitive Culture

Standard Book Number: 06–045911–5

LIBRARY OF CONGRESS CATALOG CARD NUMBER: 73–144241

To Ethnological Field Workers

Contents

PART III. CHIEFDOMS

PART IV. PRIMITIVE STATES

PART V. MODERN FOLK SOCIETIES

Author's Note

The decision to publish a paperback edition offers the opportunity to make some revisions in the text. These changes consist mainly of reducing the length and complexity of the two former *Prefaces* by separating them into a *Preface* and a *Conclusion*. Additionally, some of the individual chapters have been re-edited and the concluding sections, which relate the society to the modern world, have been updated and expanded, as have most of the bibliographies.

ACKNOWLEDGMENTS

Every chapter has been read critically by anthropologists who have specialized knowledge of the society in question. The book owes a great deal to the suggestions of the following colleagues: David F. Aberle, Robert Anderson, Richard K. Beardsley, Junius Bird, David W. Brokensha, Robert Carneiro, James B. Christensen, Gertrude E. Dole, E. Kathleen Gough, June Helm, Richard S. MacNeish, John V. Murra, Robert Redfield, Marshall D. Sahlins, Judy Samonte, William D. Schorger, William Taylor, Mischa Titiev, and Grace L. Wood.

Professor Morton H. Fried of Columbia University and my wife, Helen, deserve special mention and my deepest gratitude for the hard work they did on large parts of the manuscript—and above all for intelligent counsel and encouragement.

Preface

Mankind is proceeding toward greater and greater homogeneity —racially, culturally, and linguistically. In this process the world's ancient cultures are disappearing. Some are simply dying out or being exterminated; some are undergoing radical changes as they become involved in various kinds of functional relationships with the expanding industrial civilizations; others are being ethnically assimilated.

Most anthropologists seem to react similarly to this phenomenon —they feel disheartened, sad, or even helplessly angry. First, of course, our sympathies are aroused by the frequent suffering of the people, and by the realization that much of it is caused by the ignorance and sometimes the cruelty with which "civilized" peoples have treated them. Another feeling, less often verbalized—perhaps because it is less emotional and less immediately humanitarian—is a sense of the great loss to human knowledge, to art, history, and particularly to science, as these cultures disappear. In pre-industrialized societies we can see certain analogies to the long-vanished prehistory of mankind as a whole, and we can observe the particular ways in which customs, social systems, and even religions adapt to differing conditions of environment, to unique historical situations, and to technological developments. Modern man is losing this living evidence of his own past; at the same time he is losing the laboratory which this diversity provides.

Travel can broaden the mind, as everyone knows. To see different places and customs, however briefly, can destroy some provincial attitudes or beliefs. What is education but a widening of experience, an appreciation of the varieties and similarities of things beyond those which can be experienced locally at first hand? If one of the most important educational experiences consists of knowing personally a strange nation or city or person—Scotland, Paris, a Hindu —what an intellectual shock (not merely experience) is produced by living intimately with a truly primitive people! Thus the visitor discovers in the startling contrasts the meaning of the concept of *culture,* and is stimulated by the recognition of cultural differences to an effort to understand them. It is natural to wonder at strangeness and to query the whys and wherefores of ways different from our own. In undertaking to answer these queries the anthropologist learns to evaluate a person's explanation of his customs with the same objectivity with which he records the observed behavior itself. And if we learn to see our own civilization with the same detached attitude, then the familiar things, our everyday customs and their rationale as well, become strange, too. This new objectivity means essentially that the cataracts of ethnocentrism are removed from our eyes.

Reading is only a substitute for direct experience, but ethnology can be grasped to some extent in the library. For this reason teachers of anthropology encourage or require students to read intensively about some particular tribe. The student is taught also to understand something of the vast range of culture over the earth. This book is an attempt to provide the means for the latter kind of study by presenting a sample of the major types of non-Western cultures.

What are the major types? What are the most striking ways in which cultures differ? It would seem that there have been three great determinants, or variables, which in combination account for the most significant and most distinctive cultural differences in the world.

First, we find societies at widely varying levels of cultural and social complexity. Some are lowly hunters and gatherers with a simple *band* type of social organization. Others are hunters in a rich environment, or horticulturalists and pastoralists with a larger society compounded of several segments, forming a *tribe.* A few societies reached a productivity which permitted large populations and a hierarchical form of centralized leadership or *chiefdom*. Out of chiefdoms in some areas a more complex *state* organization developed. Finally, some are peasant or folk communities, local rural subcultures within contemporary national states. The primary consideration, then, has been to select societies that illustrate these five levels or stages of complexity.

Second, all cultures are affected in some measure by characteristics of the habitats they occupy. For this reason societies have been selected to include at each level those whose geographic environments differ radically.

A third kind of cultural diversity could be called historical. Any society has continuing contacts with other societies, and some parts of its culture may be derived or diffused from the neighboring cultures. Many of these traits are relatively non-adaptive, which is to say that their presence cannot be explained in terms of the functional requirements of a certain technology, social system, or habitat. Elements of ritual, ornamentation, design, dance, music, etiquette, and language, for example, have special characteristics in one area that are not found in another, however similar the environment and level of productivity. Regions inhabited by contiguous societies with a similarity in customs of this kind are called *culture areas*. It is presumed that the traditions are shared among the several groups because of a common historical association. Any given society, then, will have certain cultural attributes that are present simply because of its participation in a wider historical continuum of particular traditions.

Whenever possible, within the limitations of the first two criteria of selection, societies that are central or typical examples of distinct culture areas have been chosen in preference to special cases or marginal groups. Thus the Tahitians are described for Polynesia rather than the equally interesting Samoans, Maori, Hawaiians, or Marquesans; the Nootka for the North American Northwest Coast rather than the more famous Kwakiutl; the Cheyenne for the North American Plains rather than the well-known Dakota, Crow, or Omaha; and the Canadian Copper Eskimo rather than an Alaskan or Greenland group.

It was not always possible to adhere to these criteria. Some societies that would have made excellent examples had to be excluded because they have not been described completely enough.

And a few groups, such as the Arunta, the Trobrianders, and the Navaho, are included—although they are not typical of a culture area—because they have been so well described that they have become classic in anthropological literature.

Part V, "Modern Folk Societies," represents the greatest departure of the present work from its predecessors. Anthropological interest in the non-industrialized areas of the contemporary world is quite recent, but this subject is being studied increasingly, and it is desirable that students be introduced to it. Field studies in some of these areas are still rare, however, and the selections could not be made on the basis of the criteria used for bands, tribal societies, and primitive states. The main consideration is to exhibit wide geographic distribution among the four societies so that they would provide samples of four great contemporary streams of civilization. The book represents, to some extent, rural or folk aspects of Hindu, Moslem, Chinese, and European cultures. Needless to say, these are not descriptions of the nations and civilizations. The folk community is merely one local (and not necessarily typical) manifestation of only the rural phase of these civilizations. But these community studies are the contributions of ethnological field work; other aspects of contemporary civilizations are studied by such disciplines as history, economics, sociology, and the humanities. The particular kinds of contributions made by anthropological field studies are distinctive and present a perspective on civilizations or nations not provided by any other discipline.

An effort has been made to organize each chapter in such a way that the reader will see *real* differences in culture and not merely reflections of divergent interests on the part of various ethnographers. This has been a difficult and not fully attainable goal. Some monographs used in this collection have good material, for example, on ethos or world view, whereas the world view of other societies may not have been adequately described. The reader should not assume from this that only certain peoples have an ethos while others do not. In other cases, material on such topics as prehistory, child training, or acculturation is not available, but within the limitations of the literature an effort has been made to include comparable data.

Each topic is treated briefly in order to cover 21 societies. This means, of course, that depth is sacrificed. Most of the details regarding physical type and language have been omitted, and descriptions of ceremonies, ritual, mythology, and art are brief and very general. The student should be encouraged to consult the bibliographies that follow each chapter for further reading on matters of special interest to him.

So that each culture will not seem unique or strikingly unusual to the student, a brief description of the culture area to which the society pertains has been sketched in. Thus similarities as well as differences among cultures are apparent. For this reason, too, the generality of a given trait in the world as a whole has been frequently indicated. When data permit, some prehistory of each society has been described; at the end of each chapter the society's place in the modern world and its probable future are briefly considered.

Most of the chapters are written in the *ethnographic present,* a violation of the normal use of tenses which may well confuse a reader not accustomed to ethnological works. The present tense is used, but it refers to the period the monographs actually describe, no matter the changes that have occurred since then. In the chapters on the Inca and Maya the past tense is used because these cultures have not been described ethnologically, but as reconstructions from archaeological remains and historical archives. Chan Kom, though studied ethnologically by Robert Redfield in 1930, is described in past tense in order that a rather long description of the more modern society, derived from Redfield's second study in 1948, could be contrasted with it. Chan Kom is one of the few societies that has been studied by the same observer at two separate stages of culture change.

Elman R. Service

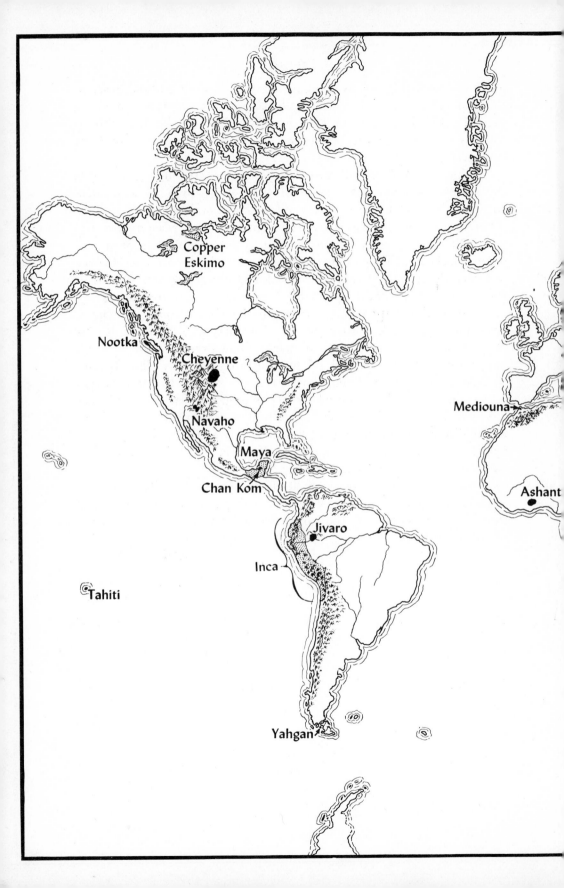

Copper
Eskimo

Nootka

Cheyenne

Navaho

Maya

Chan Kom

Jivaro

Inca

Tahiti

Yahgan

Mediouna

Ashant

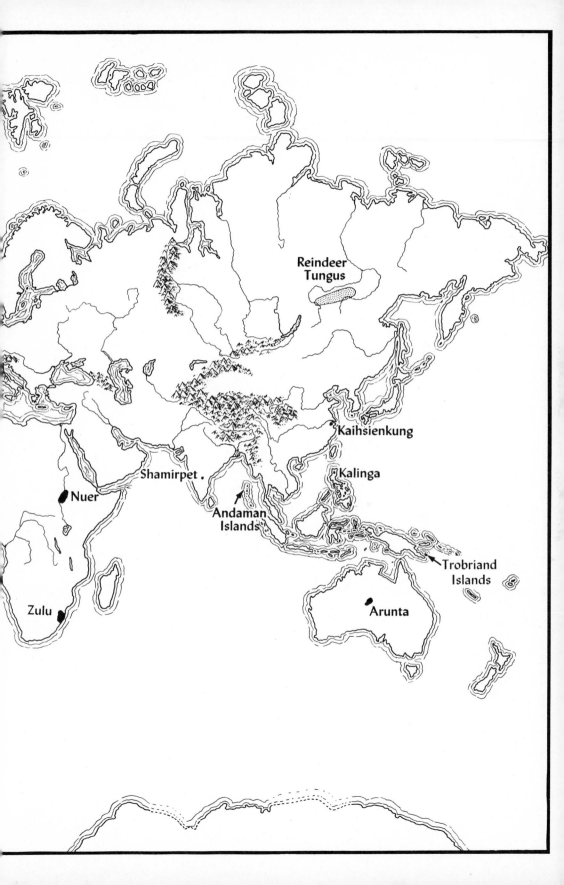

Reindeer
Tungus

Kaihsienkung

Kalinga

Shamirpet .

Nuer

Andaman
Islands

Trobriand
Islands

Zulu

Arunta

PROFILES
IN
ETHNOLOGY

PART I

BANDS

The Arunta
of Australia

Australia is the present home and refuge of creatures, often crude and quaint, that have elsewhere passed away and given place to higher forms. This applies equally to the aboriginal as to the platypus and kangaroo. Just as the platypus, laying its eggs and feebly suckling its young, reveals a mammal in the making, so does the Aboriginal show us, at least in broad outline, what early man must have been like before he learned to read and write, domesticate animals, cultivate crops, and use a metal tool. It has been possible to study in Australia human beings that still remain on the culture level of men of the Stone Age.[1]

This is the way Sir Baldwin Spencer begins his preface to the classic study of the natives of central Australia.

Australia has always been of great interest to natural scientists because of its long geographic isolation from the rest of the world. Here have been preserved early kinds of life forms which, in other parts of the earth, did not survive the struggle for existence. The landscape is characterized by plants which are survivors of ancient floral elements—types which were once more widely distributed but which were crowded into extinction by the spread of newer types in the other land masses. Australia is also the habitat of curious kinds of animals which represent early forms of mammalian evolution. The platypus, or duckbill, seems to be a

[1] Baldwin Spencer and F. J. Gillen, *The Arunta: A Study of a Stone Age People,* Vol. 1, London, 1927, p. vii. Most of the material in this chapter is from this source.

3

survival that is a kind of missing link between reptiles and mammals. The marsupials—kangaroos, wombats, opossums, and related animals—are also modern representatives of early mammalian forms.

No one knows when man first arrived in Australia. He probably came over an early land bridge from New Guinea and the chain of islands connecting it with the mainland of Asia, for this seems to be the only feasible route. The distinctive physical features of the Australians ally them with small groups now found surviving in out-of-the-way places in Ceylon, Malaya, the East Indies, and New Guinea, and this also suggests a movement of peoples between Asia and Australia.

In general, the Australian natives are chocolate brown in skin color; the mouth region projects somewhat and is rather wide; and the nose is wide at the nostrils. These are common Negroid features. But the Australian also has such typically Caucasoid features as wavy, rather than kinky, hair; facial and body hairiness; heavy brow ridges; and a depression at the root of the nose. Most physical anthropologists would not characterize him as a mixture of the two races, however, but rather as a member of a distinctive group more ancient than either of these—the Australoids.

The Stone Age culture of Australia has general features which once existed among primitive hunters elsewhere. The Australians had no access to the various neolithic inventions which diffused widely in the more populated parts of the earth. And furthermore, one wonders if they could have used most of them, considering the nature of the desert environment of central Australia, for agriculture is impossible in most parts, even with modern technology. The only domesticated animal was the native dog, the *dingo,* which was completely useless, even in hunting. Large groups of people could not be supported, and many late human inventions, such as mathematics, writing, calendrical systems, state bureaucracies—all of them products of urban life—were not suggested or necessitated by the Australian mode of existence. The wonder is that human life could be maintained at all in such an unpromising habitat.

The Australians were able to survive because they had acquired over a very long period of time a distinctive way of life, a culture, which geared their human needs with the distinctive properties of their habitat. Everything about this culture, from the technical

4

means of acquiring food from a niggardly nature to the codes of social living—the kinship system, rules of etiquette, beliefs and sentiments, religious ceremonies—seems to have been a functional apparatus which was nearly the ultimate in efficiency for survival under the conditions imposed by the nature of the Australian habitat and the limitations of the native tool kit.

Courtesy, The American Museum of Natural History

Australia is the smallest continent (or the largest island) in the world. Its area is nearly 3 million square miles, approximately the size of the United States. Geological and climatic forces have produced a relatively uniform surface over much of the land, because the ancient rock has been worn down and the lowlands filled in. Wind- and water-laid deposits cover much of the interior; Australia lies half-buried under the products of its own decay. The rim of Australia warps up like the edge of a great platter, with the result that more than half of the land surface has only internal, or basin, drainage, and much of the remainder has no regular surface drainage at all.

Because Australia is surrounded by large expanses of water, the coastal climate is fairly uniform, but temperature ranges increase toward the interior because of the largeness of the land area. In central Australia noontime shade temperatures of 110° to 113° Fahrenheit may be followed by freezing night temperatures. The climate in the interior is very dry, however, and the heat is thus more bearable than might be imagined.

Australia is bisected by the tropic of Capricorn, and lies in a transition zone between two major rain regions. This position gives Australia a large area of low rainfall, though the highlands in the east cause precipitation along the eastern rim. The coastal regions have from 40 to 60 inches annually, with the typical precipitation being irregular and torrential. The amount of rainfall decreases progressively toward the interior, where it is 10 inches or less and markedly irregular from year to year, some droughts having persisted for years. During the dry periods, the interior gives an impression of almost utter desolation, so very sparse and stunted is the vegetation. After a rain, however, the clay and sand plains flower with the glory of amazingly sudden growths of desert flowers, grasses, and herbs, which almost as quickly vanish after a few days. This vegetation is, for the most part, seasonal grasses and permanent scrub, among which various acacias are common.

It should not be surprising that Australia was sparsely populated in aboriginal times. A. P. Elkin calculated that in the year of European contact, 1788, there were only about 300,000 natives. The greatest concentration was in the coastal areas, with central Australia the most desolate and least populated part of all. Here the people had to live very dispersed, and they had to range widely to take advantage of the brief local variations in the times of seeding of wild grasses and the migrations of game.

The largest dialect division in central Australia was that of the Arunta,[2] who numbered about 2000 before 1896, when the famous study of them was made by Spencer and Gillen. The area in

[2] This group is sometimes called *Aranda,* but Spencer and Gillen called them *Arunta* and this precedent has been followed here.

which the Arunta ranged was almost exactly the central region of Australia, from the Macumba River north beyond the Macdonnell Ranges, a distance of about 400 miles. They are considered typical of the natives of interior Australia in most respects. The present account will describe Arunta culture in the ethnographic present of Spencer and Gillen's investigation; that is, as though we were observers in 1896.

The Arunta, like the other Australian natives, face their environment with a meager assortment of crude weapons and tools. Even the bow and arrow, which is so important among primitive hunters of other parts of the world, is unknown in Australia. The Arunta depend wholly on boomerangs, clubs, and spears. Added velocity and accuracy are given to the spear through the use of the wooden spear-thrower, an extension of the throwing arm which works on the same principle as a sling. The women use crude pointed sticks in digging roots and tubers. Cooking utensils are unknown; either food is eaten raw, or it is roasted directly on the embers of an open fire or baked on flat stones. The Arunta make neither pottery nor baskets; large articles are carried in netted string bags, and for smaller items, such as seeds, the shallow, troughlike wooden or bark *pitchi* is used.

A few simple cutting tools are made of local quartzite or diorite obtained from neighboring tribes. Stone tools are usually equipped with some sort of handle, although this is frequently no more than a coating of porcupine-grass resin or beeswax on one end of the tool. The most complex handle is a piece of wood joined to the stone by these plastic materials. Even axes, the only tool which may be said to be produced by specialists, are hafted poorly, and a single hard blow will loosen the blade from its handle.

The Arunta eat almost all of the kinds of animal or plant life found in their habitat. Women and children scour the vicinity of the camp for seeds and bulb roots, edible fungus, eggs of both birds and reptiles, snails, *witchetty* grubs (the pupae of cossid moths), caterpillars, beetles, *amunga* flies, honey ants, and any reptiles or burrowing rodents that they can capture. The men specialize in hunting the larger animals, such as the kangaroo and the related wallaby, the large ostrichlike emu, and smaller birds and animals.

Inasmuch as the spear is the only weapon used in hunting the larger animals, the hunter needs a great deal of stalking skill. Kangaroos are usually hunted by several men in cooperation, one remaining in ambush while the others drive the wary prey in his direction. In hunting the emu, it is a common practice for the hunter to attract the bird by dressing in a rude disguise which resembles the head and long neck of an emu. The bird seems unable to resist investigating this apparition. Sometimes emus are captured by placing

ARUNTA HUNTERS. *Courtesy, The American Museum of Natural History*

a narcotic decoction, *pituri,* in a water hole; the emu becomes stupefied and easily killed after he has drunk from the water. This bird is greatly valued by the Arunta, for it provides a large quantity of meat, prized feathers, and tendons from the long leg muscles which can be used as rope and twine. The euro, a small variety of kangaroo, and the rock wallaby, another small marsupial, tend to have definite runs; so the hunter waits immobile until one of the animals passes. Birds that assemble at the infrequent waterholes are taken by hurling the boomerang among them.

Each Arunta nuclear family unit is virtually self-sufficient economically. The only economic division of labor is by sex and age. A man, his wife, and his children provide the different kinds of labor needed for family survival. Because of various exigencies, one family may be more prosperous than another at a particular time, but rules of hospitality and generosity make for a fairly even distribution of surpluses. Giving freely is so expected, and so matter-of-fact, that the Arunta, like many primitives, accept gifts without expressing gratitude. This frequently nonpluses the Europeans in contact with them, as they mistakenly think the people therefore do not appreciate gifts.

The Arunta have no techniques for storing and preserving foods; consequently they do not try to acquire large surpluses. The quest for food is sporadic rather than unremitting, because a good-sized kill lasts a small camp for several days, and there is no point in hunting more game until the food at hand is nearly finished. However, when there is no game to be had, there is no point in hunting it— hence the common statements that the Arunta appear to have no thought for the morrow and that they philosophically tighten their belts. Much of the time, therefore, the Arunta are inactive. This is not simple laziness, of course, but a response to external circumstances. The size of the social unit, the limit of its possible growth, is set by the recurrent seasons of relative scarcity. When times are good, there is little to do in order to acquire sufficient food, and little *is* done except for visiting and the observance of the great seasonal ceremonial occasions, for in the absence of storage facilities, excess products of fruitful seasons cannot be carried over into the lean periods. The condition of the Arunta illustrates very well that it is not leisure which is responsible for cultural development, but quite the contrary. When consistent and higher productivity permits larger and larger population aggregates and when specialization is increased, then culture building proceeds, and with it forced idleness is diminished. The Arunta, because of their undeveloped technology, are literally one of the most leisured peoples in the world.

A typical encampment of Arunta consists of one family, or perhaps two or more brothers with their wives and children, living in crude shelters made by lacing stakes and sticks together into a low frame in the shape of a dome and thatching this frame with grass. If the camp is more temporary, the families shelter themselves from the wind and sun with a rough lean-to of shrubs. A small fire is usually kept burning in front of, or inside, the shelter, and the

Arunta mother carrying a digging stick and pitchi. *Courtesy, The American Museum of Natural History*

people huddle close around it. Despite the often bitter night cold, the Arunta have no clothing or wraps to cover themselves with in sleep.

The few things the Arunta wear are for decoration only—a small pubic apron for a woman and a small pubic tassel of fur string for a male; a belt of human hair, nose bones, and head and neck bands complete the ensemble for ordinary nonceremonial occasions. Sometimes ocher or pipeclay is used to make designs on the body, and scarification of the body is widely practiced, as is the custom of knocking out an incisor tooth on certain ceremonial occasions. Hair is pulled out of the forehead, giving an unnaturally high appearance to the brow.

The small migrating families feel themselves to be part of a larger whole, which has been called the *local group* or *horde* by anthropologists. This is a unity of related families who range over a territory felt to belong to themselves alone. This group is exogamous and patrilocal, which is to say that a member of the group is compelled to marry someone from a different local group and that a married couple resides in the territory of the husband's local group. The significance of this custom is that the children grow up in the locality of their father's group (hence the term *patrilocality*), and the group is thus made up of people related in a male, or patrilineal, line of descent.

In a person's own group, therefore, might be found his father and his father's father, his brother, and in time his son, his son's son, and all the brothers and all the unmarried sisters and wives of these men. The missing relatives are, of course, the married sisters of the men, who have had to go to live with their husbands' groups, and the children of these sisters. Other local groups thus contain, in addition to a person's sisters and her children (consanguineal relatives), certain affinal, or in-law, relatives. In one of these groups are found the mother's patrilineal relatives, the mother's brother and all his male ancestors and descendants. The father's brothers, as well as the father, probably married women from this group, and, conversely, the mother's brothers are likely to marry women from the father's group.

Ideally, a system of marriage exchange prevails, by which a man marries a female second cross cousin—his mother's mother's brother's daughter's daughter—and his own sisters marry the brothers of his wife. His wife comes, then, from a patrilineal group which contains his mother's mother's brothers' patrilineal relatives, which is a different group, though related, from the group his father married into. In this fashion several local groups are tied together by kin relationships of varying degrees, reinforced and stabilized by affinal ties resulting from the rule of marriage.

There is no other kind of organization, political or social, to unify the people. It is on this account that the people who roam over hundreds of square miles must pay so much attention to matters of kinship. Not only is this relationship, fictional or real, the only mechanism of intergroup unity, but various *kinds* of relationship serve as guides to interpersonal conduct, or etiquette.

Etiquette, in its broadest sense, is extremely important in a society which has no binding division of labor, no law courts or policemen, and whose unifying principles are thus completely personal. Troubles between individuals can be settled only by feuds, and feuds by their nature tend to perpetuate themselves. A society could fall to pieces unless such disorders were kept to a minimum. Under such circumstances, traditional rules of social conduct must be rigidly observed.

Like many other primitive peoples of the world, the Arunta conventionally address one another by terms denoting kinship. Personal names are secret, and even nicknames are not used socially. But also, as is the case with many other primitives, the kinship terms do not distinguish the same degrees of relationship that Euro-American peoples are accustomed to. In general, a person may refer to several individuals by the same term when the conditions of their *social* relationship to the speaker call for similar behavioral etiquette. Thus a term which might be translated *wife* refers not only to the actual wife but also to all the females of the category of relatives from which a man would be allowed to select a wife. All of their mothers are also designated by one single term, and their fathers by another. Grandparents and grandchildren address one another reciprocally by the same term. The children of brothers are treated equivalently, as are the children of sisters.

The pattern of kinship categories distinguished by the Arunta belongs to a type widespread among primitive peoples who practice local exogamy and patrilocal residence. Its most unusual feature, from a European's point of view, is that aunts and uncles, cousins, and nephews and nieces are each differentiated into two types. A paternal uncle (father's brother) is designated by the same term as the father, but a maternal uncle (mother's brother) is designated by a special term. Similarly, one's mother and her sisters are categorized by the same term, but one's father's sister is distinguished by a separate term. This may be diagramed as follows, with English words used to signify the elements of the classification:

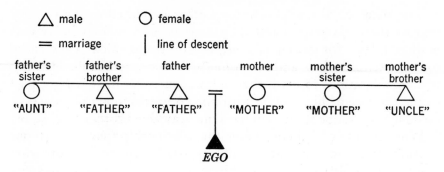

Cousins of *ego,* children of the relatives designated in the diagram above, are similarly divided into two types, one of which is merged with *ego's* lineal group, following the pattern set above. In anthropological terminology, those in *ego's* lineal group are called *parallel cousins,* while those distinguished from them (mother's brother's and father's sister's children) are called *cross cousins.*

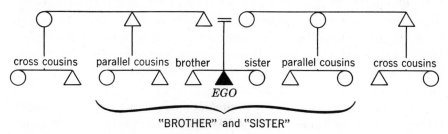

Relatives in *ego's* children's generation are also separated into the parallel category and the cross category. The diagram below shows the parallels in *ego's* local group. It is obvious that a difference in social propinquity is correlated with the separation of parallel relatives from cross relatives.

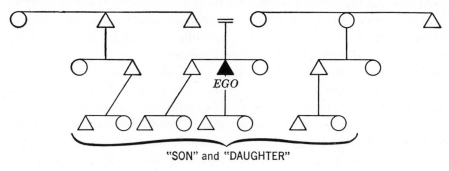

The behavior of one person to another is related to the recognition of these categories and their counterparts among in-laws. A mother-in-law, for example, must be strictly avoided; easy social contact between a man and his mother-in-law is unthinkable. He owes certain obligations to his father-in-law, especially in sharing a part of the produce of his hunting with him. A brother-in-law (actual or possible) cannot be treated in the same way as a brother, and so on.

When people who do not know the relationship they have to one another meet, an important problem arises, for serious breaches in etiquette could result. A kinship system is an *egocentric* system, which is to say that *ego,* any given person, applies the proper term and adopts the proper behavior toward another person on the basis of his understanding of that person's relationship to himself. When the range of people met is wide and the meetings are infrequent, it is difficult, and often impossible, for two people to determine the kinship terms they should use to address one another. If all important interpersonal relations can be solved only in terms of kinship, then some way of setting up named objective categories is useful. Such categories must be permanent; an individual must be a member from birth to death. Thus a limited number of categories of people is established which summarizes the kin system into objective groups on the basis of the most important criteria.

One important way of distinguishing people is on the basis of their membership in one or the other of the two groups which intermarry—one is *in-law* to the other. Distinguishing people in this way is a widespread primitive custom and is usually called the *moiety* system. Several Australian societies which have named these two groups have what is often called a *two-class system.* This is an exceedingly simple and obvious division which, from *ego's* point of view, merely separates his father's local relatives from his mother's and then develops this system to include all relatives in one or the other half. A first requisite on meeting a stranger is to decide whether he will receive the in-law treatment or not.

Another obvious way of dividing a society into two named parts is by separating the adjacent generations of people. Thus one's own generation is distinguished from one's father's generation and one's son's generation, but it is not separated from one's grandfathers' and one's grandsons' generations. Some Australians have a two-class system which is the result of naming these adjacent generations.[3] Those which have a *four-class system* have combined the naming of the moieties with the separation of the adjacent generations, thus creating four named groups. These are objective summaries of the kinship system, which universally recognize the distinction between in-law groups and which prescribe the etiquette of respect and avoidances to be observed between members of adjacent generations. This second distinction, like the first, receives widespread recognition in primitive kinship systems in the use of reciprocal terms between people of alternate generations. It is important to understand, as A. R. Radcliffe-Brown has pointed out, that all of the Australians (and, in fact, a great many other primitive peoples) have these four groupings implicit in their social order, even if they have not explicitly named the groups.

The southern branch of the Arunta has named these four groups, but the northern Arunta have named eight categories of relatives. The additional criterion which subdivides the original four is the separation of first cross cousins from second cross cousins. Among the Arunta a man should take his wife normally from the group of mother's mother's brother's daughter's daughters. In a four-class system, one and only one of the four classes of relatives would include (for *ego*) marriageable persons, but it would also include first cross cousins (e.g., mother's brother's daughters) who could *not* marry *ego*. The *eight-class system* makes the separation of first and second cross cousins, and it has significance, of course, not only in the contracting of marriage but also in the important social behavior and avoidances which accompany it.

A four-class system may be diagrammed as follows to demonstrate the relationship of one category to another in terms of generation and the marriage rule. Arunta names for the divisions are used.

	Moiety A		Moiety B
Generation I	Panunga	⟷	Purula
	↑		↑
Generation II	Bultara	⟷	Kamara

Horizontal arrows refer to marriage, and vertical arrows to inheritance of membership. A *Panunga* man has *Bultara* children, and a Bultara man has Panunga children; a *Purula* man has *Kam-*

---

[3] A great many primitive societies emphasize generational distinctions above all others. See Chapters 3 and 7.

ara children, and vice versa. The eight-class system is merely a subdivision of the foregoing, and not a particularly difficult division to make, inasmuch as the second cross cousins actually live in a different local group from the first cross cousins.

If a class system such as this is implicit in most kinship systems based on cross-cousin marriage, why then have only certain groups taken the step of actually naming the classes? Elkin has suggested that the many intergroup meetings for trade and ceremonies contribute to the use of these names:

> It is much easier for one group to learn the other's subsection system (class system) than to bother about all its kinship terms, and so mutual behavior during the gatherings is largely controlled by the subsection groupings, but only, of course, because fundamentally this is a grouping of kinship relations. . . . There is little doubt that the practical usefulness of the system at meetings of an intertribal character is the cause of its spread. . . .[4]

It seems that the class groupings are used only when necessary as simplifications, substituted for the kinship terms which are normally used. As Radcliffe-Brown describes it:

> The relationships between one person and another in the kinship system are individual relationships. In deciding what they are, appeal is always made to actual genealogical connection. Thus in western Australia the first question always asked of a stranger is who is your father's father? Similarly in all discussions as to the suitability of a proposed marriage it is the genealogical connection between the two persons that is considered. It is true that when the genealogical tie is too remote to be traced the natives fall back on a consideration of the section or subsection or the clan to which an individual belongs, but this does not alter the fact that in the minds of the natives themselves they are dealing throughout all the ramifications of the system, with real genealogical relations of parent and child or sibling and sibling.[5]

It is possible, and probable, that the large gatherings of people at certain times in central Australia and their extraordinary dispersion the rest of the time are the circumstances that dictate the use of the named classes of relatives—people meet for long periods and need to know the basic kinship distinctions to apply, but in their ordinary travels they are so remote from one another that they do not learn the specific positions they hold with respect to one another.

[4] A. P. Elkin, *The Australian Aborigines,* 3rd ed., Sydney and London, 1954, p. 101.
[5] A. R. Radcliffe-Brown, "The Social Organization of Australian Tribes," *The Oceania Monographs,* No. 1, Melbourne, 1931, p. 104. One may question the use of the expression *real genealogical* relations, and substitute *social.*

This circumstance obtains throughout central Australia, but in the coastal regions, where the population is less dispersed and the wandering is less extensive, the people use the more intimate kin terms rather than class names.

Arunta society has a further feature which is fairly usual in the primitive world; a religious concept serves as a rationale and buttress for the social order in a form known to anthropologists as *totemism*. All of the members of a local group consider themselves descendants of a particular kind of plant or animal, the totem. All of the various totems have spiritual residing places, *totem centers*, somewhere in the territory of the local group to which they pertain, and this is also the residing place of the spirits of the human ancestral members of the lineage. When a woman who has married into a particular local group becomes pregnant, the belief is that her impregnation was caused by a spirit from the local totem center which entered her body. Thus a child born into a local group is tied to that locality forever because it is the residing place of his progenitor, the ancestral spirit. A child's father is a *social* father, not the progenitor. This attitude is so firmly fixed among the Australians that it has caused controversies among observers about whether the role of sexual intercourse in conception is understood.

A person is a life member of the totemic lineage, and *home* is the locality of the totem, even in the case of women who go elsewhere to live after marriage. Thus the totemic idea, bolstered by elaborate ceremonies and rituals, plays an important role in explaining and thereby strengthening the social integration of people who are together only by the accident of place of birth. The local economic and social group becomes a religious community as well.[6]

[6] The above is in part a reconstruction of Arunta totemism rather than the situation as described by Spencer and Gillen. Among most of the natives of Australia each local group had one totem center, and the members therefore constituted a totemic lineage or *clan*. The Arunta system was apparently somewhat disturbed, however, by the time Spencer and Gillen observed it. Some Arunta local groups had more than one totem center, so that membership in a local group was not always the same as membership in a totemic group. Contact with Western civilization, with its diseases and economic dislocations, often has the effect of disrupting the functional balance of land occupancy and social organization and their religious and ritual appurtenances. Nevertheless, the majority of individuals in a local group did belong to the same totem. (See Spencer and Gillen, *op. cit.,* Vol. 1, p. 370.) Certainly this is the way things were supposed to be, for the important *alchipa* origin myth of the Arunta describes how the spirit ancestor-creator Numbakulla taught the people about the totem centers and how ultimately the countryside became dotted with local groups, each with the proper totem center associated with it.

In the absence of formal political organization among the Arunta, older men, respected for their age and wisdom, make more of the community decisions than do younger people, but there is no agency to enforce their wishes, and they are actually advisers rather than rulers. People obey tribal etiquette and customs largely because of the force of public opinion. In case of serious breaches of order, such as murder, the aggrieved family reciprocates with vengeance against the supposed murderer or his group. Warfare in the sense of organized intertribal struggle is unknown. What fighting there is, is better understood as an aspect of juridical procedure than as war. If a group, or family, feels wronged by an outside individual, it organizes an expedition to avenge the wrong. It is important to realize, however, that arbitration usually occurs instead of actual fighting; and the elders of both sides may confer and reach a decision. The wrongdoer's own group may actually aid in his punishment. In general, observers from Western civilization have been struck by the friendliness and hospitality of the Australians.

In ceremonial affairs, some sort of leadership is necessary because of the intricate coordination required of individuals and groups. Each totemic group has a leader, called the *inkata,* who takes charge of the occasional ceremonies. These ceremonies are held by the totemic groups from time to time in order to increase the fertility and well-being of the plant or animal they represent. In this fashion an important quasi-economic division of labor is maintained which promotes an interdependence among the various groups, for if a group failed to function ceremonially at appropriate intervals, it is believed that the particular food species they represent would perish.

The inkata is the caretaker of the local group's totemic center, which serves also as the storehouse where are kept the fetishes in which reside the spirits of the members, including the ancestors, of the group. Each member of the local group has one of these fetishes, called *churinga,* stored there, but only men who have been initiated are allowed to see them. The churinga are usually flat, oval pieces of wood or stone, carved with symbolic designs. Some have a hole near one end, so that they may be attached to a string and whirled in the air. The weird whirring noise made by these *bullroarers* is understood by women and children to be made by the spirits, and it serves as a sign that important rites are going on and that noninitiates should keep away.

The great ceremonies which are carried out to promote the increase of the totem are called *mbanbiuma* ceremonies. They are held normally at the time of year at which the particular totem species produces fruit or seed or gives birth to its young. The ceremonies of each group differ greatly from one another in detail, but in all of them the following features are common:

1. The heart of the ceremony is the special and very detailed ritual performance which helps increase the numbers of the totem species.

2. The inkata must eat a little of the species, as a sort of communion service.

3. Then the other members of the group ritually and sparingly eat a little of it.

4. After this, other people who are present (but who have not witnessed the secret ceremony) feast freely on the totem.

The occasion may attract people from a very wide area, and the exchanging of gifts takes place among groups which are ordinarily widely separated. Sacred churinga may be lent to other groups for certain ceremonial purposes. In general, visiting groups are received hospitably, especially if they are accompanied by women and children.

Much of the ceremonialism of Arunta life is associated with the education and socialization of children, beginning at birth and reaching a climax at the time of their initiation as full-fledged adults. Abortion is practiced only under rare circumstances. Infanticide is also rare, but twins are always killed, because they are assumed to be very unnatural. Normally, a child is born easily and accepted casually into the family. The afterbirth is burned, and the umbilical cord is made into a necklace for the child. The paternal grandfather and certain other elders from the group take a piece of wood or stone from near the totem center and secretly fashion for the child its personal churinga, which they deposit with the others. The child receives two names, a personal name and a secret, sacred name which is associated with the churinga and bestowed by the old man who made the churinga. This latter name is known only to fully initiated men (never to women and children) and is used only on important ceremonial occasions. Although an individual is called either by his kinship or class term in direct address, he may be indirectly referred to by a nickname, a personal name, and on certain occasions by a status term which has reference to his age and the degree to which he has passed through the various stages and ceremonies of the life cycle.

All children are segregated with the women from the important rituals until they reach initiation age, which is near the age of puberty. Both boys and girls go through initiation rites, but those of the boys are longer and much more complex. A boy passes through four different ceremonies, which can be summarized in terms of the central rite of each one: (1) painting the boy and tossing him into the air, (2) circumcision, (3) subincision, (4) fire ordeals and bloodletting.

The first of these is a rather small ceremony involving usually only the members of the local group. The 10- to 12-year-old boys who are undergoing the ceremony are first thrown into the air several times by the men, while the women dance in a circle around them, shouting and waving their arms. Then the boys are painted ritually on their backs by their prospective brothers-in-law, and the nasal septum is pierced for the nose bone. After this ceremony, the boys have a new status term applied to them, and they join the men in their various economic activities instead of associating only with women.

Some time after the boy has reached puberty, the circumcision ceremony takes place. Food and firewood are collected and stored at a secret hideaway, and the boys are seized and carried to this spot. After ritual dancing and singing of the myths related to the ceremony, the boys' heads are wound around with strands of fur string, and a girdle made of human hair is placed around their waists. Then the boys are removed to still another hidden place, where they are instructed for three days. This period of instruction is followed by recital of tribal myths and by ritual pantomimes, and for the first time the boys are given full knowledge of the sacred lore of the tribe. After several days, the boys are circumcised in a complicated ritual, and they remain secluded in the bush until they recover. During this period a unique custom is observed; the men visit the initiates occasionally and bite their scalps several times until blood flows freely, which is believed to promote growth of the hair.

[...]mony of subincision takes place several weeks later, after [...]tely recovered from the circumcision. The men go [...]e the initiates were secluded during recovery from [...]remony, and they again relate myths and engage in [...]es, after which the initiate's penis is slit to the [...]tone knife.

BLOOD-LETTING RITUAL. *Courtesy, The American Museum of Natural History*

Several months later the great final celebration, the *Engwura,* is observed. This is the climax to the boys' admission to adulthood, and people come from great distances and even from other language groups to participate in the various mass dances and celebrations, which may last for several months if nature provides sufficient food. This last ceremony is a complicated series of fire ordeals and blood-letting ceremonies. Various totem groups carry out special rituals, and the initiates receive the ultimate knowledge of the churinga, learn their secret names, and are accepted as full adult members of the society.

Girls undergo puberty rituals which are equivalent to the first two of the boys' initiation rites. The first rite involves rubbing the girls' breasts with fat and red ocher to promote their growth. The second ceremony includes an operation to break the hymen. Later, each girl receives a new name to signify her status as a grown woman.

A man and the woman he may marry always stand in the relationship to one another of second cross cousin. Because of the manner of grouping brothers together and sisters together along with their parallel cousins under a single kinship term, there are usually several women that a man may marry under this rule. A particular wife from this group is obtained in one of four ways. Most frequently, the decision is made by the parents, often when the boy is very young and the girl is as yet unborn. Another recognized means of obtaining a wife, and one which is often efficacious even though the girl may be promised to another man, is to charm her with magic. Her coming, of course, actually depends on her acquiescence and is therefore a sort of elopement, but, because magic was used, she cannot be held responsible for her action. Actual elopement is more dangerous, for it occurs only when there is some resistance to the marriage on the part of the parents of the couple or the parents of another man who expected to be the bridegroom. Some form of retaliation is frequent and may be the beginning of a feud. The fourth kind of marriage may be called *captive marriage,* and it is the rarest of all, as well as the most dangerous. Often the women are captured in the course of a raid connected with a feud. It is noteworthy, however, that even if the woman is a member of a distant group, she must be considered a member of the kinship class proper for the capturer to marry.

The rules of marriage, it should be emphasized, pertain only to *marriage,* not to sexual intercourse. There are many circumstances in which intercourse may occur between people not of the proper relationship categories for marriage. Incest rules relating to sexual relations prevent intercourse only between a woman and her father, brother, or son. Otherwise sexual license is allowed or even encouraged during many of the important ceremonies. It is quite obvious that marriage is not regarded as a sexual matter at all, but rather as a social and economic alliance between two people so that they may aid each other and rear children in a proper household. But not any two people; they must be of the proper kinship category for marriage, because their alliance also is a significant tie between whole groups of relatives. The Arunta are a large assortment of small local groups of patrilocally allied relatives, with many kinds and degrees of genealogical and affinal ties binding them all together. The marriage rule regulates the nature of these ties and keeps them ordered in appropriate intensity and extension. Nothing else keeps the Arunta in social order. They are one huge family.

As in a family, older members of the society are treated with great respect. The very aged and the ill and helpless are provided for with care and kindness. The people do not take a person's death with equanimity, even when extreme old age or some disease was the apparent cause. It is usually blamed on the magic of some malevolent person from a distant or enemy group. A friendly medicine man determines by magic the person at fault, and some measure of vengeance is taken.

A corpse is buried immediately after death in a sitting position in a shallow round grave. The deceased's hut is burned and his few personal possessions are destroyed, and the people move to a new camp, fearful of the spirit, which is believed to stay in the vicinity of the grave until a later final ceremony is performed. People do not refer to the dead person by name during this period, and close relatives never mention him again, for the spirit might be offended at the apparent lack of grief. During the mourning period, men of the category of sons-in-law cut themselves deeply on the shoulders, and members of the group of wives (actual and possible wives— now widows) smear themselves with white pipeclay and preserve silence until the final, frenzied end-of-mourning ceremony is performed several months later. After the end-of-mourning ceremony, the actual widow becomes the wife of one of the younger brothers of the deceased. This is a means of providing for the wife and children that is so widely found in primitive societies that anthropologists use a general term, *levirate,* for this institution.

Illness, like death, is felt to be caused by magic, and the cure for illness therefore often takes the form of divining the perpetrator of the evil. The shamans, those who specialize in magic, actually have two separate functions, which may or may not be practiced by the same men. One of these is the curing of illness, usually accomplished by pretending to suck out foreign objects which were supposedly the cause of the affliction. Should the shaman fail to cure, it is believed that the person causing the illness is possessed of stronger magic. The other function of the shaman is the use of sorcery to harm another person and to divine who is responsible for a death or illness. While shamans are specialists at this sort of thing, in actuality any person may have the knowledge to cause harm by sorcery. Most deaths are assumed to be caused by an enemy who secretly points at his victim a small bone which has been enchanted at a secret ritual. Weapons are made more dangerous by singing over them. Another important magical charm is a girdle made from the hair of a dead man and inherited by his younger brother or son.

The Arunta have a variety of myths and traditions which explain the natural phenomena of the seasons, heavens, and, in fact, nearly all of nature that they perceive. They also have a mythology which explains the origin of their ancestors and their culture. These are the various traditions which deal with the creation by the ancestors of the various totemic groups in the mythical past, the *alchera* (the *dream times,* or *the dreaming*). According to most of the traditions of the alchera, the origin of men and women was caused by self-creating superhumans who appeared on the earth and made human beings from plants, animals, and natural features which are the totems of the present groups. Various of these myths also tell of the introduction of certain important tools, ceremonies, and rules of social organization or behavior.

The most important myth of all, central in the Arunta religious system, is the *alchipa* tradition, which has associated rituals performed at the height of the initiation ceremonies. The alchipa tells of the origin of the Wild Cat group and the introduction of churinga and their local storehouses, which are so important to each of the various totem groups. In the mythical dream time, there were various supernatural ancestor-creators, but it was *Numbakulla* (which means *always existing, out of nothing*) who traveled around the extensive Arunta territory creating many of the natural features of the country, the totems, the souls, churinga, and the sacred storehouses.

The original spirits associated with the churinga all come from the body of Numbakulla, and subsequently the churinga split in two, one of each pair with a man's soul, the other with a woman's soul. Each churinga also had a secret name, given originally by Numbakulla. Eventually, the souls arose from the churinga and gave rise to men and women, each with a secret name. Numbakulla explained everything to the first *inkata alchipa* (Wild Cat totem ceremonial chief) : how to carry out the various initiation ceremonies, including the rituals of circumcision and subincision, and how to make new churinga. Then he disappeared. The first Arunta had many travels and vicissitudes, richly depicted in the mythology, which tells the story of how subsequently the whole country became dotted with the present local groups and their churinga storehouses.

Nomadic aborigines perform ancient ritual dance. *Courtesy, Australian News and Information Bureau*

The coming of European colonists to Australia was a disaster for most of the aborigines. Like other non-Europeans they lacked immunity to the common diseases of the Western World, and from a population of 3–400,000 they have declined to about 50,000. The earliest and most massive encroachment of Europeans was in the south, while the central desert and northern coasts were not heavily affected until the present century, when cattle and sheep ranchers moved into these hinterlands. Nevertheless, when Spencer revisited the Arunta in the 1920s, he found that disease already had taken a terrible toll. The band of 40 people that he had been initiated into in 1896 had become extinct, as had many others. Most of the surviving Arunta were living around a mission station.

Spencer and Gillen devoted much space in their ethnography of central Australia to the Arunta graphic arts. The Arunta seem to have had more interest in developing their artistic capacities than did other central Australians and had even manufactured several coloring materials. In recent years the surviving Arunta have been encouraged to paint with modern oils and water colors, and some of them have achieved fame in Australia for their work.

FURTHER READINGS

Adam, L., "The Abstract Art of the Aranda," *Anthropos*, Vol. 55, Nos. 3–4, 1961.

Basedow, H., *The Australian Aboriginal*, Adelaide, 1925.

Davidson, D. S., "The Basis of Social Organization in Australia," *American Anthropologist*, n.s., Vol. 28, 1926.

Davidson, D. S., *The Chronological Aspects of Certain Australian Social Institutions*, Philadelphia, 1928.

Davidson, D. S., "The Family Hunting Territory in Australia," *American Anthropologist*, n.s., Vol. 30, 1928.

Elkin, A. P., "Studies in Australian Totemism," *The Oceania Monographs*, No. 2, Melbourne, 1931–1932.

Elkin, A. P., *The Australian Aborigines: How to Understand Them*, 3rd ed., Sydney, London, 1954.

Howells, W. W., *Anthropometry of the Natives of Arnhem Land and the Australian Race Problem*, Papers, Peabody Museum of American Archaeology and Ethnology, Vol. 16, Cambridge, Mass., 1937.

Mahony, D. J., "The Problem of the Antiquity of Man in Australia," *Memoirs of the National Museum*, No. 13, Melbourne, 1943.

Mathews, R. H., "Notes on the Arranda Tribe," *Journal and Proceedings of the Royal Society of New South Wales*, Vol. 41, Sydney, 1907.

Mathews, R. H., "Marriage and Descent in the Arranda Tribe, Central Australia," *American Anthropologist*, n.s., Vol. 10, 1908.

Moorehead, A., *The Fatal Impact*, New York, 1967.

Pink, O., "The Landowners in the Northern Divisions of the Aranda Tribe," *The Oceania Monographs*, No. 6, Melbourne, 1935–1936.

Radcliffe-Brown, A. R., "The Social Organization of Australian Tribes," *The Oceania Monographs*, No. 1, Melbourne, 1931.

Spencer, B., *Wanderings in Wild Australia*, London, 1928, 2 vols.

Spencer, B., and Gillen, F. J., *The Native Tribes of Central Australia*, London, 1899.

Spencer, B., and Gillen, F. J., *The Arunta: A Study of a Stone Age People*, London, 1927, 2 vols.

Strehlow, C., *Die Aranda- und Loritja Stämme in Zentral-Australien*, Frankfort on the Main, 1907–1911.

Warner, W. L., "Kinship Morphology of Forty-one Australian Tribes," *American Anthropologist*, n.s., Vol. 35, 1933.

The Yahgan
of South America

One of the world's most miserable habitats for a naked primitive people is the southern coast of the large island of Tierra del Fuego and the smaller islands stretching southward to Cape Horn, the very extremity of South America. This uttermost part of the earth, where the Andean cordillera finally dips into the Antarctic, is a fantastically labyrinthine maze of channels, islands, fiords, and steep rocky headlands. It would be difficult to find a more depressing, unpleasant climate. Much of the rugged, forbidding landscape is drenched in cold rain or sleet and shrouded with clouds and fogs. The outer shoreline of the islands is pounded by the surf of the world's stormiest ocean, and even in more protected areas the winds howl incessantly. The temperature seldom falls much below freezing, but the climate is so wet, chilly, and stormy all the year that one wonders how a relatively unsheltered people could survive it. It is sometimes mentioned in this regard that two of Captain Cook's men actually froze to death in the highlands of this territory in January (1769), when it is summer in the southern hemisphere.

The territory of the Yahgan Indians is a rather more benign microclimate than is that of the rest of the region, but, nevertheless,

Europeans were always astonished by the hardiness of the Indians. Usually completely unclothed and often with no shelter except rude brush huts, they seemed quite at ease. Even in the worst weather the Indian women dove without hesitation into the marrow-chilling waters to bring up the shellfish that were their customary food.

The population of the Yahgan is estimated as having totaled 3000 before European diseases nearly wiped them out during the last quarter of the 1800s. At that time they were widely scattered over the miles of complicated coastline, wandering in small groups composed of two or three nuclear families, or, more often, a single family alone. The present chapter, though written in the present tense, refers to Yaghan society as it existed before the period of population breakdown.

The Yahgan Indians call themselves *Yámana* (*men* or *humans*), but the term *Yahgan*, actually their name for a particular place in their territory, has become so fixed in the literature that there is no alternative but to continue its use. They are not an organized tribe; their distinctiveness from their neighbors is primarily linguistic and to some extent cultural. The language is an isolated one, having no known affinities to any other. The nearest neighbors of the Yahgan are the Ona, who are primarily hunters inhabiting the more inland parts of Tierra del Fuego, the only large island of the archipelago, and the Alakaluf to the northwest, who are coastal dwellers and quite similar culturally, though not linguistically, to the Yahgan.

The Yahgan as a whole have no unity beyond the knowledge that they, as a group, are distinct from their neighbors and share a common territory, which means that any Yahgan is expected to defend or help any other Yahgan against non-Yahgans. This is merely sentiment, however; there is no organization for any kind of concerted action. Within the whole, there are five divisions, each composed of contiguous groups speaking a common dialect of the Yahgan language. But again there is no regular function to this unit; there is merely a feeling of closeness of relationship among members within it.

Transportation is almost entirely by water. So nearly constant is the dependence of the Yahgan on the canoe that they are often referred to as the *canoe Indians* of Tierra del Fuego, in contrast to the Ona hunters, who are called the *foot Indians*.

The physical appearance of the Yahgan is distinctively different from that of the Ona. The latter are like the hunters who once roamed much of Argentina and who became famous for their great height and general robustness. The Yahgan resemble the Alakaluf and the Chono, whose habitat extends over the Chilean archipelago father north; they are very short and squat. Judging from the statement of visitors and from photographs, the Yahgan are far from handsome by European standards. Their faces are very broad and large in proportion to their bodies. Their trunks are also broad and frequently corpulent, while their arms and legs are short and thin, giving them a rather dwarfish appearance.

The forests of the coastal regions of these islands are singularly dense and impenetrable, and for this reason the Yahgan spend most of their lives on the water or on the small, infrequent beach shelves. The most important game animal is the seal. It constitutes the principal meat in their diet; its hide is used for capes, moccasins, and tents; and the sinew, for thongs.

The whale is highly prized by the coastal people; it is so huge that it provides food for great numbers of people for many days. The discovery of a beached whale is a gala occasion. It is a time when large numbers of people can congregate free of the necessity for daily hunting and fishing. The Indians do not hunt the whale in open water, however; they merely await the providence which sometimes washes a dead one onto the shore. Less frequently a live whale is marooned in shallow water and can be killed and beached by the Indians.

Fish of many kinds abound in the coastal water, but the Yahgan have failed to develop or acquire many of the simple fishing devices, such as traps, nets, or hooks, found among most coastal dwellers of the world. The spear is the only weapon used in fishing, and some of the time the Indians merely use bait to draw fish to the surface in order to seize them by hand.[1] The day-in and day-out staple without which life would usually be impossible is shellfish, particularly mussels, conchs, and limpets. The quest for this food, more than any other factor, dictates the frequent movements of

[1] The anthropologist Junius Bird tried this technique in the Yahgan territory and reports (in a personal communication) that it was nearly as successful as using hooks.

the family groups. A few berries and a kind of tree fungus are nearly the only vegetation gathered.

Birds are plentiful, even many large ducks and geese, but again, the Indians lack appropriate devices, such as nets, for securing them easily. Simple but relatively ineffective noose snares are employed and, of course, bows and arrows, slings, and clubs are also used. One unusual method is successful with birds that roost in large groups on the rocks: the hunter steals upon them after dark and with great dexterity seizes the nearest bird with one hand around its wings and the other throttling its windpipe so that it cannot make a cry or flap its wings; he then bites its head off and goes on to the next bird. It is possible to exterminate a whole flock in this way.

The Fuegian area is savagely inhospitable in many respects, but it is not niggardly in its biological aspects. The low estate of the Indians must be understood as resulting in large part from the low development of their technology. Yahgan culture is among the most primitive known. These Indians lack agriculture and domestic animals (except the dog, which may have been a late acquistion) and, of course, the host of appurtenances associated with a sedentary life, but even as a nonagricultural people they lack several devices, such as the spear-thrower, ax, fishhook, and cooking container, commonly found among foraging peoples in other areas of the world. A commensurate simplicity exists in social organization, ceremony and ritual, art, and games.

The spear is the primary weapon of the chase and of warfare as well. The bow and arrow is known but less used by the Yahgan than by the Ona, who are primarily land game hunters. The sling and club are the only other weapons used by the Yahgan. A stick or rude pronged fork is used by the women in prying up limpets, crabs, and sea urchins. Storage devices and containers are few and crude, except for grass baskets, which are probably the most highly developed handicraft of the Yahgan. Certain mussel shells are used as knives and adz blades, and a crude bark bucket is used for carrying water. Chipped-stone knives, stone skin scrapers, and bone awls (the drill is not known) just about complete the inventory of tools.

The Yahgan practically live in their canoes; they even install a sod hearth amidships on which a fire is kept continually burning. Yet, important as the canoes are to them, and tempestuous as the sea typically is, the Indians do not construct a very seaworthy craft.

It is merely a shell of sewn beech-bark, more brittle than the birch-bark of North America, over ribs of split saplings. The canoe is crescent shaped, about 15 feet long, leaky, and unsteady. Outriggers are not known, but a sealskin is sometimes used as a crude sail if the wind is favorable. (In 1880, with the aid of steel tools, the first Yahgan dugout canoe was made and was soon copied throughout the area.)

The wife paddles the canoe, while the man stays in the bow in order to spear the fish which are frequently sighted from this vantage point. Landing from the bark canoe presents a problem, for the gravel or stone beaches would quickly destroy the fragile bark bottom if the canoe were beached. The canoe is headed toward the shore, and the bow man and any other passengers step out before it touches. The wife then takes the canoe out to the edge of the heavy kelp beds in deeper water, where she moors it. She then swims ashore; when the craft is to be used again, the wife is responsible for going out to get it. It is said that although the women are excellent swimmers, few men can swim. One can imagine that they might not be eager to learn.

The Yahgan people, males, females, and children as well, frequently go about entirely naked. The only protective clothing they have is a cape of seal or sea otter skin so brief that it does not circle the body and extends only to the waist when tied across the chest. Knowledge of tanning and softening hides is lacking, and consequently the capes are so cold, stiff, and heavy that the Indians prefer not to wear them when they are engaged in active movement. Awkward sealskin moccasins, stuffed with grass, are used for the infrequent overland walking, but they are not very serviceable. Both men and women smear their bodies with grease or oil, which offers some protection against the bitter wind and especially against the caustic effect of salt water.

Body and facial decoration is simple and of the sort fairly common among the world's marginal cultures. The women frequently wear a small triangular pubic cover of fur or bird skin. Neither sex pays any attention to headdress; no hats are worn and the hair hangs loose in a tangled mass except for bangs in front. Body hair is plucked out, mussel shells being used as tweezers. Body scarification is not practiced for decorative purposes but as a mourning observance, and tattooing is only a small part of the puberty initiation rite.

31

PRIMITIVELY CLAD FAMILY LIVES IN MODERN-STYLE HOUSE. *Courtesy, The American Museum of Natural History*

HEAVY FUR PROTECTS AGAINST HARSH TIERRA DEL FUEGO COLD. *Courtesy, The American Museum of Natural History*

There are none of the more complicated mutilations found so commonly among other American Indians, such as head deformation and ear, lip, or nose piercing. Simple designs of red, white, or black colors are painted on the body for special occasions. Red paint, made from burned earth, symbolizes peace; white, made from clay, means war; black, from charcoal, is the color of mourning. Anklets or wristlets of hide and sinew are worn as ornaments, and necklaces are made of small shells and sections of bird leg bones strung on a sinew.

Shelters, because they are intended only for temporary use, are of simple construction. There are two kinds of huts. A simple hut shaped like a beehive is made by erecting a domed framework of flexible sticks and covering it with grass, ferns, bark, or skins. The other kind of hut is shaped like a wigwam and is formed by laying sticks and poles in the shape of a cone and covering them. Smoke from the continual fire has no means of egressing except by seeping out through the roof covering. One of the typical characteristics of the Yahgan at home is their red, inflamed eyes, especially in the winter when the huts are built the most snugly.

The only division of labor or full-time economic specialization among the Yahgan is based on sex. Men do all of the important hunting and fishing, manufacture weapons and canoes, and do the heavier part of the house-building. Women are primarily in charge of children and the purely domestic activities, such as cooking, sewing, and making bags and baskets. Inasmuch as the canoe is almost a habitation, so much time do they spend in it, the wife is in charge of it and does most of the paddling and steering. As in other hunting-gathering societies, women are the gatherers, for this activity can be carried on close to the camp and does not require great speed or strength. The gathering of shellfish by women is possibly the single most important economic task over the long run.

Women enjoy particularly high status among the Yahgan, possibly because of their crucial role in providing food. It is perhaps relevant, too, that many economic tasks are joint or shared undertakings, however specialized the specific roles. When a man fishes or hunts a sea mammal, his wife is managing the canoe; when a shelter is built, the couple work on it together. The husband, in theory, is in command, but witnesses record many cases of husbands being dominated by their wives. In wider social relations, women are not expected to keep quiet or to be more demure than men.

A particularly good index of the status of women is the society's attitude toward adultery. Among the Yahgan, adultery on the part of either spouse seems to be equally disapproved, and jealousy is common, again on the part of either spouse. There is no wife-lending or prostitution. Separation or divorce occurs, of course, but it is not lightly regarded. Cruelty by the husband and marked laziness on the part of the wife seem to be the most frequent causes of discord.

Polygyny is uncommon, and when it does occur it is typically because of the *levirate* rule whereby a woman who is widowed lives with a brother of the dead man. In Yahgan thought, this is essentially the exercise of a right on the part of this brother to have possession of his fatherless nieces and nephews. Even in cases in which the widow marries another man, this brother has the right to the children.[2]

A bias toward male dominance is reflected in the postnuptial residence rule—on being married, a couple lives in the general territory of the man. Thus, the wife associates more frequently with the husband's family than he does with hers. Another aspect of this patrilocality is that, to the extent that a loose territorial group may be said to exist, membership in it is inherited patrilineally, as in most hunting-gathering societies; that is to say, male children grow up and remain among their father's relatives; only the females leave the group.

This tendency toward the formation of local groups of related families is the only suggestion of an organization larger than the household. But the organization is quite informal; association among its member families is infrequent because they range over a large territory and cross one another's paths only at irregular intervals. There is no chief or other constituted authority in the local group. The tie is essentially one of a felt relationship that includes the assumption that the individual components can call on the others for aid in case of feud or trespass or when seeking revenge against some other group. The only other function of the local

---

[2] A particularly good discussion of family rights in this and other similar matters may be found in Ruth Benedict, "Marital Property Rights in Bilateral Society," *American Anthropologist*, Vol. 38, 1936, pp. 368–374.

group is to hold ceremonial initiation rites at rare intervals.

There is no organized warfare of any kind. Battles between individuals and small groups of relatives result from some crime for which blood revenge by the aggrieved or his family is exacted. Homicide seems to have been fairly frequent in the past, but human sacrifice is unknown, as is suicide. The Yahgan were widely reputed to be cannibals after Admiral Fitzroy took four of them to England in 1829, for they had replied affirmatively to the inevitable questions about cannibalism. The family of Thomas Bridges, who lived among them for many years, deny that cannibalism existed among them, and there is abundant evidence now to support their denial.

Exchange of goods is typically initiated by the giving of a present. Later the recipient must respond with a gift equal or superior in desirability. It is as grave a social offense to refuse a gift as it is to fail to reciprocate. Hospitality is extended to all fellow Yahgans as a matter of course, and open-handedness is the rule. As in other primitive societies, generosity among friends and relatives is necessary as well as expected. It is not good manners to express thanks for a gift verbally, probably because to do so would be to indicate that the gift was unexpected—or that the recipient had had a notion the giver was stingier than he turned out to be.

Stealing is considered highly reprehensible. The precept against stealing does not extend to strangers, however, for in the Yahgan view they are possibly less than human and potentially, if not actually, dangerous. The Bridges family were finally accepted on a friendly and kinlike basis, but not until after they had suffered a long series of depredations and breaches of confidence.

Information is lacking or contradictory about much of the etiquette and many of the obligations of various categories of relatives to one another. All of the designations of kindred are bilateral—kinship on both father's and mother's side is reckoned equivalently. Aunts and uncles (mother's and father's siblings) are given distinct relationship terms, rather than being merged terminologically with the actual mother and father. Similarly, nephews and nieces are given terms distinct from those applied to the individual's own son and daughter. All cousins are addressed as *brother* or *sister*. Marriage between people of this relationship is forbidden. Inasmuch as the Yahgan live in independent nuclear families, these distinctions that separate parents from uncles and aunts, and sons and daughters

35

from nieces and nephews, are expected, for they live in different places. The fact that cousins are equated to siblings, no matter where they live, is possibly owing to the influence of the rule that prohibits marriage with them—and cousins are equated to siblings in social behavior.

A paternal uncle is supposed to take a particularly strong interest in the welfare of his nephew, especially after the nephew's marriage, and, similarly, a maternal aunt looks after a girl's welfare. A man is bound to take responsibility for parents-in-law, aiding them in time of need, giving them presents, and behaving respectfully toward them. As in many other primitive societies, this affinal relationship is considered so important, yet so sensitive, that a number of avoidance taboos (social distance) are observed. The respect of a man toward his father-in-law is most rigidly prescribed and lasts through life: the son-in-law must not look directly at the father-in-law or sit near him, and communication must be made indirectly, usually through the wife of the son-in-law.

The Yahgan clearly understand the relationship between sexual intercourse and childbirth.[3] A married couple do not normally attempt to limit births, for they greatly desire children. Unmarried girls who become pregnant practice mechanical abortion and even infanticide, however. The delivery of a baby is assisted by several female relatives of the mother, while the husband remains outside the hut. The placenta is burned, and the navel cord is dried and kept for magical purposes. Soon after the birth, the mother and the baby bathe in the icy sea, a practice which might confound modern doctors but which, as far as the evidence goes, seems to have no deleterious effects on either the mother or the child. Several dietary taboos are observed by the parents for some time both before and after the birth. After the birth, especially if the child is a first-born, the father refrains from any work for several days as though he were resting from the birth ordeal.[4]

A child is usually named after his birthplace. The giving of the name is not signalized by any special ritual, but the name does remain rather magically private; it is very bad form to address a person by his or her own name, and even the personal names of

---

[3] See Chapters 1 and 11 for contrasting beliefs.
[4] This is a ritual observance anthropologists call the *couvade,* and it is practiced by some South American tribes in a much more rigidly stylized pattern.

persons not present are not used in conversation. Kinship terms are usual in face-to-face address, and roundabout descriptive phrases are used in referring to an absent person.

During childhood, boys and girls play games together, but none are of a complex or group nature, because there are seldom any large numbers of people in a locality. After children reach the age of 7 or thereabouts, boys and girls are not allowed to play together. Corporal punishment is rare, but elders spend a good deal of time correcting a child and instructing it in the proper ways of behavior.

Many of the primitive hunters and gatherers of the world hold their most important religious ceremonies at the time a group of children reaches the age of adolescence. Among the Yahgan, these rites are a great social occasion for adults, but are seriously regarded also as a sort of graduation ceremony in the otherwise informal educational system.

The onset of puberty is observed for girls at the time of the first menses. The girl fasts for three days, and her cheeks are painted red. For several days she receives moral counseling by older women, until the end of the period is signalized by a ritual bath in the sea and a feast for all the people present. A boy's puberty is not observed by any individual rites of this sort, but eventually the several pubescent boys of the whole local group are brought together for the great *Čiéxaus* ceremony. The Čiéxaus gatherings are not held at any prescribed intervals; the food supply and the numbers of youths who are ready are the factors determining their occasion.

A special and exceptionally large hut is built for the initiation ceremony. Each of the candidates is assigned a sponsor, or mentor, who keeps up a continual barrage of practical and moral instruction throughout the many days (sometimes even months) of the ceremonial period. The candidates are subject to many ordeals and ritual prohibitions. They are allowed only a minimum of sleep and food, must sit only in a cross-legged position, must take a bath in the sea every night, and are allowed to drink only through a bird-bone sucking tube. A sort of rudimentary tattooing is made on the boys' chests early in the ceremony.

A prominent part of the ceremony consists of group singing and dancing, usually late at night. This, of course, may be a pleasurable occupation, but a serious purpose underlies it. The songs are communications to a fearful and evil spirit, *Yetaita,* who must be kept at a distance. A final ceremony presents the youths to society. One by one they are received by the ceremonial leader (who is not a chief but, as among the Arunta, a sort of master of ceremonies), who ritually makes them full members of society. Each of the mentors then presents his candidate with a specially adorned basket, a drinking bone, and a scratching stick.

Another ceremony, called the *Kina,* sometimes follows the initiation ceremony. It appears to be a diminished version of the famous Ona *Klóketen* and is essentially a dramatization of a myth that recounts the history of an earlier time when the women held mastery over the men in the society: the men were hoodwinked into their inferior status because the women used masks to impersonate spirits, which gave them control; finally the deception was discovered, and the men overthrew the women. The Kina rite can be participated in only by fully initiated men, who retire to a ceremonial hut and, secretly from the women and children, paint themselves and don the masks which impersonate the spirits. As spirits, they come out and sing and dance before the women and children and threaten to punish the women if they do not obey.

The most important rituals after the initiation rites are funeral ceremonies. The common form of disposal of the dead is cremation; the personal property of the deceased is burned at the same time. Mourning practices of close relatives include fasting, painting their bodies black, and even cutting their breasts. A formal ritual held by all friends and relatives who can attend repeats the predominant motif of the Kina—wherein the men and women engage in a mock battle.

The Yahgan believe in a host of spirits and gods. They are particularly fearful of the spirits of the recent dead and consequently abandon the camp spot where a death occurs. There is no worship of, or prayer to, dead ancestors, and the name of a dead person is never spoken. Each person possesses a friendly guardian spirit, however, which can be counted on for aid under appropriate circumstances. There seems to be a belief in a supreme spirit, sometimes called *My Father*; but because there has been an early and continuing missionary influence among the Indians, it is not known that this is a truly aboriginal belief.

The Yahgan have no priests and no dogma or formal body of beliefs. The closest approach to a religious practitioner is the male shaman—a medicine man of the sort generally common among American Indians. A man becomes a shaman by having dreams or visions that he is called to the profession by a particular spirit helper, who teaches him his shaman's song. An elder shaman then takes him as an apprentice, puts him through various ordeals, and teaches him the customary esoteric rituals. It is believed that a shaman can influence the weather, prognosticate the future of projected activities, and so on, but his principal function is to cure the sick. The usual American Indian procedures of massaging and anointing, followed by the sleight-of-hand extraction of a foreign object from the afflicted area, are applied. Illness and death are usually attributed to the machinations of an evil, or enemy, shaman. Consequently, a curing shaman is simply applying countermagic. The common Indian conception of soul loss is shared by the Yahgan, who believe that an evil shaman can steal the soul of a person, causing him to sicken and die unless the soul is recovered by another shaman.

The religious cosmogony and mythology of the Yahgan are similar to those of other primitive peoples, but lack complexity and depth. Some of the myths are explanatory of why there are spots on the moon, why the sun comes up, and so on; some are moral homilies in which a malefactor always is punished and ends in disgrace; some others are *culture hero* stories in which two brothers are described as having introduced the social rules of the society, the arts and crafts, and the names of things. *Debacle myths* include several versions of a great flood caused by the falling into the sea of the sun, or sometimes the moon. A large number of myths relate activities of feared cannibal spirits and of a race of malicious giants.

The use of narcotics plays no part in either Yahgan religion or recreation, nor is there any form of alcoholic beverage or even tobacco. Aesthetic matters, such as music and the dance, are little elaborated, and there are not even any musical instruments except rhythm-beaters. Even the nearly universal rattle, drum, and flute are not used. Games are very simple, the most popular being wrestling. The common recreation is simply chatting, but even the verbal arts are underdeveloped—there are no proverbs and no poetry, and the words to songs are simply monotonous repetitions.

The Yahgan have plenty of time to converse. Thomas Bridges estimated that they actually work only about one-fifth of the time that civilized man devotes to earning a livelihood. Other observers also have commented on the fact that these Indians give no thought to providing for the future; they eat what is available, and if they cannot find anything, they do not appear to worry about it. Of special concern to all observers has been the fact that the Indians seem so singularly uninventive. All aspects of the culture are simple, but why has not the very stringent environment led them to improvise better clothing and habitations at least? Even a professional archaeologist, Samuel K. Lothrop, who visited them in the 1920s, was led to postulate that something vital must be lacking in their mental make-up.

People who have known them well as individuals, however, have not found the Yahgan unintelligent. In fact, the Yahgan youngsters carried to England by Admiral Fitzroy between the years 1829 and 1832 adapted to English culture with remarkable quickness. Interestingly enough, they readapted to the Yahgan environment almost immediately on being returned to their people, much to the disgust of the Englishmen, who had naïvely hoped to transplant English civilization to Tierra del Fuego with these few seedlings.

It is difficult to explain why the Yahgan are so complacent and uninventive, but anthropologists know that their pattern is not exceptional in the primitive world. Certainly the challenge of a harsh environment does not always stimulate a creative response. Civilized man is always tempted to think of what *he* would do if faced with the necessity of survival in Yahgan territory. But people of Western civilization are thinking differently—that is, our views are formed by an entirely different culture, and our response to this kind of question is typically ethnocentric.

There are a few things anthropologists can say that lead at least in the direction of an explanation. First, an ancient culture, however simple, tends to reach a steady state of great inertia caused by integration of its parts and by adaptation to its environment, and it does not change without considerable pressure. Individuals in such a culture cannot easily leave it; the poor Yahgan who were returned from England had no real choice but to go back to their native culture. There is little question but that the psychic and social security which demands fitting wholly into one's native culture is more necessary than the physical comfort of being more warmly clothed, for example. Second, the most primitive cultures exist in the most marginal areas, removed by distance and geographic barriers from contact with the more populous centers of culture development. The Yahgan, like other marginally located societies, do not know about many of the artifacts commonly in use among American Indians, simply because they are so isolated. Third, the Yahgan have so much spare time because, like many other hunters and gatherers, they have no productive way of putting their time to use. There is no point in gathering more fish or more mussels than can be eaten in a day if there is no way to preserve them. And if the fish are not present in any particular period, there is no point in going fishing. The techniques of storage, such as drying and packing, made possible among the Indians of the northwest coast of North America a much fuller employment of labor, a larger and more permanently located population, and consequently a rich, intricate culture, even though it is based on a mere hunting-gathering technology, but these traits did not diffuse to southern South America.

The Yahgan had little chance to benefit from European technology after they were discovered, for the European diseases (measles, typhoid fever, whooping cough, and smallpox) decimated them soon after contact. From about 3000 people the Yahgan began sharply to decrease in 1884, and within 20 years they numbered only 130. By 1933 there were only 40 left, and the decline has been continuous, from all accounts, since then.

Ferdinand Magellan had passed some of the Fuegians in 1520 when he discovered the straits which now bear his name. According to tradition, Tierra del Fuego ("Land of Fire") received its name when Magellan noted the constant flickering of camp fires at night along the shore of the island. The rounding of the Horn by sailing ships was a difficult and dangerous undertaking, and in the centuries following Magellan's discovery a considerable number of shipwrecks occurred among the islands. The ships were plundered by the Indians, but the unsavory reputation the Yahgan acquired was probably also a result of ignorance and fear on the part of the Europeans; for in the early days of sailing, similarly wildly exaggerated fears were held about primitives encountered in many other parts of the world.

More continuous and less casual contacts of Europeans and

MODEL OF A YAHGAN CONICAL HUT. *Courtesy, The American Museum of Natural History*

Yahgan began in the early part of the nineteenth century with the coming of surveying and exploring expeditions to South America. The best known of these were the two expeditions of Fitzroy between 1826 and 1832. Fitzroy retained four Indians as hostages during his first visit and finally took them to England, where they spent three years. The two youngest ones, a girl of 9 whom the English named Fuegia Basket and a boy of about 14, Jemmy (or Jimmy) Button, were apt students, and the little girl captivated the King and Queen of England during an audience. The return voyage was made in H.M.S. *Beagle,* with the youthful Charles Darwin aboard. The *Beagle* arrived at Tierra del Fuego in 1832, and stayed for several weeks, during which Darwin compiled some interesting notes on the inhabitants.

An event of singular importance to our knowledge of the Yahgan was the arrival of Thomas Bridges and his family in 1871 to set up a mission station at Ushuaia on Beagle Channel on the south coast of Tierra del Fuego. Bridges devoted most of his life to caring for the Indians and writing about them. His dictionary of Yámana is one of the most intensive studies ever made of a primitive language.[5] The efforts of the missionaries were great, but they could not keep the Indians from contact with the increasing number of Europeans who filtered into the area. As previously related, the Indians could not withstand the European diseases, and they now are extinct.

FURTHER READINGS

Bird, J., "Antiquity and Migrations of the Early Inhabitants of Patagonia," *Geographical Review,* Vol. 28, No. 2, 1938.

Bird, J., "The Archeology of Patagonia," in J. H. Steward (ed.), *Handbook of South American Indians,* Vol. 1, Smithsonian Institution, Bureau of American Ethnology, Bull. 143, Washington, 1946.

Bridges, E. L., *Uttermost Part of the Earth,* New York, 1949.

Bridges, T., "Manners and Customs of the Firelanders," in *A Voice for South America,* South American Missionary Magazine, Vol. 13, 1866.

Cooper, J. M., "Temporal Sequence and the Marginal Cultures," *Anthropological Series, Catholic University of America,* No. 10, 1941.

Cooper, J. M., "The Yahgan," in J. H. Steward (ed.), *Handbook of South American Indians,* Vol. 1, Smithsonian Institution, Bureau of American Ethnology, Bull. 143, Washington, 1946.

Darwin, C., *Journal of Researches into the Natural History and Geology of the countries visited during the voyage of H. M. S. Beagle round the world, under the Command of Captain FitzRoy, R.N.,* London, 1845.

Darwin, C., *Charles Darwin and the Voyage of the Beagle* (ed. Nora Barlow), New York, 1946.

Gusinde, M., *Die Feuerland-Indianer,* Vol. 2, *Die Yamana,* Mödling, 1937.

Hyades, P. D. J., and Deniker, J., *Mission scientifique du cap Horn,* Anthropologie, ethnographie, Vol. 7, Paris, 1891.

Lothrop, S. K., *The Indians of Tierra del Fuego,* Contrib. from the Museum of the American Indian, Heye Foundation, Vol. 10, New York, 1928.

---

[5] Mr. Bridges' children grew up among the Yahgan and Ona and one of them has written an interesting account of his life there. See E. Lucas Bridges, *Uttermost Part of the Earth,* New York, 1949.

3

The Andaman Islanders

The Andaman Islanders inhabit a very different kind of environment from the Australian desert dwellers and Yahgan coastal peoples. They are also of a different racial type, the pygmy Negro, or Negrito, as they are called. They are apparently survivors of an ancient race of tiny forest dwellers that once inhabited much more of the globe than they do in their present distribution. In general they resemble the Negritos of remote parts of the Philippines, the African Congo region, the highlands of New Guinea, and the interior of the Malay Peninsula. Any connection the Andamanese may once have had with these other scattered groups, however, must have been in the most remote past, for they are all now quite widely separated from one another.

The Andamanese may well represent the purest, most truly original, form of Negrito forest culture. The other Negrito groups of the world typically live in some sort of contact and even economic symbiosis with more powerful neighbors. Most of them have borrowed many culture traits, even to the point of adopting a neighbor's language. The Andamanese, on the contrary, have been completely isolated, and their language constitutes a separate family or stock, having no apparent affinity with any of the known families of languages. In fact, at the time of their discovery by Europeans they seem to have been unaware of the existence of other men, and to have thought that the light-colored tall strangers were spirits.

The Andaman Islands, which together with the Nicobar Islands form a state of India, lie along the eastern part of the Bay of Bengal. Their total area is about 2500 square miles. The largest island, Great Andaman, is nearly 160 miles long, but its breadth is nowhere more than 20 miles. Little Andaman, the only other large island, is about 26 miles long and 16 miles wide. All the rest are mere outlying islets. The estimated native population before the effects of European diseases were felt was 5500.

The climate of the islands is tropical, warm and moist, with little variation in temperature. The greater part of the high annual precipitation (about 140 inches) falls during the monsoon season, from May through part of November. The rest of the year is quite dry. Streams are rare and not large, and rain water drains into large interior swamps.

Our knowledge of the Andamanese is mainly the result of the work of two men. E. H. Man was a British government official in the islands from 1869 until 1880, and although not trained as an anthropologist, he was a careful observer and meticulous collector of scientific data. A. R. Radcliffe-Brown, then a Cambridge University anthropology student, studied the Andamanese from 1906 to 1908. His work supplements Man's, and there is little conflict in their respective interpretations of Andamanese culture, except in certain aspects of kinship organization and terminology. By 1906, European diseases had reduced the native population to 27 percent of what it had been during Man's period of residence, and this reduction apparently affected the local village organization and kinship nomenclature. Even in 1880 the population studied by Man had been reduced from an earlier 1000 to only 400. Radcliffe-Brown admits difficulty and uncertainty in interpreting these matters, and the present chapter, for this reason, uses Man's data whenever there is a conflict. The present tense used hereafter should be understood as referring to Andamanese culture as of 1908 or earlier.

The Andamanese practice no agriculture and possessed no domestic animals whatever until dogs were brought to the islands in 1858. The supply of game, fish, and wild plant foods is plentiful in comparison to that of the Arunta of Australia. The largest game animal of the forest is the pig, and it is the primary hunting target, although hunters also endeavor to kill civet cats, large lizards, and even snakes and rats as opportunity affords. Birds are numerous, but the hunters have no traps or nets, and they rarely try to shoot a bird with the bow and arrow, because of the dense jungle.

Most of the islanders live on the coast or near the tiny streams, and the plentiful products of the sea are an important resource for them. The dugong (a large aquatic mammal), many kinds of turtles, an enormous variety of fish, and crabs, crayfish, and mollusks are among the most usual fare. Hunters, or anyone traveling, keep an eye open for wild honey to take home, and the women and children roam near the camp gathering such edible roots, fruits, and seeds as are in season.

Nets and short spears or harpoons are employed in fishing, but fishhooks were unknown until recently. The bow and arrow is used for shooting large fish. For hunting, the Andamanese depend entirely upon the bow and arrow. Neither traps nor spears are used, nor is the blowgun, and arrow poison is unknown. The only tool used in the women's collecting activities is a stick used for digging roots.

Wood, stone, and shell were the chief local materials used in making tools, but the Andamanese very quickly acquired the habit of making arrow points and knives of iron when it became available to them from ships wrecked along the dangerous coasts. They did not discover the use of heat as an aid in working the metal and thus were forced to shape it by crude hammering. Except in their recent and sporadic use of iron, the Adamanese make knives, adzes, scrapers, and arrow points of shell.

Canoes are of the dugout type, each one hollowed from a single log and equipped with an outrigger float which keeps it from capsizing. Otherwise, there is no mechanical transportation facility. Because of the relatively great bounty of nature, however, the Andamanese live less nomadic lives than do the Australians. Their houses are of a more permanent type, and there is a greater number and variety of household utensils.

The clay cooking pot, sometimes fitted with a wicker carrying frame, is one special device used by the Andamanese which more mobile hunting-gathering societies usually cannot afford because of its cumbersomeness and frangibility. Wooden buckets, which serve for water storage, are laboriously hollowed out of single blocks of wood. Four- or five-foot-long bambo sections also are used commonly for water storage. Nautilus shells serve as drinking vessels, and flatter shells as food plates. Baskets are woven of rattan by the women and are used for carrying food or loose articles. The Andamanese are far ahead of other more nomadic tribes in sleeping comfort, for they have woven sleeping mats and sometimes even use a wooden pillow. Curiously, though, the Andamanese are laggards in one important respect; they do not know how to kindle fire, and they have to use great care to preserve their fires. Even the many

A PARTY OF ANDAMANESE IN A DUGOUT CANOE. *Courtesy, The American Museum of Natural History*

legends concerning the origin of fire describe no feasible methods by which it was first kindled; usually the mythological creatures created it by merely blowing on charred embers.

The Andamanese village is a roughly circular arrangement of single-family, mat-roofed huts which are left open at the sides. The group of houses encloses a plazalike dance ground. Sometimes a village consists, instead, of a circular communal hut, as large as 60 feet in diameter, with locations for the cooking fires and sleeping quarters of the various individual families arranged around the outer edges, leaving the dance ground in the center. Unmarried adult men occupy a bachelors' hut by themselves. At one side of the central dancing ground near the bachelors' hut is a series of hearths which the bachelors use from time to time to cook feasts for the village as a whole. In all cases the huts are built sturdily with a view toward permanency. A village site may be occupied continuously for the several months of the rainy season. The community usually moves several times during the dry season to areas more favorably located for seasonal game or plants, but it usually returns to the original, or permanent, camp. In the temporary camps individual huts are arranged in a circle, but they are relatively carelessly and flimsily built.

The villagers—a *local group* or *band* in anthropological parlance—normally migrate in traditional routes, or orbits, the village being the relatively permanent focal point. The land over which they roam is considered their own territory, which they will defend against encroachment by outsiders. This territory and the natural resources in it are thus, in a sense, owned communally by the group as a whole, and all members have equal rights in it. The only exceptions are claims which individuals may make for certain trees. A man might discover a tree which is just right for a canoe he intends to build, or he might claim ownership of a wild fruit tree. Such a concept of individual property in trees is widely found in the primitive world, as is the concept of community right to the rest of the terrain.

Products of women's gathering activities are usually considered individual property, but a large game animal or an unusually rich harvest of some vegetable food is shared with the community. All portable items, such as tools, clothing, canoes, and ornaments, are treated as individual property simply as a matter of expediency; but the Andamanese, like all very primitive peoples, have such customs of hospitality and liberal gift-giving and so freely lend their property that the society is strongly egalitarian in the matter of wealth. People are constantly exchanging presents to commemorate even minor occasions, and it is considered a serious breach of etiquette ever to refuse another's request for anything. It is always expected, however, that equivalent return gifts will be made. Meetings between members of different villages are accompanied by the exchange of great quantities of presents.

The egalitarian nature of the village is a marked social as well as economic characteristic. Men are treated differently from women, of course, and older people are more respected than younger, but no *families* are in a higher or more powerful social or economic position than others. There is no government, strictly speaking; decisions affecting the community are made by the community, with the older men and women having more influence than the young people. There is no office of authority, no chief.

There is no true code of laws or punishment for crimes. An action which harms an individual, such as a bodily attack, theft, or adultery (which is regarded as a form of theft), is considered a matter for retribution by the aggrieved. Other actions which are regarded as generally antisocial, such as laziness, lack of respect to elders, or quarrelsomeness, are not punished as crimes, but are kept rare or within bounds by force of public opinion. A person who does not behave virtuously and properly suffers a proportionate loss in popularity and esteem.

There is likewise no government or law concerning the relations of one local group with another. Each autonomously regulates its own affairs, and relations with other groups consist only of visits between individuals and occasional meetings for feasts and dancing. A set of several local groups may be considered a unity as opposed to another set largely because they have been closely enough associated to have a common dialect and a name which identifies them, but this is only a very loose tie and the individual groups do not interfere with one another in the regulation of daily conduct. There is no such thing as true warfare between groups, or even a stand-up fight. Grievances call for countermeasures and may result in family feuds, but there is little evidence of hostilities on a village scale.

The basis of organization is kinship and kinship alone, as in other hunting-gathering societies. It is unusual, however, that the Andamanese do not use a complete set of kinship terms in addressing their relatives. Unlike many primitive peoples, they freely use personal names, although usually a title of respect is added. These special titles do not imply any specific relationship between the two people speaking. Younger people in addressing older people use terms roughly equivalent to *Sir* or *Madam* as used in our society. These two words also mean *father* and *mother,* but in the sense of *a* father or *a* mother; that is, the term *father* or the term *mother* refers to a general social, or status, position, not to biological parenthood. Another title of still higher respect (*Mam,* grandparent) is used in addressing seniors who are relatives by marriage.

It is perhaps more readily apparent among the Andamanese than among other primitives that terms of address we think of as denoting actual kinship are really status and respect terms only. They resemble terms of relationship to a degree, but they are used in societies whose only system of social relations consists of familial categories. Thus all titles of respect include the social relations and statuses that are found in a single family. But these include also all persons with whom one associates, whether relatives or not.

There seem to be special reasons why the kinship categories which the Andamanese use in address are so few and so unspecific. There is little differentiation among the children of a camp. All of them are played with, petted, and even nursed not only by their actual mothers but also by any of the mothers of the village. Babies are not weaned until they are 3 or 4 years old, and after that they are regarded as "children of the village," but even during the suckling period they are passed around a great deal.

Later a much more striking dispersion takes place. In the words of E. H. Man:

> It is said to be of rare occurrence to find any child above six or seven years of age residing with its parents, and this because it is considered a compliment and also a mark of friendship for a married man, after paying a visit, to ask his hosts to allow him to adopt one of their children. The request is usually complied with, and thenceforth the child's home is with his (or her) foster father . . . though the parents in their turn adopt the children of other friends, they nevertheless pay continued visits to their own child, and occasionally ask permission(!) to take him (or her) away with them for a few days.
>
> A man is entirely at liberty to please himself in the number of children he adopts, but he must treat them with kindness and consideration, and in every respect as his own sons and daughters, and they, on their part, render him filial affection and obedience.
>
> It not infrequently happens that in course of time permission to adopt a foster child is sought by a friend of the *soi-disant* father, and it is at once granted (unless any exceptional circumstance should render it personally inconvenient), without even the formality of a reference to the actual parents, who are merely informed of the change in order that they may be enabled to pay their periodical visits.[1]

After the age of puberty, a boy leaves the hut of his parents or foster parents and begins his life in the bachelors' hut, where he re-

[1] E. H. Man, *On the Aboriginal Inhabitants of the Andaman Islands,* London, 1932, p. 57.

mains until he is married. Information with respect to spinsters' huts for unmarried girls is contradictory. Whether or not girls live apart from their parents after puberty, it can be seen that children are thrown together into a group of age mates, with practically all members of the next ascending generation being equally "parents" and their own age mates being equally "siblings" so far as the general character of their social relations is concerned. The terminology of kinship reflects this situation, just as the terminology of other societies reflects quite different conditions. The strongest determinant of social differentiation among the Andamanese may be said to be generation-grading.

The Andamanese are quite aware of finer degrees of kinship than those few distinguished in terms of address. But, in general, the system of kinship distinctions used in reference reflects the fluidity and informality of their local social organization, emphasizing generational distinctions and relative age, but ignoring distinctions between cross and parallel relatives within the generations. The nuclear family is distinguished from all relatives of the same generation, but the collateral relatives are not sub-divided within the generation except by sex. In-law relatives in each generation are distinguished from other collateral relatives, however.

A person must be more deferential in his dealings with his in-laws than with his own family. A person's relations with his father-in-law and mother-in-law in any society are quite realistically singled out for special elaboration. The Andamanese do not address their parents-in-law with the same respect term they use for others of that generation, but use the term ordinarily used for members of the grandparental generation. The greater the age, the greater the respect; thus parents-in-law are treated as though they were actually a generation older than their true age. This sign of respect would seem outlandish in a modern city, but is quite usual in primitive societies.[2]

There are a few special kinds of etiquette applying to certain individuals. A married man is not supposed to have any direct dealings with the wife of a man younger than himself. If any communication is required between the two, it must be done through a third party. It would be an exceptionally serious breach of etiquette for him to touch her. The Andamanese say, in explanation, that a man is "shy"

[2] See, for example, Chapter 13.

or "ashamed" to have contact with a younger man's wife. On the other hand, a man can be familiar with the wife of a man older than himself, treating her more or less as he would an older sister.

A special etiquette also obtains between the parents of a married couple. The two families regularly exchange presents, but are too shy to have familiar dealings with one another. A similar respect relationship exists between any two men who, as youths, participated together in the turtle-eating or pig-eating ceremony (to be described below). The two men give one another presents of all kinds, as do families joined by affinal ties, but no direct social intercourse may exist between them.

Ordinarily in primitive society the kind of family alliance which will be made by any particular marriage is of great importance, for the marriage rule is the chief way in which the size of the total cooperating body of relatives is regulated. Among the Andaman Islanders, however, the marriage rule, like other aspects of the social organization, seems diffuse and unspecific. Marriage is prohibited with near kin, but the prohibition is not stated very precisely. It is clear that a man cannot marry his sister or half-sister, or his aunts or nieces, but evidence is confusing about whether he could marry a cousin. It is preferable, nevertheless, not to marry anyone as close as a first cousin. Foster children, if adopted at an early age as orphans, are regarded as true kin and may not marry close foster kin, but children "borrowed" in later childhood, in accordance with the custom described above, are not barred from marriage with the children of the household into which they were taken. In fact, an adoption of this kind usually corresponds to an actual betrothal, an expectation by the two sets of parents that the adopted child will later marry a foster sibling.

The largest proportion of marriages is between members of different local groups; there is a tendency, that is, toward local exogamy. This is not a strict rule, however, and its workings are probably considerably confused by the fact that depopulation has resulted in the merging of survivors of different local groups into a single one.

Marriage, essentially an alliance between families, is arranged by the older men and women, and even infants are sometimes betrothed by their parents. One of the characteristics of the marriage custom, which points up the fact that it is a family alliance rather than a compact between two individuals, is the practice which anthropologists call the *levirate*. If the husband should die, the widow is then married to a younger brother of the deceased husband, or the cousin who is the nearest equivalent of the younger brother. The complement of this custom, the *sororate*, is also practiced; a widower is expected to marry the younger sister of his deceased wife. These customs provide social security for the widow or widower, and preserve the character of the alliance between the two families. As in many other primitive tribes, a man usually marries a girl considerably younger than himself; so it is more frequent that the wife survives, and the levirate is thus more usual than the sororate.

Marriage among the Andamanese is otherwise strongly monogamous, and adultery by either partner is rigidly disapproved and punished. A marriage is not regarded as fully consummated by the marriage ceremony, however, but depends upon the birth of a child. Before marriage boys and girls participate freely in sexual experimentation.

For some time before the birth of a child and for about a month afterward, both the mother and father must observe certain dietary taboos. The infant's name is given to it before birth, and during the period of the observance of taboos the parents must be addressed or referred to always by the child's name. It is as if, for example, we named an as yet unborn child John, and from then until some weeks after the birth spoke of the parents as John's father or John's mother, being very careful, magically careful, that the father's or mother's own name never escaped our lips. This precaution insures that no harm befalls the child. This custom, called *teknonymy*, is found in many primitive societies.

The older mothers of the village attend a woman in childbirth. She is seated in her hut on a carpet of fresh-cut leaves, leaning against a wooden backrest, knees clasped by her arms. One of the attendant women aids by exerting pressure on the upper part of the abdomen. After the delivery the umbilical cord is cut, the afterbirth is buried in the jungle, and the infant cleaned by washing it and scraping it with a shell. Should the baby die in infancy, it is believed that the next baby will be a reincarnation of the first, and it is therefore given the same name. This belief in reincarnation applies only to infant deaths. It is also believed that the souls of unborn babies reside in fig trees, and that if a baby dies before weaning, its soul will go back to its tree. The tree, therefore, should not be cut or damaged.

Childhood is considered one of the three well-marked phases of a person's life, and lasts until the beginnings of puberty. The next phase is shorter, lasting until marriage, and the third is from marriage until death. As in nearly all primitive societies, these phases are demarcated by elaborate ceremonies, which anthropologists call *life crisis ceremonies* or *rites of passage*. The ceremonies occur normally at birth, puberty (the ceremonies at this time are sometimes called *initiation*), marriage, and death.

During nearly all the period of childhood, a person undergoes operations of skin scarification. A small flake of quartz is used to make tiny incisions in the skin. Incisions are made at intervals until at puberty the whole body is covered with tiny designs. It is said to improve the appearance and to strengthen the child.

The end of childhood is signalized for girls by the first menstruation. For a period of three days the girl is secluded in a hut, except when she takes a morning bath in the sea or river. She is specially adorned with bundles of leaves and must sit with arms folded and legs doubled under her. She is not allowed to speak or sleep during the first 24 hours and may not touch food with her fingers during the three days. For the next month she must bathe each morning at dawn. The personal name used by the girl during childhood is discarded at this time, and after the period of seclusion she is given a *flower-name*, the name of a tree or plant which happens to be in bloom at the time of the ceremony. This name is kept until her marriage. There is some evidence that the menstrual period is regarded as a dangerous time, but girls are not required to leave the camp as they are in so many primitive societies.

When it has been decided that a boy has reached maturity, an all-night dance is held in his honor. In the morning he must bathe for an hour or so, after which he is subjected to a final scarification of his back and, a few days later, of his chest. For a few weeks the boy's name is not used, but afterward he is addressed by his original name.

Both boys and girls are under dietary restrictions for some time after the puberty ceremony, usually for more than a year. During this period there are successive intervals during which they must abstain from each one of the important foods in turn. At the end of each period of abstention from a certain food, the youth partakes of it in a ceremony. The most elaborate come at the end of the abstentions from pork and from turtle. These ceremonies are more complex than those which mark a girl's first menstrual period, but are based on similar notions of endurance and similar taboos. A new name is given to a boy at the end of the turtle-eating.

Ceremonies celebrating marriage are somewhat variable. Usually the ceremony takes place on an evening which the two sets of parents

TEMPORARY OR HUNTING SHELTER. *Courtesy, The American Museum of Natural History*

select. The bride sits on a mat, surrounded by her relatives and friends, at one end of the village dance ground, which is lighted by torches. The bridegroom and his family and friends sit at the other end. An old, respected man then addresses the bride, describing to her what she must do to become a good wife. After speaking to the groom in a similar vein, he takes him by the hand and leads him to the bride. Friends and relatives weep loudly, while the bride and groom sit together self-consciously. Finally the officiating elder places the arms of each around the other's neck. A short time later, he again approaches and makes the bridegroom sit on his bride's lap. Thereafter it is a custom that when a man and wife greet each other fondly, the man sits on his wife's lap. Any two friends or relatives, even of the same sex, greet one another after absences of a few weeks by sitting one on the lap of the other and weeping copiously. Weeping seems to be a most frequent means of expressing sentiment, and tears can apparently be summoned at will. Radcliffe-Brown once asked several of the people how this was done, and he relates that they immediately sat down and began to shed real tears at his request.

After the wedding ceremony, the rest of the community usually hold a dance while the newlyweds retire to a new hut with their

PARTING AND MEETING BEHAVIOR. *Courtesy, The American Museum of Natural History*

wedding presents. Their friends supply them generously with food for several days. Neither one of the couple is again spoken of by his own name, but by the partner's name, as Husband of B or Wife of A, and later, when a child is expected, by the child's name.

Ritual customs related to death and burial are more complicated and of longer duration than are marriage ceremonies. After the news of a death has spread through a village, all of the women come to sit around the body, where they weep loudly until they are exhausted. After they retire, the men come and weep. All adult members of the village plaster their bodies with a wash of common clay. The corpse, too, is finally decorated with bands of white clay, alternated with stripes of red paint, and the head is shaved.

The corpse is then bundled up in a mat and tied in a flexed position. At this point the relatives make their last farewell by gently blowing their breath in the face of the dead person. All the men of the village accompany the corpse to the spot where it is to be buried in a grave three or four feet deep or placed on a platform in a tree. The body is always oriented to face the east, and a fire and a vessel of water are left with it. Plumes of shredded palm leaves are displayed at the entrances to the village to show a visitor that a period of mourning is in progress. The village itself remains deserted during this period.

Close relatives continue to mourn for several months. For the first few weeks they keep their bodies plastered with common clay, and for the remainder of the period they retain a band of clay on their foreheads. There are several prohibitions: certain foods must not be eaten, there must be no dancing, and no red paint or white clay may be used. The name of the deceased is not used during this time, nor is the name of any near relative of the deceased.

By the time the period of mourning is over, the flesh has decayed from the bones of the corpse. The ritual end of mourning is signalized by the men's digging up the bones (or removing them from the tree), washing them, and taking them to the village, where they are wept over by the women. The mourners are released from all restrictions at an evening ceremony, during which they ritually remove the clay from their foreheads and decorate themselves with the forbidden red paint and white clay. A night-long dance is then held which is like any other pleasure celebration.

The bones of the deceased are kept for many years. The skull and jawbone are decorated with red and white bands and attached to a kind of necklace. On ceremonial occasions a husband or wife, or close relative of the deceased, may wear these bones suspended about the neck, either in front or behind. Limb bones are usually kept in the roof of the hut. Small bones are strung on a string by the female relatives of the deceased and given away as presents to be worn as preventives or cures of illnesses.

The Andamanese seem to have mixed feelings toward the spirits of the dead: sometimes the feeling is affectionate toward a particular spirit; sometimes it is one of dread and fear. There are times when the spirits may be called upon to help, and times when they are apt to be angry and do harm to the community. To some extent, their will or power to do good or evil is felt to depend on the activities of the medicine man, or shaman.

The shaman is the only religious specialist in Andamanese society. He, more than other people, is able to have contact with the spirit world and thereby make use of supernatural power. A person becomes a medicine man by "dying" and then coming back to life, retaining some of the qualities of the spirit which he had temporarily become. Or sometimes a man, alone in the jungle, may be captured by spirits; and if he demonstrates his courage to them, they may let him go home. As in the first case, he has acquired power by close contact with the spirit world. A third, and less usual, way is for a person to have contact with the spirits in a dream. Sleep is believed to be close to death, and, as in the beliefs of many other primitives, dreaming is thought to be an actual set of experiences engaged in by the spirit. The idea that sleep is dangerous, incidentally, is perhaps the reason that sleep is forbidden for individuals when they are undergoing crucial parts of their initiation ceremonies.

The shaman's utility to the society is believed to lie in his ability to cure (or cause) sickness and to dispel (or arouse) storms. He can be a healer, therefore, and a useful weatherman, but he can also cause illness and stormy weather to overtake the enemies of the society. Like that of the spirit world, his power can be for good or evil.

Spirits inhabit the jungles, the sea, and the sky, and they are all the spirits of former mortals. Some of them are mythical ancestors who are more prominent and more ancient, however, than others. These *big* spirits, as they are called, are those who figure in myths and legends of the ancient past when various things in nature originated. Many of these spirits are named *totemically*; that is, they bear the names of plant or animal species, and in certain cases the spirits seem to have been responsible for creating the species. Some of the most prominent legends deal with the origin of Andamanese society (or of mankind, for the Andamanese did not know of the existence of other men until recently). The legends are contradictory, however, and extremely various; there is no universal Andamanese version of their own origin—there is no dogma or doctrine to which they are required to subscribe. No creator in the legends is worshiped, although some of the legends give one ancient spirit, Biliku or Puluga, credit for having given the ancestors more inventions than any other and for having more power over the weather.

As in primitive society generally, conceptions of the sacred, or supernatural, so permeate activities that are not specifically sacred that it is difficult to separate religious activity from such activities as music and dance, or even from play. Stories told only for entertainment are apt to be the myths of the spirit ancestors. The creativity and sheer joy which are often bound up in singing and dancing are typically felt also to be means by which humans associate with the supernatural. There is, in short, no context of events which makes any activity clearly religious. There is no special place like a church; there are no special persons like priests (even the shaman is engaged in practical, not devotional, activity); and no special days, like Sunday, which clearly demark the sacred from the profane.

Dancing is the most usual of the Andamanese entertainments and ceremonies. Weddings are celebrated by public dancing, and the occasion is one of joy for most of the people. The period of mourning for the dead is brought to a close by a dance, and all of the mourners join in. In the rare case of fighting between villages, a dance is held before the fight, but a dance is also held to ceremonialize the peace pact after the dispute. Many times a dance is held in an evening for no reason at all except pleasure.

The dance used is the same one for nearly all occasions. It always takes place in the open area in the center of the village. Near one end is placed a sounding board, a piece of wood similar in shape to a shield, upon which a man, usually the singer, beats out with his foot a rhythm to the dancing song. A row of women, who form a chorus, sit along one side with their legs stretched before them, one ankle crossed over the other. On most occasions, the women do not join in the dancing, the usual exception being the end-of-mourning dance.

Music consists of one verse sung by the man who at the same time taps the rhythm on the sounding board. The chorus is sung by the man and the row of women, who help him beat the time by clapping their hands on the hollow formed by their thighs. The dancers begin the dance when the chorus begins, hopping rhythmically on one leg until it tires, then shifting to the other. There is no attempt by the dancers themselves to form figures; only their steps are co-ordinated. The song and sounding board provide the only music among the Andamanese, and always accompany a dance. The words are not standardized—each singer composes his own song. There are variations only within narrow limits, however, for the basic characteristics of the music and dance, like all other Andamanese customs, are very ancient and thoroughly traditionalized.

The great age and stability of Andamanese culture are reflected in the philosophy, or world view. The people show no curiosity or

THE DANCE. *Courtesy, The American Museum of Natural History*

intellectual interest in natural phenomena as such, but only insofar as they affect the doings of the people themselves. Their view of the natural order is one of uniformity, of repetitive processes, as is their view of cultural matters. All things, whether in nature or in their social order, once had an origin, but once originated or set into motion, they have continued in the same path ever since. The idea of *change* (since the origin) is wholly absent. The Andamanese does see himself as part of an ordered universe, but it is not ordered in terms of laws of cause and effect. The laws of nature are rather like moral laws. Some actions are right; some are wrong. Wrong actions always lead to some kind of harm; right actions come out successfully or, at least, not harmfully. Right and wrong mean acting in accordance with, or acting against, nature; and, significantly, the rules, regulations, and etiquette, in short, the customs of the society are seen in the same perspective. Custom and law, even in the sense of natural law, are seen as exactly the same thing. It must have been difficult for the Andamanese to find the intellectual means of rationalizing their adjustments to the great changes caused by the invasion of modern men and modern technology.

Marco Polo had heard of the Andaman Islands, but his comments upon them were so wide of the mark that it is evident he was dependent on only the most derivative hearsay. The first reference made by actual visitors is by two Arab travelers of A.D. 871, who considered the natives very dangerous, cannibalistic savages. Master Caesar Frederike left a similar account from his voyage of 1566:

> From Nicubar to Pegu is, as it were, a row or chain of an infinite number of islands, of which many are inhabited with wild people; and they call these islands the Islands of Andemaon, and they call their people savage or wild, because they eat one another: also, these islands have war with one another, for they have small barques, and with them they take one another, and so eat one another: and if by evil chance any ship be lost on those islands, as many have been, there is not one man of these ships lost there that escapeth uneaten or unslain.[3]

The Andamanese were not cannibals, but apparently travelers then, like some today, were likely to adorn their adventures with lies about primitives whom they claimed to have encountered.

The islands were visited several times during the seventeenth and eighteenth centuries, accidentally often, but sometimes for the purpose of capturing and enslaving the inhabitants, a purpose not generally conducive to friendly relations. The first permanent settlement on the islands was made in 1789, when the British East India Company, under Lord Cornwallis (of some fame in the U.S.A.), sent a group of colonists and convicts to the harbor now known as Port Blair, and later transferred them to Port Cornwallis. Because of the unhealthiness of the site, the colony was abandoned in 1796, and the islands were untouched by Europeans for the next 60 years, except for occasional shipwrecks. In 1858, a penal settlement was

[3] Quoted in A. R. Radcliffe-Brown, *The Andaman Islanders,* Glencoe, Ill., 1948, p. 8.

again established at the original site, and has continued until recently.

At first the natives resisted the settlement and made repeated small-scale raids against the inhabitants. We have no information about the possible injustices and cruelties for which they may have been retaliating. An institution called Andamanese Homes was founded to provide rations and medical assistance to the aborigines, and finally friendly relations were established with all but one remote group of Andamanese.

At the present time, the Indian government has made some signs of attempting to integrate the Negritos into the nation, but the islands are so far from important areas of modern political and economic life that there is little likelihood that this can be done before the Andamanese die out. As has been usual with isolated primitives, contact with Europeans has been disastrous because the natives lack immunity to many European diseases. Syphilis has been a great killer in the Andamans consistently since 1870. Such common European diseases as measles and influenza have also repeatedly ravaged the islands. The great increase in the death rate has been more than equaled by a decrease in the birth rate. Whether this decrease is due to conscious limitation or to the effects of the various diseases is not known, but the latter is certainly an important factor. By 1953 the native population of Great Andaman had been reduced to 23 individuals.[4]

FURTHER READINGS

Man, E. H., *On the Aboriginal Inhabitants of the Andaman Islands,* London, 1932.

Mouat, F. J., *Adventures and Researches among the Andaman Islanders,* London, 1863.

Portman, M. V., *A History of Our Relations with the Andamanese,* Calcutta, 1899, 2 vols.

Radcliffe-Brown, A. R., *The Andaman Islanders,* Glencoe, Ill., 1948.

Vaidya, S., *Islands of the Marigold Sun,* London, 1960.

[4] L. Cipriani, "How to Save the Natives of Little Andaman from Extinction," *Anthropos,* Vol. 53, 1958, p. 1028.

The Copper Eskimo

From the Asiatic side of Bering Strait across the Alaskan and Canadian arctic to the east coast of Greenland—about 3400 miles —is the greatest east-west distribution of the Eskimo.[1] The longest north-south extent of their habitat is from northwest Greenland to the southern coast of Labrador, about the same distance as from northern Maine to the Florida Keys. Within this enormous area live about 36,000 Eskimo, a number that would be considered only a fair crowd at an American college football game. Before the depopulation by European diseases they numbered about 100,000, according to Vilhjalmur Stefansson.

The thin distribution of the Eskimo over enormous distances is a striking fact. Yet equally striking is the relative uniformity of linguistic, physical, and cultural characteristics throughout the whole area. All Eskimo speak closely related dialects of a single language stock; all are so clearly eskimoid in physical type that although they are representative of the great Mongoloid group, they are frequently classified also as a particular subgroup; and in many of their cultural traditions they are so similar in all areas that it would seem apparent that their dispersion over their present habitat must have been much more recent than that of the American Indians.

[1] The Eskimo's name for themselves as a people is *Inuit,* which means, merely, *men.* The word *Eskimo* is an English mispronunciation of a French mispronunciation of a Cree Indian word said to mean *eaters of raw meat.*

Archaeological studies have not determined exactly where the Eskimo came from or when they reached North America. The oldest ruins that yield a radiocarbon date are at Cape Denbigh, Alaska, a proto-Eskimo site about 4000 years old. In the central and eastern

regions of the Eskimo domain the remains are more recent. The so-called *Dorset* culture in Canada is about 2600 years old; and a later cultural phase, the *Thule,* appeared after about A.D. 1000 along the Canadian arctic coast. These and other evidences show a general eastward spread from Alaska to Greenland during these two successive phases and suggest that the provenience of the Eskimo, and probably much of their culture, was Asia.

Courtesy, The American Museum of Natural History

The arctic habitat is normally considered to be a very difficult one for human survival, and certainly one which taxes ingenuity. In a general sense, the technological means by which the Eskimo are adjusted to it are primitive, for they are a hunting-fishing people only, lacking agriculture and any domestic animals except the dog. In terms of the particulars of this technology, however, they have a much more complex development of hunting and fishing devices, clothing, housing, transport, and so on, than any primitive people of the band level—as they must, for consider the climate with which they cope. The north latitude of between 60° and 70°, within which most Eskimo live, is marked by an enormous difference between summer and winter. During the winter the more northerly Eskimo do not see the sun for weeks, except as a kind of dim twilight aura. In summer those north of the Arctic Circle (66½°) see the famous midnight sun circling the horizon, never setting. The seasonal temperatures vary accordingly. True summer lasts for only about three months, the only time when mean daily temperatures are above freezing. In winter there are several months during which temperatures normally vary between −30° and −50° Fahrenheit, though it is somewhat less cold in the territory of the

Copper Eskimo. The North American arctic is not so cold as the interior of Siberia—because the Arctic Ocean somewhat mitigates the extreme effect of latitude in the Eskimo areas—but the Eskimo adjustment to the long cold season seems more complete than that of the Siberians in view of the fact that the Eskimo are dependent completely on hunting and fishing.

The striking seasonal changes affect the habits of the Eskimo directly, inasmuch as they are so utterly dependent on game and fish. The change from winter cold, snow, and ice to summer freedom is most strikingly marked by the final breakup of river ice and the melting of snow on the land. With this change the transformation in nature's biological forms is explosive. The hardy arctic perennial plants fairly burst from the recently thawed soil; migratory birds appear soon thereafter (more than one hundred species of birds summer north of the Arctic Circle) ; and most important, great herds of caribou follow the progressively northward appearance of the plants. The "happy time" of plentiful food of land animals and fish is nigh, but it must be remarked that summer in the arctic is also awkward and uncomfortable for the people in some ways. Walking is often difficult, because the soil does not thaw as deeply as it has been frozen and the water cannot seep away; therefore this land, the *tundra,* remains a morass, except sloping areas that drain themselves and shallow soil over rock beds. A greater discomfort is caused by the dense clouds of mosquitoes, black flies, and sandflies.

Winter replaces summer gradually; nature appears to be dying away quietly. In September small lakes begin to freeze, and some snow may fall. Sea ice is usually formed before November. Snow covers everything by then, of course, but contrary to uninformed expectation, the arctic lands do not become deeply buried. The extreme cold of so much of the year drastically reduces the amount of moisture held in the air—a year's total precipitation in some places having been as little as four inches. Strong winds tend to blow the snow into great drifts in some places, but more exposed areas may be bared.

While all Eskimo have a relatively similar culture, there are differences in certain aspects of their adjustment to environment from one region to another, and of course the habitat itself is not everywhere identical. The most significant differences in cultural adaptation seem to be those related to the hunting economy. These can be characterized in terms of the degree of dependence on winter ice-hunting of the great sea mammals.

The most complete dependence on ice-hunting is that of the Polar Eskimo of northwest Greenland, whose subsistence depends almost entirely on the winter resources of the sea. K. Birket-Smith has called theirs the *High Arctic Culture,* suggesting that their

ESKIMO WOMEN SETTING FISH NET UNDER ICE. *Courtesy, The American Museum of Natural History and Hudson's Bay Company*

economy is the most peculiarly Eskimo. In southern Greenland, Labrador, and several Alaskan regions where there is open water for more of the year, there is greater dependence on fishing and hunting from boats and very little winter ice-hunting. The culture of these regions has been called the *Subarctic Culture.* Even less typical are a few groups called the *Caribou Eskimo,* who have become altogether independent of sea resources and follow an inland hunting-fishing cycle on the great Barren Grounds northwest of Hudson Bay and, in a few instances, in inland Alaska. The

Coastal Culture, or *Central Culture,* of most of the Canadian
Eskimo seems to be more average, with ice-hunting in winter but
with caribou hunting and fresh-water fishing in summer. Their
kind of economy is the most widespread, as well as being the most
unspecialized, and the other Eskimo economies may be thought of
as representing emphases varying from it in different degrees.

The Copper Eskimo of the vicinity of Coronation Gulf in the
Canadian arctic is a well-described example of the Canadian Coastal
Eskimo. Copper Eskimo differ from the others in one respect, the
use of crude copper from which some of their implements are cold-
hammered, but this technological distinction seems to have been of
minor importance, or none whatsoever, in influencing other aspects
of their culture. It would seem that a hammered copper knife or
arrowhead is superior to a stone one largely in that it is easier
to make; thus a few hours a year may have been gained for storytelling or sleeping.

The Copper Eskimo numbered between 700 and 800 in the years
1913–1916; they were divided into 14 smaller bands (averaging
about 50 persons each) named for the localities they customarily
frequented. The Copper Eskimo are not a tribe, however; there
is no form of social organization to integrate them. Only propinquity, similarity in dialect and custom, some intermarriage, and
common shifting of residence has given them a sense of oneness
setting them off from neighboring Indians and other Eskimo.

The Copper Eskimo, like almost all other coastal Eskimo, have
distinct communities in summer and winter. The longest period of
residence is at the winter site, and a larger number of people ag-
glomerate there. In late fall the different family groups collect near
known sealing grounds in a protected area where the ice will be
smoother than on open shores where the blocks of pack ice are
jumbled up and frozen together. Ice-hunting for seal then becomes
the dominant economic activity, except for, perhaps, an occasional
bear hunt.

The Copper Eskimo hunt seal in much the same manner as do
other Eskimo. Their method is called *maupok,* meaning *he waits*—
beside a seal's breathing hole. The seal, being an air-breathing
mammal, must come regularly to one of the several holes he has
maintained since the ice first formed. The hunter stands or sits

in absolute quiet until a seal comes up to breathe, and then he harpoons it as deeply as possible. Sometimes a slender bone tip-up is suspended in such a way that the seal will move it when he comes up. The hunter must respond instantaneously, which means that he cannot relax his attention. His vigil may last for hours, for each seal uses a number of breathing holes and may not return to any particular one until after a long time. K. Rasmussen tells of a man who spent two and one-half days waiting, alternately sitting and standing, but attentive all the time.

After a successful setting of the harpoon, the hunter has plenty of activity. He must carefully exhaust the seal, and finally he must enlarge the hole before he can haul out the animal. Many seals, and particularly the large bearded seals, are frustratingly lost at just the moment of near-triumph after hours of hard work.

The seal is for the coast-dwelling Eskimo the most indispensable animal. It provides the great bulk of his food, particularly in middle and late winter when it is normally the only food. Additionally, a thick layer of blubber beneath the skin of the seal reduces to a clear oil that burns nearly smokelessly and is the only source of warmth and light during the long winters. The fat of other animals is not nearly so combustible as seal oil, and wood is not only rare in the arctic but also could not be used as fuel inside the tight snow houses that are the winter dwellings of the Copper Eskimo. The hides of seals are used for water boots, kayaks, and a few other incidentals; caribou hides and occasional bearskins are used for clothing, because they are lighter, warmer, and much more flexible.

When the days grow long and the sea ice begins to break up in the channels where currents are strong, the winter community begins to move out to the inland hunting camps, after the habit of nearly all coastal Eskimo. Smaller groups of families associate in the warm seasons, the size of the groups varying in number from one place to another depending on the hunting and fishing resources.

In springtime migrating caribou are hunted in some localities, although the caribou are thinner at this season than at the time of the fall migration, and musk oxen are also sometimes encountered. Although some individual hunting is done, the greater amount of game is taken in communal drives. As many people as can be mustered station themselves so that the caribou are herded into a blind ravine or a swamp or a lake, where the floundering animals can be easily lanced by the hunters.

The main day-to-day summer activity, however, is fishing. Salmon trout (there are no true salmon on the arctic coast), lake trout, and at the coast, tomcod, make up about one-third of the yearly food intake, most of it in summer and fall. In the spawning season great quantities of salmon trout are caught with nets and impounded by dams or weirs where they are taken with the trident spear. At other times a barbless hook and line are used.

Almost no fruits or vegetables are used by the Copper Eskimo, except for a few berries in late summer. So avid is the quest for vegetable products that the partly digested contents of the caribou's stomach are the first thing eaten when one of these animals is butchered.

After the fall hunting of the southward-bound caribou, there is little to do but wait for the time of the formation of permanent ice, when the winter communities are established. During the waiting period, there is ordinarily plenty of caribou meat, some of which will be stored in stone cairns that protect it from foxes, and there is dried fish saved from the summer season. The major activity at this time is the preparation of winter clothing from the prime caribou skins, repair or manufacture of dog sleds, harpoons, lances, and so on.

All Eskimo are famous for their dextrous craftsmanship and for the remarkable tools and techniques they use in the several kinds of hunting and fishing, transportation, clothing, and shelter. In several respects modern industrial science has been unable to surpass some of the devices for arctic living which the Eskimo have used for many centuries. The most modern and expensively equipped arctic and antarctic exploring expeditions still use a large number of Eskimo items, such as sledges and dog teams, igloos, fur snow boots, and parkas. It should be remarked here, however, that the Eskimo do not use two of the devices commonly associated with the northland, snowshoes and skis.

The variation in supplies of wood in various parts of the arctic coast causes a variation in technology in certain matters. In some areas, particularly near the mouths of large rivers such as the Mackenzie, driftwood is abundant, but in many others it is scarce or nonexistent. Driftwood is very scarce in most of the Coronation

Gulf habitat of the Copper Eskimo, but there is timber available along the inland reaches of the Coppermine River, and these Eskimo make long summer journeys to get it. As a consequence of the unavailability of wood in some areas, Eskimo may make dog sledges out of sections of whalebone (the jawbone) lashed together very ingeniously, but in most areas driftwood is used for crossbars and runners, though the runners are shod with whalebone strips. In all cases, however, an extra shoeing of the runners is made by applying water which turns to ice.

The use of sled dogs is probably the most widely known of Eskimo techniques. These slant-eyed, stocky, stronghearted dogs are a single breed throughout the whole area of the Eskimo habitat. They are used as pack animals in summer; in the winter, for hunting, for smelling out the breathing holes of seals, for ice hunting, and for dragging the seals home, and also, of course, for hauling sleds. A Copper Eskimo family rarely has more than three dogs, because they consume great quantities of meat in winter and are thus a strain on the family's food supply. The dogs are usually harnessed fanwise to the sled by a shoulder-chest harness attached to the sled by a single thong trace. Ordinarily when the whole family is moving and the load is therefore heavy, the Eskimo wife helps the dogs pull the sled and the husband pushes. (The team of many dogs in a line with linked traces so familiar to modern moviegoers is not the typical Eskimo method, and in any event is more appropriate to forest travel with its deep snow trails.)

The kayak is an Eskimo device which has been copied widely. This small craft, very narrow and never more than 16 feet long, is remarkably seaworthy in expert hands. The entire light frame of wood, except for a small hatchway for the single paddler, is covered with sealskin sewn carefully to watertightness. The waterproof jacket of the paddler can be secured to the edge of the hatchway so that little or no water can enter in heavy weather; even if the kayak should capsize, the paddler can right himself with a flip of his double-bladed paddle before much water enters the craft itself (though some might enter *him*). The larger, open-decked *umiak,* or *woman's boat,* common in other coastal areas, is not used by the Copper Eskimo, and the kayak itself is used only on fresh-water lakes in summer, mostly for spearing caribou that have been driven into the water. The kayak is used in northeastern Siberia and has been claimed as an invention of the ancient Lapps of Norway; it cannot be said for certain that it is an Eskimo invention.

The snow house, or igloo, is used in much of the Eskimo area merely as a temporary dwelling, as overnight shelter during a journey; larger, permanent winter houses are made of driftwood, stone, and sod. The Copper Eskimo, however, use snow houses all winter, somewhat larger than temporary igloos, yet essentially the same. The snow house makes a remarkably sound habitation in the arctic winter. The builder selects snow from a properly compacted drift and then rapidly cuts out large blocks with a long bone

Courtesy, Chicago Natural History Museum

or copper knife. They are cut slightly beveled on one side so that as the courses are laid they will slope inward, to be finally secured at the dome by a key block. The longer an iglo is occupied the more substantial it becomes, for the slight melting inside at some times, as during cooking, turns to ice at other times, thus gradually solidifying the house. And in any case, repairs are obviously easy.

When an igloo is built for winter-long occupancy, it may be as large as 12 feet or more in diameter and 9 or 10 feet high at the dome. Sometimes several igloos in a community are built closely together with interconnecting passages, so that the families inhabiting them can visit one another easily. A large community dancehouse (for shamans' performances) is built in a central location. Benches along the sides of each habitation, for storage and for the cooking lamps, are made of wood, and a large sleeping platform is built at the rear, of wood if possible, or of snow, insulated with skins and moss. A window of an ice sheet (in other Eskimo areas more often of seal intestine) is installed over the entrance tunnel. The tunnel is long and small—one enters crawling—for the purpose of excluding the cold, and sometimes there is a bend in it to cut down drafts. A large block of snow is used to block the outside entrance. It is not to be completely blocked, however, for, obviously, some fresh air is necessary—as D. Jenness found when he was rescued one morning from a state of near-suffocation after having gone to sleep with the entry blocked.

It is not advisable to raise the temperature above freezing for very long in a snow house, of course, or an uncomfortable amount of water drips on the inhabitants. Sometimes this problem is mitigated by draping the inner walls and ceiling with skins, which are held in place by cords passed through the walls and held outside by toggles. Thus an insulating air space is made which permits a more comfortable temperature without the ceiling's melting.

In summer, tents of caribou hide or sealskin are used. They are transportable, but the skins are heavy, and when a family moves with its tent and accumulated bags of seal oil and such cumbersome household items as stone bowls and lamps, the procession is necessarily slower and more awkward than in wintertime, when sleds and dog traction can be used.

Eskimo clothing is made mostly of caribou skins; boots and a kind of waterproof coat are made of sealskin. A number of steps are involved in the preparation of the skins: first the fat is scraped from the inner side with a knife; then the skins are stretched between pegs to dry; later the inner sides are chewed thoroughly by the women to remove the rest of the fat; after further drying, the hides are flexed with a dull bone knife for further softness. Furs prepared in this laborious manner remain pliable at temperatures so low as to cause ordinary modern tanned leather to crack into pieces.

The outer parka of both sexes is brief in front, covering the chest only, but much longer in the rear. The appearance of the cut is something like that of a formal swallow-tailed coat, except that the parka is whole in front. An inner coat without the long tail is worn in winter, fur side in. Breeches are of caribou or marmot skins, and in contrast to the custom in several other Eskimo areas, they are worn high—up to their junction with the coat at the chest. As with the coat, a second pair of breeches is worn underneath in winter, fur side in. Mittens are of the gauntlet type, reaching nearly to the elbow and held by a drawstring. Men's winter footgear consists of two pairs of fur stockings reaching to the knee, so that the breeches overlap them by two or three inches. A kind of shoe of sealskin is worn over the stockings. Women wear very different boots: they reach all the way to the hips like fishermen's hip boots and are supported from the waist by thongs. According to Stefansson, these boots are as supremely irrational as the most irrational civilized clothing. They are so heavy and cumbersome that walking is difficult, and they also act as would a funnel, filling with mosquitoes and sandflies in summer and windblown snow in winter.

Eskimo fabricate a wide variety of implements used in hunting and domestic tasks. Hafted knives, arrow and harpoon points, adzes, small saws and gravers are hammered out of copper by the Copper Eskimo, and everywhere out of sheet iron since it has become available through trade. Previously bone, ivory, and stone were more widely used. Delicate articles such as needles, combs, awls, spoons, and artistic figurines, as well as decorative designs on weapons, are all cut, shaped, or incised with the rotary bow drill. Bowls for the blubber lamp and some other utensils are laboriously pecked out of soapstone. Many other household articles, such as cups, bags, buckets, and storage bags for seal oil, are made of sealskin.

Hunting weapons include the bow and arrow, lances, fish spears, and several kinds of harpoons. The harpoons are probably the most ingenious of such artifacts. A sealing harpon, for example, consists of a sharp copper or iron head fitted loosely into a socket of a foreshaft that is about two feet long. The foreshaft, in turn, is fitted to the main shaft by a ball-and-socket point. A long line is tied to the harpoon blade, brought along the shafts through lateral eyelets, and tied tautly to a knob on the main shaft; the rest of the line is held by the hunter. When the harpoon head is thrust into a seal, the force bends the harpoon at the socket point of the fore- and main-shaft so that the line is loosened and the harpoon head comes free of the shaft, though it remains attached to the line. The harpoon shaft acts as an impediment to the seal's swimming. In open-sea hunting in other Eskimo districts an inflated seal bladder and skin-covered hoop are also attached to the line to help tire the animal.

The culinary arts are not highly developed among the Eskimo. Much of the food is eaten raw or, in the case of fish, dried, and the rest is merely boiled. All parts of the animals are eaten. The internal organs are the parts most usually eaten raw, being tenderer

Courtesy, Canadian Consulate General

and tastier (to the Eskimo) than the muscle flesh. Stefansson has emphasized the significance of this factor in preventing nutritional disorders such as scurvy, but it is apparent that the Eskimo do not realize this. The Eskimo actually prefer cooked meat, but boiling meat over a blubber lamp is slow and tedious, and it is also costly, because the seal oil is the only source of heat and light and must be carefully conserved from one sealing season to the next. Many writers have described their astonishment at the amount of raw meat an Eskimo can eat at a single sitting, but Jenness observed that the amount consumed over a period of time was not abnormal, that meals were less frequently taken than in European custom.

Hospitality is considered a great virtue, and food is shared widely. In times of scarcity, as in times of plenty, a hunter is expected to divide his catch among the other households in the community. Such generosity is, of course, more than a mere sentimental virtue; it is a matter of life and death. Any hunter is lucky at some times and unlucky at others, and in an Eskimo community, there is no market or mechanism other than sharing which can average out the irregularities in the individual hunter's fortunes. Among distant communities, on the other hand, there are differences in natural products which lead toward a certain amount of specialization. Some communities are near the sources of copper, others have soapstone, and others are near the inland wood supplies. Reciprocal gift-giving of one of such items for another among the communities was the closest resemblance to trade among the Eskimo until the coming of the modern trading post.

Men and women, of course, have their specialized tasks, as they do in all human societies. The Eskimo men are the hunters and the manufacturers of their own hunting equipment. The women cook, mend, care for children, and prepare, cut, and sew skins for clothing. This division of labor is expedient, but the tasks of one sex are not rigidly tabooed to the other. If necessary, it is not beneath the dignity of a man to sew or cook, and, conversely, women help out in the game drives in subsidiary roles and also do some of the fishing. The nearest approach to specialization other than the variation in the tasks assigned to persons of different sexes and ages within the household is the role of the shaman, or *angakok,* who is given gifts for his services in curing and divination. But he, too, hunts and fishes for his living when he is not performing his sporadic services; therefore, he may be termed a part-time specialist, but not a true professional.

With the exception of shamanistic performances, all of the basic tasks in a community are relegated to the individual domestic units. The ties among the nuclear families within a community are those of kinship, cooperation in hunting and defense, and general sociability. But these ties are rather weak because of the relative self-sufficiency of each family and because of the seasonal shifts of residence. Among different communities there are no formal ties such as those that unify a tribe or make a confederacy. There may be personal friendships between certain members of different communities and sometimes marriage and consanguineal ties, but these are not regularized by any formal means or rules.

The relative self-sufficiency of the family household and the lack of regularity in consistent coresidence of the households in a community results in a pattern of kinship nomenclature similar to that of the modern English usage, and for similar reasons. Because of the lack of a consistent residential association among the families of brothers or of sisters, the actual mother and father are kept terminologically distinct from the mother's sisters and father's brothers. Similarly, in the same generation true siblings are distinguished from cousins, all of whom—no matter what the degree —are given a single term. Also as in modern English custom, one's own children are distinguished from the children of all other relatives. In contrast to most primitive peoples who require the use of kinship terms, Eskimo commonly use personal names in address.

However familiar the Eskimo kinship system may seem to the American or European reader, it is unusual in primitive societies. In most of them there is a consistent coresidential association among the families of certain siblings and sometimes even of more distant relatives, regularized by postnuptial residence rules or customs, with the result that the members of nuclear families are not demarked in the usage of kinship terms from all of those others of the wider coresident kinship group: that is, lineal descendants are not separated from collateral lines. It may well be that the Copper Eskimo system, and that of many others, was not always of the kind described by ethnographers. The drastic depopulation caused by European diseases, the despoliation of such important resources as the whales and caribou, and the influence of the fur trade resulted in the regrouping and merging of survivors into new communities that included many nonrelatives, as well as a movement of persons between communities, so that marriage customs and, in particular, postnuptial residence rules were not followed, and the nuclear family household thus emerged as the sole consistent residential group.[2]

The life cycle of individuals from birth through marriage, parent-

[2] The ethnographer Jenness believed that this fluidity of membership in the Eskimo communities was recent (*The Life of the Copper Eskimos*, p. 33). Historical research by the present writer strongly supports this judgment as well as the further opinion that Eskimo society generally was in aboriginal times more like that of other hunting-gathering peoples.

hood, and finally to death gives a perspective on the social organization from inside, so to speak. The birth of children—boys and girls alike—is greatly welcomed, and their socialization is attended with loving care. Life is harsh, however, and a sickly or deformed baby is not allowed to live. If all babies cannot be supported because of a famine, girls are the first to be sacrificed; a slight preponderance of males over females in the society has resulted. Babies are

Courtesy, The American Museum of Natural History

ordinarily suckled for more than two years, as is usual in primitive society generally, but the weaning period is gradual, and children are occasionally allowed to nurse much longer than two years.

Physical punishment of children is very rare; instead, the parents spend much time in teaching them what they *should* do. Games and other playful activity are typically imitative of adult tasks and are an important aspect of the educational process. In contrast to many primitive societies, the Eskimo do not demark the onset of puberty in either sex by ritual observances. The transition in status from child to adult is gradually acquired in the early teens and fully realized by marriage and the setting up of an independent household.

There is more freedom of choice in marriage than is common among many peoples in the world, and rules of postnuptial residence and local exogamy are absent. Inasmuch as families readily leave one community for residence in another, village exogamy would be a meaningless prohibition. Similarly, a newly married couple might choose to reside near either set of parents. There are rules against the marriage of certain close relatives, of course, as there are in all societies. Parents and children, aunts and nephews, uncles and nieces, and siblings are, not surprisingly, forbidden to marry one another. Cousin marriage is common, though not prescribed. Neither levirate nor sororate is a rule, though it is sometimes practiced.

There is no elaborate ceremony at marriage, nor even a formal gift exchange between the families. In many Eskimo areas marriage-by-capture is simulated; the groom abducts the bride while she pretends resistance to leaving her family. Monogamy is usual, presumably because it is more efficient as a form of sexual division of labor under Eskimo conditions, but there is no explicit rule against having more than one wife.

Ethnographers of the Copper Eskimo describe the frequency of divorce, general laxity in regard to sexual relations, and the custom of wife-lending (as a matter of hospitality) as being similar to practices in other Eskimo areas. The wife-lending custom, however, so often described elsewhere as a sign of the utter subjugation of the wife to the husband's authority, is considered appropriate by the whole Copper Eskimo society, rather than an exercise of male dominance. In many respects wives are treated as equals, a characteristic that Jenness attributes to the complementariness of the sex-based division of labor. There is no concept of illegitimacy of children; an unwedded woman is not scorned for having a child, nor does the child suffer any social disability.

Another Eskimo custom that has received attention equal to the custom of wife-lending is the so-called *mercy-killing* of aged or otherwise incapacitated persons. It seems clear, however, that this is not merely a curious custom, but rather a dire necessity; it happens only in times of famine or forced migration, and it is the handicapped person who suggests, or even insists on, his abandonment. Sometimes the spirit of self-sacrifice takes the form of suicide. There are no cases of mercy-killing recorded for the Copper Eskimo, undoubtedly because the necessity never arose during ethnographers' visits. At any rate, the presence of mercy-killing in any Eskimo region corresponds to very real threats to the survival of the group.

Authorities on the arctic have sometimes wondered whether nature's harshness might not be too hard to take with normal equanimity, for sometimes the Eskimo manifest brief mental disturbances that have become known as *arctic hysteria*.[3] This behavior manifests in the form of nearly complete loss of control; yet such seizures are so common that bystanders remain quite indifferent. At nearly all other times, however, the Eskimo display a buoyant lightheartedness, a good-humored optimism, which has delighted foreigners who have lived with them.

The same people who seem so earthy and funloving live all the time, however, in a pervasive atmosphere of fear of the supernatural. All illness is thought to be caused by supernatural agencies. One of the more frequent of the beliefs about illness is that a spirit has somehow enticed or stolen the soul from the ill person's body. It is also believed that illness can be caused by an evil shaman who induces a spirit which he controls to implant a foreign object somewhere in the ill person's body. This latter concept is ordinarily the explanation of a pain or ache rather than a general illness. In either instance a friendly shaman is called upon to diagnose the trouble. If it is a case of soul loss, he goes on a magical spirit-flight to recover it. If it is a case of a foreign object's causing pain, the shaman performs a ritual designed to extract the object, which he finally seeks out and displays to the patient. Inasmuch as the people have faith in the shaman's performance, there is probably some psychosomatic virtue to it, and thus there are some cures of certain kinds of illness or pain.

Eskimo shamans are similar to those in other parts of the primitive world in that they are persons who are believed to have special gifts that enable them to become more familiar in the world of

---

[3] See Chapter 5 for a fuller description of this phenomenon. It is widely found in the primitive world in many climates hence *arctic* is a misnomer for this form of hysteria, as Aberle has shown (David F. Aberle, "Arctic Hysteria and Latah in Mongolia," *Transactions of the New York Academy of Sciences,* Ser. II, Vol. 14, No. 7, 1952).

spirits than ordinary people. One of the shaman's most specialized attributes is the possession of a spirit helper or guide. Through this helper the shaman is enabled to predict things, such as what the weather will be or where something can be found or whether game is coming; above all, he is able to diagnose sickness. In all of these cases the important characteristic is the shaman's ability to fall into a trance so that his soul may journey to see other spirits, or so that the spirit helper may enter his body and thus have means of communication with people. Trances are induced, as is so usual in other parts of the world—even in a Los Angeles spiritualist meeting— by the use of a tambourine and the singing of ritual songs, all prolonged repetitiously into a drugging monotony in darkness or semi-darkness (neither Eskimo nor Los Angeles spirits like daylight), so that the people are more or less hypnotized and the relatively more unstable shaman is himself in a trance.

Death is, of course, a common result of illness, no matter what the ability of the shaman, but he is credited with cures rather than blamed for his failures. Once a person is dead, no matter how much loved in life, the grief of the survivors is soon replaced by fear— ghosts are malevolent. Among the Copper Eskimo the dead person and his personal effects are left in his house, and the people abandon the vicinity as soon as possible. Among most Eskimo societies it is believed that the ghost remains in the vicinity for five days before departing for the spirit world; therefore this is the period of greatest fear. The name of the deceased, which is felt to be in some sense supernaturally charged with part of his spirit and personality, is never to be mentioned again until it is finally given to a new baby, preferably a close descendant. Although the dead person is living in the afterworld, the Eskimo do not preoccupy themselves with that world and do not hold elaborate concepts of its nature; that is, there is no heaven or happy hunting ground.

The Eskimo's view of his own universe, on the other hand, is that it is imbued with supernatural forces. Everything in the cosmos, even an insignificant stick or stone, possesses a soul or spirit. A slain animal, for example, has left a ghost which must be placated ritually just as if it were human, and this ghost is capable of vengeance. Related to this animistic concept is a firm belief in the efficacy of amulets, various objects kept as charms. There is great variation among Eskimo groups in the specifics of this custom—

even individuals differ—but all carry a number of power-charged objects of various kinds.

In this universe of an infinity of spirits, some are more important than others, because they have direct control over things that are important to people. Sedna, the female spirit of the sea, is a very significant spirit because she can withhold the sea mammals from the Eskimo, but she is not so important that she presides over a hierarchy of lesser gods or spirits. The Sedna myth varies somewhat throughout Eskimoland, but the main essentials of it are as follows:

Sedna, who was merely an ordinary girl originally, married a sea bird and departed with him. This angered her father so much he went to bring her home. On the voyage home, the vengeful bird caused a storm at sea which so endangered the craft that the father threw the girl overboard to make the bird stop the storm. Sedna held to the gunwale of the boat, and her father cut off her fingers at the first joints. These joints fell into the sea and became whales. Sedna grasped the gunwale again and her father cut off the second joints, which became seals. The third joints were cut off, and they became walruses. Sedna then sank to the bottom of the sea, where she took up her abode and began her jurisdiction over the sea animals. She is especially angered at humans when they break their ritual taboos or misbehave, and to punish them she withholds the animals.

Sun and Moon are conceived variously as gods of one sort or another by different Eskimo groups. To the Copper Eskimo, Sila, a sky spirit who controls the sun, is the most important next to Sedna. Neither the sea nor the sky spirits, nor any others, however, bring the Eskimos any measure of comfort in adversity. They are mysterious and hostile and are not thought of as causing good things, but only misfortunes. The only way the Eskimo can keep the gods and ghosts from continually doing harm is by observing an elaborate system of taboos.

Taboos restrict activity in practically all phases of life, but inasmuch as game animals are the single important source of food and material products, the taboos surrounding them are the most significant. Probably the most widespread set of taboos has to do with the separation of all activities having to do with land animals from those having to do with sea animals. This rigid dichotomization goes even so far as to prevent the sewing of caribou skins while one is camped on sea ice or when someone is hunting walrus. Such prohibitions do not hamper the people greatly, because, ordinarily, the sharp seasonal differentiation between land hunting and sea hunting does in fact separate the two kinds of activities.

The Eskimo have many myths and tales that have been handed down unchanged for hundreds of years, as suggested by the fact that some of the myths are almost identical throughout the 3000 miles of coast. Some stories, such as that of Sedna, are regarded as historical truth. Legends, which purportedly describe the origin and history of the people, are also regarded as true. Folk tales, on the other hand, are for entertainment, and the narrator is allowed to introduce elements understood to be fictional. Some of these are told as moral homilies, but more typically the tales are offered purely as diversion.

Some stories are very brief, and might better be called poems, for it is their form and sound more than the fictional content that give pleasure. Singing, too, is a favorite entertainment. It is normally done by an individual before a group, singing or chanting a story that he has himself created. The performance is not particularly tuneful, but essentially rhythmic, accompanied by a tambourine, the only Eskimo musical instrument. The singer stays within a traditional form of composition; his artistry consists of his ingenuity in telling a new story within the limits of the pattern. Song contests are often held, the audience's response determining the winner. In some areas, grudges between two individuals are settled by a singing duel, the audience acting as a sort of jury.

The history of Eskimo contact with Europeans and of the subsequent great social and cultural changes is very different from one part of the arctic to another. The earliest European settlements were by the Norsemen in Greenland, attested by legends and by archaeological remains. By 1578, when Martin Frobisher landed there, however, he found none of the settlers. The search for the Northwest Passage to the Orient during the sixteenth century by such mariners as Frobisher, Davis, Baffin, Hudson, Munk, and others resulted in repeated contacts with many Eskimo of south and west Greenland, Labrador, and the eastern arctic coast of North America.

The diffusion of knowledge about the Eskimo, the rich whaling grounds, and the possibility of important fur trading had great consequence in the seventeenth century. The fur-trading Hudson's Bay Company was incorporated in 1670 as The Company of Merchant Adventurers, Trading into Hudson's Bay, and it established the first permanent posts in Canada. The traders of the Hudson's Bay Company and their rivals of the Northwest Company were

Courtesy, The American Museum of Natural History

later to wield enormous power over the Indians and Eskimo of Canada.

The whaling fleets of many nations had an important effect on the Eskimo of the eastern part of the Canadian arctic, particularly in the eighteenth century and the early half of the nineteenth, but none of them penetrated as far west as the territory of the Copper Eskimo. In the latter half of the same century, whalers in Alaskan waters were also very active, but their eastward movements did not reach the centrally located Copper Eskimo. Thus these remote people were for a long time spared the disasters of disease and liquor brought by the European seamen. A summary of the devastation wrought elsewhere by European diseases has been made by the famous authority on the arctic, Vilhjalmur Stefansson:

It is difficult to estimate what the population may have been before the white man came. Contagious diseases, introduced by Europeans, notably measles, have wrought great havoc among the Canadian and Alaskan Eskimos. In certain western districts a single epidemic about a quarter of a century ago is known to have killed from 25 percent to 75 percent in different places. Judging from Richardson's account, there must have been more than a thousand Eskimos in the Mackenzie Delta in 1848, and perhaps twice that number. But in 1906 Stefansson found these represented by less than thirty descendants. Fully half of that reduction appeared to be accounted for by two epidemics within the memory of people who were still living in 1906, and the preceding reduction was doubtless due to epidemics then forgotten, perhaps one or more of the smallpox plagues that have swept aboriginal Canada. Similar reductions in numbers seems likely for all sections except Greenland. Even there epidemics doubtless took toll formerly, but a strict quarantine maintained by the Danes has enabled the population to increase considerably during the last half century. Perhaps 100,000 may be a reasonable minimum estimate for Eskimo numbers before white contact began to injure as well as benefit the natives.[4]

The Copper Eskimo may well have suffered from European diseases long before traders and missionaries settled among them, inasmuch as smallpox and measles were highly contagious among these people, who had no history of exposure to them, and the diseases thus raced through aboriginal Canada by means of the contact of natives with one another. Depopulation and the merging of survivors into fluid communities of nonrelatives could well have happened long before the first ethnographic studies of them. Nevertheless, firsthand continuous acculturation of the Copper Eskimo was delayed long after that of most other Eskimo, because ships simply did not come to the region.

The first known contact of a European with the Copper Eskimo occurred in 1770 when Samuel Hearne, an employee of the Hudson's Bay Company, accompanied a group of Chipewyan Indians from the post of Fort Churchill, far inland, out to the coast in search of the rumored region of rich copper mines. On the Coppermine River, near Coronation Gulf, they surprised a settlement of Eskimo, and despite Hearne's pleadings, the Indians killed them all. Years later, in 1819 and in 1825–1826, Franklin and Richardson

---

[4] V. Stefansson, "Eskimos" in *Encyclopedia Britannica,* 14th ed., 1927, p. 708.

visited the region, but the Eskimo fled. Still later, other exploring parties in search of Franklin's lost ships were in the Coronation Gulf area. But none of these sporadic contacts had the acculturative effect that employment by whalers and fur-traders had had elsewhere and were to have belatedly among the Coronation Gulf people.

The first trading vessel did not anchor in the region of the Copper Eskimo until 1905–1906, and such ships were only occasional in the next few years so that the effect of trade was not greatly apparent during the sojourn of the Stefansson-Anderson expedition in 1908–1912 and of Jenness in 1914–1916. But according to Jenness:

> Even as we sailed away (in 1916) traders entered their country seeking fox-furs, always fox-furs; and for those pelts so useless for real clothing they offered rifles, shot-guns, steel tools and other goods that promised to make life much easier. So the Eskimos abandoned their communal seal hunts and scattered in isolated families along the coasts in order to trap white foxes during the winter months when the fur of that animal reaches its prime. Their dispersal loosened the old communal ties that had held the families together. The men no longer labored for the entire group, but hunted and trapped each one for his family alone.[5]

The fur trade has had rather similar effects in Canada wherever it has been instituted. The trader becomes the ruler—sometimes despotic and exploitative, sometimes benevolent. The first and most excited wants of the local people are for rifles and cartridges, and this latter becomes, of course, a continuous need. The sale of furs to the trader next begins to involve credit toward steel traps, knives, axes, then a tent, next a stove, and so on. And in order to trap and hunt the fur-bearing animals more effectively and more of the time, the Eskimo have had to give up much of the purely subsistence hunting, thus becoming more and more enmeshed in the cash (or credit) economy because of the necessity of buying food.

The use of the rifle in hunting has cut disastrously into the natural food supply. The great herds of caribou have been in most areas seriously depleted, and the musk oxen are nearly extinct. Purchased food is typically imbalanced nutritionally: sugar, flour, tea, and coffee have become the most usual foods; and alcohol and tobacco, near-necessities. One of the first consequences of dependence

[5] D. Jenness, *The People of the Twilight,* New York, 1928, p. 249.

on the trading post seems to be a great increase in illnesses related to nutritional deficiencies.

Courtesy, Canadian Consulate General

In Greenland and more recently in Alaska, schools, government agencies, missions, and regulated employment practices have provided some measure of protection to Eskimo as they become more and more integrated into the modern world—but this only long after the Eskimo had been despoiled, subjugated, and exploited. The central arctic coast in Canada has been much more recently penetrated; but missions, schools, and police posts are now frequent, and the postwar expansion of the Canadian economy, particularly with respect to its mineral and marine resources, has been explosive. The government now takes much more interest than previously in its Northwest Territories, the administrative district that includes most of Canada's Eskimos. In 1959 there were 19 government schools devoted primarily to education of Eskimo. Eskimo cooperatives were also formed in 1959, and a handicrafts industry provides Eskimo-made sculpture and prints to the Canadian Handicrafts Guild. It is a governmental policy to encourage the native population of Indians and Eskimo to become self-supporting, without at the same time causing them to lose their ethnic and cultural identity.

It is too early to say how this policy will work out, but it seems safe to assume that the 11,000 Eskimo of the Northwest Territories are being aided by more humane enlightenment than was practiced earlier in such regions as Alaska.

FURTHER READINGS

Aberle, D. F., "Arctic Hysteria and Latah in Mongolia," Transactions of the New York Academy of Sciences, Ser. II, Vol. 14, No. 7, 1952.

Birket-Smith, K., *The Eskimos,* New York, 1936.

Freuchen, P., *Book of The Eskimos,* Cleveland, New York, 1961.

Jenness, D., *The Life of the Copper Eskimos,* Report of the Canadian Arctic Expedition, 1913–1918, Vol. 12, Ottawa, 1922.

Jenness, D., *The People of the Twilight,* New York, 1928.

Rasmussen, K., *Across Arctic America,* New York, 1927.

Rasmussen, K., *Intellectual Culture of the Copper Eskimos,* Report of the Fifth Thule Expedition, Vol. 9, Copenhagen, 1932.

Stefansson, V., *My Life with the Eskimo,* New York, 1913.

Stefansson, V., *The Stefansson-Anderson Arctic Expedition of the American Museum: Preliminary Ethnological Report,* Anthropological Papers of the American Museum of Natural History, Vol. 14, 1914.

Stefansson, V., *The Friendly Arctic,* New York, 1921.

Weyer, E. M., Jr., *The Eskimos,* New Haven, 1932.

PART II

TRIBES

5

The Reindeer Tungus
of Siberia

The vast expanse of Siberia still contains remnants of many ancient tribes. Until the sixteenth century Siberia was peopled almost exclusively by primitive societies and had little contact with European Russia except through an occasional trading adventurer. When the great westward invasions of the loosely united Mongols or Tartars in the thirteenth century subsided, Siberia gradually became open for the Russian conquest in 1580. Since then the history of Siberia has been one of gradually increased Russian penetration and colonization, combined with a slow dwindling and assimilation of the native population.

Central Asia has for many centuries been a land of pastoral nomads, wandering seasonally in search of pasture for their sheep, cattle, and horses. Presumably, these domestic animals were derived from the great neolithic developments in the eastern Mediterranean region, in India, and in central China. With the spread of pastoral, nomadic culture, agriculture dropped out of the economic complex in the near-deserts, steppes, and mountain ranges of central Asia, except in a few favorable zones. And, as the culture based on domestic animals spread north into the great subarctic forests of

Siberia, cattle, sheep, and horses became increasingly difficult to maintain, and domesticated reindeer gradually came to take their place. Hunting, however, remained important in the economy of those tribes that were able to herd only reindeer.

The polar regions of North America and Asia contain similar latitude zones. The southern zone consists of great forests which dwindle in the north to a narrow belt of undersized trees and scrub. North of the forest zone extend the treeless plains called *tundra* or, in Canada, the Barren Grounds. Beyond this is the Arctic Ocean. But despite this similarity, the economic significance of land and sea is wholly different in Asia and North America. In North America the borders of the polar sea are inhabited by Eskimo who have made a special adaptation to the hunting of sea mammals. The tundra is actually quite barren, and only a precarious existence is provided for a few inland Eskimo and Indian groups from its scanty resources. In Asia, on the contrary, only one restricted coastal area in the far northeast is suitable for the hunting of sea mammals. Along most of the coast, the sea is shallow and the land low and swampy, and humans without whaling ships cannot reach the larger sea mammals. But the tundra and its forest border in Siberia contain a more developed culture and many more people than the northern inland areas of North America. Hunting and fishing are more productive, and reindeer-breeding is widespread.

A great arc of reindeer-herding peoples extends from northern Scandinavia through treeless tundra and northern forest margin all the way to the Chukchi Peninsula on the Bering Sea. And in modern times the reindeer belt includes Alaska, where Siberian herds have been introduced by the U.S. government to enhance the subsistence of the Eskimo. In this whole region the native peoples have had no crops and no other domesticated animal except the dog.

The uses to which the reindeer are put among the herding peoples are considerably varied, despite the similarity in habitat, and seem to reflect the different origins of the herding customs. Some western peoples, such as the Lapps of Scandinavia, depend on their deer for milk, meat, and skins and use them as traction and pack animals. It is likely that these uses were borrowed from, or suggested by, dairying neighbors to the south of them. At the eastern margin of the region, the Chukchi and Koryak near the Bering Sea have not fully domesticated their herds and use them only to pull sleds, a custom that may have been modeled on the earlier similar use of

Courtesy, The American Museum of Natural History

dogs. Between these eastern and western extremes, the Reindeer Tungus (the largest group), the Yakut, and the smaller tribe of Soyot appear to have modeled their herding customs on the habits of horsemen. The reindeer are milked, as are horses among central Asians, and the use of reindeer as mounts and as pack animals is important. Tungus saddles are similar to the horse saddles of the Mongols, and many other details of riding and packing practices suggest the transfer of customs from south to north.

Tungusic-speaking peoples, widespread in northeastern Asia, are divided into northern and southern linguistic-geographic divisions, which correspond in general to the two main types of economy among them. Southern Tungus, mainly in Manchuria and Outer Mongolia, practice some agriculture and breed cattle and horses. The Manchus, whose ancestors conquered China in 1644, are the best known of these people. Northern Tungus, believed to have been pushed into Siberia from their homeland in Manchuria, are mainly reindeer herders and hunters. A few small riverine and coastal tribes, such as the Goldi and Gilyak, live mainly by fishing.

The reindeer herders, numbering about 20,000 in all, are scattered in small independent tribes over the great expanse of eastern Siberia from the Yenisei River to the Kamchatka Peninsula. Those tribes which depend most fully on the reindeer live in northern Transbaikalia and north to about 55° north latitude. They do not call themselves Tungus and, in fact, do not have a name for the whole group. Many of the individual tribes call themselves Evenki, the original meaning of which is not clear; but judging from the contexts of its usage, it may be taken to mean *the people*. Other groups refer to the Reindeer Tungus as Orochon, *Reindeer-Keepers*.

Tungus is a term applied to them by the Yakuts and later adopted by Russian settlers. It now has become a scientific term for the language group as a whole.

Most of the winter range of the Northern Tungus is covered with forest—the so-called *taiga*—and traversed by many meandering streams which in summer help create the extensive marshlands characteristic of the broad valley floors. The soil is too thin for agriculture and the growing season very short, but the forestlands and marshes are covered with mosses, lichens, shrubs, and dwarf willows, all of which are eaten by reindeer. Winters are long and the coldest in the world; temperatures may fall as low as $-80°$ Fahrenheit, and snow and freezing weather last from early October until May and June. Snowfall is relatively light, and the absence of a deep insulating blanket of snow allows the soil to become frozen to a great depth.

All of the land in northeastern Asia except hilltops and mountains is marshland in summer. The freeze, which penetrates the ground to a great depth, is thawed only in its upper portions during the summer. The newly thawed mud of the upper few feet cannot dry out from the top down in the short summer season, and the water released by the thawing action cannot drain downward through the still-frozen lower strata. Toward the end of summer, surface drying may create an appearance of solid soil, but it is usually merely a crust, all the more dangerous, or at best exasperating, for the deception.

The treeless frozen plains, or tundra, which extend northward beyond the lattitude of the timber, make better summer pastures than the forests, and many of the herders move there for the brief warm season. There is not much grass, but willow shoots and reeds supplement the lichens. The animals must fatten as much as possible to withstand the terrible winter, when they must laboriously paw their way through the snow to find the lichens, or reindeer moss, which are nearly their only food for eight or nine months. During the winter particularly, the herds must be constantly on the move, for the snow becomes so packed from the trampling of the animals that they cannot dig through it. In consequence, the Tungus groups need to roam over a great expanse, and the population density for the region as a whole is sparse, about one person for every one hundred square miles.

In the summer the reindeer suffer terribly from the myriads of gadflies and mosquitoes. If left unattended, they would become thin and sickly from this persecution. The Tungus repel the insects by building smoky fires around which the animals congregate by day. Traveling is done mostly at night in the summer in order to avoid the pests. In winter wolves are a great scourge. A herd may lose as many as 50 percent of its number over a winter, particularly from among the young inexperienced animals. Ordinarily in the winter the herds go to pasture in the daytime only, reversing the summer procedure, and keep near the camp at night when the wolves become bolder.

The reindeer kept by the Tungus are a domesticated breed, not merely tamed wild animals. Their coloring may be black, white, or varieties of brown, in contrast to the uniform gray-brown of the wild breed. Wild bulls sometimes join the domesticated herds during the breeding season, but the Tungus try to kill them and the crossbreed offspring, because they believe the wild strain is impossible to use. The domestic reindeer have a gentle disposition and respond to affectionate treatment. They become particularly attached to the human camps because of the salt provided for them and because of their curious avidity for human urine.

Dangers to the reindeer are so manifold, particularly from wolves, that the size of the herds cannot be easily increased. The Tungus, consequently, do not slaughter their animals for meat except for rare important ceremonial occasions or in case of imminent starvation. In such cases, only the poorest stock is killed. The primary product of the reindeer is milk, which is sweet but low in butterfat. A female reindeer in the best condition can give only about a pint of milk a day after suckling her fawn. The women milk and look after the reindeer, but they do not shepherd them; the herd is left to itself to find pasture and water and usually returns by itself. The does with fawns do not leave the camp. The bucks are dehorned, because if they were not, they could injure a rider, tangle themselves in bushes, and, of course, more easily damage one another during the mating season.

The Tungus esteem their animals greatly and are affectionate and kind to them. Even in reindeer driving, a whip, stick, or goad is not often used to supplement the voice commands. The principal use of the reindeer for transportation is riding, and its use as a pack animal is secondary. In some regions the reindeer is sometimes hitched to a sledge for travel on the tundra in both summer and winter. A good-sized reindeer far surpasses the usefulness of a horse in Siberia; it can travel 50 miles a day easily, and its gait is smooth and even. It can carry a load of 175 pounds swiftly over terrain that would be very difficult or impossible for a horse. This use of the reindeer is of great economic importance to the Tungus, for it enables them to greatly extend their hunting range.

Hunting and trapping are the principal day-to-day activities of the Tungus. Squirrels, foxes, and sables are usually trapped, and larger animals, such as wild reindeer, deer, elk, bear, wolves, and boars, are hunted, in modern times with flintlock guns, earlier with bow and arrow and spear. Fishing, of course, is practiced only at times when the people have moved near a good stream. Despite the great importance of the reindeer in their affection and even in their religious ceremonies, the Tungus are essentially a hunting people; the reindeer are only the margin by which the Tungus are made more secure in subsistence and more proficient as hunters, and in this sense they have superiority over the average hunting-gathering societies of the world. The products of the hunt provide them with the bulk of their essential needs in food, clothing, and shelter. The hunting of fur-bearing animals, particularly the valuable sable and the plentiful squirrels for barter with Russian traders, has long been economically important to the Tungus. Muzzleloading flintlock guns, powder and shot, steel knives and axes, kettles and other metal utensils, and tea and tobacco are the most important goods acquired in return for the skins.

The forms of clothing are variable among the Tungus because of the different influences of neighbors on all sides. Only one peculiarly Tungusic item remains, a distinctively cut and decorated coat. It is of reindeer skins, preferably skin from fawns, tailored in a style somewhat similar to that of the European morning coat. It is worn both in winter and in summer. While the open front may have certain advantages for riding, it exposes the chest and abdomen to the cold and is therefore supplemented by a kind of leather apron which protects these parts from the wind. This style, incidentally, is found in some parts of China.

The probable southern origin of the Northern Tungus and their incomplete adaptation to arctic conditions are also suggested by

SUMMER SHELTER. *Courtesy, The American Museum of Natural History*

another clothing feature. Trousers are very brief, also of a type known in China, and have to be supplemented by extra leg protectors above and around the knee. Leggings and skin boots, however, are of the typical arctic style and were probably borrowed in their complete form from neighboring arctic tribes because the original footgear was so totally unsuitable that it could not be adapted. Protectors which shade the eyes from the brilliant springtime sun and reduce vision to a very narrow slit were also borrowed from the prior inhabitants.

The nucleus of Tungusic society is the small tent-household of husband, wife, and children, although frequently an older relative, the surviving father or mother of the husband, lives with the family. This family is the basic economic unit, and the primary division of labor in the society on the basis of sex is therein manifested. Men's activity consists of hunting and defense against dangerous animals and enemies, manufacture of most implements, loading of pack animals, slaughtering and skinning, cutting of firewood, and other arduous outdoor tasks. Women dress the skins and make clothing and tent covers, milk reindeer and care for them when they are near the camp, and undertake the usual domestic tasks associated with food preparation and care of children. The Tungus are not such sticklers over these rules as are many societies, however, and frequently a man helps his wife in any task within his competence, while women likewise help the men. An older man who can no longer hunt may take over a great many of the household tasks normally done by women.

The Tungusic home must be, of course, an easily transportable unit, and the household equipment sparse and sturdy. The winter skin tent is small; it ordinarily contains sleeping places for only two or three adults and a few children. The summer lodge is built of birch bark and is larger, because in summer a more permanent camp is established. The form of the lodge is conical, created by leaning poles together to a central apex, which is left open as a smoke hole. The furnishings are merely the skins that form the beds. The residents prefer to lie down rather than sit, in order to breathe clearer air. The tent must be kept tightly closed in winter and a fire must be kept continuously burning because of the intense cold. In summer the same procedure is followed in the lodge to inhibit the clouds of insect pests; therefore the air inside the dwellings is always very smoky. Cooking utensils are usually merely a metal kettle or two. The main element of the diet is unseasoned boiled meat. Tea and tobacco are also important and are particularly esteemed as offerings to guests.

The etiquette of the lodge is complicated. The right-hand place from the entrance is reserved for the husband, and his wife's place is adjacent. The left side is reserved for the next most senior male, who is ordinarily the eldest son. The side directly opposite the entrance is reserved for the spirits or for an eminent male visitor. Visitors are treated hospitably, but always with great respect. Conversation is formal, particularly if a visitor is older than the host, and emotional expressions of joy, amusement, or surprise are not good form. Gifts are freely given and the guest must not refuse, but he is expected to make a return gift later.

During the winter, a good three-quarters of the year, the Tungus are scattered widely over the tribal territory, hardly ever in the company of more than two or three other families. The camps move frequently as the reindeer search out new forage areas. The men of the camp are often absent on hunting and trapping excursions, while the women care for the herds and maintain the base camp, even, on necessity, moving it to a prearranged new location. When the camp consists of several families, the products of the hunt are divided among them, except for squirrel skins, which are kept to be exchanged by the individual hunter for tea, tobacco, or some such luxury.

Families tend to have customary camp sites and to keep to a fairly regular migration route, coming together in summer in more permanent and larger camps. Individual families and winter-camp groups leave stores of food, clothing, and other equipment at their accustomed sites in order to relieve the transportation problem. The storehouses are small log huts, raised on platforms as defense against animals. Any needy Tungus of the local tribal group of related clans who happens upon a storehouse is allowed to help himself. If something of value is taken which cannot be replaced before the owning family returns, a piece of wood marked to identify the borrower is left in its place. It is understood that adjustments will be made later.

The Tungus do not normally trade with one another, other than by the exchange of gifts, borrowing, and normal hospitality. Implements, tea, tobacco, and other materials from the outside world are obtained by individual Tungus in exchange for furs. This has resulted in a common respect for each individual's customary squirrel and sable trapping ground. Except for this, there is very little recognition of complete private rights in the resources of nature. The eldest son, if he is capable, usually inherits the rights and responsibilities of the family head, but there is so little important property that it is largely an informal transfer. The herd of reindeer is not a significantly permanent property of a family. The size of the herd fluctuates greatly from year to year because of attacks by wolves or epidemics, and the heads of families meet each summer in a clan council to redistribute the stock so that each household will be able to survive the next winter. In a very real sense, ownership of the reindeer is vested in the clan, even though the individual families take care of divided portions of the herd. In just the same way, the territory over which the families roam is felt to pertain to the intermarrying clans who occupy it. There are no important wealth distinctions among the people.

The Tungusic clan is made up of families related patrilineally.

Each clan has a name, sometimes that of the legendary male ancestor, and its own particular set of guardian spirits; and the clan is,
of course, exogamous. The clans vary greatly in size, from as few
as a dozen to as many as several hundred households. There is no
hereditary chief, and during the summer, when the component
households are able to camp together, the decisions of the clan are
arrived at by a general consensus of household heads. There is a
tendency for one clan to intermarry consistently with only one other.
The principle of reciprocity is strong; if one clan gives daughters
in marriage to another, the latter should give in return. In fact,
whenever feasible, it is felt proper that two single households
should reciprocate by exchanging daughters in marriage. Cross-
cousin marriage, particularly between a man and his mother's
brother's daughter, is the ideal and most common form for the
reciprocal marriages, though it is not rigidly adherred to. Parallel
cousins are members of the same clan and therefore are forbidden to
marry.

Intermarrying clans become in time composed of relatives by
descent as well as by affinal ties, and among the Tungus such clans
have become consolidated units so distinctive as to show dialectic
differentiation from others and to have a territorial unity. We may
call such an endogamous unit a true *tribe*. The Tungus tribal units
do not remain constant in population over a long period of time. It
is quite apparent from the similarity in clan names and ritual
practices in several regions that some have proliferated and broken
into separated parts and that in other cases dwindling clans have
amalgamated with others.

The pattern of kinship terms used in address reflects two main
considerations: clan membership and relative age.[1] The preferred,
and perhaps in earlier times the usual, system of marriage consistently united only two clans. From the point of view of any particular
person, therefore, there are two basic kinds of relatives, those of his
father's clan and those of his mother's clan. Each of these are subdivided into two groups, those who are senior to the speaker and
those who are junior. A change of affixes in the kinship terms

[1] The following description of the pattern of kinship terminology is S. M. Shirokogoroff's reconstruction of the proto-Tungusic pattern (*Social Organization of the
Northern Tungus,* Shanghai, 1933, Chap. IV). Various Tungusic groups have become
so influenced by different neighbors that a general description of modern Tungusic
terminology would be impossible.

distinguishes male from female relatives.

The result of the intersection of these two principles is a simple version of a common primitive pattern which separates cross cousins from parallel cousins, mother's brothers and father's sisters (whom we could term cross uncles and aunts) from the other (parallel) uncles and aunts, because they are, of course, fathers and mothers of the cross cousins who reside in the other clan. These terms are widely extended to other members of the father's and mother's clans; it is as though a term meaning mother's brother were applied to all the mother's brothers' fellow clan members older than the speaker. The only terms which refer to individuals alone are those in the direct line of descent: father, mother, grandparents, son and daughter, and grandchildren. Brothers and sisters older than the speaker are distinguished from younger brothers and sisters. Except for this small group of genealogical terms, all the other terms are best understood as respect terminology used in address. In referring to an absent person, a personal name or nickname may be used.

A person should never address his senior by name; to do so would be gross disrespect. A person should never sit in the presence of a senior person until invited and should not speak until spoken to. One never jokes with a senior, and esteem must be shown by bowing or kneeling. The definition of the junior-senior status is primarily by generation rather than absolute age. It could happen that an uncle might be near the nephew in age or even younger, but because he belongs to the father's generation he is treated by the nephew as though he were much older than his actual age. There are no customs of avoidance or taboo among classes of relatives, except for the social distance prescribed for generation differentiation.

A clan insists upon the obedience of its members to its rules and orders. The clan means everything to the individual: it provides member families with hunting territory and reindeer, it arranges marriages, it protects its members against enemies, and it enforces the rules of social behavior. A clan is empowered to punish offending members, and has three powerful measures at its customary disposal. A person may be thrashed for such crimes as refusing to obey his seniors or to follow a clan decision. More serious crimes, such as murder or incest, are rare and may be punished by death, usually by strangling. Nearly as final is the penalty of expulsion from the clan, for a person who does not belong to a clan has no one to defend him or to help him in emergencies. In modern times, the Tungus found living in Russian settlements are usually those who have been expelled from the clans. Punishment by fines or confiscation of property is unknown, because so little of the important property is considered to be individually owned. Theft, for the same reason, is not a common crime. In fact, crimes of any kind have been rare in Tungusic society until modern times, when crimes of violence have become more frequent as a consequence of a greater use of alcohol.

The Tungus are always anxious to increase the size of their clan, for the strength of the clan is directly related to the feeling of security of its members. When a woman becomes pregnant, the clan members show a great joy at the prospect of an additional member. There seems to be no preference for one sex over the other; a boy will remain a resident of the clan's territory, but the clan also needs girls to exchange for those who will come into it at marriage.

When a birth is imminent, a small tent is built near the home as a delivery room. Inside, two posts are set vertically with a crossbar suspended between them. In the act of delivery, the mother squats and leans her chest on the crossbar with her arms hanging over it. She is usually attended by an old woman, but it is said that in the old days a woman was not allowed any help. Neither then nor now are any men allowed to be present, and the husband is kept far away from the place of delivery. The Tungus do not practice infanticide even in the case of twins, although they consider twins to be abnormal and believe that, because they have only one soul between them, the death of one must soon be followed by the death of the other. The placenta is always buried, and the umbilical cord is preserved by some Tungusic groups and buried by others. The woman and child live in the small tent for a month after a birth in summer or ten days or more in winter. The mother cannot enter the family lodge until a ritual of purification by washing and smoking herself and her belongings has been performed.

Shortly after birth, the child is given a name, which, because of its magically suggestive power, is thought to have an influence on the child's development and personality. During the first few days the baby is kept wrapped in furs, but finally it is bathed and placed in a fur bag on a cradle board, where it is kept for about a year. A baby is suckled by the mother for about three years usually, but if the mother does not have another child in the meantime, she may suckle the child for as many as six years. The baby is given certain supplementary foods after about a year, however. Children frequently are exposed naked for short intervals to the bitter winter cold in order to toughen them. Bathing is rare, however, and washing the head is tabooed for two or three years. For this reason, Tungusic babies are prey to skin infections and parasites.

Parents and relatives are serious about teaching children the etiquette and skills expected of them, but training is not accompanied by punishment or any sort of rigor. Children are so greatly indulged by all the adults of a camp that they expect to be allowed to do anything that amuses them: smoke a pipe, drink liquor, or run various physical risks among the animals. Infant mortality is exceedingly high. Infectious maladies are common, and frozen hands or feet and burns from crowding too close to the fire are frequent accidents.

A girl's puberty signifies potentiality for childbearing and is recognized by the usual morphological changes. A girl is said to be *fat* when she manifests physical signs of her sexual maturity. Her first menstruation, which occurs at about the age of 14, is noted, because she is dangerous and unclean during this period, but this is not taken as the special event signalizing her maturity. A boy's approach to the status of manhood is also gradual. There are no special initiation rites; he merely grows into the increasing responsibility and status of manhood during his early teens. The true accession of both boys and girls to full membership into the society of adults is achieved by marriage and the birth of a child.

Marriage frequently takes place at an early age; sometimes one or both the partners may be sexually immature. It is felt desirable that the couple be of about the same age, and whenever possible that they be cross cousins. It is also preferred that two families should exchange marriage partners; ideally a son of one family marries the daughter of another and the latter's brother marries the sister of the former. When this reciprocity is possible, no exchange of valuables need be made between the families. Marriages are, in any case, agreements made primarily between individual families and secondarily between the two clans of which the families are members. The levirate and sororate are always an understood part of the bargain—that is, in case of the death of one of the marriage partners, a sibling of the deceased marries the surviving spouse.

Marriages which are not fully reciprocal between two families are accompanied by exchanges of property made after a considerable period of negotiation and exchange of feasts. The man's family, aided by his clan, collect a large number of reindeer, which they turn over to the girl's family. This phase corresponds to the custom misleadingly called *bride price,* which is so commonly found among pastoral peoples. The amount of the gift is an important prestige factor for both families, and it would seem that the man's clan nearly impoverishes itself to provide a rich gift. But an equivalent of about half of the gift comes back to the groom's clan in the form of the dowry that accompanies the girl. Over a period of time, of course, the gifts tend to cancel themselves out because of the tendency of the two clans to continue intermarrying and exchanging equivalent numbers of brides and associated gifts. Occasionally, a man's family and clan are so poor or so unwilling to collaborate in a particular marriage that the groom does not have an adequate gift. In such cases, he sets up his household with his wife's family in order to help provide for them economically. This custom of *bride service* is also found among some other pastoral peoples.

Wedding ceremonies are held at a time fixed as much as a year in advance and may be attended by as many as 150 persons. The two clans pitch their lodges in separate areas and begin the first day with a great feast. The ceremonial climax occurs after the groom's gifts are delivered, when, no matter how short the distance, the dowry is loaded on the reindeer and, accompanied by the bride dressed in special finery, carried to the bridegroom's lodge. The bride then takes the wife's place in the husband's lodge, at the right-hand side of the entrance, and her retinue of relatives and the husband's relatives sit around the circle. The bridegroom then enters and follows the bride around the circle to greet the guests as host. Each guest kisses the bride on the mouth and hands, and the go-betweens who carried on the marriage negotiations spit three times on her hand. This rite completed, the couple are formally man and wife. The remainder of the day and evening is spent in eating, drinking, and other diversions.

The most typical amusement at the Tungusic wedding is a dance, or *sing,* as it is called because of the monotonous rhythmic chanting which accompanies it. A large circle is formed of both men and women mixed, or sometimes of men and women in separate circles, all adjoined by locked arms. The step made in unison by the whole circle is a hop to the left with a brief forward bow of the body, so that the whole group dips and circles in a clockwise direction. A leader chants brief recitals of his own composition in time to the step, and the group keeps up an energetic refrain of meaningless words. This dance may go on for several hours.

When a girl enters into family life as a wife, she becomes charged with more duties than she had known as a daughter in her own family. She becomes the nucleus of a household and is in sole command of the tent and all its equipment; she carries water and firewood, does the cooking, looks after the animals, tans skins, and sews clothing. Her life outside the lodge also carries considerable responsibility, because the husband is often absent on long hunting trips. The frequent changes in residence caused by the needs of the deer are sometimes her duty alone. Before commencing a march, she must collect the grazing reindeer and saddle and load them. She then leads the line of reindeer, those mounted by the children behind her and the pack animals following, all linked together by their halters. She must know the country well, for she must find water, wood, and pasture for the next stop and must arrive at the appointed rendezvous with her husband at the time agreed upon.

In general, wives are deferential toward their husbands, but they cannot be said to occupy a degraded status. The formal deference is of the sort commonly found in human societies and seems related to the character of the work—his mostly outside and economically important; hers, except for childbearing, usually secondary and concerned with the household. Consequently, the wife serves dinner when the husband arrives, and if male visitors are present, she serves them and does not intrude on their conversation. Only after they have finished do she and the children eat. In some respects, the relations of husband and wife seem unexpectedly formal. They are not allowed to call one another by their personal names, for example, but must use the terms *husband* and *wife* until a child is born, after which the couple must refer to each other by a term meaning *my children's mother* or *my children's father*. This custom of teknonymy, to use the specific term, is a respectful usage found in many parts of the primitive world.

Polygyny is rare among the Tungus, but may be allowed when a man's wife bears no children or when she is older than her husband and reaches an age at which she can bear no more. It is not proper for a person to marry two sisters; nevertheless the two wives of a polygynous household call one another by the term for senior and junior sister, and the children call them both *mother*.

The Tungus seem to be more matter-of-fact about illness and disease than many other primitive peoples. Wounds and disabilities whose causes are apparent are treated according to notions about nature's properties. Contagious illnesses, of which smallpox, chickenpox, and measles are the most common, are considered the work of spirits; but isolation to prevent further contagion is practiced, and the modern practice of vaccination is welcomed. There is little concern with witchcraft, and magical treatment is attempted but rarely. Remedies, however inefficacious, are essentially naturalistic in intent. Psychological or neurotic disorders, however, are the province of shamanistic curing.

The Tungus, in common with many other peoples of the Far North, including the Eskimo, are afflicted with the psychic instability called arctic hysteria. The ways in which the temporary relaxation of self-control manifest themselves are many, but they all have in general a sort of tantrum character. The frequency of hysteria in the population as a whole appears to be related to the fact that custom does not disapprove of it; in fact, it could be said to be rewarded, for the person attracts attention, gains sympathy, and is considered remarkable. Hysterical persons are felt to be close to the spirit world, and professional shamans are largely drawn from those persons who are the most unstable. The theory seems to be that the spirits are looking for a master and attempt to possess likely candidates from time to time. Finally, from among the afflicted, a spirit finds its best medium, and that person, then, learns to call the spirit at will and control it, thus preventing its possession of other people.

The basis of shamanism among the Tungus consists, therefore, of the same notion that is found among the Eskimo and many American Indians—he is a person able to control a spirit and keep it from doing harm, and he becomes, at times, a medium for the spirit. He is also able to use this spirit to combat or guide other spirits who might be harmfully disposed. Among the Tungus, either men or women may become shamans. The word *shaman,* incidentally, is a Tungus word and was introduced to the Western world by Russians who met the Tungus in the seventeenth century.

A shaman has special knowledge, the knowledge of the spirits, when he is possessed, and consequently he may function as a diviner. As was the practice with the famous oracle of Delphi, someone must interpret his actions and the unintelligible words which he utters. But his function as a master of spirits is more important. He can prevent malevolently inclined spirits from causing bad luck, and he can remove spirits from persons suffering from mental imbalance.

The shaman uses special paraphernalia, complicated and variable from shaman to shaman, but always including the following items: a Chinese brass mirror hung with pendants, an elaborate costume, and a tambourine which he must beat in order to bring himself to a state of ecstasy and to induce a suggestible state of mind among the audience. The performance itself varies from region to region in its details and in the purposes of the ceremony, but the basic act is the monotonous drumming which finally results in the shaman's trance, during which he is possessed. A frequent purpose is his soul's journey to the lower world to accomplish some piece of business with important ancestral spirits for the good of the clan. A prior part of such a performance is often concerned with divining the causes of individual illnesses or other troubles and predicting the future. The Tungusic shaman is not, properly speaking, a medicine man or healer. In cases of illness, his role is essentially that of diagnostician. Only if he decides that a person is ill because of the action of a spirit does he intervene, and this class of illness is typically a psychological rather than a physiological malady.

Death is thought to be caused by the permanent removal of the soul from the body. It is understood that children die more easily than adults because the soul is less well stabilized in the body. Old people are expected to die as a natural form of attrition, but vigorous adults die only through accident, infectious diseases, or through the action of spirits in causing the soul to leave the body. Soul loss may be temporary, as in the cases of unconsciousness. An ill person who hovers between life and death or who has just died can recover if the shaman is quick enough in finding the soul and enticing it back into the patient's body. If the shaman is unsuccessful and the person is judged finally dead, then the attention of the people is turned to the problem of transporting the soul to the lower world.

A corpse is dressed in the best available clothing and covered with a blanket. After this preparation, the relatives begin a vigil that lasts for as long as two days if the weather is cold, but for at least 24 hours. Various foods and drinks are placed near the head of the corpse and a pipe and tobacco on the breast. Now and then the people throw bits of food and drops of milk or tea into the air in case the spirit is there. There is no obligation to demonstrate grief; the people sit around conversing in ordinary tones about everyday matters. Finally, when it is certain that the soul is not going to return, the corpse is put into a wooden coffin and the coffin elevated on posts to keep it safe from predators. A reindeer is sacrificed for the use of the spirit, and several belongings of the deceased, which will be used on his journey, are left in the coffin with him. If some trouble or misfortune befalls the clansmen after the disposal of the corpse, it is assumed that the soul was dissatisfied and is venting its anger. The shaman may be called to divine whether this is so and to convince the soul to make its journey to the lower world. Souls that do not reach the afterworld are felt to constitute a real danger to the people.

Conditions in the afterworld of the ancestors are about the same as on earth. The souls need things, they suffer from cold and hunger sometimes—it is not a heaven—and they are just as inclined to anger or jealousy as are ordinary human beings, except that somehow they seem rather more childish and thus more likely to be manipulated by shamans. Sacrifices of animals, if possible, and prayers are frequently made to the clan ancestors to keep them from bringing bad luck by coming back.

The Tungusic universe is made of three worlds: the above-mentioned lower world of ancestor spirits; a middle world in which people live; and an upper or sky world, which is where sun, moon, stars, and vague sky spirits exist. Among the Manchus and modern Tungus influenced by them, there is a concept of a Spirit of Heaven. The Reindeer Tungus, however, seem to have had no specific notions of anthropomorphic sky gods or creators, or even to have had a clear-cut mythology of creation—everything seems to have existed always in its contemporary form. The clan ancestor spirits are the primary focus of attention, but it would be misleading to call the religion ancestor worship, for the ancestors have become rather depersonalized after death and are not so much worshiped as placated and manipulated.

The cult of ecstasy and nervous hysteria of the Tungus might cause a misleading impression of the everyday average personality. Their normal social behavior has given visitors the impression of open, friendly, square-rigged honesty. Berthold Laufer, comparing them with some other Siberian peoples, stated, "I felt more at home, however, with the reindeer-breeding Tungusians, who are more alert, open minded, straightforward, and psychically more developed, and I found that A. von Middendorff was perfectly right in styling them the aristocracy of Siberia."[2]

The primitive tribes of Siberia have been subject to the Russians for several centuries, but for most of that time the consequences for native culture have not been catastrophic so much as slow and indirect. Probably the spread of European epidemic diseases was the first consequence of magnitude, for there has long been a dwindling of population. Other effects were probably generally beneficial more than deleterious, however. Guns and iron tools obtained in trade improved the natives' subsistence, and metal containers, tobacco, tea, sugar, and salt in total have not been harmful. And it should be remarked that the reindeer-breeders of Siberia did not acculturate as quickly as the partially agricultural Yakut or the semisedentary fishermen like the Chukchi, Koryak, and Goldi to the east and north. According to W. G. Bogoras:

A very important detail of the economic and political life in the north is represented by the fact that the Russian Cossacks, hunters and traders, a counterpart to the Spanish conquistadores, since they also have conquered these immense lands in almost incredibly short time, soon after that settled in the north just like fishermen. The first condition of life for them was an immovable house with a regular couch and regular heating. They were averse to wandering around the tundra with a herd of reindeer just as they have objected to the constant wandering of cattle-breeding nomads. So the Cossacks intermingled with the fishermen, took wives from among them, and assumed from the beginning their way of supporting life on fishing and hunting.[3]

The relations of the Tungus with the Russian outposts became based on sporadic trade. The sable particularly and also squirrel, fox, bear, and reindeer skins were the raw commodities used in ex-

[2] "The Reindeer and its Domestication," *Memoirs of the American Anthropological Association*, Vol. 4, 1917, p. 143.
[3] W. G. Bogoras, "Elements of the Culture of the Circumpolar Zone," *Smithsonian Institution Annual Report*, Washington, 1930, p. 475.

change for European goods. As previously indicated, most of the goods received in exchange helped, or at least did not harm, the Tungus. But one common trade item, for which it appears primitive people all over the world are avid, was alcohol—in this case cheap Russian vodka. It created the usual difficulties and disturbances, but in the frozen north there is an added danger in the use of alcohol. In the deep-freeze of winter the slightest relaxation of vigilance can result in frozen hands and feet and even death. The Tungus, whose self-restraint is apparently easily discarded, suffered considerable losses simply because of alcoholic carelessness. In some cases, fur hunters became deeply indebted through this addiction and were forced to live indentured to unscrupulous traders.

Courtesy, The American Museum of Natural History

Before the Russian Revolution, many groups of Reindeer Tungus were converted to Greek Orthodox Christianity, but apparently the conversion was nominal rather than culturally pervasive. Shamans continued to carry on their ancient profession, and so far as we know continue to do so today. Since the Revolution religious missionization has stopped, and we know very little of what may have taken its place. It seems unlikely that intellectual conversion to Marxism would make much headway among primitive hunters, and the ambitious industrialization of Siberia has been concentrated on certain restricted areas of coal and iron deposits far from the Tungusic area. It is quite probable, nevertheless, that economic change in Siberia as a whole is occurring at a much faster rate than under the Czars, when Imperial Russia was more concerned with its dependent economic relations with Europe than with developing the great subcontinent of Siberia.

As seen in other parts of the world, hunting societies in developing areas are more prone to sudden and complete obliteration than are the settled agriculturists, and we may expect the Tungus similarly to become assimilated as they find the valuable fur-bearing animals diminishing and an increase in opportunities for day labor in mining and lumbering camps. It should be noted that the Russians in Siberia do not isolate their primitives on reservations, nor are they given to racial prejudices, but attempt to draw the local peoples into national economic life as quickly as they can.

FURTHER READINGS

Bogoras, W. G., "Elements of the Culture of the Circumpolar Zone," *Smithsonian Institution Annual Report,* Washington, 1930, pp. 465–482.

Bogoras, W. G., "New Data on Types and Distribution of Reindeer Breeding in Northern Eurasia," *Proceedings of the 23rd International Congress of Americanists,* Lancaster, Pa., 1930.

Buxton, L. H. D., *The Peoples of Asia,* New York, 1925.

Cressey, G. B., *Asia's Lands and Peoples,* New York, 1934.

Czaplicka, M. A., *Aboriginal Siberia,* London, 1914.

Czaplicka, M. A., *My Siberian Year,* London (n.d.).

Hatt, G., "Notes on Reindeer Domestication," *Memoirs of the American Anthropological Association,* Vol. 6, No. 2, 1919.

Jochelson, W., *Peoples of Asiatic Russia,* New York, 1928.

Laufer, B., "The Reindeer and Its Domestication," *Memoirs of the American Anthropological Association,* Vol. 4, No. 2, 1917.

Mirov, N. T., "Notes on the Domestication of the Reindeer," *American Anthropologist,* n.s., Vol. 47, 1945.

Radloff, A., *Aus Sibirien,* Leipzig, 1884, 2 vols.

Shirokogoroff, S. M., *Social Organization of the Northern Tungus,* Shanghai, 1933.

Shirokogoroff, S. M., *Psychomental Complex of the Tungus,* London, 1935.

The Cheyenne of the North American Plains

No primitive peoples have so captured the imagination of modern Americans—and even Europeans—as the colorful warriors of the western plains of North America. When the average American hears about Indians, the image of the free-roaming, mounted buffalo hunters, with their feather war bonnets and gaudily decorated skin clothing, war paint, sun dances, sign language, the circular village of tipis, and so on, is what comes to mind. In actual fact, however, the Plains horsemen were a most special development among the many kinds of American Indians. The myriads of slow-moving buffalo which blackened the Great Plains were a unique kind of food resource in the New World, and when certain Indian tribes acquired Spanish horses and began using them in the buffalo hunt, a striking cultural transformation took place. Even the amount of warfare among the tribes in the Plains was unusually great, rather than typical of Indians, and again because of peculiar circumstances.

The famous Plains culture was not fully aboriginal nor did it last very long. The catalytic agent, the horse, was diffused gradually northward, by theft and trade, from the Spanish settlements of New Mexico sometime after 1600. Once mounted, the Indians could fol-

Courtesy, The American Museum of Natural History

low and kill greater numbers of buffalo than ever before. So productive was this new way of life that tribes of diverse cultures and languages were drawn into the Plains from all directions. The new Plains culture was a product of the functional requirements of mounted buffalo hunting and of the amalgamation of customs from diverse origins. But this picturesque life lasted only a few generations. Its fullest flowering over the whole Plains area was not accomplished until about 1800. From about 1850 through the 1870s, great battles of extermination were fought between whites and Indians as the inexorable tide of America's westward expansion flooded the area. The buffalo were soon nearly extinct, and, except for occasional outbreaks, the once proud horsemen were confined to the depressing life of the reservation.

Before the New World was colonized by Europeans, before the horse revolutionized life on the Plains, buffalo-hunting on foot was not a productive enough enterprise to support a large population. The most widespread Indian culture in the eastern United States was based on horticulture—the cultivation of maize, beans, and squash. This mode of subsistence had spread from the eastern woodlands into the Plains wherever agriculture was possible, along the rivers, especially in the Dakotas and Nebraska, but even as far west as Montana. The type of farming was gardening, not field agriculture; the Indians did not have the heavy turf-breaking implements or the draft animals to drag them in order to open the broad grasslands to agricultural exploitation. Consequently, the horticultural mode of life remained limited to river bottomlands.

In pre-Columbian times, therefore, the highest developments of culture in the Plains were the fingerlike extensions of the eastern complex of sedentary village dwellers. The village dwelling Indians of the Plains typically lived in circular houses built of packed earth, some as large as 50 feet in diameter, in villages of as many as 70 units. Their hunting incursions into the Plains after buffalo were only incidental, made usually only once a year, to supplement the vegetable diet that was their mainstay and to acquire hides, sinew, and horn. The purely hunting peoples of the further Plains were, at that time, merely marginal nomads, moving in small groups, eking out a precarious and poverty-stricken existence. The use of the horse, however, completely changed this situation.

A matter of great interest to anthropological theory is culture change—how a culture functionally adapts in its various parts to new ecological circumstances and other requirements, and how a culture borrows traits from other cultures and fits them into a functioning system. One of the most useful and interesting laboratories for such studies is found in the Great Plains. By 1800 the whole area was peopled by tribes of a striking similarity; many of the traits of the culture, even to details of ritual, and, especially, many of the forms of social organization, were nearly identical from Texas to Alberta. Yet these were tribes of great linguistic diversity, including six completely separated language stocks, and they came to the Plains from all the points of the compass and sometimes from great distances, so that the cultural differences among them were originally very great. The process of such rapid transformation from cultural heterogeneity to relative homogeneity without the various tribes being parts of a total organization, such as a nation-state, is perhaps the most unusual, and yet well-documented, case

Plains Language Families and Major Tribal Units

Language	Tribes
Algonkian	Cheyenne
	Arapaho
	Gros Ventre
	Blackfoot (Piegan and Blood)
	Cree
	Ojibwa
Athabaskan	Kiowa-Apache
	Sarsi
Caddoan	Pawnee
	Arikara
	Wichita
Kiowan	Kiowa
Siouan	Mandan
	Hidatsa
	Crow
	Dakota (often called Sioux)
	Assiniboin
	Iowa
	Oto
	Missouri
	Omaha
	Ponca
	Osage
	Kansa
Uto-Aztecan	Wind River Shoshone
	Comanche
	Ute

history of culture change on record. Only the languages did not change. But interestingly, a distinctive form of communication, the famous sign language, quickly spread to most of the Plains tribes.

The greatest period of diffusion of the horse into the Great Plains was from about 1740 to 1800. Tribes near the Spaniards in New Mexico had known of horses before 1600; but because the Spaniards expressly prohibited the sale of horses to Indians and because there were no great numbers of horses at first, the nearby Indians acquired only a few, which they slaughtered for food. Throughout the eighteenth century, however, the Spanish herds proliferated and at the same time Spanish military power waned.

By the time horses were plentiful enough to be traded throughout the whole Plains area, tribes were taking up mounted buffalo-hunting with great rapidity. It is assumed that the economic superiority of this way of life attracted the newcomers, but it seems possible too that, for the river-valley horticulturalists, the military impossibility of remaining on foot and defending their villages against mounted predators may have been the most important factor. Certainly, in the Plains, as had occurred elsewhere in the world, the horse quickly became very significant in warfare. It could fairly be called a new weapon, revolutionary in its total implications.

The Cheyenne Indians were quite typical of the horticulturalists who turned into mounted nomads. Once they became fully equestrian, their culture became the quintessence of the Plains type, partly because they came to occupy a central geographic position in the Plains, and also because (and this follows from the central location) they were middlemen in the movement of horses from south to north and finally in the exchange of European trade goods from east to west.

The legends and traditions of the Cheyenne, as well as references to them by early French explorers, locate them in the upper Mississippi River Valley on the Wisconsin-Minnesota border. The French term Cheyenne was apparently derived from the Siouan word *sha hi'ye na* (meaning "speakers of an unintelligible language"), which the Sioux Indians had applied to the Cheyenne. The Cheyenne name for themselves is *tsis tsis'tas* ("people"). The dislocation of Indians in the eastern Middle West in the 1600s, caused by the rival machinations of the British and French, apparently had repercussions farther west, for there is record of considerable disruption and warfare in Wisconsin, Minnesota, and Illinois in the latter part of the century. The Cheyenne finally moved to North Dakota and settled on the Cheyenne River sometime before 1700. Horticulture was still being practiced, but presumably a transition to Plains buffalo-hunting was in process. Probably a few of the less fortunately situated villages, or groups from them, made the change first, but by 1770 enough horses had been acquired for many bands of Cheyenne to become fully nomadic.

It must be emphasized that by 1800 life in the Plains in its most resplendent aspect—as practiced typically by the Cheyenne Indians —was not a simple consequence of the influence of the horse upon the aboriginal culture and the greatly increased hunting success it made possible. The white man's civilization figured in it in more ways than merely having originally provided the horse. Perhaps many of the Cheyenne had never seen a white man, or at most only an occasional explorer or trader, but trade in the white man's goods flowed over the entire Plains, and in this the Cheyenne participated fully. The primary currency was horses, raided from other tribes and purchased with native products. Another important item was fur. Buffalo hides, especially, were traded through other Indian tribes until they reached the westernmost white settlements through the sedentary horticultural Indians. Steel axes and knives, brass kettles, and even beads came into use all over the Plains, but above all the Indians wanted guns.

Guns, and the continuing necessity for more lead and powder, drove the Indians to ever more risky horse-raiding parties to acquire the "money." Just as Indians without horses were driven desperately to try to acquire them because of the great military, as well as economic, advantage they represented, so when competitors acquired guns, all their neighbors were driven to do so as well. A gun was a big advantage in warfare, for it could well outrange the bow and arrow.[1] All in all, the Plains area for about one hundred years was one of the arenas of the most intense tribal conflict ever known. No balance or stasis in territorial rights was possible for long because the fluctuation, first in the number of horses acquired by the various tribes and next in the possession of guns, kept the whole area in a state of turmoil.

[1] The gun was rarely used in the buffalo hunt, however. The Indians could ride close to the buffalo and discharge 20 arrows in the time needed to load the cap-and-ball or flintlock rifle of those days.

The nature of the seasonal climatic variation as reflected in the habits of the buffalo caused the social and political organization of the Plains Indians to be much looser and more flexible than the organization of sedentary horticultural Indians. In the central and northern Plains the grass grows rapidly in late spring and early summer, but in late summer it dries out, and only sparse remnants are found in the fall. Winter feed is very poor and usually covered with snow. As a consequence, the buffalo traveled in huge herds during the lush period, and by the middle of summer they were in fat condition. Later, in fall and winter, they scattered into smaller groups and ranged rapidly and widely in search of the diminishing fodder. The organization of the hunters mirrored the organization of the buffalo. They congregated into firmly structured tribes only for the organized communal hunts in summer, and during the rest of the year migrated independently in small camps, subsisting on stored meat and hit-or-miss foraging activities.

When the Cheyenne came to their habitat in the western Plains—northern Colorado, southeastern Wyoming, and east to the Black Hills—they numbered about 3500. They were joined in the Plains by a small band called the Sutaio, who spoke a dialect of the same Algonkian language and who eventually were absorbed into the society. The Arapaho, also speakers of Algonkian, had a history similar to that of the Cheyenne, and they and the related Gros Ventre maintained a close alliance with the Cheyenne that enabled them to control a large territory west of the Missouri River between the Platte and Arkansas rivers, against the incursions of their old enemies the Dakota and Crow to the north and west, the Pawnee to the east, and the Kiowa and Comanche to the south.

The buffalo is by far the chief sustenance of the Plains Indians, and the great hunts are the hardest sustained work in their economic life. No individuals are allowed to hunt buffalo as they please, for the aim of the community is to destroy a whole herd once it is discovered. The principal method of the communal hunt is the surround. The mounted men, armed with the short, powerful laminated bow, stampede the herd in such a way that is flight describes an ever-lessening circle, while the hunters keep picking off the nearest buffalo as fast as they can. If the hunt is properly organized, the animals become more and more massed in a milling jumble, and the Indians may succeed in killing all of them. Lances are some-times used from horseback, and the final killing is done with knives. The labor and excitement of such a hunt are tremendous, but the killing of the animals is only the mere beginning of the job. The flaying, butchering, and transporting of the meat and hides to the camp sometimes take days of unremitting toil, after which the meat has to be dried into jerky (an English term derived from the Span-ish *charqui*) and made into pemmican, the famous concoction of dried meat pounded with berries, which is stored in rawhide sacks. Preparing the meat and dressing the skins are women's work.

The sexual division of labor is rigid, and at some particular times it seems quite unequal. Women may be sitting warmly in the tipis gossiping while the men spend long days in freezing weather scour-ing the area for game and sometimes running considerable risks. At other times the women's activities, which include all matters considered domestic, seem exceptionally taxing, as they did to one white man who traveled with a Cheyenne camp in 1846:

After a ride of two hours, we stopped, and the chiefs, fastening their horses, collected in circles, to smoke the pipe and talk, letting their squaws unpack the animals, pitch the lodges, build fires, arrange the robes, and when all was ready, these "lords of creation" dispersed to their several homes, to wait until their patient and enduring spouses prepared some food. I was provoked, nay, angry, to see the lazy, overgrown men, do nothing to help their wives; and, when the young women pulled off their bracelets and finery, to chop wood, the cup of my wrath was full to overflowing, and, in a fit of honest indigna-tion, I pronounced them ungallant, and indeed savage in the true sense of the word.[2]

Wild sheep, deer, and especially antelope roam the foothills and Plains in great numbers. The Indians know the traveling habits of these animals and ambush them or drive them into enclosures and pits. Few of the Plains tribes use fish, but the Cheyenne are in-genious in catching them in weirs and wicker traps. Wild roots and berries are gathered in season, and small game and even dogs are used to vary the basic menu of buffalo meat.

The Cheyenne obtain most of their horses by purchase and by raiding, but some attempts to capture wild horses are made. They have not learned to use the thrown lasso of the Spaniards, but the

[2] Lewis H. Garrard, *Wah-to-Yah and the Taos Trail* (ed. by R. P. Bieber), Glen-dale, 1938, pp. 106-107.

slipnoose rope is used to hold animals. The easiest way of capturing wild horses is to concentrate on foals and pregnant mares. Horses are highly prized, and individual prestige is marked by the number of horses a person can acquire. The average number is about 10 head per family, but some have several times as many. The best horses are saved for hunting and warfare; the others are used for the transportation of household goods. Mules are highly prized for this latter purpose, but they are rare except in the southwest Plains. Household goods are packed on the animals' backs and also tied onto the *travois*—twin poles strapped to the animal with the ends dragging behind. Dogs are often hitched to smaller versions of the travois.

The skin, bone, and horn of buffalo, and to some extent of antelope and deer, provide most of the basic raw materials for the tools, weapons, clothing, and shelters of the Cheyenne. The famous conical tent—the tipi—is often so large that as many as 20 people can be accommodated in it, and it is made entirely of beautifully tanned and decorated skins. Bows are made of layers of horn backed with sinew; containers are of rawhide and horn; drills, scrapers, and awls, of antler; and all clothing is made of skins. Weaving was either unknown or was given up when the Indians became nomads. Some pottery was made in the Plains, but quickly abandoned in favor of the brass kettles acquired by trade.

The Cheyenne clothing is particulary ornate and well made. Women wear one-piece dresses of excellently tanned deer or antelope skin, reaching nearly to the feet and having open capelike half-sleeves. The dresses are fringed, and decorated with porcupine quills and beads. Women also wear leggings from the knee to the ankle and soft moccasins soled with stiff rawhide. In winter, a buffalo robe is worn with the hair side in. Men wear only a breechclout and moccasins in summer; but in winter, fringed leggings extending from the ankle to the crotch and deerskin shirts, falling below the hips, are worn by the men. These shirts have full-length sleeves, and some are elaborately ornamented with beads and fringed along the seams with the scalp locks of enemies. They are commonly called *war shirts* because of this decoration and are worn on ceremonial occasions.

The Cheyenne are fond of body decoration. Men pay particular attention to the hair, which they allow to grow as long as possible, and into it they tie various beads and crystals. Both men and women commonly confine the hair in two side braids. Eagle feathers are worn by older men. The great feather war bonnets with the two long tails are most characteristic of the Dakota tribe; among the Cheyenne they are used only ceremonially by a few distinguished men. Bracelets, necklaces, and earrings are common, as is body and face paint of many colors and designs.

The Cheyenne tribe is divided into 10 loosely organized bands, each one with its own special taboos, ceremonies, and medicines. The members feel themselves to be somehow related, and marriage between members of the same band is therefore frowned upon. There is also an informal tribal division between those who live in the northern part of the territory and those of the south. For much of the year, and especially in winter, the people travel in relatively small family groups, one sometimes meeting and camping with another for a time and then going its own way. These divisions, or camps, are named, and they function as social segments of the bands, but their composition is forever changing as small ones combine and growing ones break up.

The whole Cheyenne tribe meets in the summer for an extended cooperative hunt and for the performance of the important tribal ceremonies. The great camp is arranged in a part-circle or horseshoe shape and is three or four lodges wide. Each of the 10 bands must camp always in a particular position relative to the others in the circle. The large central area is kept clear for dances, council meetings, and public ceremonies.

The tribe as a whole is cross-cut by a series of societies which have military, social, and ceremonial functions at the time the bands are united in the summer. Most prominent are the six military societies. A youth might choose to join any one of them, but it is usual for a man to go into the society to which his father belongs. Only the able-bodied, energetic, fearless men of the tribe are accepted for membership. Among some Plains tribes (the neighboring Arapaho, for example), the societies are age-graded so that a man passes from one to the next as he becomes older until he passes into the final society, one of great prestige and political and ceremonial importance, being composed entirely of old men.

The societies are the organized military force of the tribe and its police force as well. Among the everyday duties of the soldiers are to oversee the movements of the camp, protect the moving column in its march, and enforce rules against individual hunting or other movements which might frighten away the buffalo. Each society performs special dances for the tribe, and some even have four especially selected maidens who hold honorary posts rather like hostesses for such social occasions. Each society has one elected chief, who is supposed to be the bravest war leader.

A few of the very bravest men in the tribe constitute a small group known as the *Contraries*. As the name suggests, these men always do the opposite of what is said: that is, they say *no* when they mean *yes,* approach when asked to go away, and so on. In battle, they use a special, supposedly magical *thunder bow*, which enables them to accomplish acts of extraordinary bravery. One is called to the society of Contraries by a vision, and thereafter he eats alone from special dishes, lives in a red lodge, and associates with ordinary people infrequently and in a distant matter.

The political organization of the Cheyenne, as it functions in the summer meetings, is highly developed in comparison with that of many other Plains tribes. All secular affairs are in the hands of the Tribal Council of 44 members, four from each of the bands and four general chiefs. Members retire at the end of 10 years and are allowed to choose their successors; but in practice, public opinion plays a strong part in the selection of a chief.[3] Judgments of the council are expressed through the soldier societies. The council sometimes mediates disputes and feuds, but there is no machinery to punish crimes against individuals.

Social distinctions among individuals, particularly among men, are strongly marked. Bravery, energy, and generosity are highly valued, and an individual's prestige reflects his possession of these attributes. Youths compete very actively for possession of horses particularly, for the number of horses a man has captured is a proof of his daring and energy. A man likes to display his generosity by lending fine horses and on many occasions by giving them away; also, he can trade them to other tribes for kettles, axes, knives, beads, and so on, which he can then give away. Hospitality and generosity are such strongly valued characteristics that sometimes the

---

[3] There is some difference of opinion among writers with respect to the number of years a council member serves and exactly how he is replaced.

frequent *giveaway* ceremonies are reminiscent of the Nookta pot-latch, so competitive do they become.[4]

Success in war is the primary road to achievement in status. The whole process seems, on the surface, to be so surrounded by cere-mony and so cumbered with rules as to be akin to the ethos of the legendary European knight. The primary goal, however, is to take horses; a secondary aim is to harass the neighbors by such constant deeds of daring that they stay out of Cheyenne territory. Young men often boast of their deeds of bravery while confronting the enemy, but many respected men are more interested in capturing horses than in fighting.

Nevertheless, all Cheyenne men are considered great warriors. It is man's true profession, and a love of fighting is instilled from early childhood. To die against the enemy is the noblest death. Nearly all of the Plains tribes have a series of exploits, or *coups,* ranked in order of their danger. Touching a live enemy is the greatest coup. Stealing a horse single-handed from within the enemy's camp and touching a dead enemy (which can be done by three men, with less credit for each subsequent touch) are of less importance in that order. Scalps are taken from fallen enemies as trophies, but taking the scalp is of little significance compared to counting a coup.

Raids with the primary purpose of acquiring horses are made on foot. Any man may make up and lead a raiding party, but he must have sufficient prestige so that others are willing to follow him. As leader, he has several conferences with older men, and then he makes an offering to the sacred Medicine Arrows. If the man is to be a leader for the first time, he goes into the hills to fast and tor-ture himself beforehand, in the hope that he may receive a vision of success from his guardian spirit. The night before leaving on the raid, the war party marches around the camp circle, and the well-wishers in the lodges come out with presents when they hear the war songs.

On the appointed day, the leader sets out alone, and at intervals during the day the others leave camp by different routes to meet him at some designated spot. When enemy territory is reached, the leader sends out pairs of the youngest men to scout the country mi-nutely before he allows the main body to advance. When an enemy

[4] See Chapter 10.

camp is discovered, the leader chooses a hidden spot where all extra paraphernalia are deposited; some of the men even leave their weapons. Late at night the party sneaks toward the village. The younger men are delegated to round up all the grazing stock they can, while carefully chosen older men steal into the camp to take the prized buffalo horses, which are usually tethered near the owners' lodges.

They all reassemble at the spot where the extra equipment was left and then set off, each man driving the animals he has taken. At dawn the horses are bunched into a single herd after each man has identified his own. Then the herd is driven hard for as long as 24 hours in order to put as much distance as possible between the raiding party and any pursuers. By this time danger is past, for any following Indians would have only a single horse apiece and would be outdistanced. Raids are usually successful if the exit from the camp is made without alarming anyone. On returning to the home camp, some of the men give away all their captured horses, and all give away some of them.

War parties, as opposed to raids, are usually inspired by motives of vengeance. The killing of an enemy brings consolation to the people who have been aggrieved. On rare occasions, when the provoking injury has been very great, the whole tribe may move toward the enemy. Usually, the notion of success in war consists of killing an enemy without any loss to the war party. This is, of course, most easily accomplished if a much smaller body of enemy can be surprised or ambushed. While the Indians are very brave— even foolhardy—as individuals, they are not well organized and disciplined, with the result that extended battles are rare.

A returning war party stops overnight outside the home camp to make ready for the triumphal entry at dawn, dressed in fighting attire, carrying the enemy scalps on poles. The men who showed the greatest courage in battle ride in the front rank. The whole camp welcomes them with songs and shouts. If any member of the party has been killed, the corpse is not brought home, but is left unburied on the prairie. The camp goes into mourning in such a case, and the celebration is not held.

Despite the fact that the great camp circle brings together numbers of people who are not related, most of the daily association of a Cheyenne is passed in the company of relatives. Much of the year a small group of kinsmen lives isolated from other groups, and even in the tribal camp they stay close together. This basic social segment is a matrilocally extended family which typically consists of a man and wife and their married daughters and their husbands, who come from a different group, their daughters' children, and any sons who are as yet unmarried. A single tipi shelters only a husband and wife and small children, and the extended family's camp consists therefore of a cluster of several tipis. The people of a camp collaborate in many activities, even to the point of communal cooking, though they usually eat in their separate lodges.

The terminology of kinship among the Cheyenne is of a widespread type which anthropologists call the *generation system,* meaning that the most significant distinctions are those between generations, and few distinctions are made between kinds of relatives in any given generation. This particular characteristic is found most developed in Polynesia.[5] As mentioned earlier, residence after marriage is matrilocal, but descent is traced bilaterally; that is, one's father's relatives are specified as fully as one's mother's. Cousins are not distinguished into cross and parallel types, nor are they distinguished from one's own siblings—all are called by the same basic term, although differences in sex and relative age are signified. Marriage with a relative on either side is forbidden. In the parents' generation, one calls a mother's sister *mother,* but calls a paternal aunt (father's sister) by another term. Father's brother, likewise, is called *father,* but a different term is used for a mother's brother. One's brothers' children are *sons* and *daughters,* but a sister's children have different terms.

Varying kinds of courtesy are extended to different relatives; some have to be treated with great respect (distance or social avoidance is the extreme rule), while with others one may be very familiar (a joking relationship is the extreme form). The relations of parents and children and of siblings are the closest and most constant, of course. In general, a parent and child of the same sex and siblings of the same sex are more informal with each other—have more of a joking relationship—than are those of opposite sex. Once a brother and sister have both reached puberty, they are very respectful to one another. The paternal uncle and maternal aunt are like mothers and fathers—as they are termed—respected, yet close.

[5] See Chapter 12.

The maternal uncle and paternal aunt, who are not as likely to be members of the extended family as are the paternal uncle and maternal aunt, are less formally treated by nephews and nieces. The maternal uncle is especially likely to have a mild joking relationship with his nephew, as is the father's sister with her niece. As apparently occurs in all societies, grandparents and grandchildren have a very affectionate relationship; grandparents indulge the children, and a joking or teasing relationship is common—they are more like equals than are parents and children.

The relation between parents- and children-in-law are of particular importance. Matrilocal residence causes a man to live in close association with his in-laws, but a girl does not see her in-laws frequently, and consequently the rules of decorum are not so rigid for her. A man and his mother-in-law are very respectful of one another and so distant that they may not communicate directly or be in the same lodge together. Should they accidentally meet, the son-in-law must cover his head. A father-in-law looks out for the man's interests, and they may converse directly, but he does not give direct orders or instruction. Respect and obligations between in-laws are signified by the frequent exchange of presents.

Marriage is undertaken primarily to enlarge the circle of relatives. This is so important a consideration that the Cheyenne say that this is why people cannot marry if they are already related, no matter how distantly. A young man courts a girl's relatives, rather than the girl herself, by sending presents to them. The proposal is made to the girl's parents, or often to her brother, by one of the boy's close relatives. The marriage is validated by a large exchange of goods between the two families.

A wife's younger sister is regarded by the husband as a possible second wife, because he would marry her in the event of his wife's death. Sometimes she comes to live in her sister's lodge after she has grown to puberty and is, at least insofar as the household's economics are concerned, a sort of second wife to her brother-in-law. If the husband dies, his brother is expected to take his place. Neither of these customs (sororate and levirate, respectively) is compulsory but they are expected if the alliance of extended families created by the marriage has been a desirable one. It is an especially good thing for two brothers to marry a pair of sisters, as this brings the two camps into an even closer relationship.

The two sets of relatives assemble together on the occasion of the birth of a child to the married couple, and the older women of both camps assist in the birth. The husband's sister makes a cradle for the child, and the husband himself ties the afterbirth into a tree. The naming of the child is a prerogative of the husband's family, which gives it the name of an older member of the family, and cares for the baby for the first 10 days.

Later the husband's family is in charge of such ceremonial events as the first haircut. The husband chooses a friend to perform the ritual of ear-piercing. The husband and the ceremonial friend are supposed to be like brothers ever after.[6] The wife's family is largely responsible for the day-to-day informal training of the child, for it is growing up in their camp. A child is carried in the mother's arms for the first few months, but after that, until it can run about, it is lashed to a cradle board and carried on the mother's back.

There is no special ceremony for a boy at his period of puberty, but the first menses of a girl are dramatized. The girl is

NORTHERN CHEYENNE CHIEF WOODEN-LEG. *Courtesy, The American Museum of Natural History*

painted with red paint, after which she retires to a special lodge, accompanied by her grandmother, for four days. The father makes public announcement of the event if there is a large camp and gives

[6] This is very similar to the *godparent-cofather* institution. See Chapter 18.

away a number of horses if he can afford it. A woman's menstrual periods are considered dangerous times, and a certain amount of restriction of her activity is always maintained.

The first buffalo hunt and the first war party are the big events in the coming of age of a boy. Throughout childhood children are patiently taught adult skills, and boys are quite proficient at hunting and riding by the age of 10 or 12, when they are given charge of the horse herds. By 13 or 14, they are ready for the first buffalo hunt, which, if successful, is celebrated by the father by presentation of some of his horses to people who have fewer. The first war party is the most memorable event for a youth. If he is successful, i.e., if he has counted a coup or otherwise performed bravely, he is given a new name. Following this event, he is considered to be at the age of discretion, and his parents and other relatives abruptly begin to treat him as a man rather than as a child.

A young man is expected to perform certain self-tortures in order to acquire a vision of the good-luck spirits who will safeguard him on the warpath and bring luck in hunting. Essentially, the formula consists of four days of fasting, exposed alone and naked on a hilltop. Sometimes a vision is acquired by a form of suffering which does not last so long, but which is more acute. One of the most common is to have a skewer of wood thrust under a pinch of skin, one on each side of the breast, and then to attach the skewers to a rope which is tied to the top of a pole; all day long the youth leans away from the pole, pulling and tugging in order to break the flesh. Sometimes similar strips of flesh are cut in the boy's back and a cord run through them which is attached to several buffalo skulls that he drags around behind him all day. Usually the skin and flesh do not break, and at night an older man whom he has consulted for advice releases him by cutting off the pulled-out pieces of flesh. Frequently, self-torture is undertaken in order to petition the spirits for a specific favor, as well as to have a vision. The petitioner is essentially requesting that the spirits have pity and grant the request.

While much of the training of boys is designed to teach them to be brave and hardy, a good part of it also, as in the case of girls, is designed to teach them to associate properly with their own people. They are supposed to be deferential to older people all of their lives and to be always cheerful, honest, and friendly toward their companions. Behavior toward enemies is supposed to be cruel and utterly ruthless, but within Cheyenne society just the opposite qualities are esteemed.

Etiquette as well as ethical behavior serve to make everyday life a smoothly ordered affair. For example, a visitor entering a lodge always should turn to the right and stop. The owner, who sits at the back, which is usually also the west, invites him to sit down, and if he wishes to honor the guest, he places him at his side. It is bad manners for the guest to go to the left, for that is the family's private place, and one should never pass between the fire and a sitting person. Visits of any formality are always accompanied by pipe smoking. The host begins by pointing the pipestem to the sky, to the earth, and in each of the four cardinal directions, and then by making a prayer. After the host takes a first puff, the pipe is passed around from right to left. It is very unlucky to touch anything with the pipestem, and the pipe should always be passed carefully and ceremoniously.

Prayers are made before eating, and a small offering to the spirits is placed to one side. Men and women may eat together in their own lodges, but on formal occasions the men eat alone. Feasts for some special purpose are accompanied by speeches and storytelling. A favorite evening entertainment occurs when members of two rival soldier societies meet in a competition of coup counting. Each person recounts his own deeds, but it is not done in a bragging manner. The men try to be perfectly accurate in their accounts, for honesty in such matters is highly esteemed.

The Cheyenne are, of course, accustomed to seeing injury and death from natural causes, particularly on the hunt and in warfare. But disease is understood to be a sign that the supernatural is at work, and the way to a cure is to hire a medicine man. This shaman, as among most American Indians, performs an intricate ritual, some of the elements of which are his private, secret property. First, he sings a cycle of seven different songs, accompanied by a rattle. After smoking a sacred pipe, which is a part of his personal medicine kit, he mixes a secret medicinal concoction, rubs it into his hands, and then places them on the afflicted part of the patient. Later, he sings nine songs, after which he ritually consecrates some food, of which all partake.

Sometimes the patient is placed in a small sweat lodge. Heated stones are placed inside, and from time to time water is poured on them to make a heavy steam. During the sweating, the shaman prays, sings, and shakes his rattle. A plunge in the river follows the ordeal. As in many American Indian societies, the sweat bath is felt to be a purification and is often used in purely religious contexts.

Most people have private formulas of herbal remedies which they take when indisposed. The recipes are usually revealed to them in a dream, and the medicines are viewed as a spiritual power rather than as actual drugs. Men carry a small *medicine bundle* of their private herbs, attached to their necklaces or tied into their hair.

Anyone can become a shaman, and in a sense all people have a degree of magical power. But if a person is believed to be exceptionally good at doctoring, he is called upon to help a sick person and is given gifts in return, thus becoming a sort of professional. A few shamans are believed to possess such exceptional magical powers and formulas that they can inflict disease or death on others if they choose. This ability is usually claimed in order to impress people and is seldom if ever actually put to use. The method is usually some variation of willing a foreign object to enter the victim's body.

When a person dies, disposal of the body takes place very soon, for the people are afraid of the ghost. The body is moved some distance from the camp and placed on a scaffold in a tree, or in a cave, or is covered over with rocks. A man's favorite horse is shot and placed near him, as are all his favorite personal possessions. All his other property is given away. Mourning continues for a year or more. Close female relatives cut off their hair, gash their heads and legs, and, if the deceased died in battle, sometimes even cut off a finger. Male relatives unbraid their hair and let it hang loose during the mourning period.

All of the dead go to the same afterworld, except those who have committed suicide. This heaven is in the sky, and is approached by the Hanging Road—our Milky Way—and in it the dead live as they did on earth, but as insubstantial spirits, something like shadows or silhouettes. When trade mirrors were first encountered by the Cheyenne, they were afraid that the reflection was the soul, and that it was bad luck to see it. In later years they had the same fear of photographs.

The Cheyenne believe that there are two deities more powerful than all the other gods and spirits. One lives in the sky and the other underground. Four other powerful spirits live at the four points of the compass. It is to all these that the Cheyenne are addressing a prayer or offering when they point the sacred pipestem up, down, and in the four directions.

A great many objects in addition to pipes are used by individuals as charms or amulets to ward off bad luck or evil spiritual influences. A warrior's shield, war shirt, and body decoration carry designs which are particularly sacred to him. Everyone wears or carries special charms, such as arrowpoints, bits of hair, stones and crystals, and certain grasses or herbs. Many everyday actions are tabooed for fear of offending the spirits; men who own certain shields cannot eat entrails, others cannot take food with a knife or other implement of metal, some persons cannot eat the heart of an animal, and so on.

Two kinds of fetishes are of great symbolic significance to the tribe as a whole. Four arrows—two buffalo arrows and two man arrows—are considered very sacred and are under the supervision of a special functionary. They are, in a sense, Medicine Bundles which have the same significance for the tribe as the individual's sack of herbs has for himself. Some of the most imporant of Cheyenne ceremonies are rituals designed to renew the sacred arrows. The second fetish, the Medicine Hat, was once the equivalent tribal symbol for the Sutaio, and after they were incorporated into the Cheyenne proper, the Medicine Hat was also accepted. The Hat is made of a buffalo head and horns and is kept in a bundle under the care of an official keeper. When publicly exposed under appropriate ceremonial auspices, it brings health and prosperity to the tribe. The lodge of the sacred Hat, like the Christian church, is a sanctuary for fugitives; no one may pursue an enemy or criminal into it.

The central religious acts of the tribe as a whole, those with socially integrating functions rather than individual functions, occur during the summer when the great camp circle is formed. The most famous of these, the so-called Sun Dance, is practiced throughout the whole Plains area. More special to the Cheyenne, and possibly more important to them, is the *Massaum,* sometimes called the Crazy or Foolish Dance because it involves performers acting as Contraries.

The Cheyenne Sun Dance, or Medicine Lodge, as they call it, is generally similar to others in the Plains, although among the Cheyenne it is perhaps more clearly a general petition to the spirits for tribal well-being. A large rectangular ceremonial house is constructed, its focal point being a sacred center pole around which dances are performed, offerings are made, and various rituals are performed. Toward the end of the four days of ceremony, men who have pledged to torture themselves are tied to the pole by thongs attached to skewers run through the skin on their chests. This particular aspect of the Sun Dance has attracted the fascinated attention of whites and led to the prohibition of the Sun Dance[7] on Indian reservations, although it is not the most important feature of the ceremony.

The Massaum dance is essentially mimetic magic, for its central features are impersonation of game animals and a pantomime in which the animals are hunted. Much of the ceremony is intended to increase the game, to cure the sick, and to assure success in war, and it is thus very serious; yet the Contraries are continually practicing their special type of backward buffoonery, exciting great laughter from the onlookers.

The apogee of Plains Indian life was reached at a period when contacts with civilization were increasing rapidly. In those times the Great Plains were becoming a thoroughfare between eastern cities and New Mexico, California, and Oregon, but for a while there was no true contest over the land. All the whites wanted was that the great and valuable wagon trains not be molested, and that a peaceful intercourse with the tribes continue in order that furs and robes could be acquired in exchange for cheap beads, mirrors, brass kettles, knives, and sheet iron (which the Indians particularly desired for the making of arrow points). Finally, however, guns, powder and lead, and cheap whiskey, which young Indians found to be a not so painful way of acquiring visions, became of increasing importance in the trade, presaging certain changes to follow. In 1832 the famous Santa Fe Trail opened a steadily increasing commerce between cities in Missouri and New Mexico. Indians of the southern tribes traded with the people of the caravans, and even worked for them, but some groups also attacked them from time to time—there was no tribal policy. All this was inter-

[7] The Dakota call their version of this ceremony the Sun Gazing Dance because the dancers are supposed to keep their eyes in the direction of the sun at all times. Whites have since called all tribal versions of this ceremony the Sun Dance.

esting and exciting, but at that time offered no threat to the buffalo herds in the homeland of the Cheyenne.

Soon wagons began to lumber in increasing numbers over the Oregon Trail in the northern Plains, and the United States government determined to confine the Indians to particular territories. A treaty made at Fort Laramie in 1851 assigned the Cheyenne and Arapaho a vast hunting territory between the North Platte and Arkansas rivers, from the Rockies to as far as the Black Hills. This was certainly a sufficient area, but eight years later a gold rush began in the Platte River area and the Indians were pushed farther west. Worst of all, the buffalo, that apparently inexhaustible resource of the Plains, were diminishing rapidly. White hunters shot them for hides alone, and travelers killed droves of them simply for sport. It seems that once the precarious balance of nature becomes tipped against an animal species, its decline, slow at first, finally proceeds with astonishing rapidity toward oblivion. The buffalo became nearly extinct after only a few years of these depredations.

A rapid succession of events left nearly all of the Plains Indians bewildered and furious. Ever greater numbers of whites, following new trails, did not observe, very often did not even know about, the treaties made with the Indians. When the Indians responded with attacks, government soldiers pursued them. "The only good Indian is a dead Indian" was the watchword, and peaceful groups were not distinguished from warlike groups—any Indians were likely to be punished for something they had no knowledge of. General Custer surprised a peaceful and unprepared Cheyenne village at the Washita River and nearly wiped it out. At the Battle of Sand Creek near Denver, a Cheyenne camp cordially raised an American flag to a force of U.S. soldiers, only to be shot down. The arms and legs of the victims were exhibited at the Denver Theater to great applause.

After the Civil War, a greater influx of whites into the Plains began, including more detachments of soldiers, and life was all the more impossible for the Indians. In 1867, the Indians of the southern half of the Plains, including the southern branch of the Cheyenne, accepted the reservation system and in a few years were settled in the Indian Territory of Oklahoma. In the north, the continued intrusion of whites on Indian land finally led to the climax of the Indian Wars in the 1870s. The Cheyenne, combined with some other tribes, had one famous success, the defeat of General Custer's command on the Little Big Horn; but the tide was against them, and finally, thoroughly defeated, homeless, embittered by the falsity of the promises made to them, they surrendered.

In 1878 the northern Cheyenne were moved to Oklahoma and confined there with the southern Cheyenne. So hopeless was life and so desperately homesick did they become that about 300 men, women, and children of the northern Cheyenne broke out and marched all the way to their homeland in the northern Plains, fighting their way when necessary. Once there, they laid down their arms, only to be marched back to Nebraska, under heavy guard. Again a number of them broke out, but many were killed and most of the survivors recaptured. Not long afterward the government established a reservation for the northern Cheyenne in Montana.

Most of the reservation lands were not suitable for agriculture, and farming was woman's work in any case. Even the Sun Dance was forbidden, and in all basic respects the old way was gone and there was nothing to take its place. The kind of disorientation that the Cheyenne suffered has been frequent in many parts of the world where primitives have been subdued by civilization, and a particularly striking religious reaction often has resulted. The religious movements that follow, called *revivalism* or *messianism,* are typically ecstatic, fervent sets of beliefs and ceremonies that are intended to recapture the fancied glory of the earlier existence.

Among the American Indians, a movement called the Ghost Dance Religion, which began in Nevada in 1888 (after an earlier, more limited version in 1870), swept up many American Indian tribes in the Far West and finally influenced the Plains tribes. A would-be messiah named Wovoka claimed that revelations had taught him a dance which would bring back the dead ancestors and renew the earth with game. By the time the Cheyenne and other Plains tribes has acquired this religion, they had changed its rather peaceful import into a call for a holy war against the whites. The movement was revivalistic in the special sense, too, that the new dress, customs, and tools of the white man were tabooed and the old ways fostered. The most renowned was begun by the Teton Dakota under the famous Sitting Bull, but the Dakota were massacred by U.S. soldiers at Wounded Knee. No further battle resulted, although the excitement and unrest persisted for many years.

In later times, revivalistic movements among many American Indians have been associated with the eating of *peyote*, the dried button of a small cactus plant obtained by trade with Indians of the southwest and Mexico. When it is eaten, narcotic alkaloids are released that cause visual hallucinations. The cultic practice of eating peyote spread from the south to the Plains tribes and now is almost pan-Indian in its distribution. The Plains Indians' interest in visionary experiences has caused the ritual of peyote eating to become almost as significant to them as the Sun Dance and Massaum ceremonies formerly were. Today many elements of Christian mythology have crept into the ritual and songs (it is often called the Peyote Church and is incorporated as the Native American Church) ; but people feel it is *Indian*, and because sporadic attempts have been made by the U.S. government to prohibit it, it has the peculiar attraction of clandestine ritual.

Since the government's ill-advised efforts to force the Indians in the northern reservations to farm have proved unsuccessful, cattle-raising has grown in importance.[8] It is regarded more as a man's work than farming and the country is more suited to it. Nevertheless, the reservation is too small for the 1647 northern Cheyenne to run enough cattle to support themselves. Most of the people live in clusters of small shacks in a sort of rural slum. They are very poor; some men earn wages sporadically, but there are few steady jobs near or on the reservation; a few pension checks and county relief payments come in; and now and then someone sells a few moccasins or other handicraft products. In 1945 the per capita average of earned and unearned income was only $340 per year. This money becomes distributed in one way or another, usually through sharing or gifts, for generosity and hospitality are still valued.

A few other aboriginal traits survive among the Cheyenne. The emphasis on kinship is still reflected in a pattern of long visiting journeys to relatives. A few of the old medical practices survive, and some elements of the tribal ceremonies are still practiced. Prog-

---

[8] The northern branch of the Cheyenne live on the reservation of Tongue River, Montana. Our information on the state of affairs there is recent (1951); hence, the present discussion concentrates on the northern Cheyenne. (Cf. Robert Anderson, *A Study of Cheyenne Culture History,* Ph.D. dissertation, University of Michigan, 1951.) The southern Cheyenne live in Oklahoma and their cultural disintegration occurred earlier and is more complete.

ress toward a full incorporation into modern American society has been slow, and there have been many more pitfalls than the early proponents of the reservation system would have believed. Nevertheless, intermarriage with whites continues, more Indian children are attending school, and more Indians are taking off-reservation jobs than ever before. If this trend continues, the status of Indians as helpless wards of the government may turn out to be an interim condition which will be ended within a generation or two. Meanwhile, the proud, self-sufficient warrior and hunter, the original American, has become a second-class citizen of America, typically with a more depressed economic and social status than any new immigrant has ever had.

Courtesy, The American Museum of Natural History

FURTHER READINGS

Anderson, R., *A Study of Cheyenne Culture History,* Ph.D. dissertation, University of Michigan, 1951.

Anderson, R., "The Buffalo Men, A Cheyenne Ceremony of Petition Deriving from the Sutaio," *Southwestern Journal of Anthropology,* Vol. 12, 1956.

Benedict, R. F., "The Vision in Plains Culture," *American Anthropologist,* n.s., Vol. 24, 1922.

Dorsey, G. A., *The Cheyenne,* Field Museum Anthropological Series, Vol. 9, Chicago, 1905.

Eggan, F., "The Cheyenne and Arapaho Kinship System," in F. Eggan (ed.), *Social Anthropology of North American Tribes,* Chicago, 1937.

Ewers, J. C., *The Horse in Blackfoot Indian Culture: With Comparative Material from other Western Tribes,* Smithsonian Institution, Bureau of American Ethnology, Bull. 159, Washington, 1955.

Gregg, J., *Commerce of the Prairies,* in R. G. Thwaites (ed.), *Early Western Travels,* Vols. 19–20, Cleveland, 1905.

Grinnell, G. B., *The Cheyenne Indians: Their History and Ways of Life,* New Haven, 1923, 2 vols.

Grinnell, G. B., *By Cheyenne Campfires,* New Haven, 1926.

Grinnell, G. B., *The Fighting Cheyennes,* Norman, Okla., 1956.

Hoebel, E. A., *The Cheyennes: Indians of the Great Plains,* New York, 1960.

Jablow, J., *The Cheyenne in Plains Indian Trade Relations, 1795–1840,* Monographs of the American Ethnological Society, Vol. 19, New York, 1950.

Llewellyn, K. N., and Hoebel, E. A., *The Cheyenne Way: Conflict and Case Law in Primitive Jurisprudence,* Norman, Okla., 1941.

Lowie, R. H., *Indians of the Plains,* New York, 1954.

Michelson, T., *The Narrative of a Southern Cheyenne Woman,* Smithsonian Institution, Miscellaneous Collections, Vol. 87, No. 5, Washington, 1932.

Mishkin, B., *Rank and Warfare Among the Plains Indians,* Monographs of the American Ethnological Society, Vol. 3, New York, 1940.

Mooney, J., *The Cheyenne Indians,* Memoirs of the American Anthropological Association, Vol. 1, Pt. 6, 1907.

Powell, P. J., *Sweet Medicine,* Norman, Okla., 1970.

Secoy, F. R., *Changing Military Patterns of the Great Plains,* Monographs of the American Ethnological Society, Vol. 21, New York, 1953.

Seger, J. H., *Early Days Among the Cheyenne and Arapaho Indians* (ed. W. S. Campbell), Norman, Okla., 1934.

Wissler, C., "The Influence of the Horse in the Development of Plains Culture," *American Anthropologist,* n.s., Vol. 16, 1914.

Wissler, C., *North American Indians of the Plains,* New York, 1934.

7

The Nuer of the Upper Nile River

From the southern margins of the Sahara Desert, and continuing southward into East Africa, is a long belt of tropical grasslands inhabited by tall, long-limbed, narrow-headed peoples who represent various blends of Mediterranean whites and African Forest Negroes. Most of them speak related languages, which have been recently classified as Eastern Sudanic.[1] These tribes are cattle pastoralists, most typically represented in the northern part of East Africa and becoming more and more mixed with the Bantu-speaking horticulturalists farther south into Uganda, whom they apparently conquered. Of the purely pastoral peoples, the Masai of southern Kenya and northern Tanganyika are the best known, though they are not the most typical. The Nuer farther to the north are more representative of the widely dispersed group of pastoral Sudanic tribes.

The south-central part of the Republic of the Sudan, the homeland of the Nuer, is a great open grassland traversed by the Upper Nile River and its several tributaries. The climate is tropical, and the year is divided almost equally between a very dry season and a

[1] Joseph H. Greenberg, "Studies in African Linguistic Classification: V. The Eastern Sudanic Family," *Southwestern Journal of Anthropology,* Vol. 6, 1950, pp. 143–160.

very wet one. From December to
June the rivers are low and the
blazing landscape is parched and
bare. From June to December
the rainfall is heavy, and the rivers overflow their banks and
nourish a heavy growth of high
grasses.

To a European the vista from
horizon to horizon is a desolate
wasteland, no more inviting as a
swamp in one part of the year
than as a desert the other. From
the modern point of view of agriculture or animal husbandry,
there seems to be always either an
excess or an insufficiency of water.
Insects of various kinds are constant pests. In the wet season,
mosquitoes swarm so thickly that
repose for men or beasts is impossible except in the midst of
the choking smudge of a dung
fire. In the dry season, ticks and
many kinds of biting flies harass
all animal life.

The Nuer believe that this
dreary land is the finest country
on earth. Only a few of them
have even been as far away as
Khartoum, the capital, however,
and so it is no wonder that they

Culver Pictures, Inc.

remain assured of nature's bounty to themselves. The Nuer people
are nearly as inhospitable as their land. The neighboring tribes fear
them, and civilized nations have shown very little interest in occupying the land or putting the natives to work. Consequently, the Nuer
today are one of the primitive peoples most purely aboriginal in
their social customs and organization.

139

The Nuer[2] total about 300,000 people, but there is no political unity of the whole group. *Nuer* refers not to a nation or kingdom, but to contiguous tribes who are similar culturally and linguistically and who sense this likeness to the degree that they feel distinct as a group from neighboring peoples. The Dinka, long-time enemies of the Nuer, are more similar to them than the other nearby groups, and it is probable that the two were once a single cultural-linguistic unit. Other neighbors are the several Shilluk-speaking tribes, the Galla of Ethiopia and the Anuak and Beir. To the north are nomadic Arabs, with whom the Nuer have had some contact. Generally, the character of the relations of the Nuer with any of their neighbors is hostile.

The Nuer are essentially pastoral, although, like many of the other herding peoples of the world, they grow a few crops when poverty demands and where soil and climate permit. But to the Nuer, and to all the East African pastoralists, horticulture is degrading toil, while cattle-raising is viewed with great pride. Cattle represent the main source of food in the forms of milk, meat, and blood; the skins are used for beds, bags, trays, cord, drums, and shields; the bones and horns are made into a wide variety of tools and utensils; and the dung is used as a plaster and as fuel. Cattle are by far the most cherished possession, and the Nuer seem to be interested in them nearly to the exclusion of anything else. E. E. Evans-Pritchard writes: "They are always talking about their beasts. I used sometimes to despair that I never discussed anything with the young men but livestock and girls, and even the subject of girls led inevitably to that of cattle. . . ."[3]

Milk is the staple food of the Nuer all of the year. It is drunk fresh, mixed with millet as a porridge, allowed to sour for a particularly relished dish, and churned into cheese. Milking is done twice daily by women and children; initiated men are forbidden to milk cows unless for some reason there are no women present to do it. During the dry season, when food is scarce and when cows are running dry, the Nuer bleed their cattle from a small cut in a neck vein. Blood is boiled until thick or is allowed to stand until it is coagulated into a solid block, after which it is roasted and eaten.

[2] Nuer is probably a term applied to this group by the neighboring Dinka tribe; the Nuer call themselves *Nath* (*People*).

[3] E. E. Evans-Pritchard, *The Nuer,* Oxford, 1940, pp. 18–19.

WOMEN POUNDING GRAIN WITH A MORTAR AND PESTLE. *Courtesy, British Information Services*

Cattle are not raised expressly for the meat; but when they become barren, injured, or too old for breeding, they are butchered and eaten under festive and ritualized conditions. The Nuer men are devoted to their cattle. After the women have milked the cows, the owner escorts the herd to pasture and to water, oversees them all day, and brings them back at night, meanwhile singing songs he has composed describing their virtues. In the evening he goes among his favorites, cleaning ticks from them, rubbing their backs with ashes, and decorating the horns with long tassels. The Nuer wash their hands and faces in the urine of cattle, and they cover their bodies, dress their hair, and even clean their teeth with ashes made from cattle dung.

The crops cultivated by the Nuer are millet (sorghum) and some maize. Next to milk, millet is the most important food. It is made into a boiled porridge and also brewed into a weakly alcoholic but nutritious beer. A little maize is eaten, but it does not grow nearly as well as millet under the wet conditions. Goats and sheep are interspersed among the cattle, but are not considered important. Fish is the other signicant food. At the onset of the dry season the lagoons and small rivers begin to drop and fish are easily speared in the dammed pools. The territory is rich in game, but the Nuer do not hunt intensively. Many kinds of antelope, buffalo, elephant, and hippopotamus are plentiful, but the Nuer feel that only a man poor in cattle will bother to hunt for food. Lions and leopards are a threat to the herds in the dry season, and the Nuer hunt them in self-protection, relying on dogs and the spear. The Nuer do not keep domesticated fowl, and they regard the eating of the plentiful wild birds or their eggs with repugnance.

During the rainy season, the Nuer live in villages located in the areas of higher ground and cultivate their small gardens. So rare are these spots and so uninhabitable are the extensive flooded areas that as many as from five to twenty miles separate one village from another. The size of the village is determined by the extent of the habitable and cultivable ground, and one village may contain from fifty to several hundred persons. At the end of the rainy season, after the ground has dried off, the villagers set fire to the grass to make new pasture and set off to camp near streams and rivers for the next six months. Frequent movements during this season are necessary as the pasturage becomes more and more sparse.

There are no permanent land rights among the Nuer. A village selects its site with the idea that land for all should be available. Cattle are individually owned—in fact, they are almost members of the family, so carefully are they tended—and some families are somewhat richer in cattle than others. This variation is closely related to the prestige of the owner, but it does not result in significant differences in the standard of living. The degree of sharing in a

WOMAN SPREADING MILLET TO DRY IN ORDER TO MAKE BEER. *Courtesy, British Information Services*

community, and even among neighboring communities, is such that a whole group seems to be partaking of a common stock of food. Anyone is privileged who, through luck or the possession of more or better cattle than others, is better enabled to provide for the less fortunate. There is no trade, the technology is poorly developed, and at certain times of the year, especially late in the dry season, there is a real shortage of food. The Nuer community is thus required to act as a corporate economic body. As a quick survey of the primitive world clearly shows, it is scarcity and not wealth which makes people generous.

The minimal economic unit is the household, or homestead, which is a hut or small group of huts and a cattle barn, both of wattle-and-daub construction. The homestead may be comprised of a single nuclear family or an extended family composed of a patriarch and several sons with their families. In the dry season the temporary camps of simple wind screens and flimsy beehive huts may consist of related families surrounding a common cattle corral, or of single families strung out over a wide area, depending on the conditions of the land and the proximity of pasture and good fishing sites. Usually the economic activities are individualized by homesteads during the time of residence in villages, whereas in the dry season the cattle of the associated families are herded together and, in general, there are more communal activities.

All of the members of a village or camp are kindred, as indeed, at least by fiction, are all people with whom a Nuer associates. All rights, privileges, obligations, in fact, all of the customs of inter-personal association, are regulated by kinship patterns; there is no other form of friendly association—one is a kinsman or an enemy. Genealogies are lengthy and well remembered, so that a Nuer can place into the proper category nearly any individual with whom he is likely to have contact. Nuer kinship terms are classificatory, how-ever, which is to say that the terms applied in direct address to mem-bers of the immediate family include other relatives who have an age and type of association in some measure analogous to that of a particular member of the immediate family.

On most social occasions it is a point of courtesy to designate a relative, no matter how distant, by a term denoting a member of the immediate family. Thus, all male relatives in one's parents' genera-tion are usually called *father* and all women *mother*; relatives of one's own generation are addressed as *brother* or *sister*; the children of one's own generation are called *sons* and *daughters*. The maternal uncle is, as in many societies, considered to have a rather special relationship to his nephew, in comparison to the other males of the uncle's generation, and frequently, though not always, he is designated by a separate term. There are ways, of course, of desig-nating all of these relatives more precisely. One may use a term meaning *father's brother* in addressing the paternal uncle instead of extending the term *father* to him, for example, but the use of a more precise term in address is considered bad form—it is too cold and distant.

Relative age is of great importance in Nuer interpersonal relations and seems to take precedence over genealogical considerations to a considerable degree. Every person in Nuer society is categorized explicitly in terms of an age-set system. All males are divided into age grades so that each one is a senior, equal, or junior to any other male. One is deferential to a senior, informal with an equal, superior to a junior. Women belong in the system as mothers, wives, sisters, or daughters of the particular males. The relativity of age, therefore, rather than genealogical relationship, frequently governs the use of kinship terms in address. Anyone of an older age-set is addressed as *father* or *mother,* and the younger as *son* or *daughter.* Very old people are called *grandfather* or *grandmother.* Men of the same age-set, if they are well acquainted, call one another by personal *ox names*—i.e., the name of a prize ox is applied to the owner.

Despite the generous extension of the few kinship terms to such a great number of people, there are important differences in sentiments and behavior among relatives of different kinds. A person is related to certain persons in a patrilineal line and to others through women and affinal relationships. The membership in an exogamous patrilineal descent line is the most significant relationship. This is the lineage of *closest* relatives—not necessarily closer in a territorial sense, but significantly closer in the feeling of relationship. This is why the maternal uncle is sometimes addressed by a special term, while the paternal uncle is a father; the latter is a member of the speaker's own lineage, but the mother's brother, of equal genealogical standing, is of the affinal lineage. Lineage membership means participation in a group that shares territorial rights, that has common political and juridical obligations (as in a feud or in warfare), and that owns certain ceremonial rights. Villages commonly have members of two or more different lineages within them, and a given lineage has members in different villages. The lineage thus plays, in a sense, a political role. All of the people in a village naturally have a strong feeling toward their village—it is in some ways a corporate entity whose members share many economic and social activities. So, too, they are all relatives, but the relationships may be through the mother or may be of affinal as well as genetic relationship. The lineages do not permit marriage with a fellow member, but members of the same village frequently marry. Lineage membership thus cross-cuts these village units and creates larger entities out of segments of otherwise independent villages.

Related lineages form a still larger, more amorphous group, the clan. A person knows the precise genealogical position of each member of his lineage, but clans are viewed as composed of lineages, not of individuals; the genealogical-like relationship of each lineage to another in the clan is known, but the individuals are known only as fellow clan members, all descended from a common ancestor.

Villages are units of common residence. Several villages together occupy a territory that they feel to be theirs by custom and occupation. There is a tendency for this felt relationship of villages to be signified by a common name, a district name, which is at the same time a name of the group of people in it. Several of these districts feel a kinship to others in a larger territory, and again these to another, and finally the ever more attenuated recognition of unity peters out. This final area of recognition of communality is the tribe. The Nuer, as a whole people, are divided into eight or nine large tribes, averaging about 5000 persons each, and several much smaller ones. But the tribe is the largest unit of persons who defend a common territory, who are a named group, and who act together, manifesting a sense of patriotism or belongingness. Among the Nuer tribes there is only anarchy; they are a nation in the sense of sharing a language, culture, and territory, but not a nation in the political sense.

Each Nuer tribe consists of several clans, but always there is one which is felt to be the oldest and most distinguished. It is sometimes, but not always, the largest as well. A clan tends to have at least some members in each of the many villages of the tribe, but always one particular clan is felt to be the most important in each village, another in each district, and so on, so that one may speak of the dominant clan in each of the areas as well as for the tribe as a whole. In the above sense, some social differentiation of families is therefore present everywhere. It is a matter of prestige, however, and not of privilege. There are no economic classes based on inherited differences in wealth or standards of living.

Nuer tribes have no true government or regularized authority, no laws or lawgivers. There are, to be sure, influential men, but these men have a degree of authority which rests on their individual abilities to command respect rather than on inherited status or function. Usually, a prominent leader comes from the dominant clan, but he must be of strong character and of impressive wisdom in order to attract a following. The Nuer are strongly egalitarian and do not readily accept authority except in familial ways implicit in the age and sex categories of the kinship system.

The position most closely resembling political office is that of the *Leopard-skin Chief,* so called because he is entitled to wear a leopard-skin wrap. His main function, in addition to certain ritual duties, is to mediate feuds. The most serious social disturbance in Nuer life occurs when one man kills another. As in other primitive societies without governmental institutions, this act inevitably brings retaliation from the bereaved kinsmen and is frequently the beginning of a true feud. Nuer communities do not let this situation go uncontrolled, for the society is not wholly anarchic, yet no judgment or force of a legal or governmental sort is involved in the settlement.

When homicide has been committed, the killer goes to the local Leopard-skin Chief, and if he fears vengeance at that time, he may remain with the chief, whose home is a sanctuary. The role of the chief is to go to the family of the slayer and elicit from it a promise to pay a certain number of cattle to the aggrieved, after which he attempts to persuade the family of the dead man to accept this compensation. He is only a mediator, however, and he has no authority to judge or to force either a payment or its acceptance. On the surface, there seems to be a government-like characteristic involved— a restitution rather than retribution is provided—but it is not a payment to the state or society as such, or in any sense a fine or sentence.

Occasionally the Leopard-skin Chief acts as a mediator in other kinds of disputes, such as cases involving a disputed ownership of cattle. He, and perhaps some respected elders of the community, may express their opinions on the merits of the case and attempt to argue the two sides into a settlement. But again, he has no official power. He does not summon the defendants, and he has no means of enforcing compliance with his opinion.

At certain times, men perhaps best called *prophets* have had some political influence. These men are most usually shamans or healers, believed to be possessed by one of the powerful sky spirits. A few times certain of these have been able to unite more groups in a war campaign than could have been possible in this otherwise loosely bound society. The most notable occurrences of prophets' influence were in rallying opposition to Arab and European incursions in the nineteenth century, but British rule effectively halted their activity. Warfare consists normally of small-scale raids, and only rarely in the past have several communities united in conducting wars.

It seems to the Nuer that peaceful relations should obtain between kinsmen, and that kinsmen must defend one another; the closer the relationship, the more necessary it is that peace should prevail. In general, the Nuer marry within their own tribe, so that relationship ties do not transcend the tribal boundary. On the other hand, kinship extends, in one way or another, far beyond the local villages, as a consequence of the Nuer concept of incest, which includes an extraordinarily wide range of people in its prohibition. First of all, one cannot marry within one's own lineage or clan. Inasmuch as clans may be very large, a wide segment of the population is thus prohibited from intermarriage. The rule also prohibits marriage with any of the mother's lineage, though not with other lineages in her clan, and even with those considered kindred by a fiction or analogy, as, for example, in the case of a boy and girl whose fathers are in the same age-set. There is no exogamy explicitly by locality, but a village is such a network of various kinds of kinship ties, real or fictional, that usually a mate must be sought outside one's own village. Ideally a marriage should take place between persons whose families are of villages within visiting distance.

Marriage, a home, and children are the goal in Nuer life for both males and females from early childhood. After puberty, boys and girls have a good deal of freedom in experimental love-making and usually find their lovers without any particular interference from their respective families, but marriage is the purpose behind every romance. In the final choice, however, the girl's family must approve of the suitor's family. They should be steady, agreeable people with a sufficiency of cattle.

The actual marriage is made by a payment of several head of cattle from the groom's family to the bride's family. Normally, three periods of payment and associated ritual are involved, which could be considered betrothal, wedding, and consummation. At the time of the betrothal ceremony at the bride's home, the groom's family makes a token gift of a few cattle and the groom's friend, a sort of Best Man acting as negotiator, reaches an agreement with the bride's family on the number of cattle to be given later and the dates for the subsequent ceremonies. Then singing, dancing, and feasting on an ox follow. A few weeks later, after prolonged discussions and even apparent arguments have resulted in an agreement on the complexities of how many cattle will be presented and what proportions will go to particular kinsmen of the girl, the marriage feast is held, again at the girl's home, with great numbers of relatives of both families present.

The true marriage occurs when the third feast is held, this time at the home of the groom. This ceremony is the significant one; it celebrates the final binding of the union of families, and not until this occasion does the husband have full conjugal rights over his wife; that is, he cannot punish or sue in case of the wife's adultery, for example, or prevent her from going to the dances held by unmarried people. High points in the ceremony are the first night, when the bride and groom presumably have their first sexual encounter; and in the morning, when an ox is sacrificed and a great feast is held, shared by the two families except for the bride, who is not allowed to eat in the home of her mother-in-law. On this occasion the bride is annointed with butter, and her head is shaved to signalize her change in status.

Nevertheless, the married couple do not actually live together until a child is born. The girl is given a special hut in her own family's homestead, and the husband remains with his own family, making overnight visits to his wife whenever he can. After a child is born, the husband is fully accepted as a member of the girl's family. They stay with her family, however, only until the child is weaned, and then go to live in the husband's village.

Husband, wife, and all of their respective kinsmen are most anxious for a child to be born. This is not only because they love children but also because the marriage is not stable until a child is born. Should the marriage break up because of infertility, all of the cattle have to be returned; consequently, none of the cattle may be disposed of in other bride prices or gifts in all this time.

After the weaning of the first-born, the husband builds a hut for his wife and child in his father's homestead. One of the wife's first acts in her new home is to build a mud wind screen to be the dwelling place of the spirit of her lineage. For the wife this signalizes a great change; she will now grow her own millet and milk her own cattle. The husband's father gives him a few head of cattle with which to begin his own independent household.

Sooner or later, in a normal course of events, bride prices in cattle flow into this homestead as some girls, sisters, perhaps, of the husband, go through the various stages of marriage, and he begins to acquire more cattle from his father. Eventually, if all goes well, the new couple will have both sons and daughters, so that the herds as well as the extended family maintain a balance. It should be apparent that, over time, nobody loses in the payment of bride wealth. The group receiving cattle at any particular time divides them among relatives, and when one of these later makes a bride payment, all of the relatives contribute.

The payment of cattle is therefore not literally the purchase of a bride; cattle go out of a settlement and cattle come in. The most significant aspect of these movements of cattle in one direction and women in another is their stabilizing function. It is very complicated and difficult to dissolve a marriage, inasmuch as all of the widely dispersed cattle must be returned. Thus the wife's family uses all its influence to make her remain with the husband. It is in order to avoid difficulties that so much time and so many discrete stages are involved in the making of a marriage. People want to be as certain as possible that the marriage will be stable before they fully commit themselves.

A young man must be exceptionally deferential to his in-laws, but after the birth and weaning of his first child, his status changes and he tends to become accepted as a relative rather than a mere suitor. The girl's parents call him *father of* ———— (the child's name), and social relations become structured in kinship terms. The boy does not avoid his mother-in-law any longer. They can now converse openly, though not informally, and he may visit her from time to time. Only two stringent prohibitions still obtain: the husband may not eat in his in-laws' home, and he must never appear naked before them.

A form of levirate is practiced among the Nuer in the event that the death of a man leaves a wife and children surviving. Normally, a younger brother of the deceased takes over the responsibility for the wife and her children; "he provides a hut for her." He becomes the guardian of the children primarily, for the arrangement is not, strictly speaking, a marriage. No ceremony is performed, and the widow retains her original name as the wife of the dead man.

Occasionally a man has more than one wife. The first wife has no special status; the Nuer believe all the wives should be treated equally. It is, of course, a situation which contains many possibilities of friction between the wives, and the Nuer know this well, for the word for the condition of being co-wife is also the word for jealousy. A common cause of polygynous marriages, in addition to the levirate, arises when a man dies without male heirs, for it is believed that a man's name should continue in his lineage and that his ghost will be angry should this fail to occur. Such a situation is commonly remedied by a sort of *ghost marriage,* whereby the dead man's younger brother or close kinsmen takes a wife in his name. The dead man's ghost is regarded as the legal husband, and the children take his name.

There is also a kind of marriage between two women, one of which, the "husband," is usually barren. Children are begotten to the couple by the service of a male kinsman or friend. The "husband" administers the family just as would a man and is the "father" of the children. There is no evidence that this institution is created by sexual inversion. The fact that a third person is the actual begetter is of no consequence to the Nuer in this situation, nor even in other more normal kinds of marriage, for physiological paternity is of no consequence compared to legal paternity.

Children live with their mothers in the small huts that surround the cattle barn. When boys are about 7 or 8, they are taken from the mother and come to sleep, eat, and spend their leisure hours in the barn, which, although it shelters cattle in the rainy periods, is essentially a men's club, as is a particular windbreak in the dry-season camp. The huts go with the gardens, the barn goes with the cattle; the economic division of labor—woman's gardening, man's cattle-tending—is thus manifested in the separation of quarters. But women do not have a degraded status in Nuer society. They take an active part in the daily life of the community, mixing freely with men and delivering opinions with an easy assurance.

A Nuer child's experience is not confined closely to his own family. All of the people who share the adjacent homestead take an interest in the child's upbringing, and lactating women in any part of the locality may nurse it. It falls to the mother, and to a lesser extent to other female relatives, particularly older sisters, to correct or chastise the child. Nuer fathers indulge their children and spend a great deal of time playing with them, but never really punish them.

The first-born child, especially if it is a boy, is treated in a special manner. As previously noted, he is born in his mother's family's house and is taken to his father's household after weaning. If his maternal grandmother is alive, he may remain under her care, and never live in his father's village during his childhood. If not, he stays with his father and mother until he is 6 or 7 and then goes back to his mother's home to live with his maternal uncle until initiation time, when he comes back to his father's home again.

For a Nuer boy, the most important event that occurs before his marriage is his initiation into his age-set. This, like initiation or puberty rites in many primitive societies, involves a series of severe ordeals and complicated rituals which move him from childhood into the grade of manhood. Boys between the ages of 14 and 16 are put through these rituals together, whenever there is a sufficient number of them in a village. After successive groups of boys are initiated over a six-year period, a four-year interval is kept free, after which initiations may begin again. A difference of from 4 to 10 years in age thus separates the members of any one age-set from the adjacent one. Boys who have been initiated together have a lifelong comradeship, and all the groups of a particular age-set are set off in behavior from each of the others.

The most notable ordeal in the initiation is an operation which consists of making six long cuts from ear to ear across the forehead. After the operation the boys live in partial seclusion and observe various taboos. The operation, rituals, and festivities are attended only by the fathers and their age mates. The opening and closing of the initiation period is simultaneous throughout the whole tribe and is signalized by a ritual performed by a specialist called *Man of the Cattle*.

Boys who have been initiated are eager to engage in a raid in order to prove their manhood and valor, but the age-set organization is actually not a warriors' organization, as it is among some of the other African herding societies, nor are there any other corporate activities. Even in the initiation rites themselves there is no educative or moral training; they seem to have no other meaning than to stratify the society into groups which will explicitly structure the behavior of men to one another in terms of relative age. It is chiefly in local domestic relations that the initiation of a youth into his age-set is of great importance. At this time a boy's father or uncle gives him his first spear, which elevates him to warrior status, and his first ox. At this time he takes his ox name; i.e., he is called by the name of his ox. From this time until he marries and becomes a father—a *true man*—he is heavily engaged in proving his worth as a potential head of a family and in dancing and love-making in quest of his wife-to-be.

The Nuer are meticulous about showing proper deference to older people, but except for this kind of social stratification there is no pattern of subordination or superordination; the society is eminently egalitarian, as is manifest in nearly all actions. The people are generous to each other always, but any request which has an overtone of an order quickly angers them. They are inclined to be reticent and dour with any strangers, who are always potential enemies.[4] The presence of a stranger, even as wildly strange as a modern European, does not appear to frighten them or arouse either their curiosity or hospitality: the Neur "strut about like lords of the earth, which indeed, they consider themselves to be."[5]

The Nuer have not particularly developed any of the arts except the singing of poetry, a trait they share, for some reason, with most other pastoral peoples of the world. When a Neur boy feels happy, he sings; when he guards the cattle, he sings; when he courts a girl, he sings. Some songs are traditional, others may be composed at the whim of the singer. Some are always sung by soloists; others are sung by groups. As might be expected, praise of cattle figures in a great many of them.

There is a great fear of the ghosts of the dead. Shortly after a death, the corpse is buried in the foetal position in a grave about four feet deep. A cowhide is wrapped around the body, but no possessions are placed in the grave. Relatives and age mates then allow their hair to grow and put aside their body ornaments. The most

[4] This characterization refers to the Nuer of some years ago. They have apparently become more affable in recent years.
[5] E. E. Evans-Pritchard, *op. cit.,* p. 182.

important ceremony takes place at the end of the mourning period, some six months after the death of a man and three months after the death of a woman. Bullocks are killed for a feast, and the assemblage is ritually sprinkled with milk. After the feast, the mourners shave their heads and resume wearing their customary ornaments. The main purpose of the ceremony is to placate the spirit of the deceased so that it will make no attempt to take its wife or husband, children, and cattle.

If a person is struck by lightning or dies suddenly without a previous illness, it is believed that the Sky God has removed the spirit and taken it into the sky. A mourning period is not held, inasmuch as the spirit has not lingered in the vicinity during the usual period; the sacrifice of cattle is made immediately after the burial. The Nuer do not betray great sorrow because of a death. It is the will of the Sky God if a person is taken, and to show emotion would be to complain against the action.

There are several Sky Gods or spirits. The most powerful is Deng, who is associated with sickness. Certain others are gods of war, hunting, thunder and lightning, and so on. There are also certain earth spirits, many of which are related to species of birds or animals and which function as totems of lineages. Birds are particularly sacred totems of the Neur, which is apparently the reason that the people will not eat the flesh or eggs of birds.

There is a sense, however, in which there are no particular gods at all. The Nuer hold a conception of *Kwoth*, a generalized Spirit or God-essence, reminiscent of the Polynesian *mana;* and the various named gods and totemic spirits are manifestations of the spiritual essence and not *Kwoth* themselves. Thus, in a philosophical sense the Nuer are monotheistic, but in terms of action, such as the practice of sacrifice, they seem polytheistic. Perhaps it is most appropriate to call them merely theistic.

Certain men claim special powers of healing and prognostication as a result of possession of one of the totemic spirits. Particular healers are known for their specialties; one is good at divining, another at curing constipation or headache. Divining is accomplished by reading signs, most typically by interpreting the pattern in the fall of mussel shells thrown against the side of a gourd rattle. Curing involves the world-wide technique of massage and the extraction of a foreign object from the patient's afflicted part. Some shamans have acquired wide influence and are known as prophets, being possessed of mightier spirit helpers than the ordinary diviner. Some of these men function as rain makers, conducting ceremonies that involve the sacrifice of animals to the thunder spirit. Rain makers are very important ritual functionaries among the neighboring Dinka and Shilluk, but less so among the Nuer.

The Nuer sometimes raise pyramids of considerable size in honor of a particular god-spirit. One of these is about 50 feet high and 300 feet in circumference. These monuments are built of baked earth and ashes and ringed around with upright elephant tusks. The idea of pyramids may have diffused in ancient times from Egypt; but the Nuer pyramids, in contrast to those of the Egyptians, are not burial mausoleums, nor are they built with conscripted or forced labor.

The Nuer also have a conception of *evil eye*—a person of some supernatural power who maliciously causes damage to people by looking at them. Allied to this is the notion of witches, particularly a kind of ghoul who secretly performs rites over the bodies of the newly dead in order to gain control over the souls of the surviving relatives. As is so common in human society, people who are disliked or who commit antisocial acts that arouse fear are sometimes accused of witchcraft, and it is said that in the past such witches were killed with the consent of the community.

The Nuer have many traditions or myths of their origin as a people and of the beginnings of their customs. A common feature of many of them is the idea that the original progenitors of the Nuer descended from the sky down to a very large tree and then to the ground, where they became mankind. The first descendants were all siblings, of course, but a culture hero, Gaa, divided them into two groups and decreed that they must marry into their opposite group but not into their own. By a process of growth and fission through generations, the two lineages branched into many, the more closely related ones to be conceived as clans.

The time perspective of the Nuer is limited to a very short span —in a sense they are a timeless people, as are most primitive societies. The year is seen merely in terms of the cycle of events created by the two distinct seasons. *Moons,* which are roughly months marked by the lunar cycle, are sometimes used to demark time, as are numbers of days and segments of a day. But essentially, time is marked by reference to activities. The Nuer have no word for time in the European sense. They have no conception of time as an abstract thing which can be wasted, or saved, or which passes. Activities are not coordinated with the passage of time, therefore, because the temporal points of reference are generally the activities themselves, which are conducted in a leisurely, habitual pattern.

In reckoning past events, the Nuer are not as likely to attempt to count years as they are to cite a remembered action that occurred before or after the event which is being located in time. Among the most frequent markers are the age-sets: such and such a thing happened just after a particular age-set began, or a person may say, for example, that the event occurred three sets before his own initiation (roughly 30 years). History, then, does not last long for the Nuer, at the most only about a century. Remembered events, such as famines or wars, of earlier times than that merge into tradition and are all seen in the flat time perspective common among nonliterate peoples. The shallowness of this time view may be judged from the fact that the tree under which they believe mankind was created is still standing.

The outside world has not molested the Nuer to the point of radically altering their culture. Probably the greatest change has been caused by the decimation of the cattle herds in the present century by rinderpest, an infectious disease that attacks cattle, sheep, and goats. In the past, 40 to 60 head of cattle might be included in a payment of bride wealth, whereas about half that many are all that could be expected today. The loss in cattle has caused the Nuer to plant millet to a greater extent than before to make up the loss in subsistence. Possibly the increased dependence on horticulture has had an affect on the villages, rendering them more stable.

The dwindling of the herds may, partly at least, explain the aggressiveness of the Nuer. The pastoral Dinka have been raided most persistently by the Nuer in the present century. Other tribes, such as the Shilluk, are not raided by the Nuer because, as they explain, "We only raid people who possess cattle. If they had cattle, we would raid them and take their cattle. . . ."

Arab slavers and ivory traders, who conquered many of the

Sudanic tribes in the past, had little effect on the Nuer. The Egyptian government and the later Mahdist government (the famous dervishes), which attempted to govern the Sudan between 1821 and the end of the century, had no control over the Nuer, nor did any other agency until the Anglo-Egyptian government of the Sudan finally established firm administrative posts in Nuerland after 1928. These posts are remote from everyday Nuer life, however, and the only general effect was to diminish the amount of raiding. Some effect on the religion has been caused by the government's pursuit of prophets, whom they consider responsible for uprisings; but inasmuch as the phenomenon of prophets leading war parties was a consequence of a foreign threat rather than the cause, the basis of Nuer religion is little altered.

The area contains no resources desired by foreigners; therefore the Nuer have not been pushed from their homeland. Furthermore, the Nuer have not shown any desire for modern innovations. Their fixation on cattle and their satisfaction in their simple way of life permit them to remain aloof and self-sufficient in their infrequent relations with Europeans. According to a recent work on the Nuer, the British administration finally succeeded in winning their confidence and good will: "From an excessively arrogant, uncooperative and suspicious people, the Nuer rapidly became what they are now: still proud, still intensely democratic with a fine spirit of independence, but essentially friendly."[6]

FURTHER READINGS

Evans-Pritchard, E. E., *The Nuer,* Oxford, 1940.

Evans-Pritchard, E. E., "The Nuer of the Nilotic Sudan," in M. Fortes and E. E. Evans-Pritchard (eds.), *African Political Systems,* London, New York, 1940.

Evans-Pritchard, E. E., *Some Aspects of Marriage and the Family Among the Nuer,* Livingstone, 1945.

Evans-Pritchard, E. E., "Kinship and the Local Community Among the Nuer," in A. R. Radcliffe-Brown and D. Forde (eds.), *African Systems of Kinship and Marriage,* London, New York, Toronto, 1950.

[6] P. P. Howell, *A Manual of Nuer Law,* London, New York, 1954. It should be noted, however, that the Sudan became an independent republic in 1956, which may have again altered the relations of the Nuer to governmental authority.

Evans-Pritchard, E. E., *Kinship and Marriage Among the Nuer,* Oxford, 1951.

Evans-Pritchard, E. E., *Nuer Religion,* Oxford, 1956.

Greenberg, J. H., "Studies in African Linguistic Classification," *Southwestern Journal of Anthropology,* Vols. 5, 1949, 6, 1950.

Herskovits, M. J., "The Cattle Complex of East Africa," *American Anthropologist,* n.s., Vol. 28, 1926.

Howell, P. P., *A Manual of Nuer Law,* London, New York, 1954.

Seligman, C. G. and B. Z., *Pagan Tribes of the Nilotic Sudan,* London, 1932.

The Navaho of the American Southwest

The best-preserved aboriginal cultures of the United States of America occupy the zone generally called the Southwest—mainly the states of Arizona and New Mexico, with extensions into southern Utah and southwestern Colorado. In most respects, the fund of knowledge which anthropologists have acquired about the primitive peoples of this region exceeds anything known about any other single area of like size in the world. In part this is because the Southwest was so remote and so undesirable for American commercial interests that the Indians were left relatively undisturbed for a longer time than elsewhere in the United States. The attention of investigators was drawn to the Southwest quite early in the history of American anthropology, however, and we have a long-term stockpiling of information as well as a large number of intensive modern studies.

Anthropological knowledge of the prehistory of the Southwest is also quite detailed. The arid climate has not only kept many items of prehistoric culture in a remarkable state of preservation; it has also saved for us wooden house beams, charcoal, arrow shafts, and other articles of wood, which has made possible the nearly exact dating of many Southwestern cultural remains by means of dendrochronology—tree-ring counting.

The earliest inhabitants of the Southwest were seed gatherers and hunters of small game. Eventually, the small beginnings of agriculture about 3000 years ago began to transform Southwestern society into a more sedentary form, until finally, about A.D. 1000, peoples in certain of the areas that were favorable for agriculture were living in the great stone communal dwellings of the type known as Great Pueblos. One of the better known of these is Pueblo Bonito, in northern New Mexico. One huge structure built around a central court, this pueblo covered three acres of ground and is estimated to have housed 1200 people. Like a great many other similar sites in the northern Southwest, Pueblo Bonito was built during the classic pueblo period, which lasted from about A.D. 900 to 1300. A rapid collapse and retreat to the south followed this period, and the new villages were constructed in safer localities, where a great many of them are still occupied.

The history of the Navaho[1] Indians in the Southwest begins at about the same time as the retreat of the Pueblos, which suggests the possibility that their arrival created an intensification of warfare. The Pueblos were the sedentary, wealthy agriculturalists, whereas the Navaho and related Apache were nomadic hunters, who undoubtedly found the pueblos easy to raid. During this time, at any rate, began the great cultural dichotomy in the Southwest between the intensive agriculturalists who lived in their tight little villages and the free-ranging, proud, warlike Navaho-Apache.

The Navaho-Apache apparently came down from the north, for their language is Athapascan, the language of many groups in western Canada. At that time they were simple nomads, possessing no agriculture, and no domestic animals save the dog. They did have one superior artifact which must have been of considerable consequence in their competition with the Pueblo Indians; they used a sinew-backed bow, a very much more powerful weapon than the simple warped stick which served the Pueblos.

During the years A.D. 1400–1600 the main center of Navaho-Apache dominance was in the northwestern part of New Mexico and southern Colorado. (The groups now called Apache were those who eventually moved out of this particular area). Here

[1] In older spelling, the Spanish form *Navajo* was used. It is conventionally anglicized today—the *j* written as *h*. The Navaho call themselves *Diné*, "the People."

the simple culture of the newcomers gradually underwent a considerable transformation. Most fundamental, undoubtedly, was the fact that they acquired farming knowledge from their sometime prey, the Pueblos. A considerable amount of the Pueblo ritual and ceremonial paraphernalia was also adopted. During this period, a change in the Navaho settlement pattern must have taken place as a consequence of the new farming methods. They became less nomadic; larger concentrations of people occupied areas favorable for farming. Probably this was the time at which the simple family bands became changed into matrilineal clans. Interestingly, some of the clan legends trace their beginnings to this time.

The coming of the Spaniards into the Southwest initiated the next great series of cultural changes. In 1539, with the famous exploration of the Franciscan monk, Fray Marcos de Niza, began the encroachment of Spanish adventurers, missionaries, and colonists and the steady influence of Spanish culture on the Southwestern Indians. The introduction of Spanish sheep, goats, and horses had a great effect on the way of life of the Navaho especially, for large areas of their homeland that were poor or impossible for agriculture became more economically productive. The acquisition of horses tended to revitalize the raiding habits of the Navaho, too, for settlements of Spaniards and even of other Indians were easy victims of the swift-moving horsemen.

American influence in the Southwest began to be felt after 1846, when the Navaho territory came under the jurisdiction of the U.S. government. The first task of the new government was to subdue the Navaho and Apache raiders. The U.S. troopers had little success until, during the period of the American Civil War, Kit Carson, an illiterate trapper and guide who became a colonel in the U.S. Army, aided by a handful of New Mexican soldiers, formulated a plan for vanquishing the Navaho. Instead of futilely chasing small bands of raiders, Carson struck at the roots of the Indians' subsistence. He killed their livestock, burned their fields, and cut down their fruit trees, until the people were literally starving. By 1864, large numbers of Navaho had surrendered to the government at Fort Defiance. The captive Navaho eventually came to number about 8000—probably a large proportion of the tribe at that time.

All of the captive Navaho were taken to Fort Sumner, 180 miles southeast of Santa Fe, New Mexico, in a great mass movement, which they referred to as the Long Walk. The physical suffering was very great, but probably the homesickness combined with the psychic disturbances of four long years of captivity were greater. This calamity remained alive in the Indians' imaginations for a long time, and with it began the long-standing attitudes of bitterness and distrust toward the white Americans. In 1868, after settling a treaty with the U.S. government (which did not fulfill its terms), the Navaho returned to their ruined homeland to live under the jurisdiction of U.S. government Indian agents, some of whom were merely corrupt politicians. Promises were frequently broken; land on which Navaho were living was taken for the new Sante Fe railroad; the increasing white population struggled with the Navaho over land and grazing permits—and won, more often than not.

Since the middle 1930s, from the beginnings made by the New Deal government, a more sympathetic attempt has been made to understand and aid the Navaho. But the problems are still very great. The reservation lands are arid, unproductive, and rapidly deteriorating. To help alleviate this situation, the U.S. government instituted a stock-reduction program in order to prevent the overgrazing which was ruining the land. The Indians were prevented from grazing as many animals as had been their custom, and inasmuch as they viewed their herds as basic to their lives, they felt that the government was punishing them rather than helping. This misunderstanding is the most important cause of recent bitterness. Despite grave economic hardship, the Navaho, however, have increased to more than 85,000—the largest Indian tribe in the United States. The present birth-death ratio reveals a natural increase about twice as rapid as the rest of the population of the United States. The Navaho today are threatened in two opposite ways: the steady and pervasive encroachment of the American way of life seems likely to overwhelm the Navaho culture, whereas many Navaho wish to be allowed to follow proudly the Navaho pattern of life; the increase in population and the steady deterioration of the reservation land are creating an increasing poverty which will result in a greater economic dependence and closer ties with the nation whether such a course seems desirable to the Navaho or not.

The present reservation of more than 15,000,000 acres in northwestern New Mexico, northeastern Arizona, and southeastern

Utah has a population density of 2.1 persons per square mile. This seems low, but it is actually a much greater population density than is to be found in similar surrounding areas. This rugged and beautiful country is of very small productive value; high mesas, inaccessible buttes, deep canyons, vast sand and gravel plains, and rugged mountains represent a very substantial part of the area and are nearly totally unfit for agriculture. In elevation the country varies from 4500 feet to nearly 10,000 feet in the mountains. Rainfall varies from about 5 inches annually in the lower altitudes to more than 20 inches in the mountains, but most of it falls in the torrential summer convectional storms, and it therefore runs off the land in gullies into the canyons rather than soaking into the soil. Only in the high mountains is there a plentiful supply of water, but life in winter is impossible there. Water scarcity and the seasonal nature of pasturage cause a certain amount of change in residence, in some areas standardized as a movement from highlands in summer to lowlands in winter. In no sense, however, are these movements so consistent or extensive that the Navaho could be considered a truly nomadic people.

Agriculture is the basis of subsistence generally, as it has been for hundreds of years. Maize and squash are the most frequent crops. Melons, beans, and tree fruits are also highly valued. Potatoes, alfalfa, wheat, and oats are grown frequently in areas suitable for them. The yield per acre is very low, in large part because the land is so poor, but also because modern farming techniques, such as rotation, proper fertilizer, and the best planting time, have not entirely replaced earlier methods. Wild foods are not utilized nowadays to nearly the extent they formerly were, for livestock consume most of the wild plants, and the game resources of the region are also much depleted. A few rabbits and prairie dogs may be eaten; cactus fruits and wild greens are used at certain seasons. The piñon tree provides a considerable harvest of nuts in some areas, and these are usually sold to traders for the New York market as cocktail tidbits.

The sale of livestock and by-products, such as wool and pelts, is an important commercial resource for the Navaho. Sheep are by far the most numerous of their livestock. Goats, cattle, and horses are additional prized possessions. Commercial links with the nation are also maintained by the sale of blankets and silver ornaments.

Even before the appearance of the American trader, the justly famed Navaho blanket was traded to neighboring tribes and to the Spanish settlers of New Mexico. Today, Navaho silver work has become, along with the blanket, an attractive product bought by great numbers of Americans.

Since the 1880s the trading post on the reservation has been the most significant functional link between Navaho and whites. The trader introduced the Indians to manufactured knives, axes, matches, coffee, flour, sugar, velveteen cloth (now a characteristic of Navaho dress), and a host of other odds and ends on which the Indians have become increasingly dependent. But not only did the trader stimulate the Indians' desires for American goods; he also influenced the types of things produced by the Indians. Some of the traders became very influential in Navaho affairs, for they were the only permanent white residents in many parts of the reservation, and thus the only trusted contact with the outside world. It is the long-established trader, usually, who even today advises the Indians, although some of the people employed by the U.S. government for this purpose are gaining their confidence.

The Navaho blanket (or rug) is usually made solely for sale; the blankets they wear themselves are often manufactured "Indian" blankets from Sears Roebuck, or perhaps a finer wool Pendleton. Apparently, robes of wild cotton were woven before the coming of the Spaniards, but when the Navaho acquired the Spanish sheep, they began to perfect their famous blankets. From the Spaniards they learned to use indigo blue and the brilliant scarlet made from the cochineal insects found on cactus leaves. The Indians also learned to unravel the fabric of Spanish military uniforms. *Bayeta*, they called this material, and today blankets made from it are collectors' items, for cheaper coloring methods have, of course, displaced the reweaving technique.

Silver was first acquired from raids on the Spaniards, but the Indians did not attempt to work the metal themselves until the period of American dominion, when a few Navaho began to copy the technique of the itinerant Mexican smiths, using the malleable silver coins of Mexico. Jewelry was not made for trade, but for personal adornment only. With the advent of the trading post, it became a custom for the Indians to leave their jewelry pawned as security against goods purchased on credit. The trader in this

NAVAHO HOGANS BENEATH NORTHEASTERN ARIZONA CLIFF. *Courtesy, The American Museum of Natural History*

NAVAHO SILVERSMITH AND YOUNG ONLOOKER. *Courtesy, Museum of the American Indian, Heye Foundation*

way acquired a collection of unredeemed ornaments, which he sold in town. Finally, the Indians learned that if they should grow tired of a particular piece of jewelry, they could simply leave it with the trader in return for credit and fail to redeem it—they did not know how to sell it to whites. With the great influx of tourists into the Southwest in modern times, the demand for Indian curios grew. The majority of the tourists did not appreciate the merit of the handicraft, and so the inevitable happened: white manufacturers began to make poor machine copies of the belts, earrings, necklaces, bracelets, and rings and to price them at less than the handmade articles. In recent years, the U.S. government has encouraged the Navaho to maintain the integrity of their craft in various ways, and a growing sophistication among the white population of the Southwest is helping to create somewhat of a renaissance in Navaho silversmithing.

The Navaho living quarters are usually of two kinds. The *hogan* is the more permanent house used in fall, winter, and spring. In the summer the people move to temporary camps near the areas where they cultivate their crops. Nowadays a well-to-do family may use a canvas tent, but most use a structure, common to Latin America, called a *ramada*. This consists of four upright posts supporting a flat roof of brush. It is little more than a sunshade, though sometimes a pole and brush wall is laid on the windward side.

The hogan is a low, unpretentious one-room structure built of logs, of stone, or of packed earth and brush, depending on the nature of local materials. The older type is supported by a foundation of three forked poles locked together at the apex. Other poles and logs are leaned on them, and then the whole structure is packed with clay. The preferred style today, however, is a structure having four or more sides and resembling a low log cabin with a cribbed, dome-shaped roof of tamped earth. Many Navaho houses do not have windows; the door is often made of an old blanket; and the smoke from the open fire in the center of the room is allowed to escape through a simple hole in the roof.

The house is a single-family dwelling—husband, wife, and children, usually, and sometimes an aged relative live in it. Navaho society is matrilocal, which is to say, the married couple make their home in the neighborhood of the wife's family; hence children grow up among their mother's matrilineal kindred. This order is not strict, however; for various reasons of convenience a couple may live completely separated from relatives, or even (more rarely) at the camp of the husband's parents. Usually, though, a couple live in the vicinity of matrilineal relatives in some approximation of the widespread extended family. Labor in housebuilding, roundups, well-digging, fencing, and so on is usually pooled communally by these relatives.

Men do most of the work in the fields. Women keep the dwelling in order, look after children, cook, and harvest such crops as are

NAVAHO WOMAN GRINDING CORN. *Courtesy, The American Museum of Natural History*

to be consumed immediately. Children and the aged are expected to watch over the flocks. Women are highly specialized as weavers, although a few men undertake weaving from time to time. Men are the silversmiths, but their wives may help them at times. In general, the traditional division of labor between the sexes is not as rigid as it is in many primitive societies.

There is very little conception of property's being jointly shared by husband and wife. Inasmuch as the typical household lives in the vicinity of the wife's relatives, much of the property of a household, and often even the house itself, is felt to be owned by the woman, to be inherited by her female descendants. A woman may even control more cash than her husband as well, for it is she who creates the blankets and markets the wool that are the frequent sources of cash income. It is probable, however, that in the future increased opportunities for outside wage work by men will reverse this imbalance. Because of the absence of the small courtesies that a white man ordinarily shows to his wife in public, it often appears on superficial observation that the Navaho woman has a low status,

Courtesy, Museum of the American Indian, Heye Foundation

but in many important respects the opposite is true. It has been suggested by C. Kluckhohn that the government agents, misunderstanding this, have typically made the mistake of dealing too exclusively with Navaho men, only to become annoyed later when agreements reached with the men were not carried out.

Much of Navaho property, such as farm and range land, pertains to matrilineal family lines. The husband, who may be in charge of its use, is actually little more than a trustee. Even the livestock is not owned outright by individuals. The user is not free to dispose of this property in order to satisfy some whim. Only such purely personal things as clothing, jewelry, saddles, and intangibles, such as individual songs or prayers, can be disposed of freely. Some of this personal material property is buried with the owner on his death, except for those items which he has specifically granted to a survivor. Needless to say, the steady encroachment of modern American culture is beginning already to create frictions and incompatibilities, as inheritance laws, court decisions, Indian Agency decisions, and commercial relations are based on assumptions about property which are quite foreign to the Indians.

The Navaho, like other primitives, have a social organization phrased exclusively in terms of kinship. Many categories of relatives are distinguished in Navaho usage—most of them unfamiliar to whites—and these categories reveal certain things about the conventional social life. For example, relatives on the mother's side are called by different terms from those by which the same kinds of relatives on the father's side are called. Such distinctions are related to the fact that the society is matrilocal and matrilineal—one associates with one set of relatives on a quite different basis from that on which one associates with the other. The relation of the maternal uncle to nephews and nieces is distinct from that of the father's brother. The mother's brother assumes an important role in the disciplining and rearing of nephews and nieces.

Younger and older brothers are distinguished in kinship terminology. Other relatives, among whom we would distinguish, are lumped together under a single term: a mother's sisters (maternal aunts) are called *mother,* and the children of these aunts are called by the same terms as actual siblings. These and the father's brother's children are called parallel cousins by anthropologists; the other cousins, who are children of the mother's brother or father's sister —cross cousins—are distinguished by a separate term.

Many of these categories of relationship are correlated with a prescribed etiquette, mostly having to do with variations in respectful distance. The relation between adult brothers and sisters is characterized by affectionate respect. There is considerable restriction on physical contact, and speech between them preserves many polite formalities. Similar courtesies are observed in relations between certain in-laws, the most extreme being the complete avoidance of face-to-face conversation between a mother-in-law and son-in-law. One may associate relatively freely with a cross cousin of opposite sex, and, in fact, the relationship corresponds to the standard joking relationship found among so many primitive peoples. Maternal uncles and nephews also joke with and tease one another.

Not all relatives live together in the same vicinity, of course, which is one of the causes of the distinction between father's and mother's relatives, cross and parallel cousins, and so on. Of the functioning group of relatives who regularly see one another and cooperate economically, the extended family is the basic unit. This group usually consists of parents (if living) and their married daughters with their husbands and children, all of whom live in a rather closely bunched group of hogans. Two or several extended families commonly have a sort of jurisdiction over a wider territory and engage in some cooperative endeavors, such as plowing and harvesting or giving a ceremonial. This local group of neighboring extended families is usually called the *outfit* by the white traders.

A much wider and nonlocal segment of the tribe is the clan. All Navaho belong to the clan of the mother and recognize relatives in the clan of the father on a different basis. One of the principal features of clan membership is the regulation of marriage choices; one cannot marry a person of either the mother's or the father's clan. To do so would be to commit incest, one of the most repulsive of crimes. The clans are very large, for there are only about 60 in the whole tribe, so that the link of clan membership may unite people as relatives who live many miles apart and see one another very infrequently.

In the past, the clan was the most significant agency of social control. A clan was responsible as a unit for any debts or malfeasance of any of its individual members, and consequently it attempted to regulate the conduct of all its people. Modern government officials do not recognize clan regulations, and so a Navaho judge may find himself called upon to settle impartially a case involving a fellow clan member. This is one of the many ways in which modern influences set up a conflict in the sentiments of the people.

Today tribal government is a mixture of modern imperatives and older tribal customs, and because it is a mixture and somewhat fluxlike, it appears to be quite informal. The Navaho is not accustomed to think of government as something fixed and all-powerful. The Navaho did not vest leadership in an authority. A local leader was a man respected for his age, integrity, and wisdom, whose advice was therefore sought more frequently than others', but he had no formal means of control. Group decisions were made on the basis of a public consensus, and the most influential man was somewhat more responsible than others for the decision. People were kept in line by such means as withdrawal of cooperation, gossip, and criticism, and by the belief that disease was caused by antisocial actions.

The Long Walk, the captivity, and the influence of American culture and government have created finally a nation-like unity and consciousness that did not exist aboriginally, except in the unifying result of clan membership and linkings through marriage. Today there is a Tribal Council, or assembly, of 74 elected members which makes certain decisions for the tribe as a whole, but earlier, and considerably even today, the informal decisions of the outfit—a natural community of neighbors—were basic. Much of the decision-making that involves several outfits, or even the tribe as a whole, takes place at dances, most informally, as apparently was the case in the past. The Tribal Council, however, is becoming better organized and more respected, and the tribal assets it controls are increasing in importance.

Nowadays, many Navaho children go to school and learn American ways of law, government, etiquette, and morality—but not all do, and many of those who do cannot attend regularly or for many years. Navaho ways—values, sentiments, thought patterns —are still strong and not easily disrupted. A child becomes a Navaho by a socialization process which begins on the day he is born. The Navaho people will not become thoroughly acculturated to modern life in the United States until the time that children's life in the home is very different from what it is now. The most treasured possessions of the Navaho are their children, and they go to great and careful pains to create a true Navaho adult.

According to the older but still frequent customs, a newborn child is baptized as a Navaho by sprinkling corn pollen on its head as soon as it is delivered. The baby is then bathed, the whole body is swathed in cotton cloths, and the ears are pierced for earrings. Much of the baby's early infancy passes in tight confinement wound within wrappings of cloth except during the time of the daily bath. The baby is almost constantly in close proximity to the mother, who responds immediately to any manifestation of the child's wants or discomfort. The baby is given the breast whenever it begins to cry. The nearby relatives, too, pay a great deal of affectionate attention to the baby, so that, all in all, it is fondled, patted, and cuddled during a major part of its waking hours.

After about four weeks a child is strapped onto the cradle board, and the mother then has more freedom of movement. The child is taken everywhere she goes, but the board can easily be slung from her back or suspended from a tree or wall while she attends her tasks. As the months pass, the child spends increasingly less time in the cradle board, and by the time it can toddle around by itself, the board is completely dispensed with. Each instance of increasing maturation is noted and made much of, especially when the baby laughs for the first time, which is made a minor ceremonial occasion. Any adult foods that the child can manage are given to it and, as in breast feeding, it is given food whenever it has the notion.

To a white American, it appears that Navaho spoil their children. It seems to be true that a baby is indulged a great deal. Training for the first two or three years is gradual, and gentle, and for the most part the emphasis of adult attention is on encouraging the child in favored directions, rather than on reprimanding. Partly, this may be because of the simple life of the Indians—there are few valuable objects for the baby to destroy—and partly because only few prohibitions are put on biological impulses. When the child is tied to a cradle board, of course, there is no opportunity for it to interfere experimentally with adult tasks. A great number of the frustrations and dangers of early infancy are thus eliminated, both for the child and for the mother.

The transition from infancy to childhood corresponds quite closely to the weaning period. The child tends to remain a baby until another comes along to take up the attention of the family, and the child then is abruptly denied access to the breast and, because of the various new exigencies, must act more responsibly and expect much less attention. The last child, therefore, remains a baby longest. Sometimes such a child may continue to attempt to suckle even after three or four years. Its general transition to childhood is delayed for the same reasons—the absence of someone younger to displace it.

The increasing participation of the child in everyday adult life means increasing responsibility. Watching the sheep, watering the animals, and cutting and fetching firewood may be done by quite small children. Eventually, boys and girls become fully recognized as Navaho by an initiation ceremony that introduces them to the secrets of ceremonial life. Ages of the initiates vary from 7 to 12 or 13, because of the infrequency of the ceremony.

Initiation is part of a series of ceremonies called the *Night Way,* or *Yeibichai.* Initiates are assembled around a fire, the boys naked under their blankets except for a breechcloth, the girls clothed. Two fantastically dressed figures appear, one wearing a black mask representing *Grandfather of the Monsters* and one in a white mask as *Female Divinity.* Each boy in turn is led out to the firelight, where the Female Divinity marks each of his shoulders with sacred cornmeal, the other god uttering a falsetto cry each time the meal is applied. Then the black-masked figure, making a different cry, strikes the cornmeal marks with a bundle of reeds. The boy is then struck repeatedly on different parts of his body. Onlookers joke and shout for hard or soft blows for particular boys, and the masked figure obliges by doing just the opposite.

The girls remain seated while the figure in the black mask comes to them carrying in each hand an ear of corn wrapped in spruce twigs. He presses these against the cornmeal marks which the other god has previously made on the girls' shoulders. The climax of the ceremony for both the boys and girls occurs when the gods remove their masks. The black mask is placed over the faces of the children in turn, so that each may look out of it, as the figure gives his peculiar cry. Each child is admonished not to give away the secret of the ceremony to the uninitiated. In theory, each person should go through this ceremony four times in his lifetime.

There is no particular naming ceremony either at birth or at initiation—a time when many primitives take new names. Kinship terms are always used in address among Navaho, so that so long as a child's associations are bounded by the family, there is no need for a name. As a person grows up and enters the larger society, a name is a necessity, so that people can refer to him in his absence. It is very impolite to call a person by name to his face. As among other primitive peoples, names have power. A person is therefore likely to have a secret name—a war name—which is not known to the public at large, but which gives him certain powers. Everyone has at least one nickname by which others refer to him. Now that a census is taken and many children go to school, European names have come into style, but they are often changed and have none of the surname connotations of the European custom.

A person is not fully a responsible adult until he or she has married and acquired children. The father of a boy usually takes the initiative in planning the marriage, but sometimes the boy's mater-

GRINDING CORN ON A METATE AND MANO. *Courtesy, Museum of Anthropology, University of Michigan*

nal uncle gives advice. The maternal uncle of the chosen girl is then consulted and, if the two families agree, the proposal is made and the marriage takes place.

Sometimes men have more than one wife, especially in areas where the main economic dependence is on livestock rather than farming. In such cases, the joint wives are usually sisters. In the old days, a man sometimes married an older woman and her niece, or her step-daughter, but this custom seems to be dying out. When the wives are relatives, as they typically are, they maintain separate houses, but quite close together. A ceremony is held for only the first of a man's marriages. The U.S. government, of course, prohibits polygamy and the Tribal Council has legislated against it, so that modern instances of it are kept rather secret. In the early days, if a man died, his brother was expected to marry the widow and take care of the children (the custom of the levirate). If he were already married, this amounted to obligatory polygyny.

As people grow old and more helpless, the duty of taking care of them customarily falls upon daughters or granddaughters, or if this is not possible, a niece is expected to take charge. The Navaho are extremely deferential and kindly to old or helpless relatives. When necessary, medicine men are willingly paid to perform curing ceremonies over them.

Disease is understood as being caused by the violation of some taboo, or by an attack by a ghost or a witch; therefore the process of curing must be prefaced by a ceremony of divination. This is a means of finding out the cause of the difficulty; following this, the precise ceremonial cure can be selected. There are various means of divination, but the form most frequently used is *hand-trembling.*

The hand-trembler, a specialist hired for the occasion, begins his work by sitting down beside the patient and carrying out a rite which in many respects has features recurrent in all Navaho ritual. The first thing, after washing, is to place corn pollen on certain parts of the patient's body, after which the diviner places more pollen on his own arm, tracing a trail of it along the inner arm from the elbow to the thumb and back to the elbow. A prayer is repeated as the pollen is put on the thumb, and for each finger of the hand. During the utter silence and immobility of the onlookers, the whole performance is gone through four times. (Four is a ritual number in the Southwest.) Finally the diviner begins a sacred song, and his hand and arm begin to shake and tremble. Through four verses of the song, the hand and arm tremble. This is the high point of the ritual, for the interpretation of the movements of the hand provides the information about the cause of the illness.

Following the divination, the proper curing ceremony can be selected, and the shaman (or *singer,* as he is called) can be summoned. There is considerable variation in the chants, depending on the divined cause of the illness, but all Navaho *sings* have certain elements in common, many of which are found in other American Indian curing performances: rattles, bullroarers (pieces of wood shaped to whirl and make a peculiar roaring sound when swung on

DRY PAINTING AND INCANTATIONS SHOULD RESTORE HEALTH TO SICK CHILD.

the end of a thong), burning of incense, herbal medicines, and offerings of bits of shell, semiprecious stones, and corn pollen. Most curing ceremonies also involve the use of a sweat bath, emetics, a ritual bath in yucca suds, and night-long singing. The most purely Southwestern ingredient, particularly elaborated by the Navaho, is the frequent use of dry paintings.

The Navaho dry paintings—misleadingly called sand paintings by many whites—are reproductions of extremely sacred designs made on a buckskin or on sand by pouring grains of charcoal and pulverized minerals in fine streams from the hand. The four usual colors are white, blue, yellow, and black. Some paintings are only a foot or two in diameter, and some are as large as 20 feet across. As many as 500 different dry-painting designs have been recorded, and there are undoubtedly more. All of them are highly traditionalized and old, and each painting is linked to a particular ceremony; they are not a form of self-expression.

Courtesy, The American Museum of Natural History

For the cure itself, the appropriate painting is made on the floor of the hogan, to the accompaniment of the related song and prayer. The patient is then seated upon the painting in a ritually prescribed way, and the treatment begins. First, the singer gives the patient an infusion of herbs to drink; next he touches the feet of a figure in the painting and then the feet of the patient, chanting at the same time, "May his feet be well. His feet restore unto him." The same procedure is followed for the knees, hands, shoulders, breast, back, and head, that each member be restored. When the patient has finally risen, the painting is destroyed bit by bit, following the order in which it was made.

All chants involve the notion of purification. There are taboos against certain places of sleeping and sexual acts, which all central participants in the ceremony must observe. All take sweat baths, purgatives, emetics, that they be purified of "ugly things" which are inside them. All who attend must concentrate on thinking "good, clean, beautiful thoughts." The corollary notion of the cause of illness is contamination from ghosts, witches, and the ghosts of foreigners. This latter kind of contamination is cured by one of the most famous of Navaho ceremonials, *Enemy Way*. (One of the associated public features of Enemy Way is the squaw dance, which many whites have attended.)

The chants and prayers used in the ceremonies are not prayers of supplication, nor do they manifest such attitudes as humility or gratitude, the common elements in Christian prayer. The prayers are like the other elements of the ritual; they are mechanical formulas. The universe is governed by rules. If one follows the rules, all is well. The divinities themselves follow the rules—they are compelled to act in certain ways by the proper formulas. Consequently, the chants are dangerous, for a mistake in the ritual would be a violation of the rule, and the misdirected power could cause harm.

The power of the supernatural is sometimes purposely directed to do harm. The Navaho believe firmly in witches—evil people who use ritual means to cause illness or death. Even educated Indians who have given up their faith in regard to most aspects of the ancient religion seem to find it difficult to shake off their fear of witches. The Navaho witch is believed to operate mostly at night, often disguised as a wolf or some other animal. His techniques are similar to those used by witches in other parts of the world: he may utter spells over a nail paring, hair clipping, doll replica, or some personal possession of the victim; he may magically shoot a small object, like a piece of bone, into the victim; he may introduce some magical decoction into the victim's food or drink. Witchcraft is combated by ceremonies designed to cure the bewitched, and by using various substances as a protection. If the people are quite convinced that a certain person is a witch, they have even been known to kill him.

The Navaho do not believe in a happy hunting ground type of life after death. Death is a horrible fate, and the people do not freely speak of death or of the dead. A corpse is buried as soon as possible, and elaborate precautions are taken against contamination.

The afterworld is located in the north and under the ground. The recently deceased are guided to it by their dead kinsmen, a journey which takes four days. It is regarded as an uninviting, shadowy place, though it seems to be somewhat of a replica of this earth. It is assumed that the dead may return as ghosts to injure the living. No matter how affectionate and helpful the dead person may have been while alive, he is always likely to return to avenge some neglect or wrong. Ghosts appear only at night, and even adult Navaho are quite fearful of traveling alone in the dark.

The universe of the Navaho contains two classes of beings. Ordinary human beings and their ghosts in the afterworld are the Earth Surface People; the others are the Holy People. The Holy People are mysterious supernaturals who have the means to give great aid or cause great harm to Earth Surface People. The relation between the two kinds of beings is not like the relation in modern Christian theology of God and man, the former an all-powerful symbol of righteousness, the latter attempting to live up to His revealed precepts. The supernaturals are not all-powerful or particularly moral, and they may even be manipulated and coerced as though they were children.

According to the Navaho creation myth, the Holy People first lived underground, ascending from time to time through 12 (some versions say four) distinct superimposed worlds. Finally, they were caused to ascend through a reed to the present world because of a great flood. Natural objects were then created, and, at about the same time, Changing Woman was born. Changing Woman became the mother of the *Twin Heroes* and also played a leading part in a great ceremonial conclave of the Holy People, at which they created the Earth Surface People and taught them how to live. The myth about this event is the foundation for one of the key Navaho ceremonials, the Blessing Way.

The most important supernaturals in Navaho religious lore are, first, Changing Woman (sometimes called Turquoise Woman) and next her husband, the Sun. The Hero Twins—Monster Slayer and Child of the Water—also figure in a great many Navaho myths. In telling of their adventures, most of the stories establish the Navaho ideals for the conduct of young men. So much of their activity had to do with warlike adventures that they could be called war gods. But the Twins are not dependable, nor are any of the other Holy People completely so, except Changing Woman. She is almost always pictured as benevolent, and she gave perhaps the greatest gift of all, maize.

The origin myth, which tells of all this, is by far the most important of any of the myths, for it is nearly always the final authority for the ritual prescriptions. Beyond this, however, the Navaho have an extensive and rich set of oral traditions. Any ceremonial practice is rationalized by a corresponding myth, most of them of great dramatic and emotional artistry. Many of them contain passages of fine ritual poetry as well. The following passage, taken from the myth of the Mountain Top Way, may serve as a more or less typical example:

But instead of looking south in the direction in which he was going he looked to the north, the country in which dwelt his people. Before him were the beautiful peaks of *dibenca* with their forested slopes. The clouds hung over the mountain, the showers of rain fell down its sides, and all the country looked beautiful. And he said to the land *"ahalani"* Greeting! and a feeling of loneliness and homesickness came over him, and he wept and sang this song:

> That flowing water! That flowing water!
> My mind wanders across it.
> That broad water! That flowing water!
> My mind wanders across it.
> That old age water! That flowing water!
> My mind wanders across it.[2]

Some of the chants are impressive liturgies; and when they are accompanied by dry paintings, dramas acted out by masked god-impersonators, and lighted by open-air fires in the desert night, a witness can have a most moving experience.

Ritual and singing are also integrated into the affairs of everyday life. Group ceremonials are special religious occasions, and religion in these contexts seems readily separable from economics or normal social life. But there is another aspect of the religion, a personal or folk practice of ritual, song, and belief, which is a nearly indistinguishable part of almost any activity. Some of these practices take the form of taboos, some are of a more positive sort—i.e., some are *pro*scriptions, some are *pre*scriptions.

The former may be illustrated by a few random examples. Wood may not be used for building fires or as timbers for a hogan if it has previously belonged to a dead person, or if it has been struck by lightning, touched by a bear, or rubbed by the horns of a deer.

---

[2] Washington Matthews, "The Mountain Chant: A Navaho Ceremony," *5th Annual Report of the Bureau of American Ethnology, 1883–84,* Washington, 1887, p. 393; reprinted in C. Kluckhohn and D. Leighton, *The Navaho,* Cambridge, Mass., 1946, pp. 134–135.

One must not step over a fire, except during ceremonies, nor may one step over a recumbent person. Hair should not be cut, or a dry season will result. Food must be stirred only in a clockwise direction. Designs on pottery or baskets must never form a completed circle, for the maker would become ill.

Songs are probably the most common ritual prescriptions. Certain songs bring good luck, good harvests, or good hunting. Blessing Way songs are sung before retiring and on arising in the morning to insure well-being. In short, nearly every common act of daily life is prevaded by some sort of ritual patterning. Most primitive peoples of the world attempt, in some measure, to cause harmony between the rules of the supernatural realm and those of everyday, natural life, but to many observers it seems that the Navaho have merged the two more completely than most.

It is apparent that the Navaho have maintained this harmony by continually making adjustments. Their material culture, especially their economic technology, has undergone several great transformations: first, when they acquired agriculture from the neighboring Pueblo Indians and adopted a more sedentary mode of life; next, when they acquired sheep, goats, cattle, and horses from the Spaniards; and lately, as they have become more concerned with handicrafts, marketing methods, and modern machinery. They have made all these transitions without greatly altering their conceptions of supernaturalism or their ideals regarding the right way to live. Today they are on the brink of their greatest, and final, transformation—they are still captives, in a real sense, of the American people and American culture, and their release seems to be imminent, but the liberation will occur progressively as they stop being Navaho and become modern Americans. America has always, sooner or later, absorbed its diverse cultural aliens. The process can be retarded by isolation, as the Navaho have demonstrated, but this growing tribe cannot maintain itself much longer without becoming involved more and more in the American economy. And this has always been the fundamental way in which both alien groups and individuals began the process of Americanization.

The tempo of Navaho involvement in the national economy and culture has accelerated considerably since World War II. In part this has been owing simply to an increase in the opportunities for individual Indians to obtain off-reservation employment and to a greater willingness of more individuals to risk such an adventure. But in addition there have been three kinds of developments of significance for the people who remain on the reservation—developments which affect them no matter how great their conservatism. These are a change in the Indian Service program; the increased effectiveness of the Navaho Tribal Council; and the growth of mining and other enterprises on the reservation.

In 1950 the U.S. Congress enacted a long-range program for rehabilitation of the Navaho and Hopi reservations, which included an appropriation of $88,570,000 to be spent over a 10-year period. This program has not been fully implemented as yet, but considerable progress has been made in planning such things as improvement of the range, extension of irrigation and water supplies, exploitation of coal and timber, increase in production of arts and crafts, road construction, and off-reservation settlement of Navaho families.

The Navaho Tribal Council was organized in 1923, because the discovery of oil on the reservation made it necessary that some elected body should be able to speak for the tribe as a whole. Since 1949 the Indian Service has strongly encouraged the Council, and it now assumes a major responsibility in Navaho affairs. The Council comprises a chairman, vice-chairman, and 74 district representatives. In 1956 the tribal budget managed by the council totaled more than $3 million. The Council nowadays makes nearly all the major decisions with respect to oil and mining leases and royalties.

Since 1942 income from vanadium-uranium leases have provided about $2.5 million to the Council. In addition these enterprises employ a great many of the reservation Indians. Oil and gas leases were worth more than $1.5 million to the tribe in 1955.

Today nearly all Navaho children go to school for at least several years. One important consequence is that the younger people are increasingly bilingual, which of course makes off-reservation employment more possible. Perhaps this foretells an increasing acculturation rate. Yet in the long history of Navaho accommodation to alien cultures—the Pueblo, the Spanish, the modern American—the capacity for the Navaho to remain Navaho in certain distinctive ways at the same time that they incorporate alien elements in their culture is a striking characteristic. Arthur Woodward said:

It has always seemed to me that the Navajo man is a living exponent of acculturation. He wears on his person in his various garments visible evidence of the accumulation of material culture from alien sources. First of all, a Navajo wears underneath his outer garments his native breech clout. This he does not remove, unless he takes a bath, and even then some of the men do not take it off. Over the breech clout is a pair of calico drawers fashioned rather fully and being slightly more than knee length. These are slit up the outer seam from the bottom for about six or seven inches. These were his pantaloons in the days when Mexican costume was in vogue. . . . Over the aboriginal and Spanish-Mexican garb the Navajo has placed his latest acquisitions, the American jeans, shirt, shoes, and hat. Thus we have in him a living exponent of three layers of culture; he has absorbed them all and discarded none.[3]

The Navaho have built up similar layers of aboriginal and various foreign elements in economic, social, political, and religious aspects of their culture as well. How long they will continue to do this and still maintain some distinctiveness as Navaho cannot be estimated. The rate of change has been accelerating with increased economic opportunities and educational facilities, and probably will continue to do so. But there is another very important variable, the attitude of the white-American people toward the Navaho. So far, the Navaho engaged in off-reservation employment—the best candidates for assimilation—are not secure in it, and most families prefer life on the reservation to the extent that economic conditions permit. The Navaho remain so strongly corporate as a people, because so far they do not have full freedom to choose. Such freedom requires that the Navaho be prepared with education and skills to move into American economic and social life, but it also requires that the white-Americans be prepared to accept them.

FURTHER READINGS

Adair, J., *The Navajo and Pueblo Silversmiths,* Norman, Okla., 1944.
Amsden, C. A., *Navaho Weaving: Its Technic and History,* Albuquerque, 1949.
Dyk, W., *Son of Old Man Hat,* New York, 1938.

[3] Quoted in E. Z. Vogt, "Navaho," in E. H. Spicer (ed.), *Perspectives in American Indian Culture Change,* Chicago, 1961, pp. 328–329. Most of the information in this section was taken from Vogt's article.

Hall, E. T., Jr., "Recent Clues to Athapascan Prehistory in the Southwest," *American Anthropologist,* n.s., Vol. 46, 1944.

Hill, W. W., "The Agricultural and Hunting Methods of the Navaho Indians," *Yale University Publications in Anthropology,* Vol. 18, 1938.

Hill, W. W., *Some Navaho Cultural Changes during Two Centuries,* Smithsonian Institution, Miscellaneous Collections, Vol. 100, Washington, 1940.

Kluckhohn, C., "The Navahos in the Machine Age," *Technology Review,* Vol. 44, 1942.

Kluckhohn, C., *Navaho Witchcraft,* Papers of the Peabody Museum of Archaeology and Ethnology, Vol. 22, Cambridge, Mass., 1944.

Kluckhohn, C., "The Philosophy of the Navaho Indians," in F. S. C. Northrup (ed.), *Ideological Differences and World Order,* New Haven, 1949.

Kluckhohn, C., and Leighton, D., *The Navaho,* Cambridge, Mass., 1946.

Kluckhohn, C., and Spencer, K., *A Bibliography of the Navaho Indians,* New York, 1940.

La Farge, O., *Laughing Boy,* Boston, 1929.

Leighton, A. and D. C., *The Navaho Door,* Cambridge, Mass., 1944.

Leighton, D. C., and Kluckhohn, C., *Children of the People,* Cambridge, Mass., 1947.

McCombe, L., Vogt, E. Z., and Kluckhohn, C., *Navaho Means People,* Cambridge, Mass., 1951.

Reichard, G. A., *Social Life of the Navajo Indians,* New York, 1928.

Reichard, G. A., *Spider Woman,* New York, 1934.

Reichard, G. A., *Dezba, Woman of the Desert,* New York, 1939.

Reichard, G. A., *Navaho Indian Religion,* Bollingen Series, Vol. 18, New York, 1950.

Spencer, K., *Reflections of Social Life in the Navaho Origin Myth,* University of New Mexico Publications in Anthropology, No. 3, Albuquerque, 1946.

Vogt, E. Z., "Navaho," in E. H. Spicer (ed.), *Perspectives in American Indian Culture Change,* Chicago, 1961.

9

The Jivaro
of South America

The Amazon basin is one of the most extensive alluvial plains in the world. Moreover it is the world's largest area of tropical rain forest—being nearly the size of Europe. From a highland periphery in eastern Brazil across the lowlands to the steep sides of the Andes at the western edge of the continent is a distance of more than 2000 miles. The Amazon forest is one of the most sparsely settled regions of the world. In this regard it might as well be considered a desert; yet it would appear, as it has to so many visitors, that the land is exceptionally fertile. It would seem that decaying vegetation could have built up a great thickness of soft black soil; rain is abundant, and, judging from the size of the trees and their density, it should be a land of great agricultural potentiality. But despite the fact that the mysterious forest has stimulated a great deal of interest, there are probably more myths, or at least misinformation, about it than about any other region of the world.

First of all, the soil is not fertile or deep in humus; it is very poor for most agricultural uses. Trees grow vigorously, but trees are more dependent on ground-water conditions than on the quality of the surface soil. The tropical soils are very deficient in mineral salts, primarily, and the organic material is quickly destroyed because of the combination of the tropical temperature and the leaching action of rain water. The only advantage the rain forest has is the looseness of its soil; primitive peoples whose only gardening implement is a sharpened stick are enabled to work the surface of the soil, whereas the much more fertile grassy plains remain impervious to their efforts.

Another widely held misconception of Amazonia is that the temperatures are unbearably high. Actually, a summer heat wave in a northern state of the United States frequently attains much higher temperatures. The temperatures of the rain-forest floor rarely reach 90° F., even though the equator cuts nearly exactly through the middle of the region. The most noteworthy effect of the latitude (to a North American) is monotony. The temperature variation between dawn and afternoon on any one day may only be about 25°, but even this is greater than the mean variation from season to season. For a stranger to the tropics, another depressing characteristic of the climate is the excessive humidity and the great amount of rainfall. One can stand the heat, but, as one North American puts it, the problem is "whether man can be happy in the rain." At the equator there is no seasonal variation, and nearly every day the rain comes as a sudden, violent shower, followed by equally rapid clearing. This is normally a daytime phenomenon; the nights are usually bright and clear.

Two other misconceptions about the jungle are common. One is that there is an abundance of large animals—that hunting is good. But on the whole, the Amazon forest is notably deficient in large land animals. One is conscious of a teeming animal life; monkeys and a great variety of birds and insects are present, to be sure, but they live almost entirely in the treetops. The best wild-food resource is in the rivers, which abound with fish, turtles, and, in the larger rivers, even large fresh-water mammals. For this reason the primitive peoples of Amazonia are most concentrated along these rivers.

Another misconception of Amazonia is that it is an impenetrable jungle of trees, vines, shrubs, and plants. Actually the vitality of plant growth is concentrated in the very high, very thick canopy of interlaced tree branches. Underneath, where man lives, a dark tomblike silence prevails. The absence of sunlight prevents the undergrowth of plants and seedlings from growing thickly. Only along rivers and in cutover areas or uplands is there enough sunlight for thickets to grow. The absence of grass and shrubs accounts for the scarcity of herbivorous animals and of the carnivores that prey upon them.

The tropical forest tribes are of a bewildering variety of language stocks, but physically and culturally they are quite uniform. They conform to the general racial characteristics of the American Indians, but are somewhat shorter than the Plains Indians of either North or South America, the males averaging about five feet four inches in height. The Amazonian Indians subsist largely on vegetable crops, and the Plains Indians on meat, which may explain the consistent difference in stature. The relative uniformity of the environment throughout most of the Amazon basin is matched by a cultural uniformity. The most significant ecological difference is in the location of the tribes with respect to good fishing resources. As the Amazon and its many tributaries become smaller and smaller toward the upland borders of the basin, so the characteristic culture of the lowlands becomes progressively more attenuated in some features.

The eastern slope of the Andes, in the region belonging to Ecuador and Peru, is generally called the *montaña*. It is basically a tropical rain forest similar to Amazonia proper, but here the rivers are smaller and run faster, making navigation difficult, and the land is somewhat more broken up. The region is difficult of access, and the tribes of the *montaña* have been much less disturbed by Europeans than the tribes near the great navigable rivers.

The Jivaro are typical of the tribes of the *montaña,* and dissimilar to the general Amazonian type in only a few minor respects. They are a well-known group, for their famous custom of shrinking and preserving human heads has long excited the imagination of Europeans, and a large amount of both scientific and journalistic literature concerning them has been published. Head-shrinking, however, is not a purely Jivaro trait. They are merely a people who, because of their relative isolation, have retained a custom which once was widespread in northwestern South America. The method of preparing the trophy heads, contrary to popular belief, is not a mysterious and carefully guarded secret. It has been known for centuries, and the Jivaro make no attempt to conceal it.

The Jivaro[1] are a linguistic and cultural entity of about 20,000 people. There is no political unity of the whole, but there is a feeling that they, the *Shuara* (as they call themselves), are distinct from other peoples. The language has no known affinity to any other. There are four main divisions of Jivaro, corresponding to geographical locations, but even within these areas there are smaller independent tribes moving in orbits that center about a stream that they consider their own. These groups make war incessantly on one another and on any outsiders who threaten them. The aboriginal Inca Empire never conquered them, nor have the later whites in 400 years of effort made any significant progress. "The Jivaro does not have the submissive, humble, cringing appearance, I might almost say servile, of the civilized Indian; much to the contrary, everything in him reveals the free man, passionately loving liberty, incapable of putting up with the slightest subjection."[2]

A YOUNG JIVARO MOTHER AND CHILD. *Courtesy, The American Museum of Natural History*

The basic subsistence of the Jivaro is the garden crops cultivated by women. Game and fish are highly prized foods, however, and the men spend a great deal of time hunting. Monkeys and birds are the most frequently hunted game; they are plentiful, and monkeys especially

[1] Jivaro (*jíbaro*) is a Spanish word meaning "uncivilized".
[2] P. Rivet, quoted in M. W. Stirling, *Historical and Ethnographical Material on the Jivaro Indians,* Smithsonian Institution, Bureau of American Ethnology, Bull. 117, Washington, 1938, p. 3.

are considered exceptionally tasty. Peccaries make a desirable food, but they are dangerous to hunt because they are so vicious and run in herds which attack in unison. The usual method is a communal hunt. The animals are enticed to attack, and the men ascend to the lower branches of large trees, from which they can shoot or spear the animals as they rush past in a blind charge.

The blowgun, lance, and in modern times an occasional cheap trade gun, often a muzzle loader, are the usual weapons used in the chase. The blowgun is the most valuable of these—particularly for small game, such as monkeys and birds—in the deep forest. This weapon, widely used in the Amazon region, consists of a hollow tube, 10 to 15 feet in length, through which a poisoned dart can be propelled by a puff of breath up to an effective range of 45 yards. The Jivaro are among the most expert blowgun hunters in South America and are also justly famed for their great skill in the manufacture of this complicated device.

The main problem in making an effective blowgun is in creating a perfectly straight, smooth bore. This problem is met in an ingenious way. The manufacturer first cuts to the desired length a section of chonta palm, a kind of wood that is very hard and characterized by a straight, longitudinal grain. Two strips of this wood, each about three inches in width, are cut and then carefully shaved until they are straight. One side of each strip is left flat and the other rounded; when the two flat sides are placed together, a round pole is formed, tapering in diameter from about one and one-quarter inches at one end to three-quarters of an inch at the other. Next a slightly longer, perfectly straight rod of chonta is shaved and smoothed to about one-fourth of an inch in diameter, the size of the intended bore of the blowgun. The flat sides of each of the long blowgun strips are then scraped down the length until the two together form a groove slightly smaller than the rod. Finally the rod is sandwiched between the two strips and tied. Fine sand and water are poured in and the rod is worked back and forth until the abrasive action has smoothed away the grooves to the point where the two longitudinal halves of the blowgun meet. The rod can then be removed and the two strips wrapped together with fiber and glued with melted latex. A bone mouthpiece is fixed at the larger end.

The dart is made from the midrib of a palm leaf, about a

forearm's length and of the diameter of a matchstick. The point is coated with poison, and to the butt is attached a bit of floss from the silk-cotton tree. The poisoned dart varies in effectiveness depending on the size of the animal and the location of the wound. Monkeys frequently live for nearly half an hour and large birds less time after being wounded by a dart. The dart is so small and light that the blowgun would be useless without an effective poison.

The blowgun is not used in warfare. The Indians say it would bring bad luck to use it against a man, but it is possible that the dart would be ineffective because of the size of a man and perhaps because a man, understanding the danger, would immediately extract the dart. The typical weapons of war are the lance and shield and, increasingly in modern times, various kinds of firearms. Apparently, the Jivaro once used the bow and arrow and also the spear thrower, but after they acquired the blowgun in the seventeenth century, they gave up the other two weapons.

If the Indians are located on a large stream, they employ several devices for catching fish. Sometimes, if the water is low, a dam is constructed and a poisonous sap from the barbasco shrub distributed above the dam. As the juice permeates the water, the fish rise to the surface in a stupefied condition and are gathered by the assembled villagers. Fish are caught sometimes with rude traps and nets, or speared. In the larger rivers the manatee and fresh-water porpoise can sometimes be speared. Giant reptiles, such as caymans, turtles, boa constrictors, and anacondas, abound in some regions and are eaten when more desirable game is absent. Various insects and grubs, frogs, lizards, and snails are relished. Bees' honey is considered a great delicacy, as are various wild fruits. When seed- or fruit-eating birds are killed, the contents of the crop are eaten immediately.

The day-to-day mainstay of Jivaro subsistence, however, is the garden produce. The most important item is, as elsewhere in Amazonia, the manioc root, a large, very starchy tuber that resembles the parsnip in color and texture. The Jivaro make it into a flour, as is done elsewhere, but their manioc is of the nonpoisonous variety, and so they do not go through the process of volatilizing the poison that so many of the other South American forest tribes do. A common use of manioc is for a drink, called *nijimanche,* which women and girls prepare by chewing up mouthfuls of manioc and spitting it into a large jar where it ferments slightly.

Maize, sweet potatoes, squash, and peanuts are also cultivated. Bananas, plantains, and papayas are planted, but receive no additional care. The bananas and plantains are picked green and pre-

JIVARO WARRIOR. *Courtesy, The American Museum of Natural History*

pared for eating by boiling or roasting. Cotton and tobacco are the principal nonfood items grown. The latter is smoked in the form of cigars but also is made into a juice which is blown up the nostrils by a helper. The planting, weeding, and harvesting of the gardens are women's work, and the only aid in gardening is a simple digging stick.

The original clearing of a garden and house plot in the jungle is

men's work, done in the typical slash-and-burn fashion of the tropics. The large trees, which are frequently of extremely hard wood,
are felled only with great labor. First the undergrowth is removed
from the whole area, and then the smaller trees are ringed so that
they will weaken and be toppled by the felling of the largest trees.
Then several men attack the remaining giants. Before the modern
acquisition of steel axes, a tree was not truly chopped down, but
patiently beaten through by the constant hammering of the rude
stone hand axes. It sometimes took weeks for a small party of men
to fell one of the ironlike monsters in this fashion.

When the tree finally falls, it drags with it all of the smaller
trees in the vicinity, for they are all bound together by a complicated network of creepers and vines. As the tree crashes down, the
Indians run for their lives to escape the torrent of aroused ants,
bees, hornets, scorpions, and centipedes that infest the upper canopy
of the forest. After the trees and brush have lain for several months
in the dry season, the Indians set fire to the area, after which crops
can be planted and houses built. Some of the Jivaro have two or
three gardens going at the same time, planted at different times of
the year. Their residence at any one coincides with the period of its
greatest productivity. A large garden plot lasts five or six years
before it loses its fertility and a new one must be chopped out of the
virgin timber.

Usually only a single large house stands in the clearing. It is an
elliptical, palm-thatched building about 40 by 80 feet in size, housing a number of patrilineally related families. At one end are split-
bamboo platforms that serve as beds for the men. The women, who
sleep at the other end, have similar beds, but they are separated
by bamboo walls into tiny cubicles for greater privacy. Children
sleep at the women's end of the building, and boys move to the
fathers' end when they are about 7 years old. Large jars of
nijimanche are kept in the middle of the house, and the walls are
lined with personal possessions.

Cooking is done by the women on fires built near their own end
of the hut. The usual dish is simply a continuously cooking peppery
stew into which new ingredients are added each day. A wooden
mortar and pestle is used to mash maize, and sometimes a flat
wooden slab is used for finer results.

Men fill their spare time by spinning cotton thread and weaving cloth, two tasks which in many American Indian tribes are woman's work. The loom is small and nearly vertical, with a continuous warp that produces a cylindrical piece of cloth. The cloth may be colored brown with a vegetable dye. Men wear a knee-length wrap-around skirt of this cloth, and women use a larger square that is wrapped around the body in such a way that two of the corners are pinned over the right shoulder, leaving the other shoulder bare.

The Jivaro are attentive to their personal appearance, and the men tend to outdo the women in vanity. Hair is worn long, except for low bangs cut over the eyebrows. The rest of the hair is left free by women, but men commonly braid theirs or gather it at the back of the neck. Both men and women wear bamboo tubes thrust through the lobes of the ears, and girls also have the lower lip pierced for a small cane plug. Necklaces, bracelets, and belts made of seeds, shells, teeth, and bird bones are worn by both sexes. Iridescent beetle wing covers and bright toucan feathers are attached to many of the ornaments, and the men sometimes wear a sort of crown made from them. Men also wear a distinctive girdle made of the hair of a courageous Jivaro who has been killed in battle. Its purpose is to transmit some of the spiritual qualities of the hero to the wearer. Both men and women paint their faces and sometimes their arms and shoulders with an oily red pigment made from the seeds of the prized *achiote* plant. The juice of the *genipa* plant is used for black paint, which is frequently applied over the red in a series of simple designs.

The Jivaro are one of the largest dialect groups in the Amazon basin, but they are spread over such a large territory that local groups are largely independent. Each community, or *jivaría,* is economically autonomous, although alliances are frequent among several *jivarías* of a district. These alliances are for purposes of warfare. The closest thing to a chief is the war leader, or *curaka,* who has authority only in cases of hostilities; he has no power beyond his personal ability to command the respect of his followers. There is a tendency for several communities to be related to one another by blood and affinal kinship ties because of the rule of local exogamy, which requires that a man marry a woman from a village other than his own. There is, therefore, a more or less natural grouping of contiguous communities into a loose tribe, but cooperation among them is almost entirely limited to collaboration in feuds or in head-hunting against more distant and unrelated communities.

The Jivaro have long been considered one of the most bellicose peoples in South America. The normal form of warfare is a never-ending cycle of blood-revenge feuds between unrelated groups of Jivaro. Action against non-Jivaro groups is less frequent, depending on the sporadic and rare invasions of such strangers into the territory. At these times, blood feuds are suspended, and large bodies of Jivaro unite in a common purpose and plan.

The greatest aspiration of a Jivaro man is to be renowned as a warrior, a status which he acquires and increases in proportion to the number of heads he takes. As a rule, Jivaro raiding conforms to a curious pattern. After a group decides to make a raid and appropriate ceremonies and an all-night dance have prepared the warriors, an emissary is sent to the enemy's camp to warn them to get ready. This message is sent despite the fact that all plans and subsequent actions in the raid are designed to surprise the enemy. In the case of a war against whites or other non-Jivaro, however, this courtesy is not observed, and every attempt is made to ambush and completely exterminate the intruders. In a successful blood-feud raid, men and old people are killed, but young women and children are usually taken as captives. Later they are adopted into the raiders' group as wives and sons and daughters. The captives rarely attempt to escape.

The ostensible purpose of a raid is to take the heads of the hostile warriors. As soon as the brief battle is over, each raider sets about cutting off the heads of those he has slain. Later, after the raiders have traveled to a safe place, they set up a camp and begin shrinking the heads. The *tsantsas,* as the tiny shrunken heads are called, are really only the skins that have been peeled from the skulls. The complete head skin is boiled for several hours until the skin is about one-third its original size. Heated stones or sand are placed inside the head to complete the drying and shrinking process. Finally, the head is smoked for about eight hours for purposes of preservation, and the face skin is polished. The raiders' arrival at home, bearing the *tsantsas,* is the signal for a great victory celebration, including as a high point a warlike dance around the *tsantsas,* which dramatizes the battle.[3] In contrast to the customs

[3] Tourists in Ecuador and Peru have provided a lively market for *tsantsas,* and thousands of counterfeit Jivaro heads have been sold by enterprising manufacturers during the past 100 years. Most of them are monkey or sloth heads; others are from unclaimed hospital dead.

of many warlike Amazon tribes, captives are not tortured and sacrificed, nor is cannibalism practiced.

All communities spend considerable effort in elaborating protection against surprise attack. Great hollow-log signal drums are ar-

SHRUNKEN HEAD OR TSANTSA. *Courtesy, The American Museum of Natural History*

ranged to summon neighbors, and the approaches to a village are honeycombed with pitfalls and booby traps. Frequently the great house itself is surrounded by a palisade fence of upright logs, and escape tunnels are dug from the house to a river bank if one is nearby. A foreign visitor must be prepared to spend many hours in approaching a *jivaría*. The approaching party shout and fire guns to give notice of their presence, after which the host group adorn themselves to the fullest, and finally welcome the visitors with elaborate, time-consuming ritual courtesy. If the approach is not made properly, the visitors may be attacked from ambush.

Constant warfare has caused a considerable numerical predominance of women in Jivaro society, and a consequent prevalence of polygyny. A young man usually courts his first wife, who is preferably a cross cousin from a neighboring friendly village, but other wives may be acquired by capture on a raid. There is no formal marriage ceremony. It might appear that romantic love is absent in Jivaro society, inasmuch as all that is formally required is the groom's gift and the consent of the father or brother of the girl. Normally, however, a man does not want a woman who does not reciprocate his affection; consequently, elaborate courting campaigns are frequent before the contract is actually made. A married couple live in the man's *jivaría,* but visits are frequently made to the girl's family, and the man and his parents-in-law and the girl and her in-laws observe most of the courtesy and respect rules so widespread in the primitive world.[4] A further cause of polygyny is the practice of the levirate. When a man dies or is killed, the brother who is closest to him in age takes care of the widow and children. It is not compulsory that she become his wife, but usually she does so.

The frequency of polygyny should not be taken as evidence that the lot of women is an unhappy one in Jivaro society. Husbands and wives are usually deeply affectionate toward one another. Jealousy among a man's wives is very rare. The typical household of an older man consists of one wife of about his own age, another of 15 to 20 years of age, and the last an immature child. These women almost always become very fond of one another and share their duties equably. The character of the husband's affection for three women of such disparate ages is different for each of them; therefore there is little clash of interest.

Although a group of relatives is suspicious and frequently ruthless and bloodthirsty toward outsiders, within the kinship group friendship, trust, and affection prevail. Great emphasis is placed on hospitality, generosity, and good humor. In common with most

---

[4] Reliable information is lacking on Jivaro kinship terminology, clans or other sodalities, and many related social customs.

American Indians, the Jivaro are fond of singing and of instrumental music. Dances and ceremonies are always accompanied by group singing, and particularly talented singers are often called upon to perform solos. There are many kinds of songs, for love, war, mourning, and so on. Men play bamboo flutes of various kinds, usually for sad occasions or when they are in love. Trumpets are made of the shell of the giant land snail, but these are usually used for signaling rather than for music. Hollow-log drums are also used for signaling, but can be played for the accompaniment of ceremonial dances as well. Small cylindrical drums about 10 inches long are used for most dancing occasions. The most unusual instrument is a small primitive violin called a *querquer*. The sounding box is made of cedar or balsa and has two fiber strings that can be tuned. It is played with a small bow that has a string of rattan. This instrument can be played only when the musician is alone in the house and is mourning or recalling sad occasions. The music is very sad and the musician weeps as he plays.

The Jivaro are very fond of children and regard the purpose of marriage as begetting children. A barren woman is discarded as a wife for this reason. When a woman becomes pregnant, particularly if it is her first pregnancy, the husband and all the relatives are attentive to her. When the time for the birth approaches, she is given a drink that includes shavings from the spine of the cashparay, which deadens the pain of the birth. Delivery is made from a sitting or a half-standing position. Apparently no ritual disposal is made of the placenta or the umbilical cord. The old women take the child and mother to the river for a bath. After this, the mother resumes her lighter duties.

Until the child is able to walk, the father abstains from animal flesh and certain plants because of the danger to the child's spirit. The father is not confined to bed at any time, although this custom, called the *couvade*, is prevalent among neighboring societies and is found in many areas of the world; for example, among the Basques of Spain.

All of the adults of the community give attention to the children. They are rarely punished and have great liberty; yet like most children in the primitive world, they are well behaved and respectful toward adults. As they grow older, girls spend most of their time with the women, learning by imitative play most of the tasks that will fall to them later. Small boys stay with men, accompany them on hunts, and even on war parties after they reach 7 or 8 years of age, although they do not fight until they are older. Puberty initiation rites are not elaborate. After a girl's first menses she is "invigorated" by a ceremony which involves the blowing of tobacco juice up her nostrils. Boys are initiated into manhood by a feast, but there is no secret cult, and no ordeals are involved.

In contrast to many primitive groups, the Jivaro do not ascribe all illnesses to the evil magic of a witch, shaman, or enemy, although some shamans claim the power to cause illness and death. Colds, fever, and dysentery are regarded as natural sicknesses. The Jivaro seem to have an understanding of contagion, probably stemming from their experience with European diseases, and they abandon a house or isolate a person who has symptoms of one of the contagious diseases. Many illnesses are caused by particular spirits which enter the body. The shaman cures these by the typical American Indian sucking ritual. After he has sucked the afflicted part for a long time, he suddenly rushes from the house, gagging and retching because he has sucked the spirit into his own stomach. Outdoors he vomits and spits the spirit out, and with great gesticulations he orders the spirit to leave the vicinity. All of the people of the house help out at this stage by shouting to the spirit to go away.

When a Jivaro dies, his body is placed in a small dugout canoe or in a log hollowed out for the purpose. His favorite weapons are placed with him, and the coffin covered over with a slab of bark. The coffin is then suspended from the ridgepole of the house and mourning goes on for six days. If the man has been a *curaka* of the household, the building is then abandoned after a supply of food is placed on the floor. Every month thereafter for a period of two years someone comes to replenish the food supply. If the dead person is not so important, the house is not abandoned, and after the six-day period, the coffin is put in a smaller house built nearby for the purpose. The bodies of women are treated in the same manner as are those of ordinary men. It is believed that children change into small birds after death, so that no attendance to the body is necessary. The mourning customs are not particularly elaborate. During the first six days after death the women of the house weep and lament, but the men absent themselves. Keepsakes are treasured in memory of the dead for many years.

The Jivaro believe that the dead are reborn in some form of animal life. A *curaka* or famous warrior is likely to be born as a jaguar and go to live in the forest near the enemy to continue harassing them as he did in his human life span. The two-year period of feeding the corpse is said to be necessary in order that the jaguar may grow large enough to fend for himself. After this period the coffin is taken down, and the bones are buried.

The mythology of the Jivaro contains a few traces of Christianity. The Jivaro were subjected to sporadic missionary influence in some parts of their territory for several hundreds of years and, like most other primitive mythologies, theirs has tended to incorporate disparate foreign elements rather easily because the myths are not dogmas. The aboriginal creation myth is the story of Cupara and his wife who created the Sun and the Sun's wife, Moon, out of mud. Children of the Sun and Moon were various plant and animal species, including Sloth, who became the first Jivaro, and Nijimanche, the manioc plant and an everlasting friend of the Jivaro. A great many tales recount various adventures of these figures who, one way or another, created characteristic elements of Jivaro culture. One of the most typical is reminiscent of the widespread American Indian stories of the Twin Gods. In the Jivaro version, Jaguar killed his Jivaro wife, but Jaguar's mother secretly reared his twin sons, who finally became two stars. When they grew up, they came down to earth and avenged their mother by killing Jaguar, and then ascended to the sky again by an arrow chain. Another common tale concerns the universal deluge, but it is uncertain whether this tale is a result of Christian missionizing.

Jivaro religion is based on two related concepts of impersonal supernatural power and of the souls that embody and manifest it. The impersonal power is called *Kakarma* and resembles the well-known Polynesian concept of *mana*.[5] Some of this power is acquired by means of rituals, and some people therefore have more of it than others. The best way for a person to increase his power is to acquire an *arutam* soul, for one of these can so increase his intelligence and strength that it is impossible for anyone to kill him with either sorcery or physical violence.

The *arutam* souls are free ranging and eternally living. No person is born with this kind of soul, but must acquire it in a vision.

[5] See Chapter 12.

A boy begins his quest of the vision at about the age of 6, when, accompanied usually by his father, he goes to a waterfall where *Arutam* souls tend to congregate. There he fasts and drinks tobacco water, awaiting the vision for as long as five days. If the vision comes—and usually it does not until after many quests of this sort and the boy is much older—it is a very frightening apparition. If the seeker finds the courage, he runs up and touches it, and then it explodes. The next night the *arutam* appears in the boy's dream as an old man who gives up his soul to the dreamer. The boy must not reveal to anyone that he now has an *arutam,* but it is apparent to people that such is the case because of the greatly increased self-confidence and forcefulness in his demeanor. He now has the power to kill without danger to himself. The only way he can ever be killed is for an enemy, by magical means, to induce the soul to leave him.

A second kind of soul is the *muisak,* the avenging soul. Should a person who once had an *arutam* lose it and be killed, the *muisak* is formed and leaves the corpse through the mouth, after which it is capable of causing various kinds of "accidental" death to the murderer or one of his family. The rationale for the preparation of the shrunken head so quickly after a killing is that it is necessary to seal up the victim's *muisak* within the head.

There is still another kind of soul, the ordinary personal soul, that everyone acquires at birth. The residing place of this soul is in the blood. When a person dies, it leaves the body and returns to the site of the house where it was born, to live there with the other liberated family souls in a spirit house identical with the original, but invisible. They and the neighboring souls that have also returned go on living, recapitulating the moves that they made from one house site to another in life. When the entire life history of the deceased has been repeated, the soul turns into a demon and unhappily roams the forest, longing for the companionship now lost forever. It is now a danger to children, because it is so lonesome that it sometimes carries them away. After a life span as a demon, the soul changes into a kind of giant butterfly. Later it dies, and the soul then is transformed into mist. All fogs and clouds are made by souls in this final and eternal form.

There are no gods which play ethical or moral roles in the Jivaro pantheon, nor are there any priests or other religious specialists except the shaman, whose primary function is magical curing. His power lies in his knowledge of the spirits. Essentially he is a diagnostician. Once he has identified the particular spirit that has caused an illness, he knows the method to apply in order to call it forth from the patient. Inasmuch as this knowledge controls the spirit, the shaman has the power to send sickness into people as well as to expel it. Thus the shaman may be the most feared as well as most respected member of his community.

A young man who wishes to become a shaman goes to an older shaman whom he respects and asks for instruction. If the older man agrees, he subjects the neophyte to a rigorous course of training for one month. Much of the training consists of fasting and taking various narcotics, including the curious tobacco infusion which is blown into the nostrils. At a final point of becoming light-headed and exhausted, the pupil feels that the spirit of the blowgun dart has taken possession of his body. Following this experience, instruction is concerned with practical methods of controlling the various sickness spirits. Prominent in these methods is the singing of special songs accompanied by a shaman's drum.[6]

If a shaman wants to send a disease spirit into the body of someone in order to make him sick, he goes alone to the river to call the spirit. Tobacco smoke is ritually blown toward the residing place of the spirit, and the special songs that attract it are sung. The spirit is sent as an allegorical blowgun dart into the body of the victim. Once the spirit is sent into a victim, the same shaman has no power to recall it—a cure must be made by a different shaman.

A shaman has certain other duties besides his main function of curing, because he is considered wise as well as powerful. Often, because of the absence of any true political organization among the Jivaro, the shaman may be the most influential individual in the community. Frequently he is the *curaka* as well as the shaman. Some of his knowledge of the supernatural is also put to the service of the community in various ways besides healing. He can prepare a love potion for a young man which will help him acquire a wife he wants. Some of the Shaman's other tasks are to control rains and floods, divine the activity of enemies, interpret omens of success or defeat in warfare, and make designs for shields which will make them contain power for success in warfare.

[6] See Chapter 4 for a further description of shamanism.

The first record of the Jivaro in modern history appeared in about the middle of the fifteenth century when, according to Inca chronicles, several attempts were made by the Inca to expand their empire into Jivaro territory. These campaigns were unsuccessful, perhaps because of the unfamiliarity of the climate and terrain as well as the fighting skill of the Jivaro. About a century later, after the Spaniards had conquered the Inca Empire, an expedition under Benavente encountered the Jivaro in what the leader described as "the worst land that I have seen in all the days of my life, either in Spain or in all parts of the Indies in which I have traveled . . . and the people of this province are all naked and very independent. . . ."[7] In his account of the expedition, Benavente applied to the Indians the name "Jivaro" by which they have been known ever since.

Subsequent attempts by the Spaniards to occupy the Jivaro country were inspired by the discovery of placer gold in the upper reaches of the many rivers. The Jivaro did not attack the new-comers in force at first; but as the Spaniards came in greater numbers and apparently practiced certain cruelties on the Indians, including enslavement in some instances, a series of local revolts and raids were begun which culminated in a great coordinated Jivaro uprising in 1599, the same year as the great revolt of the Arauca-nians in Chile. This revolt ended in success for the Jivaro; all of the Spaniards were killed in several localities, and the remainder fled for their lives. Later punitive expeditions of Spaniards were caught in ambush and destroyed, and Spanish penetration of the region was halted.

Several attempts by Jesuits to establish mission towns were made, but none of them got a foothold until the second half of the eighteenth century. One intrepid Father, Andrés Camacho, travel-ing alone, finally won the confidence of several groups of Jivaro and made considerable progress with them. The Jesuits were expelled from the New World in 1767 by Charles III, however, and the period of evangelization came to an end. Sporadic incursions by Dominican Fathers made little headway, but did introduce small-pox, which decimated the Jivaro, who had no resistance to this disease. The upheavals of the Wars of Independence in Latin Amer-ica so disturbed Ecuador and Peru that no further attempts at paci-fication of the *montaña* country were made until the latter half of

---

[7] Quoted in Stirling, *op. cit.,* p. 7.

the nineteenth century, when two small missions were established. In 1902 a mission run by the Gospel Missionary Union of the United States was established and has continued ever since. None of the missions has influenced any substantial numbers of Indians, however.

The most important and influential period of white contact with natives of the *montaña*, as in many other regions of the Amazon basin, was that of the great rubber boom. The *montaña* region was particularly rich in wild rubber, and when the great world demand for crude rubber began in the 1870s, one of the most spectacular booms in the history of the Amazon began. Adventurers of all stamps and nations came into the region. In many parts of the Amazon the brutality of the whites toward the Indians was unmatched in all of the unlovely annals of European colonial expansion. During this relatively brief period of the boom—it lasted until about 1910, when it collapsed suddenly because of the great success of the rubber plantations in Indonesia, which were begun from Brazilian wild-rubber seedlings—the Jivaro had access to more European trade goods, cheap muzzle-loading shotguns, axes, knives, and machetes than at any other period of their history. Their warlike propensities, the remoteness of the country, and transportation difficulties preserved them from more than sporadic contact with the whites, however, and they were spared the disasters which overcame the Indian tribes of more accessible regions of the rubber country.[8]

Since the rubber period, the Indians have had occasional access to European goods from distant posts, but have remained intransigent against all attempts to control them. Occasional travelers and ethnologists have made contacts with groups of Jivaro and have been treated hospitably by them, but the essential anarchy of the society and its independence from the authority of modern government continue. The Jivaro remain one of the most warlike, as well as most purely aboriginal, peoples on earth.

[8] F. W. Up de Graff and a few companions spent several years in the Jivaro country during this period. The record of his adventures contains interesting descriptions of the Jivaro (particularly a head-taking expedition he accompanied) as well as information on the rubber-gathering economy. See *Head Hunters of the Amazon: Seven Years of Exploration and Adventure*, Garden City, N.Y., 1923.

FURTHER READINGS

Harner, M. J., "Jívaro Souls," *American Anthropologist,* Vol. 64, No. 2, 1962.

Karsten, R., *Blood Revenge, War, and Victory Feasts Among the Jivaro Indians of Eastern Ecuador,* Smithsonian Institution, Bureau of American Ethnology, Bull. 79, Washington, 1923.

Karsten, R., *Headhunters of Western Amazonas: The Life and Culture of the Jibaro Indians of Eastern Ecuador and Peru,* Societas Scientiarum Fennica, Commentationes Humanarum Litterarum, Vol. 8, No. 1, Helsinki, 1935.

Rivet, P., "Les Indiens Jiberos," *L'Anthropologie,* Vols. 18, 19, 1907–1908.

Steward, J. H., and Métraux, A., "The Jivaro," in J. H. Steward (ed.), *Handbook of South American Indians,* Vol. 3, Smithsonian Institution, Bureau of American Ethnology, Bull. 143, Washington, 1948.

Stirling, M. W., *Historical and Ethnographical Material on the Jivaro Indians,* Smithsonian Institution, Bureau of American Ethnology, Bull. 117, Washington, 1938.

Up de Graff, F. W., *Head Hunters of the Amazon: Seven Years of Exploration and Adventure,* Garden City, N.Y., 1923.

PART III

CHIEFDOMS

The Nootka
of British Columbia

The Northwest Coast of North America contains a series of similar peoples very distinct in culture from the rest of American Indian tribes. Along with the many unique features of material culture, the patterning or organization of the culture, especially as manifest in social organization and attitudes toward individual status, is so strikingly foreign to aboriginal America and so reminiscent of Polynesia and parts of Asia that some anthropologists have speculated on the possibility of the late provenience of this culture from somewhere in Oceania or the Orient. The Nootka Indians of the seaward side of Vancouver Island are representative of these interesting Northwest Coastal peoples.

There are, of course, many particular differences among these groups, including a considerable variety of language families and dialects; but where similar habitat and contiguity have obtained, the Northwest Coast is clearly distinct as a culture area from the rest of North America. From northern California to southern Alaska the western shelf of the continent is a narrow strip of land between the coastal mountains and the sea, where nature has presented primitive hunting-fishing societies with an abundance of food and materials

TOTEM POLES AND REMAINS OF HOUSE. *Courtesy, Museum of the American Indian, Heye Foundation*

perhaps unsurpassed anywhere in the world, and, consequently, with a standard of living which can be matched only by societies possessing agriculture and domestic animals. The warm Japan current running along the coast keeps the climate equable (though rather chilly) the year round, as the coastal ranges cut off the interior continental winds. This mountain barrier also causes the warm, moisture-laden winds from the ocean to tarry over the coastal strip and drop most of their rain on this narrow region—as much as 100 inches a year.

One consequence of the relative warmth of the climate and the heavy rainfall is the tremendous growth of splendid forests of hemlock, fir, and cedar, and a resulting abundance of big game, especially elk, deer, and bear. Berries and edible roots grow vigorously, and many species of large waterfowl, such as duck, geese, heron, and grouse, are plentiful. But in addition to this particular bounty of nature, and of much more importance to the life of the Indians, are the sea and coastal resources. The many streams and rivers emptying into the ocean are so packed every fall with huge salmon on their way to the upstream spawning grounds that in a few weeks the natives with their ingenious traps, nets, and weirs literally harvest a crop of fish which provides them with food for all the year. The shore waters contain shellfish which can be gathered in great amounts with but little skill or effort. The sea swarms with such fish as halibut, herring, and cod. A commensurate wealth of aquatic mammals, hair seals, sea lions, whales, and porpoises, feed on the fish. The now nearly extinct sea otter was once abundant, and its rich fur was the object for the trading parties of whites who first contacted the Indians in the vicinity of Nootka Sound in the 1770s. The country is so indented with bays and fiords that the natives actually have recourse to several times the length of coastline than appears on maps.

The term *Nootka* refers to all of the 6000 or more people who speak the Nootkan language, which is a member of the Wakashan stock.[1] This name is not a native word, but is Captain Cook's rendering of what he mistakenly thought was the Indians' designation for themselves or their territory. Like so many other primitive peoples, they have no term for themselves as a nation, but only local designations for their component social groupings. The cultural and linguistic unit of people that we call Nootka has no reality to the natives themselves, for there are no social and political bonds uniting them all. The area as a whole, being composed of separated inlets and sounds, tends to create a comparable separation among the various groups of Indians, so that local confederations are created among the people of a single inlet; but these usually remain independent of the people at the next inlet, for the wooded, rugged land between them makes a considerable barrier.

Descriptions made by modern anthropologists, including the excellent recent one by Philip Drucker,[2] do not carry us back to the truly aboriginal, before certain kinds of contacts with whites had changed some aspects of the Indians' culture. There have been

[1] The population figure of 6000 is from A. L. Kroeber, *Cultural and Natural Areas of Native North America,* Berkeley, 1939, Table 7, p. 135.

[2] P. Drucker, *The Northern and Central Nootkan Tribes,* Smithsonian Institution, Bureau of American Ethnology, Bull. 144, Washington, 1951.

several well-marked periods of disturbance. There was, first of all, the short-lived but intensive trade between Indians and whites for sea-otter furs, then a period of less frequent contact, and finally the modern period of permanent trading posts, the gradual encroachment of white settlers and missionaries, and the sporadic employment of the Nootka in fish canneries. The account which follows is drawn largely from Drucker's material, which refers to Nootkan life from the 1870s to the early 1900s, shortly before the full effects of the modern period were felt. The present tense used hereafter should be understood as referring to this period.

Before the modern changes took place, the Nootka had achieved some measure of cultural balance and stability after the first great shocks of white contact. Some of the tools and techniques acquired from the ocean trade were used, but they were essentially fitted into an aboriginal cultural context. Some of these technological items were used in the food quest; others, such as the steel ax, knife, and adz, created a great efflorescence in woodcarving, housebuilding, and the making of the famous totem poles.

Perhaps the most important of the aboriginal devices are those used in catching the salmon. At the beginning of the salmon spawning season, tidewater traps of considerable size are set to catch the fish as they congregate at the mouths of the larger rivers. In the rivers themselves, cylindrical latticework traps are placed so that the fish are guided into the trap mouth by systems of weirs. Harpoons of several types are in common use, as are varieties of hooks and lines, herring rakes, and dipnets. A barbed sealing harpoon, of a complicated three-part construction—detachable head, shaft, and line—is also an important tool, mostly used in the hunting of hair seal, sea lion, and porpoise. The Nootka once also used to do a considerable amount of whaling, using for this purpose a huge whaling harpoon with a lanyard and a line with inflated skin buoys. Bows and arrows, spears, and various traps and deadfalls are used in hunting the elk, deer, and sea otter.

There is one class of technological items which deserves special mention, the preservative or storage techniques. Any people who depend on wild food are usually at the mercy of the great extremes of nature's prodigality. One fall season may provide a prodigious salmon run, but the whole winter season may be almost completely unproductive. Without storage techniques, a society is set in its demographic limits and consequent general cultural advance, by the seasons of scarcity unless it can carry over surpluses from the periods of plenty. Most hunting-gathering societies lack efficient storage and preservative techniques, but the Nootka are especially proficient at preserving fish, a notoriously quick-spoiling food. Salmon are dried, smoked, and stored by pressing them together and baling them. Salmon roe is packed in wooden boxes, or some-times in seal bladders, to be smoked into a mass called in English Siwash cheese.

NOOTKA MASK. *Courtesy, The American Museum of Natural History*

Nootkan clothing and orna-mentation are simple on ordinary occasions. In pleasant weather men wear nothing at all except a few ornaments. For warmth, a robe woven of shredded cedar bark is worn, and in rainy weather a bark cape and cone-shaped hat provide some protec-tion. Women wear robes similar to men's and always an apron of shredded cedar bark. Men cut their hair at shoulder length and women make two braids and tie the ends together. Face painting, earrings, and nose ornaments are common decorations for both sexes, and women in addition wear bead and shell necklaces, bracelets, and anklets of various mate-rials. Ceremonial dress is much finer than the everyday dress; the most prized robes are worn at such times, and particular interest is shown in those woven with shredded bark mixed with mountain-goat wool. Elaborate masks and headdressses carved to represent the heads of various animals are a striking addition to the costume at most ceremonies.

All of the natives of the Northwest Coast are adept woodwork-ers. Even before steel tools were acquired, the great trees of the Pacific Northwest provided easily made planks to the native carpenter. Houses, furniture, canoes, most containers, masks, and many other objects are made of wood, and very well made, too, considering that the carpenter's kit is limited to a few chisels, adzes, wedges, simple bone drills, and mauls.

The plank houses are huge, from 40 to 100 feet in length and 30 to 40 in width, sheltering a number of nuclear families. The houses are set in permanent frames at the two principal village sites, which are the summer and winter homes and the most important fishing stations. The plank roofing and siding are removable and are often transported from village to village in the seasonal shifting of residence. In each of these long houses resides a group of families who are related patrilineally, and the family spaces, each with its own cooking hearth and low plank beds, are allotted according to an invariable plan. The chief of the lineage occupies a rear corner to the right (of a person inside facing the door). The man next in rank, normally a younger brother, occupies the opposite corner, and the two front corners are next in importance. These spaces are marked off by storage boxes stacked at the boundaries.

Early travelers were bothered by the filthiness of the Nootkan households. "They invariably complain of the disorder of the houses, with bladders of oil and bundles of greasy fish dangling from overhead at just the height to smear one's face as he blinked his smoke-irritated eyes; baskets, boxes, dishes, mats, and tools scattered about the floor; and the floor itself a seething stinking mass of trash, fish guts, shellfish, and other refuse."[3]

Women do the usual family cooking, although young men often are the cooks for feasts at which large quantities of food are to be served. The cooking process is simple. Fresh fish are broiled over an open fire, while dried items and fish roe, molluscs, and meat and fowl are boiled in a watertight wooden box into which hot stones are dropped. Roasting in coals or ashes is rare, but some foods, such as clover roots, clams, and sometimes fresh meat or fish, are steamed by laying them in seaweed over a pile of hot stones. The Nootka are very fond of oils and greases, possibly because their diet is so lacking in starch and sugar carbohydrates. Whale oil, and in modern times dogfish oil, are served in separate receptacles, into which the diner dips each morsel of food before eating it.

[3] *Ibid.*, p. 72.

The household lineages are the fundamental social and political units of the society. Each lineage is typically associated with several others that occupy adjacent houses at the permanent winter village, which is usually located in one of the sheltered coves of the upper reaches of one of the inlets. In summer, people of several villages move down to the open beaches and lower parts of the inlets to engage in sea fishing and sea-mammal hunting, carrying the plank siding of their houses with them. Thus another and much larger village is formed for the summer season.

In this way, locality becomes the basis for a rather formal political arrangement. The basic unit above the level of the nuclear family is composed of kinsmen who inhabit a common long house. These lineages are united into villages because they inhabit a common winter locality, and these winter villages into confederacies because of the use of a common territory in the summer. There are clearly three ascending levels of social integration created by the factors of terrain and economic life. The arrangement is formalized, but it is probably better to think of it as a social order rather than a planned political order. The members, actually, consider themselves kinsmen, and the forms of association are all based on the analogy to family life.

Two basic principles govern the interactions of any two people, of any two lineages, or of any two villages of the confederation. These are relative rank and closeness of relationship. All persons are graded by the principle of primogeniture just as it might be applied in an individual family. The eldest son is the most important, and it is he who succeeds his father as head of the family. The next brother is of little importance except as a possible successor should his elder brother die so young that his own son cannot yet inherit the position and responsibility. A still younger brother, of course, has little chance of ever succeeding to the father's position. He can only form his own little family, starting from scratch, as it were. If there are certain privileges and rights pertaining to his family line, he is not likely to inherit them. A similar gradation from older to younger separates sisters, as well, but it is less important in the total scheme, because women do not occupy the important positions in the society. Inasmuch as the whole integrated society is based on the family analogy, individual family lineages are also graded with respect to one another, depending on the assumed birth order of the ancestors. Such an arrangement of society is rare among true primitives, but is familiar to us in our history. The closed society of the recent European nobility was similarly graduated, as were the Scottish and Irish clans, the Semitic tribes, and the Polynesians.

The recognition of categories of kindred is not carried to the degree of specificity observed by many primitive peoples. Nootkan kinship terminology is similar to that of Polynesian societies in that the significant discriminations are based on generational and sex differences. Parents' siblings and cousins are designated by the same term, with no distinction as to cross and parallel categories or variations in degree of collaterality. One's own siblings and cousins are not separated terminologically, nor are nephews and nieces distinguished from sons and daughters. The term for grandparents or other relatives of that generation merely means ancestor. In all these generations, of course, males can be distinguished from females by adding the appropriate affix. Any particular person's relationship to the speaker can be specified in a roundabout way by using qualifying words and phrases. Concordant with the generalized nature of the kinship categories, the Nootka are not specific in their patterns of avoidance, distance, and familiarity with any particular kinds of relatives. Apparently the ranking of people in terms of birth order has cross-cut the usual kinship categories and superseded them as determinants of etiquette.

All economic resources such as fishing, hunting, and gathering grounds are under the jurisdiction of individuals. This is not ownership exactly, for kinsmen have an inalienable right to the exploitation of any of the resources; but, rather, certain individuals hold the right to direct or manage the use of the resource. This right, a sort of stewardship, is inherited from father to eldest son and is never divided among brothers. This situation is directly related to (if not the cause of) the complicated system of social rank and etiquette on the Northwest Coast. A line of eldest sons inherits an important chieftainship and economic patrimony. Other patrimonies are subdivisions of this, and the offices are held by lesser lines of descent. Thus it is that while the society is entirely based on kinship relations, an important attribute of primitiveness, the individual descent lines are always ranked differentially, and the differences are typically expressed in terms of wealth.

On the surface, it would appear that while Nootkan society is a primitive one in the sense that there are no organizational principles above the level of kinship ties, there is a strong modern flavor to it. The society is not egalitarian, and there seems to be an overweening interest in wealth and the distinct social prerogatives associated with it. The competitive giveaway feasts—the famous *potlatches*—have suggested such phrases as *capitalist ethic* and *conspicuous consumption*. The society has also been characterized as divided into feudal-like social classes.

As Drucker has pointed out, however, such characterizations are superficial and misleading. Social classes or castes exist in only one sense; there is a primary division of the society between freemen and slaves. Slaves are war captives from another tribe; they are not kinsmen and thus not regarded as a part of the society. They perform drudge labor or degrading tasks around the camps and are the property of the captor. To term them *slaves* is probably incorrect, for they are not a productive part of the economy; this is not a *slave society*. These captives are more truly trophies of war, and their possession proves that the owner is important enough and wealthy enough to be able to keep them. Except for these few chattels, the distinctions in rank and wealth do not correspond to the European concept of social classes.

The society does not consist of two or more social strata, but rather of a series of individual status positions all ranked in order. No two individuals are precisely equivalent in rank. If this is a system of social classes, then each individual is in a class by himself. Furthermore, all individuals, from the most highly ranked to the lowliest, are considered kinsmen. Status distinctions based on the purely familial criteria of birth order and marriage are extended to include the whole functioning village. Distinctions such as these are, of course, implicit in any family in any society. The essential characteristic of societies like the Nootkan is that managerial rights to property are inherited undivided by individuals. Primogeniture seems bound to occur if there is no *frontier,* that is, no possibility of younger brothers equaling the older brothers' patrimony in some other area or new enterprise.[4]

This means, too, that until depopulation through the effect of

[4] See Chapter 12 for further description and discussion of this kind of social system.

European diseases left high positions open for lesser relatives to succeed to, statuses were frozen; there was no social (or economic) mobility. Thus, ambition, hard work, competitiveness, were not means to enhance a socioeconomic position. The capitalist ethic is out of place in this society wholly based on an aristocratic principle of inherited positions. As a matter of fact, the predominant, sanctioned pattern of social behavior strongly condemns aggressive behavior and regards as ideal the individual noted for his mildness.

The most usual symbolic expressions of differences in inherited rank are sumptuary customs in dress, the use of special names, economic privileges, potlatch rights, and various ceremonial privileges. The most visible everyday symbols of rank are found in differences in dress. In general, the higher the rank, the more ornate the costume worn. Only chiefs of lineages may wear ornaments of dentalia and abalone shell, sea-otter-fur trimming on their robes, and particular decorations on their headdresses.

The names bestowed on individuals are a hereditary right. These are the names of ancestors which descend through a line of first-born sons, and they symbolize a particular social position. The very process of coming to assume a particular status position consists largely of the ritual of having the particular name bestowed on one. For this reason, *title* is perhaps a better term than *name,* for the particular designation is not applied to an individual from birth, but only when he comes to acquire the position it symbolizes.

Status rights and privileges are also expressed in economic form. The various grades of chiefs have various amounts of territory over which they act as executives for their lesser kinsmen. Those who use the resources formally acknowledge the positions by paying sorts of tributes, such as first fruits of the salmon catch or berry-picking, certain choice parts of sea mammals killed, blankets, furs, and so on. Many economic products are acquired by the chief according to strict and complicated custom, but quantities of goods are also given to the chief more freely, when there is a surplus beyond the donor's subsistence needs. The chief has no means to enforce these divisions of the products, of course, and thus, in a strict sense, the process should not be considered a tax or a tribute. Furthermore, and importantly, these gifts do not function particularly to increase personal wealth which the chief might consume, for it is understood that he will later give away a comparable amount of goods in a great feast or potlach. The chief's function is to redistribute goods, a not unusual feature in the primitive world.[5]

The economic function is clear: different individuals, families, and groups have varying degrees of luck at hunting or fishing at any given time, and may also be engaged in quite different pursuits. One way to get rid of a surplus of salmon and acquire some needed oil, for example, would be to trade for it, as in a market. This method of distribution would be familiar to members of European society, but many primitives distribute goods in quite a different way. The surpluses are given to the chief, who may redistribute them to the members of his group at an occasion (typically made festive) or may exchange with another group by giving the products to them at a feast in their honor, later to receive some of their surpluses at a reciprocating feast. Contrary to the attitudes in Western civilization, competitiveness in such a culture lies in trying to give away the most, rather than in trying to get the better of the bargain.

Gift-giving as a means of economic trade can serve functions that a market cannot. Peaceful relations between groups are created and good fellowship enhanced by festive giving, and social solidarity among the members of a group is strengthened by the noncompetitive interdependence. The potlatches also are highly ceremonialized, and in such a way that the various ranks are clearly delineated. So social and ceremonial are the potlatches, in fact, that their economic function can be easily overlooked by the observer.

One of the most striking social aspects of the potlatch is its use as a manifestation and validation of rank. Each individual receiving at a potlatch occupies (and owns by hereditary right) a particular seat, and all seats are arranged with respect to others in an order equivalent to the status positions of the occupants. Ritual homage accompanies the taking of the seat, almost as though it were a throne, and the gifts are distributed in appropriate order and appropriate quantity or value. Constituent members of the social groups of the various chiefs sit in the rest of the long house, undifferentiated, except that men sit on the right and women on the left. The people seem to feel that the purpose and function of

[5] For close parallels of this, see Chapters 11 and 12.

the potlatch is to validate hereditary privileges, or at times to bestow them, rather than to accomplish a mere economic exchange of surpluses.

Inheritance of an office and associated status does not take place after the death of an incumbent, but is more or less gradually assumed by the child, who, as he becomes older, is increasingly given more and more of the various rights and privileges belonging to the father, until he is finally experienced enough to assume all of the burdens of his father's position. This might occur long before the father becomes too old to continue in his position. He merely retires to a more and more advisory capacity.

The formality by which an heir is invested with a part of his inheritance is typically the potlatch feast. Some of the inheritance, however, consists of certain supernatural attributes and ownership of supernatural songs and dances. The acquisition of these is made by a ritual called the Shaman's Dance, which is followed by a potlatch. In brief, supernaturals (wolves, according to the origin myth which is the basis for the ritual) kidnap the youngster and take him to a place where a particular ancestor of his supposedly lived, and there they bestow upon him the name of the ancestor and the associated supernatural rights. When the boy is restored to society, he sings his ancestor's supernatural song at the potlatch and recites the various rights which he has inherited.

The frequent potlatches are the high points of the life of the social group, but they are also the important steps by which an individual ascends from birth to maturity, especially if he is the eldest son of a man of rank. Such a person is involved in a seemingly endless round of festivals, celebrating such things as his first tooth, the first solid food he eats, the first bird he shoots, and so on almost infinitely. Less important children have less frequent festivals, and fewer people are involved.

Childbirth always takes place in the seclusion of a small hut of brush prepared for the occasion. For four days after the birth, the mother has to remain in the hut, and both the mother and father observe restrictions on their diet and movements. The new baby, meanwhile, is attached to its cradle board and a shredded-bark cap is tied firmly on its head in order to form it into the ideal long, narrow shape. Magical formulas are used to insure the development of desirable qualities in the child. Some of the most usual involve the means of disposing of the afterbirth after the four-day taboo period. If songs are sung as the afterbirth is buried, the child will be a good singer; if carpenter's tools are buried with it, he will become a skilled artisan; bits of basketry and matting are customarily buried with the afterbirth of a girl baby so she will become a good weaver. Also, at the fourth day the child's ears are pierced, and a potlatch is given to mark the event.

In case of twin births, special and severe observances are necessary, for the people feel that supernaturals have intervened to cause the unusual births, as in the case of deformed children. The parents and children are forced to remain in seclusion for four years, subsisting by themselves except for the occasional aid of kinsmen who pay them brief visits. Twins are supposed to have more luck and supernatural power than other people and often become shamans after maturity.

By modern American standards, the Nootka are affectionate and indulgent toward children. Toilet training does not begin until late, and physical punishment is not used—nor are children ever slapped or spanked for any other reason. The only means of correction, even for older children, is talking to them, attempting to shame them. This does not mean that the parents are careless, however, for they give great attention to the proper care and education of children. Instruction in etiquette and morality begins very early in life, and the children are patiently corrected over and over again.

Mythology is always an important oral teaching aid, and probably a very successful one, for listening to tales is one of the most frequent forms of amusement. Family traditions are handed down in this way, the tales usually describing the origin of the customs. Contemporary anecdotes and plain gossip are indulged in for the usual reasons, but are also recounted to children for instructional purposes whenever it seems that either ideal or antisocial conduct is revealed in some clarity. Instruction of the young by these varied means is not the duty of the mother and father alone; aunts and uncles, older siblings, and especially grandparents are all active in the training of the child.

A fuller participation in adult activities begins at the age of puberty, and thereafter a great change in the nature of the learning process takes place. At a girl's first menses she is secluded for four days and may eat only dried fish, may scratch only with a stick, and must always sit with her legs together in front of her. Many other taboos are like those observed by a mother during her four-day seclusion after giving birth to a child. At the end of the four days, the girl is given a ceremonial bath, and her hair is dressed with a special ornamentation to be worn for several months to signify her new status as a woman. The occasion is typically marked by a feast or, if she is the eldest daughter, by a full potlatch. From then on until marriage a girl's activities are much more restricted and chaperoned than during her childhood; most of her time is spent in the house learning the various domestic arts. Premarital chastity is insisted upon.

No particular rites mark the boys' arrival at man's estate. Boys are kept busy learning hunting and fishing techniques, and serving as novitiates in social and ceremonial life. Young men, like young women, are supposed to assume a retiring and unassertive manner in the presence of their elders. Young men play an increasingly active role in all affairs, but never take the spotlight away from the elders, who are always the major figures. Only at the marriage ceremony does a young man occupy the center of the stage.

As among other primitives, marriage is conceived of as a formal alliance between two family groups rather than between two individuals. Marriages are arranged by the elders soon after their children reach puberty. The proposal is made by the boy's parents and involves a visit to the girl's home, during which the visitors present a few gifts, describe the groom's ancestry, and recount previous marriages between the two family lines. Marriage is always between distant relatives; it is rare for first cousins to marry. It is customary for the girl's father to refuse the gifts and the marriage offer the first time. Only after two, sometimes more, visits may he accept. All parents want their children to make a good marriage to someone of higher rank and wealth. Such desires on the part of all the people, of course, tend to cancel out, so that most marriages are actually between men and women of equivalent rank.

The marriage ceremony itself revolves around the presentation of the gifts which are brought to the bride's village by the groom's party. As on the occasion of the original proposal, the bride's father steadfastly refuses the presents for several days. After the presents are finally accepted, the bride is ceremonially welcomed to the groom's village. The dowry is usually paid by the bride's parents at this time, though sometimes they wait until the birth of the first child.

An important aspect of the dowry is the presentation to the son-in-law of some of the bride's father's privileged names, special dances, potlatch seats, and even territorial rights. These represent an inheritance to be passed on to the child of the marriage, and if no son is born, they revert to the donor. Similarly, the groom formally presents to the bride all of the rights he owns, to be passed on to their child.

Polygyny is sometimes practiced by important chiefs, for to have several wives is a sign of wealth. Polyandry is not in favor, however: "A man wouldn't stand for that," it is said in explanation. Divorce is quite common and accomplished simply and unceremoniously. Childlessness is the most common cause. On the death of a husband, one of his brothers is expected to marry the widow; and similarly, if a wife dies, the husband might marry one of her unmarried sisters or other close relatives. Both of these kinds of remarriages are regarded primarily as a means of taking care of the children.

Death inspires considerable fear among the Nootka. A corpse is always disposed of as soon as possible, so rapidly, in fact, that white observers have wondered whether some unfortunates might not have been sealed up in the coffin-like boxes before they were dead. The boxes are usually deposited in a remote cave or lashed onto the upper branches of a tree. The mourners, men and women alike, cut their hair short and, following the disposal of the body, gather to sing the mourning songs. Some few days later, a *throwing away* potlatch is held, during which the deceased's possessions are given away or destroyed. From this time until a year or so later, the deceased's name should not be pronounced; if it forms an element of a commonly used word or expression, some substitute has to be found. The mourning period even for close kin is not especially long; the close relatives are expected to stay indoors for a few days and to appear sad for a somewhat longer time.

Houses are not burned or abandoned because of a death, although this is a widespread primitive custom. Probably because the houses represent so large an investment for a numerous group, abandonment or destruction is not feasible. In modern times, individual family houses "white-man style," have become quite common and are frequently burned following the death of an occupant at the same time at which the deceased's personal effects are destroyed.

The Nootka believe that each person possesses a sort of soul which resides in the brain and that on the death of the body the soul is liberated. It does not reside in any particular afterworld or heaven, but simply goes away. This soul is distinct from the *vital spirit*, or *life*, which is seated in the breast.

The Nootkan cosmology reveals something of the peoples' basic experience in the world. They have a minute, firsthand knowledge of the seashores and inlets, but have rarely ventured into the rugged, nearly impassable inland jungles and rugged mountains. The inland fastnesses are thought of as populated by tremendous numbers of malignant supernatural beings, whereas the coasts and inlets are all well known and safe; the behavior of the tides, currents, and storms is accepted with naturalistic understanding. In general, the perspective of their cosmology is provincial; there are no involved explanations of heavens, underworlds, or other lands.

Unlike some seafaring peoples, such as the Polynesians, the Nootka seem to have little interest in the heavenly bodies; even the idea of steering by the North Star was introduced by white seamen. In general, the supernatural beings personified from natural phenomena are vague beliefs, unsystematized, and not organized into groups or hierarchies. Nor is there any worship and so it would be an error to call the spirits *gods*. There are many kinds of spirits, to be sure, and some are dangerous, others more pacific, but these correspond to modern superstitions rather than to modern religions.

A large part of Nootkan belief consists of mechanical means to guide or channel supernatural power. This is essentially ritual technique and is approached in a practical and direct manner; there is nothing of awe, ecstasy, or devotion in the attitude of the Indians. This manner is so common among primitives, and so different from what Europeans consider a religious frame of mind, that the practices have often been called *magic* rather than *religion*.

Yet the peoples of the Northwest Coast do have the beginnings of a priesthood, which makes them distinctive from the tribally organized American Indians and more like such developed chiefdoms as the Polynesians. In this case it is the chief himself who performs certain rituals for the welfare of his people. The main occasion on which the chief acts as priest is at the beginning of the seasonal salmon run, when he is ritually cleansed and then performs a complicated ceremony to insure the coming of the salmon. This is essentially the same in spirit as the First Fruits ceremonies held before the harvest in so many agricultural societies.

Man is served by supernatural means, according to Nootkan belief, in ways which serve three principal social ends. One set of rituals has as its aim the securing of good luck in all the various realms in which nature has to be coped with by man. Weather is controlled in this way, as is health, the behavior of game, and so on. Another kind of ritual practice is the acquisition from the spirit world of the various rights and privileges with which a man displays his rank. The third is the curing of the sick—i.e., prevention of death—which is, of course, regarded as an extremely important activity in any society and is such a noteworthy aspect of primitive religious practice that early thought about cultural evolution was inclined to credit this preoccupation with being the very basis of religion and perhaps its first manifestation. Certainly curing deserves some kind of special attention as a cultural phenomenon, for it is in the shaman's activity that is manifested the first beginning of professionalization in primitive society.

The medicine man, or shaman, being a specialist whose gifts or knowledge can be acquired rather than inherited, is one of the few Nootka who can earn power and prestige by his own efforts. For this reason, shamans are often of humble origin or younger sons of important people, usually of high intelligence and ambition.[6] A person who wishes to become a shaman first undertakes various rituals that will aid him in his spirit quest, his encounter with the supernatural whence his power to cure will come. The preparations for the encounter begin with ritual bathing for four nights during the waxing of the moon, to be repeated each moon until the spiritual quest is finished. Strict continence is mandatory, and food is eaten only sparingly. The coming of the spirit is dramatic; it is said that the power of the apparition is such that often the seeker faints dead away, blood trickling from his mouth, nose, and ears. The seeker, after his encounter, is supposed to make a certain ritual cry and

[6] Drucker's description of the qualities of the Nootkan shaman conflicts with the common view that shamans are unstable, psychotic, or epileptic persons. Drucker, *op. cit.,* p. 182.

perform a secret trick that will conquer the spirit, which then disappears, leaving behind some token or fetish—usually a rattle—which gives the seeker control over the supernatural power. It is understood to be a very dangerous procedure to seek to control a spirit, for one may be defeated and killed or left deranged. Only daring and ambitious people attempt, therefore, to become shaman's.

Next the neophyte must learn to use the power to call the spirit to him. This he does with songs and dances which the spirit has revealed to him. The period of practice comes to a close finally with a formal feast given by the chief, when it is announced that a new-fledged shaman is ready to begin his duties, and his new shaman's name is given him.

Shamans are called to cure only serious illnesses; cuts and bruises and the like are treated with home remedies, and even in more serious cases the shaman is not called until these have failed. The curing performance always takes place at night, the patient lying on a pile of mats before a fire. It always attracts a large crowd, for it is very dramatic. The shaman, seated in the firelight beside the patient—the onlookers outside the circle of firelight—feels over the body, searching for the seat of the trouble, shaking his head sadly. ("You should have called me sooner.")

Finally the shaman feels ready to begin:

He gave a few tentative shakes of his rattle and began to hum a spirit song, deep in his throat. It took a while to get in good voice. His humming became bolder, the clicking of his rattle sharper. By this means he called his spirit to his aid.

Now the time had arrived for the immediate relative of the sick person to stand up and call his offer of payment: blankets, furs, canoes, or, recently, money. According to conventional belief, the shaman himself had nothing to do with accepting or refusing the offer. His spirit attended to that. . . . Should it be insufficient, the supernatural being would draw away, removing his aura of power. The shaman's throat weakened, his song died away to a low hum again. The patient's relative then had to increase his offer. When at length it satisfied the spirit he drew near once more, and the shaman's song welled forth.[7]

From then on the performance consists usually of the location of the foreign object causing the pain and its extraction by sucking

[7] *Ibid.*, p. 203.

it out. Some serious illnesses are caused by spirit contamination or by soul loss, and then more special techniques are necessary. The offending spirit has to be driven away by ritual techniques, and in the case of soul loss, the shaman's spirit helper guides him to the place of the wandering soul.

Black magic, or witchcraft, is a common source of trouble. An evil shaman, or someone who possesses supernatural power, can cause illness by sending pieces of bone, or duck's claws, or some such objects into a person's body. There is, consequently, sometimes the notion that the curing shaman has actually sent the offending objects into the patient in the first place in order later to collect a fee for curing him.

Witchcraft seems to be the principal crime against the society, but this does not mean that the Nootka are an especially double-dealing, suspicious, witch-ridden society. Murder, theft, and other crimes common to organized society are in fact very rare among the Nootka. There is no formal machinery of social control; most disputes are settled by public dressing-downs at a feast or potlatch if nothing else, such as private counsel, suffices. Revenge by an individual seems to have been rare, and suicide, the ultimate protest against society, had not occurred within the memory of any of Drucker's informants.

Battles with neighboring societies are fought for a variety of reasons, but economic motives are by far the most common—most typically a simple *lebensraum* justification. There are no protracted wars; simple raiding, a single battle, is the norm. Curiously, there is no record anywhere on the Northwest Coast of a conquest resulting in suzerainty of a victor over the vanquished, or of any form of tribute. It is possible that, as in the Polynesian islands, permanent conquest is too difficult because the social groups are so separated by geographical hindrances.

The Nootka wage war quite effectively and mercilessly, compared to the inefficient war games of so many American Indian tribes. Once a plan of attack is approved at a council of chiefs, the Nootkan warriors bathe ritually for several nights. If the plans permit time for preparations, a course of practical as well as ritual training is undertaken: dry runs of the assault landing, and so on. Slings and bows and arrows are carried for long-range fighting, if necessary, but the favorite weapons are stone clubs and spears or pikes with fire-hardened, sharp points. Only the chiefs wear body armor, usually of several thicknesses of elkhide.

The favorite tactic is the night assault on a sleeping village. For this to be successful, of course, well-geared timing and organization are essential, and accurate information on the location of the houses and even of the interior sleeping arrangements is needed. Other tactics are ambushes and surprise attacks on isolated parties. When a Nootkan village goes after another group's territory, the aim is complete destruction of the enemy. Whole heads are taken as trophies—even of women and children—and carried aloft on the points of the spears, and after the return home, a great dancing celebration is held around them. The booty is later distributed at a potlatch.

The ruthlessness of Nootkan warfare should not suggest that among themselves aggressive and savage behavior is condoned, for the ideal personality type is friendly and generous. It is perhaps difficult to think of such a people as warlike, but, even as in modern society, diametrically opposed principles to these can be called forth and praised in the context of warfare. Even a war chief, famed as a savage warrior, can never use his strength or reputation to bully his own kinsmen.

Observers have noted that the Nootka are a strikingly light-hearted people, with a highly developed sense of humor. Horseplay, buffoonery, and ribald anecdotes are very common, and satirical clowning is often a motif in otherwise serious ceremonies. The Nootka are also greatly interested in theatrical ceremonies; such performances seem to be the axis around which social life revolves. All in all, the typical personality of the Nootka Indians stands in striking contrast to the gloomy sullenness which has been attributed to other peoples of the Northwest Coast.[8]

The Nootka saw a white man for the first time when the Spanish mariner, Juán Pérez, anchored briefly at Nootka Sound in 1774 and the astounded but unafraid natives climbed aboard his ship to offer gifts. Four years later Captain Cook, on his famous third voyage of exploration in the Pacific, stopped at Nootka Sound and there acquired a few sea-otter pelts, which were later discovered

[8] This description of the Nootkan public personality conflicts with that ascribed to the neighboring Kwakiutl by the late Ruth Benedict. The above characterization follows Drucker, *op. cit.*, pp. 453–457.

A MODERN NOOTKA VILLAGE. *Courtesy, The American Museum of Natural History*

to be immensely valuable in world trade. Soon ships of many nations were frantically competing for this wealth. The "Nootka Sound Controversy" nearly caused a war between Spain and England, and it has been said that Boston was saved from commercial ruin by the sudden success of its traders in exchanging sea-otter pelts in China for tea and silk. Several ships came each year until, after about forty years, the supply of sea otter was nearly exhausted.

From the white traders the Nootka acquired firearms, steel axes and knives, and great piles of cheap blankets and ornaments. And as everywhere in the aboriginal world subjected to this kind of contact, the population rapidly declined because of the many diseases that were introduced for which they had no immunity. Indirect social repercussions of these two effects of white contact must have been considerable. The great abundance of certain kinds of white man's goods, and the immediate effect on subsistence of steel tools and firearms, resulted in an increase in the number and size of the exuberant giveaway feasts, the potlatches; and the concomitant decline in population disrupted the rigid system of inherited statuses, creating a certain degree of mobility as positions became open to lesser relatives through the dying out of some family lines.

From about 1820 through the rest of the century trade dwindled considerably as the sea otter neared extinction. From 1875 the Indians were influenced somewhat by a Catholic mission, especially because the wars were halted. Since 1900 commercial fishing, wage working in fish canneries, a government school, the establishment of a white community, and Canadian laws against potlatching have resulted in many changes. In the main, the surviving Nootka are on their way toward an identification of themselves as Canadian *citizens,* however much identifiable as Indians.

FURTHER READINGS

Barnett, H. G., "The Nature of the Potlatch," *American Anthropologist,* n.s., Vol. 40, 1938.

Boas, F., "The Nootka," *Report of the 60th Meeting of the British Association for the Advancement of Science,* London, 1890.

Curtis, E. S., "The Nootka," in *The North American Indian,* 1907–1930, Vol. 11, Cambridge, Mass., 1916.

Drucker, P., "Wealth, Rank, and Kinship in Northwest Coast Society," *American Anthropologist,* n.s., Vol. 41, 1939.

Drucker, P., *The Northern and Central Nootkan Tribes,* Smithsonian Institution, Bureau of American Ethnology, Bull. 144, Washington, 1951.

Drucker, P., *Indians of the Northwest Coast,* New York, 1955.

Drucker, P., *Cultures of the North Pacific Coast,* San Francisco, 1965.

Hawthorn, H. B., *et al., The Indians of British Columbia: A Study of Contemporary Social Adjustment,* Berkeley and Vancouver, 1958.

Jewitt, J. R., *Narrative of the adventures and sufferings of John R. Jewitt; only survivor of the crew of the Ship Boston, during a captivity of nearly three years among the savages of Nootka Sound . . . ,* Middletown, 1815.

Koppert, V. A., "Contributions to Clayoquot Ethnology," *Catholic University of America Anthropological Series,* Vol. 1, Washington, 1930.

Moser, C., *Reminiscences of the West Coast of Vancouver Island,* Victoria, B.C., 1926.

Sapir, E., "A Girl's Puberty Ceremony among the Nootka Indians," *Transactions of the Royal Society of Canada,* Ser. 3, Vol. 7, 1913.

Sapir, E., "The Life of a Nootka Indian," *Queen's Quarterly,* Vol. 28, 1921.

Sapir, E., "Sayach'apis, a Nootka Trader," in E. C. Parsons (ed.), *American Indian Life,* New York, 1925.

Sapir, E., and Swadesh, M., *Native Accounts of Nootkan Ethnography,* Indiana University Research Center in Anthropology, Folklore, and Linguistics, Pub. 1, 1955.

Swadesh, M., "Motivations in Nootka Warfare," *Southwestern Journal of Anthropology,* Vol. 4, 1948.

The Trobriand Islanders of Melanesia

Melanesia means *dark islands,* and they were apparently called this because the dark-skinned peoples of this southwestern Pacific region differed so strikingly from the earlier known Polynesians of the Central Pacific. These islands were regarded as dark, too, because of the tales about the savage cannibals of the dank forests who practiced malignant witchcraft and ambushed landing parties from European ships. The experience of the American armed forces in World War II finally brought the region to public notice in the United States, but these experiences were not of the sort to create the impression of romance and carefree happiness that accompanied the acquaintance of Europeans with the Polynesians.

Some parts of Melanesia were so little colonized by white settlers during the last 100 years of great European expansion that the aboriginal culture of the inhabitants remains today, along with that of neighboring Australia, one of the last on the face of the globe which ethnographers can study as truly primitive functioning societies. New Guinea had been sighted as early as 1527 by the Portuguese Jorge de Menezes, and later was rediscovered by ships of several different countries, but the coast had so few harbors and the natives seemed so poor that little exploration was done. Not until 1700 was any part of New Guinea charted. Captain Dampier explored the north coastal waters in that year, and 67 years later another Englishman, Carteret, explored somewhat farther. Captain Cook, and the Frenchmen Bougainville and d'Entrecasteaux, later discovered some of the other important islands of Melanesia. During the nineteenth century whalers and traders sometimes visited certain large islands for water and trade with the natives. Not all of the islands were touched, however.

Some of the larger Melanesian islands, the Solomons, New Caledonia, and New Hebrides, were subjected to slave raiding, or *blackbirding,* in the latter part of the nineteenth century. European ships made a business of capturing Melanesians and selling them for work on the great cotton plantations in Fiji and sugar plantations in Australia. The natives' fear of these depredations had, of course, a direct effect on subsequent relations between them and all Europeans; the Melanesians, because of their experience, were little inclined to adopt European customs. Indirectly, however, the effects of white contact were considerable, especially those resulting from a continual decrease in native population due to foreign diseases.

The people of Melanesia are of three distinct racial strains in varying degrees of mixture. The first arrivals to these islands were probably short-statured Negroes—usually called Negritos—from the direction of Malaysia. Today Melanesian Negritos are found only in tiny groups in the remote mountain fastnesses of central New Guinea. Next seems to have come a lighter-skinned, wavy-haired, bearded group from probably the same direction, which has been called variously *Proto-Caucasoid, Archaic White, Ainoid,* and *Veddoid;* these latter two names have been used because of the posited affinity of this stock to the present-day Ainu of northern Japan and the similar Vedda of Ceylon. Apparently, they mixed to some extent with the Negritos, for the greater part of the modern population of New Guinea, the so-called *Papuans,* resembles a mixture of these two. The antiquity of these movements is suggested by the tremendous diversity of languages in the Papuan area; assuming they were once related, a great many have diverged so far that there is now no evidence of affinity.

The third group, the Melanesians, apparently arrived much later. These peoples mostly inhabit the small islands and the coastal regions of the larger ones, and the different groups of them resemble one another quite closely in physical appearance, language, and many features of culture. They are black-skinned, but seem to be generally less heavy-featured and more lightly built than the Papuans; they speak dialects of the Malayo-Polynesian language family; and their culture seems to be more adapted to seafaring than that of the Papuans. Their physical appearance and cultural emphases suggest that, as in language, they have some old affinity to the Polynesians. The Trobriand Islanders are rather typical representatives of this last type found in the Melanesian islands.

The Trobriands, a small group of islands of coral formation lying off the southeastern extremity of New Guinea, are probably more widely known in the English-speaking world than any other islands in Melanesia, for the natives have been immortalized in several intensive descriptions by Bronislaw Malinowski, who lived among them during the years of World War I. Fortunately, these islands were so unimportant during the lawless years when the larger islands were being plundered of their

A MODERN MELANESIAN GIRL. *Courtesy, Marshall D. Sahlins*

populations that Malinowski was privileged to live among a people whose way of life had not been altered in most important respects.

The bulk of the Trobriand population lives on one large island, Kiriwina (or Boyowa), which is 30 miles long and quite narrow. The rest of the archipelago consists of many tiny coral islands near it. The soil of Kiriwina is very rich, and produces some of the finest yam crops known to the tropical world. The population, consequently, is very dense, and all of the land is under intermittent cultivation, except a few places where there are coral outcrops and brackish swamps. The relative absence of primeval jungle means that hunting is of scant importance and the gathering of wild produce of little more. Fishing is an important occupation in villages located near the coast, and a lively trade exists between them and the inland villages.

The larger inland villages are typically built on level ground in a geometrical plan. In the center, or plaza, is the level, well-trodden ceremonial court and dance ground, the whole area surrounded by a concentric ring of yam storehouses. These are built on piles, with walls of large round logs laid with the ends overlapped so that wide interstices leave the stored yams visible from outside. Most of the storehouses have small platforms fronting on the plaza which are used as benches.

Behind the yam houses is a ring of dwellings. These huts are built directly on the ground rather than on piles and are quite dark—the only opening is the door in front. Each is a single family unit and quite small; only a married couple and their small children, if any, occupy it. Boys and girls beyond the age of puberty live separately in communal houses until marriage. The chief's house, larger and more decorated than the others, usually is placed in the central ring of storehouses. The dwelling units are really only sleeping places and most of the daily life, including even such typical household occupations as cooking, takes place out of doors among the groves of trees behind the houses.

The surrounding countryside is neither varied nor picturesque, for the island is one large flat plain. In any given year about one-fifth to one-quarter of the whole island is cultivated, while the areas left fallow grow into a low tangle of bush and vine scrub. The cultivated land, according to Malinowski, produces much more than the people actually require for subsistence; an average harvest might provide twice the quantity needed. Perhaps the reason for this over-production, or at least one reason, is the great competitive displays of yams. The quality and size of a man's yam crop is the most important single means of acquiring prestige, and he is likely to produce more than he needs for subsistence. His own level of consumption, or wealth, incidentally, is not raised directly by any extra effort he puts into the garden work, for about three-fourths of his harvest must be given away, part of it to the village chief for later redistribution, and part to his matrilineal in-laws (his sister's or mother's husband and family).

The yam is the foremost staple, but other plants of tropical Oceania are also grown, notably taro, sweet potatoes, bananas, and coconuts. The island lacks materials such as stone, clay, rattan, and bamboo, but these are obtained by trade with peoples from other islands. On the island of Kiriwina, intervillage trade also is of great importance. The coastal communities specialize in fishing along with their agriculture, and the various inland communities often have their own local specialization in arts and crafts.

As in the other areas of Melanesia, trade between villages and between whole island groups has been developed to an extent very unusual in the primitive world. Partly, this can be accounted for by the diversity of the environment; some local areas have fine clay, others exceptional wood, others have a prized kind of stone, and so on. But the greater specialization is in skilled craftsmanship. The concentration of skill in a particular line, such as woodcarving, pottery decoration, or canoe building, usually is found in the areas where the required raw material does not occur; in other words, a kind of division of labor and district specialization has come about which far transcends the environmental determinants of local specialization.

The interisland trade which links the various groups of islands off eastern New Guinea is overlaid with such an elaborate ceremonialism that its basic economic nature has been often lost sight of by those Europeans who have familiarized themselves with it. The *kula* ring, as described in Malinowski's famous *Argonauts of the Western Pacific,* is a splendidly ornate example of the essential difference between the phrasing of the exchange of goods in primitive societies and that of modern Western civilization. Whereas in modern commerce goods are exchanged explicitly to produce an immediate profit—"Buy cheap and sell dear"—primitive exchange emphasizes reciprocity and social obligation. The ideal is to give more than to receive. In both cases one result is identical; people are able to get rid of a surplus they do not need and acquire something they do need. But trade as practiced by most primitives has a social purpose; it can be accomplished as a form of reciprocal gift giving, as in the northern European and American custom of the Christmas exchange. It is, perhaps, a rather inefficient form of trade, as trade, but it serves the additional function of creating a friendly atmosphere rather than a competitive one. The kula ring is unusual in the primitive world only because it is so extensive,

Courtesy, The American Museum of Natural History

uniting so many independent societies in its orbit. The phrasing of trade as gift exchange, however, is not unusual; it is typical of primitives, who, in the absence of police and enforced law and order among communities, must evolve mechanisms for economic exchange which minimize competition and enhance solidarity.

From the point of view of the natives' own phrasing, it seems that the most important aspect of the kula is the highly ritualized exchange of nonutilitarian "valuables" rather than the exchange of basic subsistence goods. Two kinds of objects, symbols of the reciprocal relationship of all the trade partners who are links in the whole ring, circulate in opposite directions among the islands. Bracelets, made of a special white shell, are given by Trobrianders to their trade partners at Dobu, who will later give them to their partners on the other side of them, and so on around the trading ring. The Trobrianders will receive from the Dobuans, in turn, necklaces made of red spondylus shell, which they later present to their partners in the other direction, to be passed on around the circle. These two kinds of objects thus circulate in opposite directions, linking up the whole chain of trade partners as a double ring, symbolizing reciprocity—an exchange of equivalent but not identical goods—which is the characteristic of social interdependence. But it is essential to remember that the kula objects are not *goods* in the usual utilitarian sense; they are symbols, and their value is perceived much as modern man values such things as heirlooms and souvenirs. Partners who exchange them feel that they are united in lifelong brotherhood.

While the exchange of these objects would seem to be the reason for the trading expeditions, especially because the act of exchange is surrounded by so much careful etiquette and the objects themselves have honorific names and a carefully recounted history, there is, nevertheless, an important trade in large quantities of purely utilitarian handicrafts, raw materials, and foodstuffs accompanying it. These, of course, do not circulate continuously as do the kula symbols, though there is some considerable movement of them. There is a nearly continuous trickle of exchange going on between individuals in a district and between villages of various districts. The group of people who go on the overseas expeditions to visit their kula partners expend much time and effort in bringing together by local exchange the large quantity of goods that will be useful to their hosts on the islands they visit. They bring home in return a more or less equal amount of needed goods which they then exchange on the same local basis.

In a sense, nearly all the trade which goes on in the Trobriands is gift exchange; but we must understand it as always reciprocal. Spontaneous gifts, such as alms or charity, do not exist, for anyone in need is cared for by relatives. A gift of valuables from which no return is contemplated is found only in the relationship of parent to child. Even such an obviously routine utilitarian exchange as that of fish for vegetables between a fishing village and a neighboring inland horticultural village is invested with many of the same characteristics as the kula. Each man has his partner in the other village, and following a harvest the inlander puts a large quantity of vegetables before his partner's house. The fisherman later reciprocates with some approximation of the value in fish. This is distinct from barter in two respects: the element of trust is involved, for the amount of the repayment is left up to the receiver; and the gift cannot be refused.

It is only under certain circumstances that exchange takes the form of barter. Sometimes some of the inland families who specialize in making wooden dishes, combs, lime pots, and the like, hawk their surplus articles through the other villages. In these cases, haggling over equivalences takes place. It is also distinguished from the normal exchange because any two individuals may do it, even strangers. Ceremonialism is absent, and, significantly, the inlanders who peddle goods in this way are regarded as pariahs; the form of exchange has a special name, *gimwali,* which is used scornfully to characterize an exchange carried out in an improper manner.

The social divisions of the Trobrianders are of the sort widely found among primitive horticulturalists. In the main, the levels of social integration extend from the nuclear family of husband, wife, and children to the subclan (or lineage), and then to the full clan. The latter two kinship groupings are cross-cut to some extent by local ties based on village membership, district, and tribe. These two sets of affinities are quite distinct, for the groups based on kinship are not local; a person may find kindred in different villages and districts. Furthermore, membership in a family line is inherited matrilineally; a person is a member of his mother's lineage and clan. Inasmuch as a bride moves to her husband's home, the ties of matrilineal kinship cut across those of locality. Each village always contains members of two or more clans, for these divisions are exogamous—a husband and wife cannot be members of the same clan.

When a person belongs to a matrilineally traced kindred, position, possessions, and social identity pass from mother to daughter, and from a man to his sister's son; consequently, a boy looks to his mother's brother as the source of his inheritance. This is *matriliny,* once postulated by anthropologists during the early days of the science to be the earliest form of kinship reckoning. From the point of view of inheritance, then, and from the point of view of the matrilineal kindred, a husband is the merest appendage. He is the husband of the mother, but that is all; he is not a link in the transmission of the combined resources of the matrilineal kindred.[1]

Inasmuch as kinship is counted only in the maternal line, the children of any union are considered to be related solely to the mother and in no way to the father. It would appear (as it did to Malinow-

[1] For further discussion of the principles of matrilineal inheritance, see Chapter 8.

ski) that the Trobrianders are ignorant of the facts of procreation—as though sexual intercourse were unrelated to pregnancy.
This apparent ignorance of the paternal role in conception has been
much discussed also with respect to the Australians. But it is important to understand that these peoples are not describing a *biological* relationship, but rather a kind of *social* relationship. The
physiological aspect of kinship is unimportant and irrelevant.

Considering just the above characteristics of matrilineal inheritance, it is no wonder that some early anthropologists were led to
suppose that it could only have occurred because of a political dominance of women—that matriliny means *matriarchy*. In the Trobriands, as elsewhere in the primitive world, however, we find this
to be far from the actual situation. So far we have been referring to
the aspects of life which could be called social inheritance. There is
another part of day-to-day social life which is functional in the most
immediate sense, that of the nuclear family. Here we meet just the
opposite emphasis from the foregoing—a patriarchal principle, in
fact. Marriage establishes a new household in the community. Each
household is an economic unit, among other things, and the husband
is the dominant member of it. Men also hold the important offices
of the community, lineage, and clan. When these are heritable positions, they descend through females, to be sure, but the offices are
held by the brothers to the line of women; thus we see clearly that
matriliny is not matriarchy and that it can coexist with many patriarchal characteristics.

The terminology of kinship is widely generalized and closely related to residential units. A child, normally born in his father's village, refers to all the older men of his clan and village as *father* and
to their wives as *mother*; people of his own generation are equated
with siblings. The sisters of the village men, among whom are the
father's sister (the boy's potential mother-in-law), are married into
other villages, and their daughters are equated as possible wives
and their sons as possible brothers-in-law. All women of the father's
matrilineal lineage are referred to by the same term. The lack of
preciseness in categorizing relatives may be related to the fact that
there are no strict rules of avoidance and privileged familiarity
among different kinds of relatives. The strict etiquette governing
interpersonal relations is determined largely by a system of personal

rank instead, and this feature, which cross-cuts the usual kinship categories, may have subordinated and weakened them as guides to social behavior.

Individuals, whole villages, and clans are all ranked in terms of varying prestige. The rank of individuals is manifested by titles, the right to wear certain ornaments, and, most important of all, by forms of etiquette. This latter characteristic deserves special consideration, especially because it is an important culture trait among the several which closely resemble Polynesian and Indonesian customs.

A person of rank must always be in such a position that his head is higher than that of a person of lesser rank. For example, when commoners are present, the chief sits on a high platform. When a chief is standing, commoners in his presence bend low. When commoners have to walk past a chief who is seated, he must rise and they must bend; should he prefer to remain seated, they must crawl. There are also some sumptuary taboos, reminiscent again of Polynesia but generally absent from the rest of Melanesia. Certain kinds of foods and actions are forbidden to people of a particular rank, and the higher the rank the more stringent and numerous the prohibitions.

The position of women with respect to the inheritance of rank and privilege is similar to that of men. A woman of rank is treated by commoners with the same deference as would be accorded a man of the same rank. Women also take full part in many of the public ceremonies, a contrast to many primitive societies. Further evidence of the relatively high position of women is that their chastity is not insisted upon so rigorously as it is in many other societies.

The island as a whole is divided into four great clans with different grades of prestige. These in turn are divided into several subclans, or lineages, each of which is also ranked with respect to the others. A village headman is, as a rule, the eldest male of the most important of the subclans of the village. Some villages have many members from an important clan, and other villages may be predominantly composed of members of a lesser clan. This complicates the classification of individuals, for two persons from different villages might be of equally high rank within their respective villages but be unequal with respect to one another because of the inequality of their respective clans and lineages. When two strangers meet, it is necessary for them to establish the proper formalities to be used toward one another in accordance with their respective ranks. The first question to be settled is, therefore, which clans they belong to and, following this, their respective positions in the sub-clans and villages.

Some villages are larger than others and are higher in rank; so it appears that a feudal-like relation exists among them. This impression is strengthened by the fact that the lesser, or vassal, villages pay tribute to the leading village in the district. This payment of tribute, however, appears to be less a payment under duress through force or conquest and more a payment of kinship obligations. From each village subject to him, the headman of the ranking village takes a wife. This wife is always the sister or daughter of the chief of the subject village. Inasmuch as a wife's family has to supply the son-in-law with a large proportion of their produce at harvest-time, the ranking chief thereby receives a considerable amount of food. And because the wife is from the ranking family of the subject village, nearly the whole community is involved in this production.

In this way, a chief's prestige may be appraised in terms of wealth—the amount of produce deposited in his storehouse. But this is not his personal wealth, for he redistributes this store to pay for the many services he receives; he has to furnish food for the big feasts and ceremonies to which his far-flung in-laws must be invited. In this situation, again, the emphasis is not on the economic aspect as much as it is on reciprocal social obligations. In a sense, the chief's right to practice polygyny, forbidden to others, is the basis of his position and power.

Warfare seems to have occurred occasionally in the old days and may, perhaps, have led originally to the division of the society into ranked villages and districts. But the more recent battles, described to Malinowski by aged informants, seem not to have been oriented toward conquest. They were neither bloody nor of long duration, and were fought rather in a sporting manner. This is not to say that defeat was not a serious matter, for it meant destruction of the losers' villages. But after a year or so, a ceremony of reconciliation took place, and the former enemies together rebuilt the villages that had been destroyed. Unlike many other societies of Melanesia and Polynesia, the Trobianders did not practice head-hunting and cannibalism.

A chief has no formal mechanism for maintaining his rule—no police force or law courts to punish offenses. In the Trobriands, the power of a chief to punish individuals is largely an indirect one. Should anyone offend or defy him, the chief summons one of the sorcerers to kill the offender by black magic. This is done openly, which is perhaps an important reason for the efficacy of the magic. The people are genuinely afraid of magical spells and thus often doom themselves through an excess of fear.

Magical rituals and ceremonies pervade all of the activities of the Trobrianders. Even the simplest of the day-to-day activities, such as garden work, involve magic as a practical technique. Each village has its special garden magician, who inherits his position and special knowledge from his mother's brother. All phases of the garden work, from the burning and clearing of the land through the successive phases of planting, weeding, and harvesting, are inaugurated by the magician who presides over the ceremonies. He also magically assists the plants themselves to accomplish their successive phases of growth. In addition, the magician regulates the behavior of the garden workers, seeing that work is done on time and that no one shirks or lags behind the others. Fishing and canoe building, in fact all aspects of life, are similarly interwoven with magical practices.

Childbirth, too, is phrased as a supernatural event. New life—procreation—is believed to be caused by a spirit of an ancestor who, desiring reincarnation, finds his way back to the islands and into the womb of some woman of his clan and lineage. There is, however, no consciousness of personal identity; the spirit is of an unknown ancestor, known only as a clan and lineage member.

Malinowski relates in this regard the difficulties encountered by the Christian missionaries in the Trobriands. Christian morality is, of course, closely associated with the sacredness of the father-son relationship. This reflects the organization of European society, which is strongly patriarchal as well as patrilineal—the father is not only the undisputed master of the household but also the progenitor of the children. The Trobrianders, having an almost opposite notion, found the Christian dogma an absurdity. Unwilling to accept the idea of fatherhood, the natives held a strong dislike for the missionaries because of their "lies." One of Malinowski's informants, indeed, gave empirical evidence of the falsity of the notion that sexual intercourse had any relation to pregnancy by recounting that he had, on one occasion, been absent from home for over a year and, on returning, found his wife pregnant—final proof that only spirits could be the cause.

Once a child is born, however, the mother and the father share fully in giving it loving care. Every baby should have a father, according to the Trobriander. What, then, is a father, if they are unaware of his role in procreation? "If there is no father, there is no man to take the baby in his arms," they say. A baby needs a father, just as much as a mother, to aid in its care and upbringing. Here kinship is clearly demonstrated to be a sociological rather than a biological matter.

The true guardian of the child's interests in relation to the whole matrilineal kindred is the mother's brother. It is from him that the child takes guidance, and it is this uncle's position in society for which he is being trained. The mother's brother, in many respects, fills the role of the father as it is defined in a patrilineal society. But this brother cannot approach his sister, the child's mother, in one extremely important area of existence—sex. This means that he is debarred from being a part of her household. Thus the child in Trobriand society, or in other matrilineal society, has in a sense two fathers. The mother's husband is bound to the child by very strong ties of personal attachment based on the intimacy of the household. He is the loving father. The mother's brother, on the other hand, has great responsibilities in guiding and instructing the child. Who can say this is a bad arrangement? One of the most frequent psychological disturbances in a patrilineal society, such as that of modern Europe and America, is related to the ambivalence of a child's attitude toward the father, who, perforce, fills two roles: the guide, lawgiver, and punisher, on the one hand; and the loving parent who "takes it in his arms," on the other.

Only matrilineal kinsmen are considered entirely reliable; a husband is only a husband—not a blood kinsman of the children. Thus, when a pregnant woman is in her seventh or eighth month, she leaves her husband's hut and goes to her mother's or mother's brother's hut for safety until after delivery. When labor begins, all the males leave the hut armed with spears to guard the approaches against sorcerers who might come close enough to cast an evil spell which would make the delivery difficult. The husband, who has been summoned to help guard his wife, is actually controlled and ordered by the wife's male relatives.

Inside, the woman in labor is made to squat on a raised platform which has a small fire burning under it. The heat is to increase the flow of blood, which is believed to be helpful. Three days or more after the delivery the umbilical cord and the afterbirth are buried in the garden so as to "keep the child's mind on the garden." Mother and baby spend most of their time for about a month baking themselves on the heated platform. Later, after several ceremonies, they go home to the husband's hut, where they spend another month in nearly total seclusion. Not until the baby is weaned, about two years later, are conjugal sex relations reestablished.

Childhood is passed much as anywhere in the primitive world. Restriction on activity is largely absent, except for insistence on matters of etiquette. As the child approaches puberty, however, more and more freedom is acquired simply because he spends increasing amounts of time in the company of age mates. With adolescence, this community of children becomes almost an independent society, for at this time they quit the homes of their parents and begin to live almost exclusively in the communal huts provided for each sex. Part of the reason for this is the extremely rigid taboos which separate brothers and sisters. From puberty until death they may not approach one another and may not therefore continue to inhabit the same household. There is, incidentally, no ritual or magic connected with the beginnings of puberty; there are not even the restrictive taboos on menstruating girls so common in primitive society.

Except for the strict prohibition against incest, there is no restriction on sexual activity. A number of trial liaisons take place, often involving brief cohabitations in the bachelors' house, but sooner or later a fairly constant attachment forms between a couple, and sometimes, if certain other conditions are fulfilled, it leads to marriage. An attachment before marriage can never involve sharing a meal; married people eat together, unmarried couples do not. The Western custom of taking an unmarried girl out to dinner would be profoundly shocking to a Trobriander.

Despite the fact that sexual activity is freely indulged in before marriage, and even long-term attachments are countenanced, most youngsters desire marriage. An unmarried person, no matter how old he or she may be, has no household and lacks many privileges

associated with adulthood. (The word for *male adult* in the Trobriander's language is the same as the word for *married man.*) A
woman, of course, wishes to marry in order to have a household in
which children can be properly cared for. Men, in Trobriand society,
have an especially good reason to approve of marriage, for the
woman's kindred, as mentioned earlier, must provide him a considerable amount of yearly tribute—a sort of periodically renewed
dowry.

The most desirable marriage, from the point of view of the families involved, is a kind of cross-cousin marriage; a man should
marry the daughter of his father's sister. This is apparently desirable because of the conflicting interests in a matrilineal family. The
law of matrilineal succession contradicts a father's interest in passing on all possible privileges to his son. In this form of cross-cousin
marriage, however, the boy's father is simultaneously the maternal
uncle of the boy's wife, and, hence, her guardian, from whom she
receives her share of the heritable goods and privileges. Obviously,
this kind of marriage serves best a family of high rank, for by this
means the holdings are consolidated, but apparently other families
prefer it, too. Therefore, whenever there is a possibility for it,
such a marriage is always arranged as soon as possible. Typically,
this arrangement takes the form of betrothal of the couple while
they are still infants.

Many marriages cannot, of course, take this form, usually because there are no candidates of the proper relationship. There are
many considerations, however, which restrict the range of choices a
person can make even if a marriage had not been arranged. Persons
who belong to the same clan or subclan cannot marry, which auto-
matically excludes parallel cousins (father's brother's or mother's
sister's children). One may not marry a person from a different
political district. One should not marry into a lower social rank.

Hardly any rite or ceremony is associated with the beginnings of
marriage. A woman simply joins her husband in a house he has
taken in the village of his matrilineal kinsmen. Patrilocal residence[2]
usually carries certain social liabilities for the woman, for she finds
herself surrounded by her husband's relatives and must please them.

[2] This is patrilocal residence from the point of view of the children born of the
union. Some anthropologists would call it *avunculocal residence* because from the
point of view of the couple themselves they are living near or with the man's mother's
brother rather than his father.

But a Trobriand woman retains a considerable amount of independence. If her husband does not treat her well, she simply leaves him. The husband, of course, does not want this to happen, for he would then lose the renewable and considerable dowry his wife's kin give him.

Within the household the woman owns all the property and utensils pertaining to her own work; that is, she may dispose of them as she pleases, as the man may do with his own belongings—there is no household property held in common. The larger valuables, the house, garden land, trees, canoes, and livestock, are owned by the man. At the death of either one the spouse does not inherit anything of economic importance pertaining to the deceased. The goods go to the matrilineal kindred, just as do the privileges and rank mentioned earlier. The ownership of these two classes of goods is perhaps best thought of as an aspect of the familial division of labor. Men do the heavy outdoor work, with only the weeding of the gardens allocated to women. Men handle the trading, the manufacture of stone implements, and the woodcarving. Women do the cooking, the housework, and the weaving of mats, armlets, and belts.

The relations of husband and wife and of the two groups of their respective kindred involved in the marriage are most dramatically symbolized when the husband dies. The wife is the chief mourner, and she must play this role most ostentatiously and dramatically for many months—sometimes even for years. A widower is not required to make such an elaborate burden of his grief, but he puts on a considerable show.

A dead person's spirit is not aware of the various and complicated rituals carried out over the physical remains. At death the spirit goes to the timeless netherworld, where it takes up a happy existence entirely oblivious to the former life on earth. The mourning rituals are carried out quite frankly to impress the living observers. The matrilineal kinsmen of the deceased behave quite differently from the conjugal relatives. The matrilineal kin, who might be expected to feel the loss the most deeply, nevertheless do not display any sign of mourning in dress or ornamentation, and they are not allowed to come near the corpse, even to aid in the burial. The surviving spouse, the children, and the other relatives-in-law, however, must display their grief. They must shave their heads, cover their bodies with soot, and howl their grief as though in utmost despair. It is, then, the conjugal relatives who appear most bereaved rather than the matrilineal kinsmen.

A corpse is subjected to a great number of rites before it is finally laid to rest. First it is washed, anointed, and ornamented. The legs are tied together, and the arms are bound to the sides of the body. A row of female relatives-in-law then sit in the hut with the corpse lying on their knees, the widow or widower holding the head. Wailing goes on for hours while these women pet and fondle the corpse. Outside the hut other female relatives-in-law perform a slow rhythmic dance. The sons of the deceased meanwhile dig a grave, and after a few hours of mourning the body is wrapped in mats and buried. All night long a wake is held at the grave, the widow lying on the grave with her closest relatives around her. The other villagers and guests are beyond them, all wailing and singing disconsolately.

On the following evening the body is exhumed and examined for signs which will reveal what kind of sorcery was the cause of death. Sons of the deceased have the duty of removing many of the bones and cleaning them, after which they are kept as relics. The skull, if the deceased was a male, is made into a lime pot for the widow's use, and the jawbone becomes an ornament to hang from a necklace. The smaller long bones are used as lime spatulas. Certain intimate personal possessions of the deceased are distributed to the in-law relatives to be kept as mementos.

After this, what is left of the body is reburied, and the wake is over. The widow, who all this time has remained beside the corpse, now enters a small cage built inside her house, where she lives in the dark during her mourning period, forbidden to speak aloud, and accepting food and drink only as it is placed in her mouth by the kinsmen of the deceased, who are in constant surveillance of her. After a time, from six months to two years depending on the rank of the dead man, she is finally released and ceremonially washed, anointed and dressed in an especially gaudy grass skirt. She is then considered to be marriageable again.

The Trobrianders have none of the fears of ghosts so common in primitive societies. There is, however, a great concern with sorcerers and witches, and every death that does not result from an obviously natural cause is considered to be the consequence of their black magic. The ghosts of the dead do not influence human beings, either for better or for worse. Sometimes, in magical formulas, there may be an invocation to ancestral spirits, and in several rites they receive offerings. It is also believed that the ghosts return to their own villages once a year and take part in the big annual village festival, but there is no real intimacy or collaboration between living people and individualized spirits of the dead. Apparently the ghost affects human existence clearly on only one occasion, when the vague ancestral spark of life is transferred from the spirit world to the womb of a woman.

The most prevalent form of black magic is that of the *black sorcerer,* or *bwaga'u.* Nearly every village has one or two men dreaded for their supernatural power. This form of supernaturalism is quite distinct from religion; any person may become a practitioner by learning the formulas of the black art. One may acquire this knowledge from a father's teachings or by purchasing it from a maternal uncle.

A sorcerer kills in the following manner. First he must cast a light spell over the victim so that he will be indisposed enough to keep to his house. The next stage is somehow to approach the house in the dead of night in order to insert into the victim's fire a bundle of specially charmed herbs. The fumes from the herbs cause the victim to be seized by a deadly disease. Naturally, a sorcerer has a difficult task in accomplishing his design, for any indisposed person is alert to prevent it. Male relatives and friends guard all the approaches to the hut during an illness, and a friendly bwaga'u is usually hired to make counterspells against any attempt on the life of the sick man.

A sorcerer thus frustrated can turn to his last resort, the rite of the pointing bone. First, he and an accomplice or two go to a remote secret spot, where they boil up a concoction of special herbs in coconut oil. The herbs are then wrapped around the sharp pointing bone and deadly incantations are chanted over it. Then the sorcerer steals into the village and waits in hiding until he sees his victim. Aiming the bone at him, the sorcerer violently stabs and twists the bone as though to make a deep wound. It is believed that this ritual will never fail to kill unless the victim is sufficiently aware of his danger to have hired a more powerful magician to counteract it.

The bwaga'u, while a frequent danger, is not the only source of fear, death, and disease. All very sudden and violent diseases are assumed to have been caused by the flying witches, who come from faraway localities in the dead of night to pounce upon a person and remove some of his vital organs, such as the brains, lungs, or heart. The victim will die shortly, unless another witch can be prevailed upon to discover and restore the missing parts. Epidemic diseases are caused by certain nonhuman beings which come from the south. They are invisible as they march through a village striking all persons who are abroad at the time. Certain light illnesses may be caused by the *tokway,* a wood sprite, which is not malevolent so much as mischievous, stealing food and playing tricks.

Another class of beings are those culture heroes who existed in the past and who, according to present-day myths, are responsible for the origins of particular aspects of Trobriand culture. Each·of the subclans was created by a separate ancestress who came out of the underworld through a hole in the ground, usually at a spot located near the largest concentration of members of the group. It is believed, also, that the subclans belong to one or another of the four major clans because of the common relationship they have to a certain plant or animal species; i.e., the clans are totemic.

The practice of agriculture itself was a gift from a mythological being, *Tudava.* In one tale this hero was the first man to emerge from the ground, but others followed him and to each he assigned a totem. There was no land except Kiriwina, and so Tudava threw stones into the sea and other islands were brought into being. Tudava taught some people the magic of making gardens, and others to fish and to exchange the fish for garden produce. He taught the people to cook and to eat fish, oppossums, and pigs, but to stop eating rats, snakes, and iguanas. Similar stories explain the origin of characteristics of the region. These stories do not involve gods who are to be worshiped or placated, or who can, in short, intervene in present affairs. The myths are merely explanatory and often rationalizations of some contemporary state of affairs.

In the world view of the Trobrianders, the origin myths are not history in our sense of the word. In fact, the Trobriander is distinctly unhistorical in his cosmogony. Agriculture, magic, law, the people themselves, islands—everything—came into being once, full-blown, and that is the way they *are.* The Trobriander, like so many primitive peoples, does not view phenomena as being in a process of change through time. A being is changeless; therefore, the Trobriand language has no word for *to be* or *to become*. The English language, on the other hand, suggests that we think in terms of temporality and place things in terms of a temporally developing sequence. Allied with this consciousness of chronological sequence, we have our notions of causality; the temporal relatedness of events leads us to seek antecedents and consequences. The Trobriander states the essence of the thing itself. Dorothy Lee pointed out that the persistent question "why" of our younger children would probably be matched in the Trobriands by the question "what."[3]

Trobriand culture had, of course, no fundamental changes over a very long period of time, which may be why the conception of historical change was so foreign to them. Even today, the great shocks of contact with Western civilization, which have so profoundly altered or destroyed most of the primitive cultures of the world, have not destroyed the Trobrianders' age-old way of life. The depopulation so widespread in Melanesia has not affected the Trobrianders to any great extent, and they still number about 8500 persons, as compared to a count of 8000 made in 1906-1907.

Methodist and Roman Catholic missions have taught many of the people to read and write, but the modern world economy has not affected them profoundly; so there apparently has been as yet no drastic cultural breakdown. The islands are governed by an Australian magistrate, but the rule is locally quite indirect, through the chiefs, which tends to preserve, if not enhance, their power. The kula trade was continuing as of 1936, and chiefs were still concerned with making their garden magic. The government prohibited malicious magic, however, which prevented the chiefs from using sorcerers as a form of political control. Several of the old ceremonies, especially those which make use of the bones of dead relatives, have been given up as Christian ideas have been accepted by more of the people.

The Japanese occupied the Islands during World War II, but no battles were fought there. There is no available account of what the more recent acculturation has been.[4]

[3] D. M. Lee, "Being and Value in Primitive Culture," *The Journal of Philosophy,* Vol. 46, No. 13, 1949.
[4] H. A. Powell completed a field study of the Trobriands in 1952, but his full work is still unpublished.

FURTHER READINGS

Austen, L., "Cultural Changes in Kiriwina," *Oceania,* Vol. 16, 1945.

Belshaw, C. S., *Changing Melanesia,* Oxford, 1954.

Codrington, R. H., *The Melanesians,* London, 1891.

Elkin, A. P., *Social Anthropology in Melanesia,* London and New York, 1953.

Hogbin, H. I., "The Trobriand Islands, 1945," *Man,* Vol. 46, No. 67, 1946.

Keesing, F. M., *The South Seas in the Modern World,* New York, 1941; rev. 1945.

Lee, D. M., "Being and Value in Primitive Culture," *The Journal of Philosophy,* Vol. 46, No. 13, 1949.

Malinowski, B., *Argonauts of the Western Pacific,* London, 1922.

Malinowski, B., *Crime and Custom in Savage Society,* London and New York, 1926.

Malinowski, B., *The Sexual Life of Savages,* London, 1929.

Malinowski, B., *Coral Gardens and Their Magic,* London and New York, 1935, 2 vols.

Oliver, D. L., *The Pacific Islands,* Cambridge, 1951.

Powell, H. A., "Competitive Leadership in Trobriand Political Organization," *Journal of the Royal Anthropological Institute,* Vol. 90, Pt. 1, 1960.

Robson, R. W., *The Pacific Islands Handbook: 1944,* American ed., New York, 1945 (Australian eds. titled *Pacific Islands Year Book*).

Seligmann, C. G., *The Melanesians of British New Guinea,* Cambridge, 1910.

Sider, K. B., "Affinity and the Role of the Father in the Trobriands," *Southwestern Journal of Anthropology,* Vol. 23, No. 1, 1967.

12

The Tahitians of Polynesia

The romantic South Seas of fiction, cinema, and daydreams typically refers to the great triangle of Pacific islands called Polynesia ("many islands"). From the era of the first great explorer-navigators of the seventeenth and eighteenth centuries to today, the gemlike islands, the nearly perfect climate, and above all the handsome, laughing natives, living an apparently carefree Eden-like existence, have intrigued all observers. The island of Tahiti, one of the Society Islands near the center of the far-flung Polynesian group, was so beautiful, the natives were so remarkably hospitable, and the women were so captivating that the sailors of the famous *Bounty,* under Lieutenant Bligh, were inspired to mutiny rather than continue their long voyage. Tahiti is also famous as the refuge of the distinguished French painter, Paul Gauguin, and a number of others have followed since.

The Polynesian islands are dispersed over a huge area of the Pacific Ocean. From the Hawaiian Islands at the northern apex to New Zealand in the south is a distance of about 5000 miles, and the greatest east-west distance is over 3,000 miles. The major island groupings are the Hawaiian, Ellice, Samoan, Tongan,

Cook, Society, Tuamotuan, Marquesan, and New Zealand. Of isolated islands, the most important are Easter Island and Niue. There are also a great many tiny islands. With the exception of New Zealand, which is a much larger land mass than the others, and in a more temperate climate, the various larger groups do not greatly differ geographically from one another. Within some groups, however, there are significant variations.

The greatest difference among the islands is between the large *high islands,* which are of volcanic origin, and the *low islands,* which are tiny coral formations. Many of the major island groups include both. It was on the high islands, however, where most of the population of Polynesia lived, that the classic Polynesian culture was manifested. The low islands were peopled by groups from nearby high islands, but because the islands were small and the subsistence was more limited, they lacked several of the usual features of high-island culture.

Courtesy, The American Museum of Natural History

The high islands are rugged, eroded remnants of great volcanic cones. There is often very little level land in the interior, but on some islands, such as Tahiti, there are coastal flats and broad river estuaries. The arable land is very rich; the soil is weathered out of the volcanic rock, and is well covered with a dense tropical growth. Rainfall is plentiful on the high islands, and greater than on the coral atolls, because the interior peaks are usually so high that they can push the rain-bearing winds upward to cooler altitudes, causing the precipitation on the land to be much greater than at sea. Voyagers often can recognize the presence of a distant high island by the clouds hovering over it. The climate of most of Polynesia is tropical, but the heat is not particularly oppressive. The average temperature on Tahiti is 77°, with a yearly range of 69°–84°.

Courtesy, The American Museum of Natural History

The Polynesian population is often described as a blend of at least three racial types, Caucasoid, Mongoloid, and Negroid. Whatever the mixture, however, Polynesians are quite homogeneous in physical traits. In general, they are light brown in color, tall, beardless, with wavy brown hair and brown eyes, and a facial configuration suggestive of the Mediterranean white type. The Polynesian language is also relatively homogeneous over the entire triangle of islands, and the physical type is nearly coterminous with the language type. The near congruence of physical type and language, and the fact that but little local differentiation in either has occurred, suggest that their dispersal over the great geographic range of the islands was relatively recent.

The prehistory of the Polynesians has long been a fascinating problem, and many hypotheses have been suggested regarding their original provenience. Thor Heyerdahl has argued that Polynesia was populated from the New World. His intrepid raft voyage from Peru to Tuamotu showed that contact *could* have been made from the Americas. But it does not demonstrate in a way convincing to anthropologists specializing in Polynesian researches that any substantial part of the population of Polynesia actually did come from the New World, or that any important cultural exchange was made in that way.

A great body of evidence of several kinds links Polynesians and their culture to Asia, most probably to the southeastern part. The mixed Polynesian physical type could be accounted for by the presence in southeast Asia of a variety of racial groups. Even more significantly, the language affinities of Polynesian are with Malayan; they belong together in the Malayo-Polynesian language family. Most conclusive of all is the fact that the great majority of the distinctive culture traits of Polynesia have their counterparts in Indonesia. Some investigators believe that even the actual waves of migration and their routes can be established. These reconstructions depend heavily on the genealogies and legends of the Polynesians themselves. But certainly most anthropologists would agree now on the following minimal conclusions: the settling of Polynesia occurred recently, probably not more than 2000 years ago and perhaps less; the Polynesians came from some part of Indonesia; the Society Islands were one of the earliest settlements in central and eastern Polynesia, and here the characteristic Polynesian cultural patterns emerged and were elaborated out of the basic Indonesian traits; and from central Polynesia the people spread outward from island to island until they occupied such distant points as Hawaii, the Marquesas and Easter Island, and New Zealand.

Most of the islands of the Society group in central Polynesia are high islands, although there are a few small coral islets. The total land area is about 600 square miles.[1] Tahiti, the largest island, is about 35 miles long and half as wide at its greatest breadth. Its twin volcanic peaks are over 7000 feet high, and the island is covered with a dense growth of grasses, ferns, and trees. Most of the shoreline is protected by an outer coral reef, creating a beautiful calm lagoon. The people live mostly on the coastal flatlands and for short distances up the stream valleys. At the time of its discovery by Europeans, Tahiti had a population of about 100,000 people.

The native flora and fauna of all the Polynesian islands, except New Zealand, were so meager in variety and utility that a purely indigenous civilization could not have developed very far. There were no edible wild plants, with the possible exception of the pan-

---

[1] O. W. Freeman (ed.), *Geography of the Pacific,* New York, 1951, p. 367.

danus, very few birds, and no other game. The prolific sea was the only natural resource rich in food. The basic domesticated foods of the Polynesians were brought with them from Indonesia: coconut palms, breadfruit trees, taro, yams, sweet potatoes,[2] bananas and plantains, sugar cane, and the two domestic animals, the pig and the chicken.

As elsewhere in Polynesia, except inland New Zealand, sea food is by far the most important natural resource exploited. The fishing technology is highly diversified and elaborated; complicated weirs, basketry traps, many forms of nets and seines, fish poisons, harpoons with detachable heads, and many kinds of hooks and lines are used. Polynesians of both sexes are excellent swimmers. Women dive for slow-moving crabs and other shellfish, and even capture the octopus by inducing it to twine its tentacles around a stick so that it can be drawn out of the water. Men and boys spend a great deal of time diving to greath depths for the pearl oysters, the flesh of which is used for food and the shell for many kinds of implements and ornaments.

The coconut palm is the most versatile domesticated plant. The meat from mature coconuts is a nourishing food, and also yields an oil which is used in cooking and as an ointment. The liquid, or milk, of the young nuts is a delicious and refreshing drink. Palm leaves are used as thatch, and the fiber for cordage and for the manufacture of mats and baskets. The plants grow well, even on poor soil, and need no care except during the first few years of growth, when they must be fenced against pigs.

Breadfruit is the most important single food in Tahiti. The breadfruit tree begins to bear its large, globular fruit at about five years of age and may continue to yield for 40 or 50 years with little care. The fruit is plentiful and nutritious, but probably its greatest value is the fact that it stores well, whereas most other Polynesian staples do not. In fact, under the Polynesian method of storage, breadfruit will keep almost indefinitely, and the people particularly relish the older, fuller-flavored stock. At the height of the ripening season, great piles of the fruit are roasted whole or baked in great stone ovens, after which it is placed in large

---

[2] According to some authorities, the sweet potato was native only to the Americas, and therefore was either introduced into Polynesia by early European seafarers or by Polynesian contacts with natives of the New World.

leaf-lined pits and covered over. The breadfruit tree also provides valuable timber for canoes and houses.

The Tahitians are excellent farmers and make very efficient use of the small amount of arable land for their gardens by terracing hillsides, diverting streams for irrigation where necessary, and enriching the soil by various means. The cultivated plants are mostly the root crops, taro, yams, and sweet potatoes, along with bananas and plantains, sugar cane, and gourds. A sharpened digging stick is the primary agricultural implement. The main source of protein aside from sea food is pork, and pigs are carefully fed and tended. Chickens are eaten, but the eggs are not. Dogs, kept as pets, are also occasionally used as food.

A variety of pepper tree is planted along the streams for the roots, which are used to make kava, a slightly intoxicating drink which tastes like soapy water. The roots are chewed by young girls and then placed in a large container. Water is added, and the mixture is strained. The saliva releases an alkaloid from which the drink derives its mild potency.

Another useful tree, the paper mulberry, is cultivated for its inner bark from which is made the famous bark cloth, or *tapa*. Overlapping pieces of bark are beaten together with a striated club to form a light paperlike material which is surprisingly strong, although it is not water-resistant. All of the Polynesians decorate it by painting and stamping it with dye. There is no fiber suitable for weaving, but mats are plaited from the coarse pandanus fiber and from coconut fiber. Elaborate ceremonial cloaks are made of feathers by securing the quills in the knots of netting.

Tahitian technology is complex, even though it is limited by the lack of certain resources on the island. There are no metals, and so all tools are made of shell, stone, or wood, and there is no clay for pottery. There are many specialized kinds of woodworking tools. Adzes of ground stone and shell, socketed and hafted, are of many sizes and types. The pump drill is one of the more ingenious Polynesian contrivances. It consists of a straight shaft tipped with a drill point of hard stone or bone. The shaft passes through a heavy horizontal disk of wood or stone which acts as a fly wheel, and at the top of the shaft cords are fastened which are wrapped around the shaft and tied to each end of a short wooden bar. As the bar is pulled downward, the cords unwrap, causing the shaft to revolve.

The flywheel keeps the shaft revolving so that the cords will wrap around it again. A light rhythmic pumping motion against the bar is all that is needed to keep the drill spinning. Other carpenters' tools include gouges, chisels, knives, rasps, and files.

Boats and canoes are the most skillful works of the carpenters. Small dugout canoes, hollowed from a single log and equipped with an outrigger, and often with mat sails, are used for local voyages. More seaworthy vessels are made by building a deck over two canoes. Vessels as much as 100 feet long are made by fitting planks together and caulking the seams. Canoe building is in the hands of a special class of artisans who employ a great deal of ritual and prayer in their work. So much prestige, as well as ceremony, accrues to these craftsmen that as a group they have been likened to a priesthood and to a guild.

The Polynesians have no mechanical navigational devices, but depend solely on their knowledge of astronomy and geography. They know all of the planets and fixed stars, and they reached the conclusion that the world is round long before contact with Europeans.

Housebuilding, like boatbuilding, is a specialized craft in the Society Islands. The dwellings of the chiefs are built by these professional craftsmen, and are frequently very large and ornate. One house in Tahiti is 397 feet long. Most of the people build their own houses, which are small, square, and relatively undistinguished. Typically, houses are constructed by erecting heavy corner posts and ridgepoles, fitted into notches. Rafters and side poles are put in place and thatched with pandanus or coconut leaves. Doorways are closed with trellised bamboo cane. An inner lining of coconut mats or of tapa cloth is used in a chief's house. The area for several yards around a house is leveled and covered with pebbles, coral, or flagstone.

Household furnishings are meager, for much of the domestic life, such as cooking, takes place out of doors or in a cooking shed. Occasionally the head of a family sits on a stool, but people usually sit cross-legged on the floor. Bundles of clothing are hung from a sort of clothes tree. Beds are merely mats thrown down at night, and pillows are slightly concave wooden blocks. Despite this comfortless arrangement, the Polynesians are famous sleepers; some missionaries have regretfully noted men sleeping as much as 15 or 16 hours without awakening.

Cooking is done mainly in an earth oven, a stone-lined pit in which a fire is burned for some time before the food is lowered into place and covered with leaves and earth. The only other important cooking method is stone boiling. Heated stones are dropped into a waterproofed basket or wooden bowl to make the water boil. This device is a common one throughout the world where pottery or other fireproof containers are absent. Fish and shellfish are usually eaten raw, but all meat and vegetable foods are cooked. Vegetables are usually pounded into a paste and are often mixed with coconut milk or oil. Food for men is prepared by men; women and children eat separately, and their food is cooked by women.

Ordinarily, the people take two meals a day. The first is a light one eaten in the morning, unceremoniously and whenever the individual wants it. The heavy dinner is always at night. Polynesians are prodigious eaters; their performances at community feasts have astounded Europeans. Food is served on leaves or in carved wooden bowls and coconut shells, and is eaten with the fingers.

Tahitians have little clothing. Men wear a loincloth and women a kilt, both usually made of tapa cloth. Feather cloaks are worn only on special occasions. The art of body decoration, however, is highly elaborated. Tattooing is universal in Polynesia, although it varies in style from place to place. In the Society Islands men are heavily tattooed, sometimes over the whole body except the face, while women usually are tattooed only on the hands and feet. The designs are made by driving carbon into the skin with a sharp bone tool.

Hairdressing varies a great deal in Polynesia, but everywhere it is an important form of personal decoration. In the Society Islands women bob their hair in a simple style, but men may braid their long hair into buns or pigtails, or shave one part of the head, making varied and complicated coiffures. On some occasions, as when preparing for war, the men of Tahiti wear tall, ornate headdresses of dyed feathers. Nearly always, men and women wear wreaths of flowers around their necks and often place single flowers in their hair or over one ear. Necklaces of shell or teeth and semicircular breastplates of fiber overlaid with feathers and pearl shell are also worn. Both men and women spend much time in bathing, anointing and perfuming themselves, and caring for and decorating their hair.

Considerable attention is given also to caring for the beauty of the habitation areas. House interiors and immediate surroundings are kept very clean by frequent sweeping. Paths and assembly areas are pebbled and kept free of debris. The dwellings of chiefs and the assembly houses are elaborately ornamented, and at intervals over the whole locality of dispersed settlement are luxuriant growths of flowers and shrubs.

The basic domestic unit of Tahitian society is an enlarged or extended family, frequently composed of two or three brothers and their wives and children. A number of these households scattered over a given territory are usually related in the patrilineal line, thus forming a local lineage. Descent may be traced from both the mother's and the father's patrilineal kindred, and it is kept account of for many generations, inasmuch as social status, privileges, and land-use rights are acquired only through inheritance. Usually a person's position depends on the rank inherited from his male ancestors, but sometimes, when a mother or more remote female ancestor comes from a family line of higher rank than his father's, an individual may bolster his claim by citing this relationship. It is expected, however, that marriages will be contracted between persons of equal status; thus there would normally be no need for marking out both descent lines in order to validate a particular status.

All individuals in Tahiti occupy a single pigeonhole of status. Consequently a father can pass on his rank and responsibilities to only one son—the position can be occupied by no more than one incumbent. The widespread Polynesian emphasis on primogeniture is related to this fact.[3] The first-born son at full maturity has the adult responsibility over his brothers and sisters, and is accorded obedience and deference by them. The second son is a sort of deputy and takes the position should his older brother be absent or die, up to the time when the older brother's first-born son is old enough to succeed to it. The youngest son in a large family is a woebegone figure, for he has little chance for distinction in the line of succession; his status will always be lower than that of his older brothers as long as they live.

In any large family almost anywhere a hierarchy becomes established among the brothers and sisters in the sense that the older ones have some authority over the younger. But this kind of social ordering among the group of brothers and sisters is elaborate and

[3] A further discussion of this practice may be found in Chapter 10.

intricate in Tahiti, and it establishes the position of the individual for his whole life and in relation to the entire body of related families. Each individual family, and even a line of descent, within a lineage holds a rank with reference to all others depending on its origin and position relative to the main line of descent. Descent through a line of first-borns is a complete recapitulation in each generation of all of the original power and status of the founder of the lineage, with a sort of compounding of status the further back it can be traced.

In this kind of society, the ability to recount an extensive genealogy is of great importance, and people of high status can trace their ancestors as far back as 50 generations. The main line of descent and each branch are named, and a first-born son takes his name from his father when he succeeds to his father's position. A subsidiary personal name allows individuals in a line of descent to be identified in each generation. This system of names or titles is exactly like that of the European nobility, and the titles are always evocative of specific status privileges, duties, and responsibilities.

The subdivisions of rank are a continuous gradation from top to bottom, but it is conventional to describe the society as being composed essentially of three grades of people. The immediate families of the chiefs of the paramount lineages in the larger districts are called the *Ari'i,* the heads of lesser lineages and their families are of an intermediate group called *Ra'atira.* The remainder of the population are classed as *Manahune.* It should not be overlooked, however, that Tahitian communities are a kindred; the social differences among them are like differentiations within a familial system. The three-class society of feudal Europe, with which Polynesian society is sometimes equated, was clearly demarked into classes to each of which whole families belonged. A closer parallel to Polynesia would be the social differences among branches of interrelated noble families of Europe, specifically excluding the middle and lower classes.

Social rank in Tahiti embodies simultaneously economic, political, and religious powers—in short, a theocratic principle. A kind of spiritual power or force called *mana* is possessed by all individuals, but in varying degrees, corresponding to rank. An *Ari'i* possesses a great amount of this sacred power, because he is closer to the ancestral gods who are the source of it, and lower ranks have relatively less. Mana is thought of as a contagious power which could be harmful if passed to a weaker, less highly endowed person. The concept of taboo, an elaborate series of *thou shalt nots,* was in origin essentially a prohibition of contact between those with more mana and those with less.

Some of the early missionaries in Tahiti regarded Tahitian chiefs as tyrannical and despotic after witnessing the considerable deference their subjects offered them, and after noting that the people also apparently paid their chiefs a sort of tribute. A fuller consideration of the situation suggests, however, that, inasmuch as the deference is religiously inspired, *despotic* is therefore not the proper term. Similarly, the so-called tributes could perhaps more accurately be classed as offerings (many of them are literally first fruits) rather than as a regularized tax, particularly because the great bulk of the gifts are soon redistributed to the people.

There is no market exchange among the people of Tahiti. The gifts to the chief, and from lower chiefs to higher chiefs, can be seen as a means by which an exchange of goods is accomplished. The chiefs accumulate the surplus of products given them and then redistribute it at great feasts. Some early writers, noting this particular feature of Tahitian life, described the society as communistic. The other observers, who called attention to exploitation by the chiefs, were apparently viewing the accumulating aspect of the process rather than the redistribution. It seems that the society cannot be accurately generalized as either exploitative or communistic; it is something else—a system wholly new to the experience of Europeans.

The early European visitors were bothered by another Tahitian custom—it appeared that the natives gave away their children with great frequency. This turns out on analysis to be a very important social phenomenon, in its own way redressing economic inequalities. Inasmuch as all land, as well as statuses, is strictly inherited, there is no way to maintain balance and stability in the system unless all families continue to be of an equal size through time. But a normal tendency is for some lineages to proliferate and some others to diminish in size, circumstances which, in the absence of a frontier or idle land, would result in new and uncontrolled economic differentiations. Unless the land itself is subdivided and redistributed periodically, as it is in many primitive agricultural societies, control of family size is the only means of preserving a *status quo* in the lineage throughout the passing generations. The Tahitians have practiced infanticide to some extent in order to control population size, but more usually have passed children from families which are too large to those which are too small. An adopted child receives his title and share of land from his foster family, just as though he were their own child, despite the fact that he may spend considerable time visiting the members of his original family.

It is not surprising that the religion reflects the important social, economic, and political role of inheritance and genealogy by emphasizing ancestor worship. In Tahiti, each family has its own sacred place dedicated to the ancestors, and each larger group of affiliated families also has its *marae,* as this spot is called. Typically, it is an open area with a low stone wall around it, with a raised section, or sometimes a small pyramid, at one end. The marae is a mortuary and also an assembly place for religious ceremonies.

An interesting representation of the social system is found in the marae. Here is laid a ring of stone seats, each inherited by the various chiefs, who sit on them at the religious assemblies, arranged in the order of social importance and sanctity. In the early days of the expansion of Tahitian society, kinship groups which emigrated to another place took with them the stone of their own leader from the ancestral marae to establish a new one where they settled. The position of the stone in the original marae was retained, however, so that the precise social position of a new lineage settlement relative to the original families was never lost. Thus, by visible objective means, the whole genealogical system is graphically symbolized, no matter how widely separated in space the component lineages become.

In the days of expansion, there had apparently been a normal tendency for the younger brothers of chiefs to move to new places and begin new communities, so that more recently settled localities had less distinguished social positions than the older society, and likewise the newer maraes had less sanctity than the parent ones. The fact that the largest marae on the nearby island of Raiatea is considered more sacred than any on Tahiti suggests the possibility that the earliest settlement in central Polynesia may have been established there.

Patterns of etiquette and general social conduct, tied as they are to the rank system and to religion, are exceedingly intricate. The ranking of individuals is so overriding a principle that kinship terms of the generalizing kind so typically a part of the etiquette of personal address in the primitive world are not in use in Polynesia—personal, honorific titles are used instead. The recognized categories of relatives are comparatively simplified. All cousins, whether cross or parallel, are classed under the same designation as siblings. The relatives in the generations above and below are referred to similarly by single general terms. Distinctions of generation, sex, and relative age are the only significant features of the classification of kindred, but the importance of primogeniture and the inheritance of rank is reflected by the use of titles instead of kinship terms in direct address.

Possibly the best-known feature of social conduct in Polynesia is associated with the idea of taboo. All of the people have sumptuary prohibitions associated with their ranks. At mealtimes, for example, lower ranks cannot eat with higher ranks (and on some of the Polynesian islands are not even permitted to observe persons of higher rank eating), and because men are of more sanctity than women and children, they are required to eat separately. Many ordinary foods are tabooed to women and children, as well, and certain special foods are tabooed for particular ranks. The highest ranking *Ari'i* is so sacred that anything he uses becomes tabooed, and any food he touches is a deadly poison for those below him in rank. On some Polynesian islands this complexity is solved by keeping the highest chief almost completely inactive. He is carried on a litter, bathed and fed by an attendant, and in western Polynesia he is not even allowed to speak in public—an *orator chief* (often his younger brother) speaks for him. A frequent custom, too, is for the highest chiefs to speak with an archaic vocabulary of words tabooed to commoners. This language could be called a religious vocabulary, as well, as it is frequently the language of the liturgies.

The social ordering within a local kinship group, made coherent and stable by the genealogical system, is matched by a wider intercommunity, and even interisland, order, based on more tenuous but essentially similar arrangements. It is possible, however, that in the Society Islands, before the coming of Europeans, this pattern was not stable, inasmuch as warfare seems to have frequently altered the social hierarchy. Large-scale warfare involving coordinated land and naval forces sometimes occurred between whole island groups, and tributary relations were frequently set up which put the vanquished in an inferior political and economic position. In Hawaii, permanent conquests of this sort resulted in a somewhat stratified society, inasmuch as the lineage of the conquering group became superior to the lineage of the conquered. There is no clear evidence that this occurred often in Tahiti, but it must be considered a possible result of the warfare.

Weapons of war are slings, javelins, thrusting spears, short wooden swords, and clubs of various types, often intricately carved and sometimes with a serrated or toothed cutting edge. The bow and arrow are known in Polynesia, and often used in games and in hunting, but not widely used in war. Defensive armor, such as shields and helmets, is not used, but the Tahitians sometimes encase a few of their warriors in layers of cord network. Fortified villages are not normally used in Polynesia except in New Zealand, where the Maori surround their villages with moats and stockades, but the Tahitians build refuges where they can retire to withstand a siege. The Tahitians sometimes keep war captives as hostiges and as drudge slaves. Cannibalism practiced in connection with slain enemies is widespread in Polynesia; but if our information is accurate, the Tahitians are horrified at such an idea, although they do make sacrifices of captives in religious rituals.

A sort of moral equivalent of war occurs in the practice of competitive athletics. Nearly all games are aggressively conducted, and some are quite dangerous. A sort of soccer football is popular in Tahiti, and sometimes whole districts oppose one another. A group sport something like shinny is also played. There are individual sports of many kinds, wrestling, bare-fisted boxing, foot races, and swimming races being most popular in that order. Archery contests in Tahiti are a curious mixture of sport and sacred ritual. The game is simply shooting for distance, but the ritual accompaniments are elaborate, involving ceremonies in the temple, a special ceremonial costume, and purifying rites after the contest.

Other popular diversions are cockfights accompanied by wagering, many kinds of children's games, and, above all, music and dancing. All Polynesians are particularly fond of music and have elaborated this art far beyond most other primitive peoples. Large and small drums, flutes, hand clapping, and voice are the usual musical accompaniments of the dance in Tahiti. The Hawaiians and Tahitians have developed vocal music to an unusually high art, and even have choruses which sing parts. Modern Hawaiian music is heavily Euro-peanized, however, and the ukulele and "Hawaiian" guitar are of Portuguese origin.

The dance is usually the graceful *hura* (hula), performed by chiefs' daughters who are specially trained in the art. The costumes are composed of an intricately pleated long skirt, and of feathers fixed to the dancers' fingers. Dancing performances are often part of a fuller variety performance which includes pantomimes and dra-matic skits. As in much of oriental Asia, men are the singers and in-strumentalists, and the only actors, even for female parts.

Some public performances are the work of a specialized traveling entertainment troupe, the *Ariori* society. This is a religious cult group whose patron is Oro, the God of War, in whose name plays, dances, songs, and poems are made. Far from being religious in the Euro-pean moral sense, however, this group is associated with obscenity, sexual license, and the general inversion of all taboos. Once the Ariori arrive at the local Ariori house, it is as though a sort of Mardi Gras had begun. The players are beyond all restriction and make fun of the most serious social rules. They are the perpetual, irresponsible adolescents, at whatever age, for they own no property and have no children. Although it is not known who is eligible for membership, or exactly how one may become a member of the Ariori group, it is apparent that it is frequently a refuge for younger sons of large families.

Some of the earliest missionaries in the Society Islands assumed that the Ariori society was primarily addicted to sexual license and birth control. And inasmuch as they had also witnessed the giving away of children, it was widely believed that the islanders did not feel parental affection. Actually, as in other primitive societies, babies are usually considered a great blessing, and children are the objects of much attentive love.

The birth of a child is accompanied by many ritual observances by family members, and if the baby is of high rank, a commensurate amount of public ceremony is performed. Ordinarily a priest-doctor presides at the delivery, which is attended by a crowd of relatives. The afterbirth is buried near the marae, and the umbilical cord (the essence of the child) is placed in a small box and buried in a cham-ber in the marae. The naming ceremony at the marae is one of the high points in the ceremonial proceedings if the baby is a boy of high rank.

A child spends most of its time with other children, and the first years are relatively carefree. As a child grows older, more and more tasks are assigned, and also more adult-like responsibility in general social conduct is expected. First-born boys of upper-ranking families are given special training, for they are to inherit the full prerogatives of the family's position. Part of this training is a natural result of being the eldest son, for he has nearly complete responsibility over all the other children. Some of his instruction is by precept; he is drilled in a nearly feudal-like code of honor, in *noblesse oblige,* dignity, courtesy, pride, and generosity. The higher the rank, the more stringent is this training.

A boy's puberty, or coming of age, is ceremonialized by making an incision in the foreskin of the penis. A feast is then given during which the food taboo is imposed. Never again can the boy eat food cooked by women, nor can he eat in the company of women. Tattooing is the general sign of the beginning of adolescent status for both boys and girls.

Children are often betrothed in infancy, especially if they are of high rank, but marriage is normally postponed until late adolescence, or even later for men. The years between puberty and marriage are a comparatively carefree time of experimental love affairs. Lower-ranking individuals have some freedom in choosing a mate, because so little inheritance is involved, but marriage between close relatives is discouraged. At higher ranks the number of social equals is more limited, and cousin marriage is frequent.

The marriage celebration consists of a great feast, accompanied by exchange of gifts, and songs and dancing. After that the major preoccupation is the birth of the first boy, and insuring that he will have the proper qualities for his position. A chief and his wife are secluded and relieved of all duties, given special fattening foods, and anointed and bathed, while temple rites are performed to aid in the conception of the first-born son.

Marriages are easily dissolved, especially among commoners. After divorces, children remain with the mother or are adopted by other families. Families are not large; if adoption cannot function to limit sufficiently the number of children in a household, the family resorts to abortion or infanticide.

At death, babies and adults of low status are buried rather unceremoniously. The bodies of chiefs, on the other hand, are preserved as long as possible in a specially built shelter. There is an attempt at mummification, for the viscera and brains are removed and the skin oiled and baked in the sun. After the body has disintegrated, the skull is kept in the marae. Mourning is noisy and lasts for a long time, and the close relatives frequently wound themselves with knives. The chief's wife lies beside his body for a time, perhaps as a symbolic survival of a more ancient custom of killing the widow. The priest calls upon the dead man's soul to be satisfied in the afterworld and not to come back to his loved ones. If the deceased is an important chief, all activity in his district is tabooed for several days while his soul begins its journey.

It is believed that the seat of the soul, and of thought, perception, and emotions, is in the bowels. At death, the soul comes out of the mouth or nostrils and goes away. According to some stories, the soul goes to a paradise or a homeland of the ancestors somewhere in the west.

The details of cosmological belief vary greatly in Polynesia, but all have certain common, general elements. The creation myths are all of the sort called *evolutionary,* and the various gods have the same names, although the specific acts attributed to them are distinctive among the several island groups. Even among the Tahitians alone, there are several different creation myths. As a rule, the myths include the idea of void or nothingness in the beginning. Natural phenomena, people, and culture were created by gods, and finally specific events occur which tie in with the known history of the people.

The total number of gods in the pantheon is enormous and variable from place to place, but a few of them are revered in one way or another all over Polynesia. Ta'aroa is considered the creator in Tahiti, and is usually a high god elsewhere. Oro, Tane, Ro'o, and Tu are other important, widely known gods. Some gods, often one of the above, are considered to be patrons or titular dieties of some cult or locality. Various others have jurisdiction over some aspect of nature, such as the sea, thunder, or wind, and others are patrons of certain occupations or amusements. In the Society Islands, the most important god of the latter kind is Oro, patron of the Ariori society and God of War. Besides these, there are many lesser gods, divine ancestors, and a myriad of simple spirits.

Each of the Society Islands has its own oracle, which is consulted before any important activity. Certain priests also practice divination by interpreting omens and by experimental augury. The examination of the characteristics of the inside of a newly cut coconut and the interpretation of the motions described by a coconut half as it sinks in deep water are the most common methods. Sometimes special priests become possessed by a spirit and bound around in a frenzy, muttering indistinct sounds. These sounds, which represent the voice of a god speaking through the medium, are interpreted by other priests. Some men are considered to be sorcerers who can cause death by performing magical rites over a victim's nail clippings, hair, or scrap of clothing. These men demonstrate their power by walking over hot stones.

There is no particular moral or ethical content in Polynesian religion. The religion buttresses the social order primarily by establishing the sanctity of the rulers and thereby reinforcing their authority. The gods also function as morale builders to individuals. Prayers, which are essentially petitions to the gods, are said on arising, before meals, and before any significant undertaking. Offerings of food, from which the gods partake of the essence, are laid out every day, as well as at any kind of ceremony. Human sacrifice of war prisoners and criminals sometimes is offered at the most important ceremonials, but more often pigs and dogs are sacrificed. The fact that the Tahitians pray so frequently impressed the early Christian missionaries sent to convert them, but most of the native religion seemed to be particularly heathenish, amoral, and barbarous, and the Christians set about to change it as quickly as possible.

The first Europeans to touch any of the Society Islands were probably Spaniards, under the navigator Quirós, around 1606. Much later, in 1767, the English Captain Wallis formally took possession of Tahiti, which he called King George Island, but his stay was brief. Bougainville, a French explorer, touched on Tahiti the following year and claimed it for France.

To the English-speaking world, the most famous of the early explorers was Captain James Cook, who came to Tahiti in 1769 in H.M.S. *Endeavour* on a commission of the British Royal Society to observe the passage of the planet Venus across the face of the sun. It was in honor of the Royal Society that Cook named the island group the Society Islands. Scientists from the *Endeavour* explored all of the larger islands and became well acquainted with the friendly, hospitable natives. Cook and other persons on the voyage later published descriptions of the islands and the people which are still important scientific documents. Cook made three voyages to Polynesia in all, and on his final visit in 1778 met his death in Hawaii during a brief skirmish with the natives.

One of the most fascinating events in the history of Tahitian-European relations occurred in 1788 when Lieutenant Bligh, who had been on one of Cook's voyages, arrived in Tahiti in command of H. M.S. *Bounty.* The *Bounty* crew spent five idyllic months there, and so hospitable were the islanders that many of the men had settled down and married into chiefs' families. The sad farewells when the ship finally sailed away, the subsequent mutiny and the return of the *Bounty* to Tahiti without its captain, the later settlement of Pitcairn Island by a small mixed band of Tahitians and English mutineers, and the final development of a utopian social system by the inbred descendants of the mutineers are salient features of a story far stranger than fiction.[4]

A few other explorers visited Tahiti before the close of the eighteenth century, but all of the contacts were sporadic and relatively brief. There were no true settlements, and no long-term jurisdiction over the Tahitians was achieved; consequently there were no consistent clashes of cultural systems of the type which alters native cultures in significant ways. The fullest effect on Tahitian culture was later imposed by English missionaries. In 1797, the London Missionary Society's ship, the *Duff,* arrived in Tahiti. These Protestant missionaries who settled in Tahiti had rapid success with the natives, partly because of the receptive attitude of the Tahitians, and partly because of local political events. The natives were tremendously impressed with the technological equipment of the Europeans, and with their spiritual strength, or mana, as well, for the Europeans repeatedly flouted the local taboos with impunity. The Polynesians were therefore quite willing to accept the Christian gods into their own pantheon. A local *Ari'i,* Pomare, became an early convert to Christianity, and with the aid of European economic power and firearms quickly established himself as sovereign over Tahiti. Through Pomare, and later through his descendants, the Missionary Council controlled Tahiti as an independent state for nearly 40 years.

[4] An anthropologist, Harry L. Shapiro of the American Museum of Natural History, has made an intensive study of the *Bounty* descendants and recounted their history faithfully and interestingly. See *The Heritage of the Bounty: Six Generations,* New York, 1936.

The missionaries changed many of the local customs which seemed to them immoral. The native women were induced to wear the loose "Mother Hubbard" dresses, the temples were destroyed, dancing and much of the music was forbidden, and marriage and courtship customs were altered. But one fortunate result of the firm control over Tahiti was that the islanders were protected from many of the depredations inflicted on other islands by the great influx of carousing European sailors.

A French Roman Catholic Mission attempted to settle in Tahiti in 1836, but it was driven out by the natives. French naval forces followed a few years later, however, and by 1843 established control over the island, which has been a French colony ever since. The French regime was considerably more lax than the English missionaries had been, and did not control the traders and adventurers who began to pour in.

As in other parts of Polynesia, European diseases exacted an awful toll of the native population. Meanwhile, Chinese labor was imported to work on the newly established plantations. These Chinese quickly became influential in commercial enterprises, and now constitute about one-fourth of the population and are practically in control of the internal markets of French Oceania.

Papeete, the chief town of Tahiti, is the administrative as well as the economic capital of the French colony, and French civil servants, retired people, and artists have settled there. Caste lines between natives and Europeans never developed in Tahiti, and the population now includes many persons of mixed descent. On the relatively metropolitan island of modern Tahiti, the pure Polynesian seems destined to disappear by much the same process as is occurring in Hawaii, by racial mixture and by absorption into modern commercial life; but on some of the more distant and less important of the Society Islands, the natives have preserved some of their aboriginal ways. The population is increasing in many of these out-of-the-way areas, and perhaps they may be able to continue their independent ways for some time to come. They have learned to market copra (dried coconut) and pearls independently in order to purchase certain European goods they now find necessary, but their subsistence is assured by their own efforts and so, therefore, may be their continued cultural integrity.

FURTHER READINGS

Arii, T. E., *Tahiti,* New York, 1947.

Bell, F. L. S., "A Functional Interpretation of Inheritance and Succession in Central Polynesia," *Oceania,* Vol. 3, 1932.

Buck, P. H. (Te Rangi Hiroa), *Vikings of the Sunrise,* New York, 1938.

Burrows, E. G., "Cultural Areas in Polynesia," *Journal of the Polynesian Society,* Vol. 49, 1940.

Cook, Capt. J., *The Journal and Voyages of Captain Cook,* London, 1773, 1777, 1784.

Crossland, C., "The Island of Tahiti," *Geographic Journal,* Vol. 71, 1928.

Ellis, W., *Polynesian Researches,* London, 1831 (various later eds.), 4 vols.

Freeman, O. W. (ed.), *Geography of the Pacific,* New York, 1951.

Furnas, J. C., *Anatomy of Paradise,* New York, 1947.

Grace, G. W., "Subgrouping of Malayo-Polynesian: A Report of Tentative Findings," *American Anthropologist,* n.s., Vol. 57, 1955.

Handy, E. S. C., *History and Culture in the Society Islands,* Bernice P. Bishop Museum Bull. 79, Honolulu, 1930.

Henry, T., *Ancient Tahiti,* Bernice P. Bishop Museum Bull. 48, Honolulu, 1928.

Keesing, F. M., *The South Seas in the Modern World,* New York, 1941.

Keesing, F. M., *Native Peoples of the Pacific World,* New York, 1945.

Linton, R., *Ethnology of Polynesia and Micronesia,* Field Museum of Natural History Guide, Pt. 6, Chicago, 1926.

Oliver, D. L., *The Pacific Islands,* Cambridge, 1951.

Oliver, D. L., *Ancient Tahitian Society,* Honolulu (in press).

Piddington, R. (ed.), *Essays in Polynesian Ethnology,* Cambridge, 1939.

Robson, R. W., *The Pacific Islands Handbook, 1944,* American ed., New York, 1945 (Australian eds. titled *Pacific Islands Year Book*).

Sahlins, M. D., *Social Stratification in Polynesia,* Monographs of the American Ethnological Society, Seattle, 1958.

Shapiro, H. L., *The Heritage of the Bounty; Six Generations,* New York, 1936.

Sharp, A., *Ancient Voyagers in the Pacific,* Wellington, 1956.

Williamson, R. W., *The Social and Political Systems of Central Polynesia,* Cambridge, 1924, 3 vols.

Williamson, R. W., *Religion and Social Organization in Central Polynesia,* Cambridge, 1937.

Wilson, J. (ed.), *A Missionary Voyage to the South Pacific Ocean . . . in the . . . "Duff,"* London, 1799.

The Kalinga of the
Philippine Islands

The Philippine Islands are a part of the great culture area generally called Indonesia. Despite the long colonial epoch of over three centuries of submission to Spanish authority and later to that of the United States of America, the basic cultural substratum of the Philippines is generally similar to that of the large islands southwest of them. This ancient culture, however, is not simple and undifferentiated. As in the larger islands of Indonesia, several racial strains have occupied the land and mixed in varying proportions, and the aboriginal cultures received further influences from India, China, and the Islamic World before the Spaniards discovered the island group in 1521, subsequently occupied it, and named it in honor of their Philip II.

Of the peoples now found in the Philippines, the pygmy Negroes, or Negritos, were probably the first to arrive. These are shy hunters and gatherers who have retreated into the depths of the heavily forested areas and are found mainly on the northern island of Luzon. Indonesians[1] were next and probably brought a primitive horticul-

---

[1] This term has been used in a variety of ways. Krieger, for example, uses it to designate the dominant physical type over Indonesia, a type more commonly referred to in the literature as *Malay*. In general, however, *Indonesian* is used to specify a

ture to the islands, where they came to occupy the mountainous areas of the larger ones. Finally came the modern Malays, or *deutero-Malays* (as they are called to distinguish them from the *proto-Malays*), who are found generally along the coasts and in lowland areas and whose cultures show some influence from India, which long had a dominant influence in the islands of western Indonesia. Chinese trade later also added to the cultural complexity of the Philippines. Before the arrival of the Spaniards, a further cultural influence, Islam, was brought to the southern Philippines by Malays from Indonesia who had been converted through contact with Arab traders. When the Spaniards encountered the Islamic peoples in the Philippines they called them *Moros*, as they had called the Moslems in Spain and in North Africa.

The modern population of the Philippines is usually classified into four types which primarily reflect cultural differentiation, but to some extent their distribution suggests the historical sequence given above. The Negritos are the most remote and the least assimilated into Philippine national culture. At the other extreme are Filipinos, the peoples of the central islands (known collectively as the *Visayans*) and the coastal and valley peoples of Luzon, who were converted to Christianity early in the Spanish colonial period. The Moros occupy an analogous position in the coastal and lowland areas of the southern Philippines, although they have less influence on the national level than the numerically superior Filipinos. The other peoples are the so-called pagans, or wild tribes, who occupy large areas of the southern island of Mindanao and most of northern Luzon, as well as isolated positions on a few of the other islands. These latter peoples, of whom the Kalinga are one, are in large part Indonesians.

Luzon is the largest island of the Philippine archipelago. The northern half of the island is, except for coastal flatlands and lower river valleys, ruggedly mountainous, and it is these fastnesses that the pagan tribes inhabit. The basis of life is agriculture, which is practiced so intensively by means of irrigation and terracing that the population of northern Luzon is remarkably dense. All of the peoples of the region are quite similar to one another and have be-

---

type that is less Mongoloid (according to some authors, it is predominantly Caucasoid) than the Malay. Cf. H. W. Krieger, *Peoples of the Philippines,* Smithsonian Institution, War Background Studies, No. 4, Washington, 1942.

come famous, or notorious, in history for their head-hunting procliv-
ities.[2]

The Kalinga speak a language related to the far-flung Malayo-
Polynesian family. They number about 24,000 persons (as of 1939)
and occupy the approximate geographic center of the northern
Luzon pagan area. At Lubwagan, where the ethnologist R. F. Bar-

MOUNTAINS BECOME ECONOMICALLY USEFUL AS RICE PADDIES. *Courtesy, Pan American World Airways*

ton lived, the mountain ranges are somewhat less precipitous than
those occupied by the adjacent Tinguian and Ifugao, the soil is
richer, and there are greater water resources for irrigation. The
Kalinga of this region produce so much large-grain rice, characterized by Barton as possibly the finest in the world, that they have
been able to export some of it to the lowlands.

The Kalinga, like the other Indonesians, are typically less Mon-

[2] The names of the principal groups are Igorot, Tinguian, Kalinga, Ifugao, and
Apayao. Subgroups of the Igorot have been described in the literature as Bontok,
Nabaloi, and Kankanai. Sometimes all of these people are collectively called *Igorot*
(mountain people) by Filipinos.

goloid than the average Filipino, although they too have straight black hair, nearly hairless brown skin, and some occurrence of the distinctive eyefold. The Kalinga are relatively tall and, as described by Barton, "broad-shouldered, narrow-hipped, graceful, and strong." They, like the other mountain peoples, are much

given to elaborating on nature by tattooing the body, blackening and filing the teeth, and bedecking the hair and the pierced ear lobes with flowers. The hair of both sexes flows loose and long behind and is cut in bangs in front. Clothing is simple; a G string or breechclout for the men, and for women the brief sarong. Sometimes both men and women wear a tiny shoulder jacket, so short that it leaves much of the chest exposed.

The principal agricultural product of the Kalinga is rice, followed by the much less important production of bananas, sugar cane, sweet potatoes, and peas. Areca palms are planted for the nut (often miscalled *betel* nut), which is chewed everywhere in the Indonesian culture area. Coconut palms and bamboo are also planted. Domestic animals are the carabao, or water-

Courtesy, Chicago Natural History Museum

buffalo, pigs, fowl, dogs, and a few cattle. All of these animals are eaten, including the dogs, but the principal use of the carabao is in plowing the terraced fields. The eggs of chickens are prized, as is the milk of the carabao and cattle, but production of milk and eggs is poor, and they are used only as medicine for sickly children.

Although agriculture is intensive and productive, the farming implements are simple. The complicated terraces and the irrigation canals which water them are constructed entirely by hand labor aided only by a simple wooden shovel. The preparation of a field, once it has been leveled and the terrace wall built, is done by driving several carabao around and around it until the soil is trampled deeply to a thick paste of mud. The rice crop is planted and transplanted by hand—"stoop labor" of the most onerous kind—and weeded and harvested by hand. After the harvest, before the ground is flooded for a new crop, the topsoil is gathered and heaped into low mounds, into which a few garden vegetables are planted.

The Kalinga of Lubwagan make good, substantial, and roomy houses, again, like their subsistence generally, superior to those of their neighbors. The house of the ordinary Kalinga is a square of 15 to 20 feet across and raised on piles several feet above the ground. If the owner is wealthy, his house is octagon-shaped. The floor and walls are of split bamboo, and an inner ceiling is made of reeds. There are several additional refinements: the crest of the roof may be made into a long smoke trough; the floor along the sides òf the house is raised slightly to make sleeping platforms; a fireplace is located toward the rear; and in the front of the house a rather narrow veranda is built. The bamboo floor is removable, and the housewife transports it to the spring or brook several times a week to wash it.

Kalinga social organization is based primarily on kinship principles. The simple family of husband, wife, children and sometimes a dependent relative is the household group, the basic economic unit, and the nucleus of the kinship society. A number of households together form a kindred, the recognition of which is based on a bilateral rather than a unilateral, i.e., patrilineal or matrilineal, principle. A person recognizes as a relative anyone who is a descendant of one of the great-grandparents, which is to say that relationship in one's own generation is recognized as far as third cousins.

The kinship terms used in address follow the Polynesian principle of separating the generations, but generalize within them. Thus *apo* refers to grandparent, or to any other lateral kin of that generation. It is a term of greatest respect as well, so that a distinguished stranger is addressed by this title, even by people of his own age. *Ama* and *ina* are used for *father* and *mother* respectively, but are frequently applied to other relatives of that generation. Similarly, the terms for siblings and sons and daughters are used for relatives of those generations in addressing them. There are other terms which are used in reference rather than in address to distinguish more precise relationships—cousins from siblings, second cousins

Courtesy, Chicago Natural History Museum

from first, nieces and nephews from own children, and so on—but no terms which distinguish cross from parallel cousins, which is possibly a consequence of the lack of local exogamy. The terms of address are so simple and generalized also probably because they function as titles of respect rather than as names. Personal names are used in address as well as reference, except in the case of the mother- and father-in-law, for as in all primitive societies they must be shown great respect, and kinship terms rather than personal names are used in addressing them.[3]

Households and kindreds are interlocked by means of marriages which create in-laws ties with unrelated or distantly related households. The countryside is densely populated, compared to most primitive areas, and so long as kinship remains the basis of the local social organization, it is desirable to extend the bonds as far as possible.[4] Hence the Kalinga prohibit marriage with any relative nearer than second cousin, and with any affinal relatives. This latter rule is unusual. Levirate, sororate, and brother-sister exchange, all common forms of marriage in primitive cultures, are thus forbidden to the Kalinga. Affinal ties between different kindreds are of course strengthened by every subsequent marriage between them, but the Kalinga apparently want to diffuse the ties more widely—"Why waste a marriage? The other family would be ours with only one marriage!"

The region, the political and geographic unit of the society, is thus composed of households and kindreds, all of whom have some measure of affinal and consanguineal ties among themselves. This situation is created by the rule of endogamy; marriages outside the regional boundary are disapproved. The region, therefore, is autonomous in all practical respects.

The economy of Kalinga society is in many ways a primitive one based on the distribution of goods along kinship lines; but like the sociopolitical system, it also has certain modern characteristics, probably because the Kalinga have been for so long in partial adaptation to the national economy, which has stimulated their interest in commodity exchange. The primitive traits involve such things as free access to hunting and fishing territories and pasture lands, the division of game among relatives by the hunter, and the great emphasis on hospitality, on gift-giving, and on the general interest of the whole kindred in any transaction made by one of its members. Primitive communalism in one way or another enters into all of economic life; no man is a self-sufficient entrepreneur. The concept of private property, however, is highly developed in certain aspects of the economy, so that a noticeable difference has

[3] In many societies, the respect for them is carried so far that they cannot be directly addressed at all.

[4] The population of Lubwagan, a typical region of intermarrying families, was 2400 during Barton's period of residence there.

arisen in the relative wealth of individual families.

Private-use rights over land exist when a person has expended labor on it to make it productive. For example, a wild bamboo clump is free to all, but if a man cleans and clears it, he thereby establishes an exclusive right to it. Land in the Kalinga mountains is, of course, utterly useless for irrigation farming until it has had an enormous amount of work done on it. It must be cleared, leveled, terraced, and plowed, and irrigation canals must be brought to it. Inasmuch as the labor takes a long time and frequently involves several members of a family, it is regarded as family property after the labor is invested. Because the irrigation renews the soil, a rice field does not wear out, and tenure rights are perpetual in the family line. Unirrigated hill land, where sweet potatoes and peas are grown, loses its fertility after two or three years and is then abandoned. The original cultivator retains some equity in it, and if he chose, would have the right to cultivate it again. If it lies fallow long enough, however, and someone else wishes to plant it, the previous occupant is expected to give permission. That is, he must either cultivate it himself or give up his equity in it.

An individual owner of a rice paddy does not have complete rights over it. He cannot dispose of it as he wishes. The land belongs to the family line, and the present owner can sell it only in case of a crisis so serious that influential kinsmen concur in the sale. Nor can he bequeath the land freely to those who are not the customary inheritors, the next of kin.

Inheritance is a peculiar combination of primogeniture and parental interests. The oldest son inherits the best fields of his father at the time when he sets up his own permanent household. The oldest daughter inherits the best land of her mother. Younger children get less desirable lands. The youngest child, son or daughter, normally stays with the parents after marriage, and acquires in time the property the parents have retained for their own subsistence and any other property they may have acquired after the previous divisions among the other children.

As a consequence of the emphasis on primogeniture, eldest sons and daughters occupy a favored position in the society, but they do not have nearly so complete a predominance as, for example, in Polynesia, where the property and social position of the father are passed on undivided to the eldest son, with the younger children remaining as the merest satellites to him. The position of women in Kalinga society is a remarkably secure one, inasmuch as they inherit on equal terms with men. The presence of two parallel lines of property, mother's and father's, makes the marriage bond a rather fragile one because of the absence of conjugal property. A woman can divorce her husband freely without worrying about economic difficulties, because she retains control of her own property. When a married person dies, the surviving spouse does not inherit any of the deceased's property, for it is vested in the children. Should the widow or widower marry again, no property accompanies the move. If the deceased was childless, the property reverts in its entirety to the deceased's parents to be divided among their children.

Ownership of water rights is acquired in the same way that equity in land is established. The first to develop a water system has the prior right to its use, and subsequent cultivators must pay him for permission to divert water to their fields. Over a large area of fields using water from a single stream the flowage rights become complicated, but always the system of priorities is followed in order of original users, and each has the power to prohibit any additional diversion of water upstream from him. In the rare cases where a single source of water supplies more than one region, disputes are frequent. It seems likely that inasmuch as the water is so essential to the economy, and because feuds and long-term struggles or warfare between regions which share water would be so disastrous, political relations between otherwise autonomous populations are in some measure consequences of this interdependence.

Another factor which is related to the interregional political relations is the amount of trade which occurs internally and between autonomous regions. The idea of transferring property for a consideration is well established. Most primitive peoples trade by merely exchanging gifts, but even if the trade is an immediate exchange of one thing for another, it is direct—that is, money does not intervene in the process. The Kalinga do not have, natively, a fully developed money, a single kind of commodity specialized as a medium of exchange and measure of value, but they are nearing it. All large values are calculated in terms of carabao, and payment is frequently made with carabao. The next smaller units are pigs; and finally there is a sort of quasi-currency, called by Barton, *heirlooms*.

The Kalinga heirlooms tend to function as currency because they are not consumable and hence lend themselves to accumulation, and because they are of so many kinds of objects of great variation in value that they are quite divisible. Some of their value, incidentally, is like that of modern currency, merely symbolic, involving public acceptance rather than a readily apparent or intrinsic value. As in much of Indonesia, almost any object—a bead, gong, jar, plate, pair of earrings, necklace, or whatever—which has remained in the family for a long time acquires a kind of antiquarian value. A set of gold earrings, or string of beads, may have a history which everyone knows and consequently a conventional value. Identical objects which are new or of unknown history have much less value.

When an important piece of property is sold by an individual, portions of the purchase price must be given as gifts to a circle of relatives, varying in amount depending on the closeness of the relative. The more important the object sold, the wider is the circle of relatives involved. A significant amount of primitive communalism stands revealed here; the owner (occupant) of a rice field really has only the most significant share in it. Fully individualized property exists only as personal clothing, tools, and ornaments.

Sales are effected by two agents of the seller, one representing the wife's kin and the other the husband's. The formalities of the sale are elaborate. When agreement has been reached among the relatives that the object may be sold, and a price has been set, the agents look for a buyer. At the home of the buyer, after some formalities, the agent takes a bowl from the buyer's shelf and puts it on the floor, where it is contemplated by everyone for several minutes in utter silence. If someone sneezes during the interim, or some other incident regarded as a bad omen occurs, the deal is off. If not, the buyer finally picks up the bowl and presents it to the seller. This is the beginning of a long series of ceremonially conducted payments. The relatives of the seller come individually later on to bargain for their own payments. There is in this matter an understanding on the part of the buyer that he makes these payments to clear the title. The buyer himself, of course, normally acquires parts of the payment from *his* relatives; consequently he is not finally a sole owner of the property after its purchase.

Inasmuch as payments are piecemeal and delayed, a conception of debt is involved. Unpaid debts do not end with the life of the debtor—all obligations are inherited. Sometimes a debt is collected by seizure of property by the kinsmen of the seller, but more frequently an attempt is made to shame the debtor. Dunning is resorted to at first, but later, especially if the debtor is from another region, the *sit-down* is employed. The creditor goes to the home of the debtor and installs himself in it. He cannot be forced or even asked to leave because he is in the sacred status of guest. This is so embarrassing to the host that he makes a great effort to raise the payment from his kinsmen, who, of course, are also ashamed, though somewhat less so, depending on the closeness of the relationship.

Exchange between independent regions has been a powerful deterrent to war, and out of it has risen an interesting Kalinga interregional institution, the peace pact. The widespread institution of trade partners has been elaborated and formalized, frankly in the interests of trade originally, into a peace pact between them which involves the regions which they each inhabit. Pact-holders have the duties of enforcing peace between their two regions. This is a political function in one sense; a pact-holder is spokesman for his own region in relation to others, and for the others in his own. A strong element of primitive society is present in the institution, however, for pact-holders are ceremonial brothers with all the appropriate ritual obligations and incest prohibitions (their children must not marry) of true brothers.

Barton thought that the regional autonomy and the instituting of supratribal relations between regions meant that the Kalinga had an inchoate state, or civil society. This idea has been disputed by Edward Dozier, a more recent investigator, who finds nothing statelike in this situation.[5] The relations between regions are normally hostile unless economic exchanges are so important that arrangements must be made to foster them. There is nothing unusual in this, especially among chiefdoms. A chief can make arrangements with another chief so that reciprocal exchanges can take place between them. This is difficult at the tribal or band level, because ordinarily there is no individual with the authority to make treaties or pacts with another such person and keep his word. He could only guarantee the behavior of his own family, whereas a

[5] E. P. Dozier, "The Territorial or Regional Unit of the Kalinga," unpublished manuscript.

chief can speak for all the people in his region. It also should be emphasized how advantageous such reciprocities are to the chiefs themselves, for the goods they exchange with their partner-chiefs are redistributed in the regions, to the further enhancement of the authority and prestige of each chief.

The regional chiefs, or *Pangats,* as they are called, have of course an important role in the internal functioning of the society as well as in external economic relations. Primarily, the Pangat acts to keep peace within the region. In the course of helping to maintain order in the society, the most usual role of the Pangat is as a mediator in disputes. An injury done one group by a member of another is usually, in primitive society, rectified by retaliation, a course of action which frequently leads to feuds. A Pangat, however, tries to settle the case by means of some form of payment or restitution satisfactory to the aggrieved. Such settlements, as opposed to retribution in kind, are an eminently civilized recourse, and in Kalinga society fail to be fully realized as a form of state control over domestic affairs because of the lack of organized legal force that can be applied to cause the judgment to be accepted by either or both parties.

A payment (*wergild*, in old Europe) levied against a person guilty of homicide, adultery, or some such injury is frequently accepted in Kalinga society. It is not necesarily a guarantee that no retaliation will ever be attempted, but it does give a person an opportunity to refrain from vengeance without loss of prestige. In general, it seems that the Kalinga political order, as suggested by this freedom to undertake retaliation or not, merely exercises a moderative and mediative function rather than a truly legislative one. The nearest approach to the use of legal force, the simple prerequisite of the state, is the personal threat of the Pangat, who is respected and feared, to force acceptance of his judgment.

The typical Kalinga regional territory is a supratribal society in another respect. A purely tribal society does not have *classes* of families in the modern sense, but the Kalinga kindreds, although basic and powerful, are cross-cut by an alignment of nuclear families which occupy distinct levels of political and economic strength and of related social status. Pangats, the most powerful men, are few, but they are at the apex of the stratification. Below them are the *Kadangyan,* wealthy aristocratic leaders of the kinship groups. The middle or average group is called *Baknang,* and the poor are called *Kapus.* The differences between the upper and lower extremes are considerable, judging from the fact that many of the Kapus are completely propertyless and must find work as tenants while some of the wealthy have enough land to allow several tenants to crop the land at half-shares. The relationship between master and tenant is feudal-like; a tenant must help avenge an injury to the master, help him in emergencies, and so on, while the master is expected to help avenge the tenant and assist him in time of illness or other crisis. It is a relationship of propertied master to penniless serf, but the phrasing of the relationship is that of kinship, and more often than not the two are actually related in some way.

The day-to-day life of the Kalinga is regulated by the kinship regulations of a typical tribal society, however, for it is only at a few points, and infrequently, that the activities of chiefs dominate kinship interests. In most respects the Kalinga have not lost any of the characteristics of a primitive tribe; they have merely *added* the few quasi-political features of chiefdoms in order to master special problems. The role of the kindred in taking vengeance, for example, is not halted by the peace pacts or by the influence of the Pangat. Negotiation and such payments as wergild are undertaken when both sides prefer not to feud for special reasons. Actually, a considerable prestige is associated with head-hunting, and it is one of the primary means of acquiring greater status than one inherits. Only one who has accompanied a head-taking expedition may wear the distinctive tattoo and be accorded respect in important discussions.

A head-hunting expedition is always phrased as an act of vengeance, but it is to a considerable extent quite impersonal. A grudge against another kindred or even people of a distant region is remembered for generations, and so the vengeance may be taken against descendants of the original offender. Additionally, any relative, male or female, of the offender may be killed. Thus feuds are easily perpetuated, inasmuch as one group may retaliate against people who may never have heard of the act which is being avenged, and these then desire revenge for what seems to them a wholly unprovoked aggression.

A head-taking expedition normally consists of five or six men who steal into enemy territory and wait in ambush until some resident comes by. After the victim is killed, the head is cut off and taken home, where a great celebration is held. The head is stuck on a stake, and pantomime dances are enacted, and later the members of the war party drink the brains mixed with fermented sugar-cane juice. The rituals are performed in the belief that bringing in an enemy head increases the fertility of fields, domestic animals, and women, and promotes the general welfare. Younger sons are particularly anxious to engage in such expeditions because their status is lower thān first-born sons. Their enterprise is frequently rewarded by proud parents, who present them with choice fields, sometimes even fields previously allotted to another son.

The birth of the first child to a married couple is a very important event; the birth, in effect, establishes the family, whereas each subsequent birth to them is progressively less significant. A Kalinga marriage is merely tentative, a sort of trial marriage, until a child is born. The series of celebrations and feasts which relatives of both kinship groups give to signalize the birth are not merely to welcome the tiny new member, but more significantly to demonstrate and celebrate the fact that the two groups are now effectively cemented in a union symbolized by the child.

The socialization of a Kalinga child is informal. The child becomes a Kalinga by easy stages, mainly by imitating older people. The only purposely imparted feature of the education is the history of the kinship group, particularly that relating to the troubles, enmities, debts, and so on involved in its relations with others. Other matters—geography, folk tales, myths, dances, religion—are learned from the public at large, more or less haphazardly. Children are not purposely taught to walk or talk, and there is no conscious prohibition against any kind of behavior, even if dangerous to the child. Barton relates: "I have taken awls or sharp knives away from children or jerked them back from steep places, and the action has always provoked rage in the child —used to having its own uncontrolled way—and surprise in the elders, who regarded my solicitude as supererogatory."[6]

As children grow into later childhood, they begin to participate more and more in adult activities. Boys are particularly encouraged to be brave and to not be afraid to kill. When an enemy corpse is

[6] R. F. Barton, *The Kalingas,* Chicago, 1949, p. 42.

brought home to the village by a head-hunting party, the boys are allowed to spear the enemy and to hack flesh from the bones. A Pangat, being very influential, can even go a step farther and train his boys on living subjects. For example, the boy might be encouraged to sneak upon some unsuspecting villager and jab a spear into his buttocks. The Pangat then pays wergild to the victim, and all is well. The boy can attain great prestige among his age mates by such an action.

By the age of about 10, children leave their parents' homes and go into a sort of dormitory residence with a group of chums of the same sex. Soon boys and girls are freely flirting and philandering, and generally having a good time. The irresponsibility of adolescents, which is such a problem to parents in modern urban society, is here apparently recognized as normal, and their freedom is insured by their being moved out of the parents' homes. But marriage, which comes as soon as a boy is considered mature, brings a considerable change.

Kalinga children are usually engaged to be married when they are small. Parents may even make a conditional engagement of a son before the girl is born. The boy's parents make the proposal, at first indirectly, feeling their way so as not to be shamed by a direct refusal from the girl's family. If the proposal is accepted, gifts are exchanged and a feast is given. Thereafter the two groups exchange presents frequently for as long as the engagement lasts. A great feast which includes all the relatives of the two groups signalizes the marriage ceremony of the boy and girl. The newlyweds then live with the girl's family for three or four months and finally set up their own household, often in a nearby house that the girl's father has built for them. After the birth of their first child, a feast is held at which the girl's relatives are all given presents by the boy's family, and the marriage is then considered established on a firm basis.

Divorces are common among childless couples, but also occur after children are born. The cause usually is the failure of one of the spouses to assume the proper duties in the household division of labor; divorces due to infidelity or sexual jealousy are very rare. The husband does the heavier work in the fields, such as plowing, terracing, and clearing, and carries on all the family business, whether buying and selling, politics, or avenging wrongs against the kinship group. The woman's work is largely domestic, and she also helps with the planting and harvesting.

Among the aristocracy, men sometimes keep mistresses, or concubines, most usually in other villages than their own. This is a recognized institution, and a wife's feelings against her husband on this score are discounted. The semilegitimate children of concubinage are not discriminated against, but they never are very high in status because they cannot inherit more than a small share of the property of the family. If the man's wife is childless and he does not divorce her, he is expected to take a mistress, and often the wife helps him to make a choice.

Illness and death from sickness are believed to be caused by unhappy or jealous souls of the ancestral dead. Healing rites involve sacrifice of animals to these souls and are accompanied by prayers to them. Healing shamans sometimes put on ritual performances lasting as long as a day and a half in order to exorcise the evil spiritual influence from a patient. Among the Kalinga, shamanism is almost entirely in the hands of old women. They say that their souls have married the supernatural spirits and that the rituals are given to them by the spirits. Male priests officiate at head-hunting rites, but with the decline of head-hunting, this office has nearly ceased to exist.

When a sick person dies, a long wake is held in order to forestall the visitation of certain ghoulish spirits who would eat the dead. The corpse is placed seated in a wide chair, and the widow or widower sits beside it for much of the time, wailing and lamenting. The deceased's mother and father and close relatives stand in front of the house, also loudly grieving. If the funeral is for an aged person, however, the wake has a festive character, and songs and chants are sung and a feast is given. The corpse is kept for as long as three to ten days before it is buried in the rice fields. On the tenth day after interment, a shaman chants a dirge which dispatches the soul to the Skyworld, the region of the ancestral spirits. Cooked rice, fermented cane juice, and sometimes a hat are placed on the grave for several weeks.

The Kalinga pantheon includes many classes of beings. The most important is the god Kabungan, to whom sacrifices of pigs and chickens are made to insure the fertility of the fields. The usual

departmental gods are present: gods of thunder, lightning, rain-
bows, howling winds, and particular sicknesses and various gods of
geographic features and regions. Curiously, for an agricultural
people, there is no concept of sun and moon dieties. One class of
gods or spirits is greatly feared—the *bulaiyao,* who capture and
eat souls of the dead. The *anitu,* the ghosts or souls of the dead, are
frequently blamed for sickness and bad luck. Even those who are
ancestral seem to be considered malevolent, and Kabungan is frequently called upon to put an end to their depredations. A few of
the ancestral spirits have a special function of punishing their
descendants for wrong actions, particularly those actions which
are against the family interest. This is as close as Kalinga religion
comes to having a moral or ethical content.

Kalinga music and dance are highly ritualized, but seem to have
only a distant relation to the religion. As with many Indonesians,
gongs and various bamboo lengths which give different tones when
beaten are the main instruments of orchestral music. Nose flutes,
pipes made of bamboo flutes tied together, and bamboo harps are
also frequently used. The dance is, according to Barton, a beautiful
thing to see—"the men lunging and retreating, while beating gongs
suspended from human jawbones, and encircling the women, who,
marking time without much locomotion, revolve in their places to
face the warriors dancing around them. The Kalingas are fond of
bright colors and, for the dance, thrust hibiscus blossoms or sun-
flowers through their punctured earlobes or wear them in their head-
bands. . . . More beautiful than the gay ornamentation, however,
were the gracefully moving, sinuous, muscular bodies of the dancers
and the streaming hair of both women and men. . . ."[7]

But this aspect of Kalinga life does not exist in modern times.
The narrow-hipped, finely muscled bodies of the men are now
dressed in baggy, dirty khakis, and the lithe symmetry of the women
is concealed under long shapeless "Mother Hubbard" dresses.
Christian mission schools have had an important influence. Additionally, mines have been opened in Kalinga territory, and the
construction of automobile roads is bringing to a close the relative
isolation of the Kalinga.

Head-hunting was, of course, the first Kalinga institution which

[7] *Ibid.,* p. 12.

the Americans tried to stamp out when they extended governmental rule to the highlands of northern Luzon after 1901. But the custom of private justice, of which head-hunting is the most striking manifestation, was so important to the Kalinga that even as late as 1940 local feuds were still occasionally arousing the authorities to action. In 1947, under the headline, "Kalinga Tribal War Is Narrowly Averted," a Philippine newspaper carried the following item:

A feudal war in Kalinga between the villages of Mabongtot, Lubuagan and Mangali, Tanudan was recently averted by the timely intervention of Lt. Mario Bansen and Mr. Antonio Kanao, mayor of Lubuagan.

According to information these two villages had continually fought each other in the past, but in recent years there had been a peace pact or "bodong" between the two. However, last August the Mabongtot chief who had made the pact with Mangali died, in which case a successor had to be appointed and a new pact made. Otherwise the old feuds would come back into play.

In this particular case no effort was apparently made to renew the pact between the two villages and trouble started when an attempt was made on the life of the mayor of Tanudan. From then on the situation got worse until both villages were prepared to fight it out on the traditional battleground as their forefathers had done, except that now they have the better tools and ways of killing each other that modern, civilized warfare has brought them. Foxholes and shells of various calibers were found on their proposed battleground when this was inspected.

Fortunately, the intervention of Lt. Bansen and Mayor Kanao averted any actual bloodshed, and now it is reported that a new pact is in the making. The village chieftains have already exchanged spears which is a sign for truce. The first ceremonies for the new bodong are scheduled for this week.[8]

Some Kalinga institutions have proven to be exceedingly viable. The practice of paying a wergild indemnity had always been an acceptable substitute for vengeance, and now it has increased in frequency as retaliation is suppressed. For a long period such institutions continued in full operation despite the fact that the government of the islands had superimposed its own law—and perhaps they continue even today. A Kalinga offender, consequently, often is punished twice for a single act, by the government and by his own people independently.

Kalinga religion is dying slowly, but Christianity does not easily

[8] *The Baguio Midland Courier,* October 26, 1947; reprinted in Barton, *op. cit.,* p. 256.

replace it. Many Kalinga have accepted membership in the Christian Church, but find the moral code curious and difficult to follow. As a young Kalinga Pangat explained to Barton:

I believe in the Bible, yes, but I do not agree that only white men can interpret it. I believe that Kalingas have a part of the truth and that that truth is embodied in the Bible. . . .

[For example] . . . the Christian opposition to the *dagdagas* system of legalized mistresses is contrary to the Bible. Not long ago, a Catholic Kalinga was reproved by the priest for having taken a *dagdagas*. He answered, "What does it say in the Bible? 'Increase and multiply.' My wife cannot bear children—therefore I have taken a *dagdagas* as Jacob did. I should be disobeying the Bible if I did otherwise. You who do not marry break the command—not I who take *dagdagas* and fulfill it."[9]

The idea of sin, particularly, is difficult for the mountain men to comprehend. The above speaker, in discussing sin, apparently equates it with his own culture's conceptions of wrong, which are almost entirely wrapped up in the ideas of vengeance, feud, and, particularly, the strong tribal notion of collective responsibility of the kindred, including the ancestors.

Then, too, they tell us that we have sinned against God. What sin have *we* committed against *Him*? The Bontok man was right who, when the priest told him he had sinned against God, answered: "The holy pictures that you give us show that they who killed God's son were bearded men. You yourself have a beard. Maybe your ancestors killed God's son. But we Igorots have no beards. Therefore, those slayers of God's son were not our ancestors. Therefore, we Igorots have not sinned against God."[10]

In the main, however, the influence of European civilization has not had all of the devastating effects on the Philippine pagans that other more primitive peoples have suffered elsewhere. There have been occasional epidemics, but, as of 1941, Barton was convinced that the Kalinga population was increasing. Nearly all of the young men work in the mines, and the added wealth has improved Kalinga subsistence. Rinderpest, which formerly decimated the cattle herds, has now been wiped out, and an increase in the amount of modern medical facilities available to the people has cut down the number of deaths of young children. Wage work, combined with a public-school system, has always been the most rapid means of transform-

[9] Barton, *op. cit.*, pp. 30-31.
[10] *Ibid.*

ing a primitive community; therefore it seems safe to predict that the Kalinga will soon become complete citizens of the Philippines, culturally as well as legally.

FURTHER READINGS

Barton, R. F., *The Half Way Sun: Life Among the Headhunters of the Philippines,* New York, 1930.

Barton, R. F., *The Kalingas: Their Institutions and Custom Law,* Chicago, 1949.

Beyer, H. O., "The Non-Christian Peoples of the Philippines," *Philippine Census of 1918,* Manila, 1921.

Dozier, E. P., "Land Use and Social Organization Among the Non-Christian Tribes of Northwestern Luzon," in *Symposium: Patterns of Land Utilization and Other Papers,* Proceedings of the 1961 Annual Spring Meeting of the American Ethnological Society, Seattle, 1961.

Dozier, E. P., "The Territorial or Regional Unit of the Kalinga," unpublished manuscript.

Eggan, F., "Some Aspects of Culture Change in the Northern Philippines," *American Anthropologist,* Vol. 43, No. 1, 1941.

Keesing, F. M. and M., *Taming Philippine Headhunters,* Stanford, 1934.

Krieger, H. W., *Peoples of the Philippines,* Smithsonian Institution, War Background Studies, No. 4, Washington, 1942.

Kroeber, A. L., *Peoples of the Philippines,* New York, 1928.

Scott, W. H., "A Preliminary Report on Upland Rice in Northern Luzon," *Southwestern Journal of Anthropology,* Vol. 14, No. 1, 1958.

Scott, W. H., "Economic and Material Culture of the Kalingas of Madukayan," *Southwestern Journal of Anthropology,* Vol. 14, No. 3, 1958.

Worcester, D. C., "Headhunters of Northern Luzon," *National Geographic Magazine,* Vol. 23, No. 9, 1912.

Worcester, D. C., "The non-Christian Peoples of the Philippine Islands," *National Geographic Magazine,* Vol. 24, No. 11, 1913.

PART IV

PRIMITIVE STATES

14

The Zulu
of South Africa

One of the most dramatic and famous instances of the rise of a primitive conquest state occurred in South Africa between 1816 and 1828, when the Zulu military chieftain Shaka consolidated his hold over the large territory that today is known as Zululand and Natal. Shaka's domain was maintained by succeeding kings until a war with the British began in 1879. In 1887 Zululand was placed under the jurisdiction of the British Governor of Natal. The life span of the independent Zulu kingdom was thus about seventy years.

The Zulu belong to the Nguni branch of the Bantu language family so widespread in Central and South Africa. Prior to Shaka's time the Zulu proper were only a small relationship group subject to the Mtetwa chiefdom. So great was the prestige of the word *Zulu* after Shaka's exploits, however, that today more than 2,000,-000 people of disparate origins call themselves Zulu.

The chain of circumstances that led to the suzerainty of the Zulu actually began before Shaka's time. A claimant by descent to the Mtetwa chieftaincy, a young man named Dingiswayo, quarreled with his father and became a refugee among alien groups who were in contact with the Portuguese trading port at Delagoa Bay. After several years he came home and became chief of the Mtetwa. Presumably because of the influence of foreign ideas, Dingiswayo set about reorganizing his people. One of his most important acts was to systematize trade relations with Delagoa Bay. It seems probable that this trade greatly strengthened his position among his people, inasmuch as he could consequently redistribute to them many prized objects of European manufacture, such as brass, beads, and cloth.

Once his civil authority over his own people was consolidated, Dingiswayo reorganized the military arm. Principally this consisted of using age grades as the basis of conscription, so that regiments were formed of young men who lived together for several years as militia. The tactics of warfare were also altered to include encircling movements, which resulted in more conclusive victories. Before this, warfare had been highly ceremonialized and not very bloody, often involving only single combat by champions.

Between 1806 and 1808 Dingiswayo conquered his neighbors and incorporated them into his nascent kingdom. During this time Shaka, the Zulu, was distinguishing himself as a young warrior under Dingiswayo. Shaka was a descendant of the chiefly line of the Zulu, but for some reason (legends vary on this point) he and his mother had fled from home and sought the protection of Dingiswayo. When Shaka's father, chief of the Zulu, died in 1816, Dingiswayo helped Shaka take over that office.

Shaka, a bold and enterprising young man, then had an army of his own to command. He had learned the successful new principles of Dingiswayo's organization, which he instituted. Shaka also added some tactical innovations of his own. The most important of these was the conversion of the light, javelin-like, throwing *assagai* to a short, heavy, stabbing one. Hand-to-hand tactics, combined with the enveloping maneuver, completely transformed warfare; it lost its former inconclusive and ritualized character and became total war, requiring unconditional surrender. Shaka literally crushed his opponents.

While Shaka was building up the power and local prestige of his Zulu, he was still subject to Dingiswayo of the Mtetwa. But Dingiswayo was not watching Shaka, for his paramount rival was another large chiefdom, the Ndwandwe, led by a strong military leader, Zwide. Eventually they fought, and Zwide defeated and killed Dingiswayo. Noting that the Zulu seemed to be waxing in strength, Zwide next invaded their territory. Shaka's unusual tactical sense saved the Zulu, for he kept retreating as though unprepared or demoralized until he had lured the enemy far beyond reach of their supplies. Finally it was the troops of Zwide who were demoralized, mostly because of hunger, and Shaka fell upon them and defeated them thoroughly, although many, including Zwide, made their escape.

The next order of business was political consolidation of the kingdom. Shaka annexed the Mtetwa, putting his own man in office as successor to Dingiswayo and incorporating the Mtetwa troops into his own regiments. Similar arrangements were made with other neighboring peoples, some of whom joined the Zulu voluntarily. The conquest of those who did not submit was always ruthless, but once peace was achieved, the people were left in possession of their own lands under leaders loyal to Shaka.

Zwide attacked the Zulu again in 1819, but this time Shaka not only defeated the Ndwandwe army but also followed to Zwide's homeland and destroyed it. Zwide escaped and settled down later as a powerless refugee about 200 miles to the north. Shaka then controlled the territory of what is today called Zululand. His triumphs through the innovation of total war, meanwhile, had far-reaching effects in South Africa and as far north as Lake Victoria Nyasa. Peoples fleeing Shaka set others in motion, and the shock waves of conflicts between marauding newcomers and settled tribes resulted in new conquest states of later fame, such as the Matabele, Nguni, and Shangana.

Shaka fought a campaign every year until finally he was master of the greater part of Natal as well as Zululand, and it seemed for a while that he was like Alexander, with no more worlds to conquer. It may be supposed that because there had been no anterior state-governmental organization, the huge territory and the many formerly independent peoples it included posed many new problems of governance for Shaka, who now had somehow to rule rather than merely to direct his fighting armies. It is a matter of great fortune for us that this period of Shaka's reign is well documented, for in 1825 two Englishmen, King and Fynn, arrived for a long stay and another, Isaacs, came a little later. Fynn and Isaacs left interesting accounts of life in Shaka's court.

The previous Bantu method of governing had been according to well-understood concepts of customary law. In case of any necessary departure from custom, the chiefs had been advised by a council of old men. But Shaka ruled totally, as he had made war totally.

For a time the morale of the inchoate nation was high, because Shaka's genius had made it so successful at war. While the campaigns were in process, there was little difficulty with dissident kinship units or factions at home. After the conquests were over and the problems of consolidation of the whole had to be met, Shaka's impulse was to govern by terror. Cruelty begets cruelty, and terror, counterterror, and in the end Shaka's tyranny was so great that his own brother, Dingane, assassinated him in 1828 with the apparent approval of the people.

It may be that governance by terror is a sign of the weakness of the state, that arbitrarily used personal force signifies the relative absence of established law and order that is impersonal and institutionalized and therefore more stable. This is suggested by the fact that King Dingane continued to rule by terror in the same way that Shaka had even though he had ostensibly overthrown Shaka in order to abolish such rule. The results of his tyranny were the same as Shaka's, as the people turned from him to his brother, Mpande, who defeated Dingane in civil war.

Mpande ruled for 32 years in comparative peace, both internal and external, until his death in 1872. That the kingdom had achieved internal order during this time must mean that certain features of the state, incipient in Shaka's kingdom, had later become established firmly enough to make relatively peaceful rule possible. King Mpande has usually been called a weak king, in contrast to the great Shaka, apparently because he was not such a ruthless exterminator. But it can be as reasonably guessed that he did not need to use such force.

The innovations begun by Dingiswayo and Shaka, continued by Dingane and finally consolidated and institutionalized in the time of Mpande are essentially those which make a state a *suprakinship* society. Some of the elements are organizational, and others are ideological and ceremonial. When these latter are first instituted, of course, they do not have the unifying significance that they acquire after a generation or more of use, for finally they become traditional, more fully religious, and related to a growing national consciousness. This may be one of the reasons that Mpande did not need to rule by terror. Another reason may lie in the external situation. Whereas Shaka was all-conquering and the Zulu finally faced no external threat whatsoever, by the time of Mpande the

Zulu were virtually impounded on three sides by strong states and by the Indian Ocean to the east. To the north the Swazi and Thonga kingdoms stood firm, and to the southwest were the powerful Basuto. Most important of all, however, was the presence of Europeans. The well-armed Boers had settled to the west and were already beginning to encroach on Zulu territory. Adjacent to the Zulu at the south, the territory was ruled by the British, whose power had long been known to the Zulu. Such a foreign-political situation must have been distracting, to say the least, so that internal problems that might have caused trouble under earlier conditions were insignificant. It may be supposed, too, that being enclaved among strong neighbors, and particularly being in contact with neighbors so different from themselves in race, language, and culture as the Europeans, the Zulu found a newly heightened consciousness of themselves *as* Zulu, as members of a nation.

The original small Zulu chiefdom had subjugated neighbors quite similar to themselves so that the creation of suprakinship, national culture and institutions was not so difficult as in many areas where conquest states arose after the subjugation of unlike peoples. The same language, the same customs, and the same religion prevailed throughout the Zulu kingdom, so that national institutions were made of already-existing ingredients, and if the institutions were new, they did not conflict with cultural elements of one area and not another—the overlay of national culture was thus not a replacement of older culture for the subjugated peoples, only an addition. No caste lines reflecting the ethnic or cultural identity of conquerors as opposed to conquered ever arose among the Zulu. The only problem in the beginning was to overcome the tendency toward autonomy of the original chiefdoms composed of related people, for the unity of the nation exists in exactly inverse proportion to such autonomy.

The organizational innovations that helped make a nation out of separate kinship units were several. First in time and perhaps also in significance was the military organization based on age-graded regiments of men who lived as bachelors in barracks. They were directly under the king's orders rather than the orders of their own chiefs and thus were not only a standing army but also a state police that could be dispatched to any rebellious quarter with confidence that they would remain loyal to the king. At the same time, of course, the local chiefs were left without a substantial part of their own warriors. Many regiments were also used as a labor force by the king, so that his own revenue was increased and his power therefore enhanced. By the time of King Mpande the threat of the Boers had caused the barracks to be more closely centered near the king, which further concentrated his power.

A second organizational matter of significance that was intensified by the time of King Mpande was the centralization of trade. As noted earlier, Dingiswayo had seen the advantages that would accrue to himself if he encouraged trade with Europeans that would pass entirely through his own hands. By Mpande's time this foreign trade had increased greatly in amount and importance, and the king was therefore able to better consolidate his hold over the various districts as the chiefs became increasingly dependent on him for the goods he redistributed.

Another organizational change had consequences that may not have been intentional. The earlier chiefdoms had been composed of related patrilineal lineages that were local units and adjacent to one another. As time went on, most of these lineages grew, fissioned, and became more dispersed until they were only vague clans, exogamous and named, but having no such precise functions as the original lineages had had. The main local unit of the society was the *kraal,* a small, village homestead usually composed only of a patriarch and his several wives and perhaps a married son or two. Those that were closely related patrilineally formed lineages, but the clan of related lineages was weak. Meanwhile the state had apportioned subordinate political power to chiefs of territorial districts and to subchiefs of wards within the districts. These territorial subdivisions in the beginning had probably corresponded rather closely to the actual areas inhabited by the various chiefdoms and their lineages, but as time went on people moved around for various reasons, and some lineages grew and others declined until there became no close congruence between kinship group membership and political subdivision. Thus as the political territorial divisions grew in importance through time, the larger kinship units themselves came to have less and less political significance.

Of all institutions that are related to statecraft, the law is the most distinctive. A chief invokes custom, the gods, councils of elders, and so on in support of his authority, but a state as large and complex as that of the Zulu forever faces internal problems that are so unprecedented and so dangerous that some machinery of adjudication has to be instituted. A state must take measures against actions that threaten its integration. These are of two major kinds: actions against the state itself (or the king) and actions of groups against one another in which the state must intervene to prevent feud—or that ultimate result of feuds, civil war. In one way, law enforcement was simpler than in modern states and somewhat decentralized: responsibility was held to be collective, so that a crime by an individual involved restitution and fine to be paid by the kraal, or perhaps the whole lineage; thus individual crime was often effectively prevented by the collectivity. Local crimes were tried and punished at the local or district level, depending on who was involved, but any judgment could be appealed to a higher authority and ultimately to the king himself. All fines for murder and all fines from cases tried at the king's court belonged to the king. Next to the monopoly on foreign trade, this was the most important source of the state's revenue.

Ideological or symbolic innovations became in time very important factors in the consolidation of the king's position and in the unification of the nation. First of all, the king symbolized the nation itself; his good health was the nation's well-being. This identity of king and nation was dramatically represented in the First Fruits Ceremony, when the king was treated with magical medicines in order that the nation be strengthened. The king was also the custodian of various sacred fetishes that symbolized the nation's ancestors; thus he and only he could communicate with them in order to aid the nation—to ask for rain, for example.

Most of the characteristics of the Zulu political organization mentioned above were begun during Shaka's reign, but it was not until later, most clearly in the peaceful times of King Mpande, that they were fully coherent, elaborated, and traditionalized. In the following description of Zulu life, the present tense is used with reference to the period of Mpande's rule.

The territory inhabited by the Zulu comprises some 80,000 square miles and includes from one-quarter to one-half million people. Except in some low, marshy valleys, the land is fertile and watered adequately for gardens and pasturage. The dominant features of the topography are the rolling hills and valleys.

Occasionally there are forests, but the land is mostly open park, except for various bushes. Numerous streams wend their way from the interior upland eastward to the Indian Ocean.

Scattered over the landscape are the Zulu kraals. These are always a circle of several beehive-shaped grass huts surrounding a fenced area where the small herd of cattle is kept at night and confined for milking at midday. An outer hedge of planted prickly pear or mimosa fences in the whole kraal. The Zulu are normally polygynous, and each hut is the home of one wife and her children.

ZULU WIVES BREWING KAFIR BEER. *Courtesy, The American Museum of Natural History*

The kraal is largely a self-sufficient economic unit. Cattle provide daily milk used in the form of soured curds, but beef is eaten only at special ceremonial times. Goats, sheep, fowl, and dogs are also common. The day-to-day foundation of Zulu subsistence, however, is the garden, which is always tended by women. *Mealies* (maize, which was introduced from the new world and spread rapidly over much of Africa), kafir (a kind of grain sorghum), pumpkins, sweet potatoes, watermelons, plantain, sugar-cane, and calabashes are the most usual products. Some tobacco is grown, which both men and women take as snuff. Men smoke hemp, a narcotic known as hashish in the Near East. Despite the much greater use of vegetables and grain, cattle are the focus of interest and of more of the work. Cattle represent wealth, and are important as gifts, bride wealth, restitution, or payments of any kind; they are also ritually important and are the sacrifies that ancestral spirits demand.

There is some recourse to hunting for additional meat, for there is large game in Zulu territory: elephants, rhinoceroses, buffalos, various large antelope species, pigs, and the great feline carnivores. These animals are taken in large game drives, sometimes as a Royal Hunt involving thousands of people. Elaborate prehunt work involves erecting fences, digging pitfalls, and building ambuscades.

Like many other African peoples the Zulu know ironworking, which is the only professionalized craft in the economy. An ironsmith, using bellows and charcoal to heat the iron to malleability, can hammer out very finely made projectile points, knives, and ornaments. (Products of European metallurgy, including even some firearms, were becoming plentiful during Mpande's reign, however).

But most of the economic life of the Zulu takes place within the organization of the kraal. The division of labor by sex is strictly demarked, as are the tasks appropriate to children. Women, in addition to the expected housework and cooking, do all of the gardening, brew beer (from sprouted maize), and make pottery and mats. Men, as expected, do the fighting, hunting, hut-building, and such heavy work as clearing the land. Men are ritually associated with cattle, which are taboo to women, so they not only herd cattle but also do the milking (including the washing of the milking utensils) and the dressing of skins. Children gradually take up adult tasks as they mature, but boys are not allowed to herd cattle until after the ear-piercing ceremony at the age of 9 or 10.

All of the land is thought of as the property of the king. The distribution of the land for use, however, is more directly the responsibility of district chiefs, who allot it in the names of individual kraals. The kraals use the land as they see fit, but cannot alienate it. Land not in use as gardens is public grazing land. The property of the kraal itself is under the jurisdiction of the senior male and is inherited by primogeniture. Individual property includes, of course, such things as weapons and clothing. In addition, each wife owns her own hut and its utensils. The cattle are herded together and the headman of the kraal has ultimate jurisdiction over them, but they are thought of as individual property, and each wife is allotted some small proportion of the herd.

The huts of the kraal are always arranged in a circle on sloping ground with the entrance at the lowest point. The hut of the first wife of the headman is at the point opposite the entrance, on the highest ground overlooking the rest of the kraal. In this hut is kept the ancestral assagai to which sacrifices of animals are dedicated. The headman is the officiating priest at such ceremonies for he is the direct representative of the kraal ancestors.

The etiquette in the hut at mealtimes reflects the strict division of status and authority in Zulu society by sex and age. All men and boys occupy the right side of the hut, the headman nearest the door and the others ranged from him in descending order of seniority. The wife takes a similar position opposite, with the daughters also seated by seniority. Small children of both sexes take the rear position on the women's side. Directly in the rear of the hut is a storage place which is also a sacred area where offerings to the ancestors are placed.

On ordinary days the inhabitants of the kraal rise at dawn and disperse to their several tasks. The heaviest work is usually done in the cool of the morning. At about eleven o'clock the herdboys bring the cattle in and milk them, and the people go to their huts for the first meal of the day. The afternoon is given to lighter household tasks or working at the various crafts, while the herdboys take the cattle out to pasture and guard them until sundown when they are again brought into the kraal. The second meal of the day is eaten after this.

The organization of the kraal in terms of patrilocality and patrilineality combined with strict genealogical seniority is the same as the organization of the wider kinship group, the lineage. Thus there is a kraal in the lineage whose head is senior in the lineage because he is a first-born son of a line of first-born sons from the common ancestor of the lineage. Then there are other kraals in hierarchical order depending on the birth order of their headmen. A lineage is ordinarily a discernible residential unit like a dispersed neighborhood. The members of a lineage have many privileges with respect to one another's herds and lands; they help one another, and arbitrate disputes among members.

Clans are like higher-order lineages; lineages are related to other lineages by a common ancestral figure from whom the lineages descended. Clans are so large and dispersed that they are not primarily residential groups, but their identity is preserved by a clan name, a sacred clan song, and ceremonies of sacrifice to the ancestors. Clan members cannot intermarry, and they have family-like mutual obligations of hospitality and aid. Only clan members can drink milk together, for milk symbolizes intimate family relationship and is treated as sacred.

The whole Zulu nation of hundreds of clans is united politically and with true political forms, and yet there is a sentiment of the kinship of the whole. Although *Zulu* was once the name of but a single clan, an ideology has been fostered which makes the king not only the head of the Zulu clan but also the father of the whole people. For many occasions a polite form of address to a person is *Zulu*, no matter his clan affiliation.

The pattern of kinship nomenclature used among relatives reflects the three important status considerations that are below the level of actual political and military status. These are sex, relative age, and clan relationship. *Ego's* own father, father's brothers, and father's male parallel cousins are all given the same term, but their relative seniority is indicated by an affix. The eldest of these is always shown the greatest respect, even if he is not close genealogically. The same term is also used in address to a district chief, even when actual relationship is not known. Similarly, mother and mother's sisters and her female parallel cousins are given the same term and distinguished by age if *ego* is a female. This age distinction is not explicitly recognized by males, because male status is higher than that of any female. Grandparents are distinguished from one another by sex only, although *ego's* father's father is the patriarch of greatest authority.

In *ego's* own generation the children of all of his fathers are the same as his own brother and sister. The children of mothers' brothers, of course, are cross cousins and members of his mother's lineage and clan. Fathers' sisters' children are also cross cousins and often, but not always, members of his mother's lineage and clan. All are given the same term, which is different from the term for the parallel cousins. The marriage rule forbids the marriage of *ego* into both own clan and his mother's; thus, an individual does not marry a cross cousin. This fact is of some interest, because it reveals so clearly that it is the distinction between the affines in *ego's* parents' generation—father's clan as opposed to mother's clan—that creates the distinction in *ego's* generation between parallel cousins (members of own clan) and cross cousins (members of mother's clan) and not any form of marriage relationship involving himself.

Children of all siblings and all cousins are simply *my child*. All of the children of these are equally generalized terminologically as grandchildren, which is to say that children's and grandchildren's terms merely signify their generation. Sex differences and more precise linkages can be stated, however, with descriptive phrases— the generalized character of these kinship terms is in no sense caused by ignorance of, or lack of interest in, exact genealogical connections.

The terminology used for affines is generalized at all generational levels except that a wife's actual father and mother are given specific titles. A female *ego,* however, because she lives after marriage in close proximity to her husband's family, tends to adopt the same terms for his mother and father that he uses. The social relationship of affines is one of formal respect. A wife must be particularly circumspect, because she is living under direct surveillance of her in-laws. She cannot use the personal names of her father- or mother-in-law, or even any word that contains the radical of such a name. After she has been in residence among her husband's people for a long time, and particularly after having raised children, she will be considered more fully a part of the lineage.

The kinds of status discussed above are essentially those based on kinship and marriage. The Zulu however, also have status deriving from political position. Shaka's immediate family, and ultimately the important members of his clan, acquired high status because of his exploits. Neither he nor his successor, his brother Dingane, left any descendants, but Mpande formed a true royal family, so that any children of this line form a ruling class of princes and princesses, superior in all cases to district chiefs, the next highest rank, unless a prince is himself settled into a district as chief. The descendants of the king are differentiated among themselves in terms of birth order.

For all people, kindred or not and whatever the rank, the overriding principle is that of seniority, manifested in the birth order in a family, age grades in the broader social context, and relative age in any meeting of strangers. The most rigid structuring of seniority is that of the age grades, and the various ceremonies of the individual's life cycle serve to demark the important stages by which his age status changes.

The birth of a child not only marks the beginning of a new individual's life cycle, but if it is a first-born child, the birth is celebrated because it marks a very important stage in the life cycle of the parents themselves. A marriage is literally not complete or consummated until a child is born. The birth of a first-born takes place in the husband's mother's hut, and it is only after the birth of the first child that the wife has jurisdiction in her own hut. A barren woman is regarded as the most unfortunate kind of person in Zulu society. In some cases, however, if the marriage is important as an economic or political alliance, an absence of progeny can be compensated for by the adoption of a child of the wife's sister.

Pregnancy is a period attended by a great many taboos and rituals, primarily because of the belief that the foetus can be easily marked by things that happen to the mother or are seen by her. Delivery of the baby is attended by women only, and the oldest ones ordinarily act as midwives. As in a great many primitive societies, great care is taken in disposing of the umbilical cord and afterbirth. These are buried in the rear of the hut, the area where ancestor spirits reside, and carefully covered over so that no stranger may find them. Again, as in primitive society generally, it is strongly believed that harmful magic can be worked with bodily effluvia. The child is strengthened against harm by being held in the smoke of burning charms made from parts of "unlucky" animals—animals that may have marked the child if seen by its mother. Some dirt is scraped from the father's body, also, and mixed with the other medicines. Some of this is given in a drink, and some is rubbed into small incisions in the baby's skin in order that the baby acquire the personality of the father as well as be linked with the paternal ancestors. Mother and child are then isolated until the navel cord withers and drops off, a period of 8 to 10 days. The baby is considered weak and susceptible to evil influences, and the mother is ritually unclean, until this period is ended with purification rites.

Children are mostly under the jurisdiction of women until the emancipation of boys is celebrated by the ear-piercing ceremony at the age of 9 or 10. All the boys in the vicinity, sometimes all those of the lineage, who are approximately of that age are gathered together at the time of either the full moon or the new moon to have their ears pierced. This ritual excludes all women except those past child-bearing age. An ox is sacrificed to the ancestors, and then the beloved feast of roast beef and beer is held. (The boys were allowed to herd only goats and sheep before, but now they are ritually introduced to man's work, cattle herding.) All the boys who have undergone this ceremony, but not the later puberty ceremony, are members of an age-set sodality.

The puberty rituals are based on physiological signs of maturity and thus not strictly on age. When a boy has his first nocturnal emission, he steals out of the hut and takes all of the cattle out of the kraal and drives them as far away as he can. In the morning the men go to find him, and the longer he can evade discovery, the more praiseworthy his deed. At the subsequent ceremony and feast he is given his first assagai, after which he dives in the river to emerge newly born. He is given a new name, and for the rest of his life his age-mates and all people younger must call him by that name. People senior to him continue to use his baby name.

Girls' puberty is also determined by physiological signs. The girl runs away after discovering her first menstruation and hides while her female age-mates look for her. After she is found, they escort her to her mother's hut and seclude her in the sacred rear area behind a screen. After several days she is brought out and her new status signalized by a feast.

Within a few years after puberty all boys join the local company of the age regiment that is formed simultaneously throughout the nation. Regimental songs and insignia are assigned and also a regimental name, which is a title of individual address as well as the name for the regiment as a whole. All the regiments of unmarried men are called Black Regiments (signified by black shields) and live in barracks. These form the standing army, police, and king's labor force. Older married men of the White Regiments live at home but can be called up, like militia, as needed.

In Shaka's day the Black Regiments were kept in barracks for many years before marriage was allowed, so that more troops would be under arms at all times. In later, more peaceful times the men were dismissed for marriage at an earlier age, ordinarily in their middle twenties.

Marriages are essentially arrangements between lineages, but within the lineages a great many negotiations take place between the particular families of the betrothed. It should be remembered that a man cannot marry into either his father's or his mother's clan; hence the marriage does not involve families of any very close degree of relationship. The negotiations involve the number and condition of the cattle to be transferred from the groom's family and lineage to the bride's, presents of beer from the bride's family to the groom's, a present to the bride from her father of a few cattle and goods that will go with her to her new home, and particular presents that go to important members of her new family.

Before the actual marriage the girl's hair is put up in a topknot, and after the marriage the groom always wears a head-ring. The *lobola*—in Zulu thought, the cattle given to the bride's family in exchange for rights to the progeny—are brought to the bride's family kraal, after which the bride, escorted by age-mates, but not by her own family, sets out for her new home. She is kept secluded by her friends even during the next day's wedding celebrations. An interesting feature of the celebrations is that ritualized

Courtesy, The American Museum of Natural History

insults are exchanged between the groom's family and her own family, after her family arrives for the feasting. One aspect of the overt antagonism is apparently that it dramatizes the significance of the loss of the girl by her family. It is also demonstrated at the ceremony how difficult is the acceptance of a new member into the husband's kraal. The bride must be very demure, and even stays in seclusion for a while after the wedding. For some time highly ceremonialized visits and gift exchanges are maintained between the two in-law groups. The husband is supposed to be helpful to his father-in-law at all times and to expect aid in return.

The Zulu are highly moral about marriage obligations: divorce and desertion are very rare, as is unchaste behavior. In case of any difficulty caused by the wife that results in divorce, her family must return the lobola. The lobola also might be returned if the wife should die before children are born to her, but usually a younger sister is sent to replace her. This custom of the sororate is matched by the levirate—if the husband dies, his brother accepts the care of the widow and children.

Kings and high chiefs have more wives and more elaborate ceremonies and give larger lobolas than do persons of lower status. Additionally, the kings often choose, or accept as gifts, large numbers of girls who are quartered together and called the *King's Sisters.* In many cases they are simply concubines, but often they are given by the king in marriage to someone favored by him. Thus the king's royal herds are increased by lobolas from the grateful husbands.

Death is ceremonialized by frenzied demonstrations of grief and by purification rituals. The corpse is a source of magical pollution, and a great many taboos are invoked. The relatives shave their heads, all ornaments are discarded, and the name of the deceased cannot be uttered until after the Bringing-Home Ceremony a year or two later. In early times corpses were hidden in the bush, and in later times, buried, but in either case the place remains secret, because if a magician can acquire a part of the body, he can harm the surviving relatives. The Bringing-Home Ceremony is held to retire the spirit (of males only) in the ancestral spirit-residing place in the kraal. The main elements of the ceremony are the taking of purifying medicines by the relatives and the sacrifice of an ox. A part of the ox is placed in the sacred ancestral area. The feast is a joyful one, for it celebrates the spirit's joining the ancestors, and normal life can be resumed in the kraal.

The death of a king is, of course, a very important event. A very large tomb is prepared, and his favorite wife and a large number of retainers are strangled and buried with him. Inasmuch as the ancestral spirits of the royal line control the destiny of the whole nation, the Bringing-Home Ceremony for his spirit is the most important ceremony that ever occurs.

The ideology of religion is above all centered on the patrilineal ancestors, both local and national. In most cases, the ancestors were real persons, although standing above all is a Creator or First Cause, *Unkulunkulu* ("the old, old one"), who made all things. As an object of worship or prayer, however, this god is too remote and nonfunctional to command much attention. There is also a vague conception of a Lord of Heaven who can cause thunder or rain, and a Princess of Heaven who presides over the growth of crops.

Supernaturalism includes the belief in spirits, omens, sympathetic magic, and spirit possession that are so widespread as elements of shamanism. In Zulu society there are several different kinds of shamans and magicians. The most common is the shaman proper, or diviner. Like shamans elsewhere, he is essentially a diagnostician. His special ability comes from being possessed by a spirit who speaks through him or gives him messages in a dream. Knowing the cause of an illness, he can prescribe the cure. He also sometimes functions as an agent of government in that his special powers enable him to find, by "smelling out", treasonable people and other criminals.

Another common medicine man is not a diviner, but merely an herbalist. He is less important and less awesome, because he does not claim spiritual power, but only superior knowledge or experience with natural medicines. A Heaven Doctor is specialized for controlling thunder and lightning by magic; his close counterpart is the Rain Maker, who by magic can induce rain.

In contrast to all of the shamans and magicians mentioned above, whose aims are to benefit society, the wizard, or witch, uses magic for antisocial ends. He (or she) can cause no end of misfortunes. His deadliest practice is obtaining some part of a victim's body, such as hair- or fingernail-clippings, and mixing them with herbs in a secret formula and burying the mixture in a hole, over which he builds a fire; the victim feels a burning sensation at first and soon dies unless a shaman can effectively diagnose the trouble and make countermagic. The wizard can also do harm by using soil from a person's footprint or by introducing a magical decoction into his food or beer.

But these are local, or folk, aspects of supernaturalism. The Zulu state is quite properly to be considered a theocracy; hence there are also many elements of supernatural belief, ritual, and ceremony that are aspects of statecraft. The beliefs that are most functionally connected to the social order generally and to the state in particular are those that center on the cult of the ancestors. The ancestor-gods are arranged in hierarchical order, as are the people on earth, and the most significant ceremonies—and those including the most people—are, of course, directed to the most important ancestors. The king himself is the center of these ceremonies, for it is he who is the direct descendant of the highest ranking ancestors. The king is also the custodian of the sacred fetishes symbolic of the nation and its ancestors. The belief in the close connections of the king with the ancestors makes him directly responsible for the growth of crops, rainfall, fruitfulness, and good luck generally, because only he can petition the ancestors for aid.

The most impressive national ceremony is the yearly First Fruits Ceremony, which initiates the period of the harvest. No one may harvest any crops until the king has conducted the ceremony. The whole nation assembles before the king, with the army regiments dressed in splendid ceremonial array and drawn up in ranks between him and the multitude. A special rain-making song, sometimes called the King's Song or national anthem, is used only on this occasion. It is accompanied by a rhythmic stamping of the right foot, and when it is begun by one regiment and then taken up successively by others until the whole army and then the whole assemblage is in full voice, the ancestors are highly honored. A First Fruits feast follows, and then the army, numbering perhaps 20,000 soldiers, performs its leaping, whirling dance before the king and the rest of the nation.

The late history of the Zulu, which led to their modern predicament, is a part of the history of European colonization in South Africa. The first European settlement was at the Cape of Good Hope in 1652 on behalf of the Dutch East India Company, which needed a supply station on the route to the Far East. This colony was joined by Huguenot settlers in 1688, and became the farming nucleus of the population known as Boers, later as Afrikaners. In 1795 the British occupied the Cape, and in 1814 Holland ceded the territory to Great Britain by the Treaty of Vienna, after which a number of British settlers arrived.

There had been an indirect trade between Zululand and the Portuguese post at Delagoa Bay in Dingiswayo's time, but the first direct contact of Zulu and Europeans occurred only after 1824 when a small English group formed a settlement at Port Natal (now

Durban) to trade European goods for ivory and skins. Shaka accepted them because of the obvious advantages of the trade. He was also much impressed with their firearms, and a few English sailors helped him win some important battles by using their muskets at critical moments.

This peaceful relationship between the few Europeans and the Zulu was altered by the arrival of Boer settlers in Natal beginning in 1838. These were outliers of the Great Trek, in which numbers of Boers left the British-ruled Cape to set up their own government in the north. King Dingane reacted against the incoming Boers by killing most of them, but the English, contrary to expectation, took the side of the Boers and retaliated with a raid into Zululand, where they were soundly defeated. But more Boers came, defeated Dingane, and took possession of Natal. Inasmuch as the whole Zulu army was defeated by only 400 mounted Boers, it became clear to the Zulu that times had changed, that they could not withstand European military technology.

Great Britain took possession of Natal (but not Zululand) in 1843, and the Boers retired to the Transvaal. But eventually troubles occurred at the border of Natal and Zululand, and the British invaded Zululand in 1879. After an initial defeat administered by King Cetshwayo, the British conquered the Zulu, exiled the king, divided the kingdom into 13 independent parts, and then withdrew. Naturally enough, this was not a viable arrangement, and numerous small wars broke out among independent Zulu factions. Meanwhile, the Boers were again entering the region, and finally the British government, responding to the pleas of many Zulu as well as of humanitarian groups in Great Britain, reoccupied Zululand in 1887 and set up a centralized administration with a British magistrate who worked with the district chiefs. The king, though still honored by the Zulu, was relegated to a chief's status in one small district.

The subsequent years of close contact with European government, missionaries, and economic institutions altered Zulu life in much the same way as native life was altered elsewhere in South Africa. The plow was introduced, which greatly increased the amount of land under cultivation; but because oxen were used for traction, men became the agriculturalists. Meanwhile the growth in population— the Zulu now number more than 2 million, as contrasted to one-quarter to one-half million in King Mpande's time—has greatly overburdened the Reserve in which the Zulu are confined. The recourse, as elsewhere, has been for men to leave the Reserve periodically to work for wages on plantations, in mines and factories, and as servants. At first, such work was necessary in order to pay the hut tax that supported the cost of government administration, but eventually the desire to purchase European goods, as well as the increasing attrition of population on the limited land, has made at least some wage labor almost universal among Zulu men.

In modern times the economic relations between South African whites and the native Bantus have reached the point of their being integrated into a single system. Each needs the other and the economy would not function without both Bantu labor and European capital, technology, and management. This is not a happy symbiosis, however, for necessary as Bantu labor has come to be, the relations of the two groups are on a caste basis, with the white caste maintaining a total political, social, and economic monopoly of power.

The Zulu on the Reserve have very many grievances, most of them products of economic and political helplessness. At the same time that they grow more educated generally, and ever more enmeshed in the economic and political system, so does their understanding of their helplessness, so that their consequent reaction against the whites takes more overt form. Thus as they become more Europeanized in certain respects, there is also an increase in sentiment and emotion toward what are perceived to be old Zulu customs. It is often the most educated who have reacted against the new and who advocate most strongly a return to Zulu culture. This phenomenon of revivalism or revitalization is characteristic of an oppressed nation or race and has been observed among American Indians, Melanesians, and Indonesians, as well as in Africa.

The Bantu natives represent a great majority over the whites in South Africa today; yet the whites hold utter dominion over them. The whites are not simply colonials of a European power, however, for they have been there for so many generations that they consider themselves to be natives of South Africa, an independent nation that their own ancestors created. The solution of the problem of Negro-white relations in South Africa is not like the relatively simple one carried out in Ghana, for example, or Nigeria. There the British frankly held an administrative and economic colony that did not include great numbers of settlers, and in response to native nationalism they finally granted independence and withdrew. In South Africa, however, the nationalism is manifested by the long-settled Europeans, former colonists but now South Africans, more than by the Bantu.

There are in South Africa a great many white people of good will and good intentions toward the Bantu. But the majority political party, the Nationalists, largely composed of Afrikaners, descendants of the early Huguenot settlers, have maintained a policy of segregation and suppression of Bantu aspirations—the policy of Apartheid. By this policy the Bantu are confined to their overcrowded Reserves except when they go out to work on a highly restrictive pass card. Meanwhile, the progress of such peoples as the Zulu is supposed to take place independently of the whites—on their own Reserve, which is their nation's homeland.

Inasmuch as any such arrangement in South Africa also includes the retention of the Bantu as a low-paid proletariat caste, clearly an independent development in the Reserves will not result—in the off-hours, so to speak. It is impossible to predict what will happen, or when, but we may be certain that whatever does happen will not be pretty. Ronald Segal, a famous South African journalist (now in exile) said: "Whether or not revolution will come to South Africa has long ago given place to the question of what form revolution will take. The arrogance and rigidity of white domination have made fundamental reform synonomous with Armageddon, and it has become apparent to all but a choir of moral re-armers that the whites will surrender their monopoly over the places of power only when the ushers have finally forced them to make room."[1]

Meanwhile, what is the attitude of other nations to this situation? For most Western nations the standard diplomatic attitude is an ambivalent one. The problem is particularly acute for the United States of America, the self-proclaimed leader of the Free World. The United States faces in several world areas the dilemma of supporting a repressive, antidemocratic regime for the sake of its anti-Communist strategic alliance, thus at the same time fomenting an anti-Americanism among the newly independent democratic nations. In the case of South Africa the dilemma is absolute, for, as Mr. Segal puts it:

[1] R. Segal, "The Free World's Other Face," in J. Duffy and R. Manners (eds.), *Africa Speaks,* London, Toronto, New York, 1961, p. 219.

. . . South Africa not only produces most of the West's gold supply and a substantial slice of its uranium, as well as nearly all its diamonds, but its administration is anti-Communist to the point of derangement. Here in truth is a Gibraltar of the West. Yet on this rock, 3,000,000 whites dominate some 10,000,000 Africans, over 1,000,000 Coloureds [mixed white-Negro], and just under 500,000 Asiatics; and the dominion is not only absolute, it is malevolent. Stripped of all franchise rights and all but a mockery of civil liberties, the Africans are hounded by "pass" laws into silent serfdom on the white-owned farms or slow starvation in the suffocated Reserves. . . . No wonder then that the Africans stream into the urban areas, whether their papers are in order or not, risking jail for the average city wage of $45 a month. No wonder that 95 per cent of the Africans living in the city of Durban were authoritatively reported in 1959 to be living below the bread-line, and that official estimates place the African infant mortality rate as somewhere between 200 and 300 per 1,000.[2]

FURTHER READINGS

Bryant, A. T., *Olden Times in Zululand and Natal,* London, New York, Toronto, 1929.

Bryant, A. T., *The Zulu People as They Were Before the White Man Came,* Pietermaritzburg, 1949, 2 vols.

Gibson, J. Y., *The Story of the Zulus,* London, 1911.

Gluckman, M., *The Kingdom of the Zulu of South Africa,* in M. Fortes and E. E. Evans-Pritchard (eds.), *African Political Systems,* London, New York, Toronto, 1940.

Gluckman, M., *Kinship and Marriage among the Lozi of Northern Rhodesia and the Zulu of Natal,* in A. R. Radcliffe-Brown and D. Forde (eds.), *African Systems of Kinship and Marriage,* London, 1950.

Gluckman, M., *Analysis of a Social Situation in Modern Zululand,* Rhodes-Livingstone Papers, No. 28, Manchester, 1958.

Isaacs, N., *Travels and Adventures in Eastern Africa . . . ,* London, 1836.

Krige, E. J., *The Social System of the Zulus,* Pietermaritzburg, 1957.

Kuper, H., *The Uniform of Color,* Johannesburg, 1947.

Ritter, E. A., *Shaka Zulu: The Rise of the Zulu Empire,* London, 1955.

Segal, R., "The Free World's Other Face," in J. Duffy and R. Manners (eds.), *Africa Speaks,* London, Toronto, New York, 1961.

Shapera, I. (ed.), *Western Civilization and the Natives of South Africa,* London, 1934.

Shapera, I., *The Bantu-Speaking Tribes of South Africa,* London, 1937.

[2] *Ibid.,* pp. 205–206.

15

The Maya
of Mexico

The cultural development of the American Indians had two great historical crests. One culmination was the civilization of the Andes, dominated at the end of its course by the Inca dynasty. The other was the civilization of Meso-America, the region encompassing the central plateau of Mexico and the area to the south including Yucatán, Chiapas, Guatemala, and part of Honduras in Central America. These were two civilizations in the most literal sense of the term; for society was organized on a civil basis, the principle of the city-state, rather than the kinship principle alone, which was charactertistic of most of the other American Indian tribes.

The Meso-American region was a cultural unity, but kept from perfect homogeneity by geographic variation and by the political sovereignty of the several petty empires which waxed and waned in the area. But all of the separate civil entities that occupied the region shared the definitive essentials of the Meso-American civilization. Some of the most famous of these states are the Aztec and earlier Toltec of the region centered around Mexico City. Others are less well known, but include some impressive developments. In the Mexican state of Michoacan, north and west of the Aztec, Tarascan-speaking Indians were part of an empire that, at least in military strength, was able to hold its own against any of its neighbors. East and south of Mexico City, impressive archaeological sites, particularly at Cholula, testify to similar cultural developments. Zapotec and Mixtec remains in Oaxaca, farther south, and Olmec, Totonac, and Huastec along the gulf coast of Tabasco and Vera Cruz again are reminiscent of the more northerly ones, although much less archaeological work has been done in those regions. Finally, in the jungle lowlands of Yucatán, in the Petén region of northern Guatemala, and in neighboring British Honduras are the impressive stone pyramids and temples of the mysterious Maya.

The lowland Mayan outposts of the general Meso-American civilization have had a longer and more intensive amount of study by professional archaeologists than has any other comparable region in the New World. Even in the sixteenth century the Spaniards were impressed by the striking architecture of the Maya civic centers and left several interesting accounts of Mayan life—most of which, unfortunately, lay disintegrating in archives for centuries. Among these, the most famous and most useful was the history and description of Yucatán written by the Bishop Diego de Landa about 1560 and based on observations made shortly after the Spanish conquest.[1] Other written sources from the early days are the summaries of ancient Mayan history and historical legend set down by Maya Indians in the Spanish alphabet but in the Mayan language.

After the Spanish conquest European diseases ravaged the native population and even today hookworm and malaria make a great part of the lowland jungle nearly uninhabitable. As a consequence, the great number of Mayan ruins remained lost cities until the nineteenth century, when several explorations attracted the attention of the outside world to this interesting area. Probably the most important, and one of the earliest, of these was by John Lloyd Stephens, who made two arduous explorations between 1839 and 1841. Stephens was an educated American diplomat and amateur archaeologist who traveled in the company of Frederick Catherwood, an English artist. Two books written by Stephens and illustrated by the fine drawings of Catherwood were widely read in the mid-century and were responsible for an awakening of scientific

[1] See A. M. Tozzer's translation of Landa's *"Relación de las Cosas de Yucatán,"* Papers of the Peabody Museum of American Archaeology and Ethnology, Vol. 18, Cambridge, Mass., 1941.

and scholarly interest in the Maya in both Europe and America.[2]

The first truly scientific work on the Maya was done by the English archaeologist Sir Alfred Maudslay in the period 1881–1894. The first scientific organization to support intensive Mayan studies was the Peabody Museum of Archaeology and Ethnology of Harvard University in 1892. In modern times, beginning in 1915, the Carnegie Institution of Washington has continued a pro-

MAYAN PYRAMID AND TEMPLE, CHICHEN ITZA, YUCATÁN. *Courtesy, Mexican National Tourist Council*

gram of studies and excavations ranking as the most intensive concerted drive even made on one archeological region. Other research centers have also contributed to our knowledge of the Maya: the Instituto de Antropología e Historia de Mexico, the University Museum of Pennsylvania, the Middle American Research Institute of Tulane University, the British Museum, and the Chicago Natural History Museum.

Mayan culture has been very exciting to those several scholars who have devoted their lives to its investigation. The ruins of great pyramids and temples are grandiose, surprisingly numerous, and

[2] John L. Stephens, *Incidents of Travel in Central America, Chiapas and Yucatan,* New York, 1841, 2 vols.; *Incidents of Travel in Yucatan,* New York, 1843, 2 vols.

beautiful as well. How could they have been built by American Indians in such a fiendishly difficult jungle? Perhaps more striking and wonderful are the intellectual characteristics of the Mayan culture. The calendar system, though complicated, is as accurately geared to astronomical cycles as any in the world; the hieroglyphic writing is reminiscent of that of the ancient eastern Mediterranean classic civilizations; in mathematics, the principle of the zero and the related positional numeration was used before the savants of India grasped it and passed it on to the forebears of Western civilization.

Nothing is known, unfortunately, of the origins of these cultural phenomena. They are not necessarily specifically Mayan. Calendars, counting systems, pyramids, hieroglyphs, and so on were common to the Meso-American area as a whole. The ruins of a few other great and ancient civilizations of the world, such as those of Cambodia and Java, have been found in tropical forests, but these were introduced into the area from outside, already in full bloom. It may be presumed that the conditions requisite for the development of a civilization must be more special and fecund than those required for its later perpetuation. It seems likely, therefore, that the basic elements which go to make up civilization were developed in highland parts of Meso-America where water control (irrigation and/or drainage) made primitive agriculture so prolific that urban civilization and its various concomitants followed more understandably than they could in the lowland forests.[3]

Foremost experts on the Maya, it should be remarked, believe that the Maya developed their own civilization to maturation in the tropic zones, somehow as a product of unusual Maya genius or character.[4] But there is no evidence that the Maya developed the essentials of their civilization themselves or earlier than some other regions of Meso-America (and the above-mentioned works describe the possibly contemporaneous development of other parts of Meso-America); hence our suggestion that it is better to think of the Maya as presenting an aspect of general Meso-American civilization, rather than to accept the more standard conclusion exemplified by the following statement from Thompson: "Maya

[3] Betty Meggers, "Environmental Limitation on the Development of Culture," *American Anthropologist*, Vol. 56, 1954. See particularly pp. 817–820.

[4] Sylvanus G. Morley, *The Ancient Maya*, Stanford, 1946, 1947, or 1956; J. Eric Thompson, *The Rise and Fall of Maya Civilization*, Norman, Okla., 1954.

civilization, I believe, was the product of Maya character, but there was another essential ingredient—a creative minority with the imagination and mental energy to start Maya lowland civilization on its course and keep it on that course for several hundred years."[5]

The culture of the ancient Maya occupied three rather distinct ecological zones. The southern area is mountainous, composed of the Guatemalan highlands and the adjacent and similar region in El Salvador. Here Mayan-speaking people survive in greater numbers today than they do in the lowlands. This was not the area of greatest prominence in the spectacular pyramid- and temple-building period, however, and therefore has not been a focus of archaeological interest. The central area, the lowland region of which the core is the Petén district of Guatemala, is now largely uninhabited but once was where some of the largest Mayan cities were built. The northern division is the peninsula comprising the Mexican states of Campeche and Yucatán, and the small territory of Quintana Roo. The Classic Mayan city-building occurred in the central region and later appeared in the northern area in somewhat less fulsome degree. It is this latter area, however, that is the best known, primarily because it was the one about which the Spaniards have left the fullest information.

Both the central and northern areas are low-lying tropical forests, the soil thin and built over a limestone base. The central area is slightly higher than the northern with some undulation so that streams flow and shallow lakes are formed. Rainfall is very high near the highlands during the wet season. A dry season lasts from January until May. Proceeding into the northern region, the rainfall lessens progressively, the country flattens, and, because of the more porous limestone base, streams perish and the sole source of water consists of deep pools—*cenotes*—where breaks in the limestone crust expose ground water.[6]

In the lowland environment the limestone is perhaps the natural resource responsible for giving Mayan civilization characteristics that distinguish it most clearly from other Meso-American cultures. This stone, when fresh, is easily quarried, cut, and carved; when exposed to the elements for a time, it hardens. When it is burned,

[5] Thompson, *op. cit.,* p. 268.
[6] For further discussion of the geography of Yucatán, see Chapter 18.

it reduces to lime, and mixed with granular limestone, it makes a fine mortar. Mayan architecture and carvings, as distinguished from those in the highlands of Meso-America, certainly must be understood as dependent in some measure on the distinctiveness of this resource.

In other respects the lowlands offered no apparent stimulus to cultural advance. Animal life in the jungle was more plentiful than in the highlands—jaguar, deer, peccaries, tapirs, monkeys, and a great many kinds of birds were the largest or most important as game, and numerous wild fruits were found, but hardly enough of either to make the population as dense or as secure in food as that in certain of the highland areas that had water-controlled agriculture. The crops grown by the Maya were of the kind known to many other American Indians. Maize, beans, and squash were the classic American trinity usually planted together, but maize was considered the most important. The American tubers—sweet potatoes, yams, and manioc—were probably next in importance. Several spices, particularly chili peppers, allspice, and vanilla, were grown, as were cacao, cotton, tobacco, and gourds. The forest itself yielded fine hardwoods, leaves for thatch, several fibers, refuge for the honeybee, and (of considerable negative importance) great numbers of insect pests. Yet none of these was distinctive of the area; other tropical forest regions in Central and South America were similar.

The history of the occupation of the lowland Maya region as revealed by archaeology does not take us back to the origins of the basic features of Meso-American civilization. For that matter, these origins have not been discovered in other parts of Meso-America either; the earliest sites now known, while somewhat simpler and smaller than the later and more numerous ones, all indicate that a community life based on agriculture was already present. This period, generally dated as from about 500 B.C. until about A.D. 300, and usually called the Formative, already manifested such special features of characteristic Meso-American culture as pyramids, elementary hieroglyphs and calendrical computations, pottery and figurines, and such art motifs as grotesque masks of jaguars and snakes.[7]

[7] The dates, based on the interpretations of Maya calendrical carvings, are those of the generally accepted Goodman-Martínez-Thompson correlation formula. Recent

The Classic Period, the time of great spread and efflorescence of the Mayan culture centered in the central area, dates from about A.D. 300 to a peak about 800 and was followed by a period of senescence and political collapse between 800 and 925. In Yucatán, meanwhile, a period of domination by northern Mexican invaders, apparently Toltecs, began and persisted until, after 1200, the Mayan culture (and probably political rule) gradually reasserted itself. But in the fifteenth century, local warfare and a general decline were again evident. But the time the Spaniards arrived in Yucatán in 1527, there was apparently no political unity, empire or confederation, left in the region. The possible causes of the decline of the Old Empire of the central region and the later disruption of the New Empire in Yucatán have been a major interest of many experts on the Maya, and a great many explanations have been made, ranging from deforestation, peasant revolts, failure of leadership, and so on, to warfare. There is evidence of warfare to be sure, and, interestingly, it appears that certain other empires, such as that of Teotihuacan near Mexico City, were undergoing similar hardships at about the same time that the Classic Maya culture was having its difficulties. But it is possible to regard warfare, particularly civil war, as a frequent *result* of political breakdown, rather than its cause. At any rate, the causes of the political disintegration remain unknown, and we must simply add the Maya to the long list of ancient civilizations that rose only to fall.

It appears that the waxing and waning of the two phases of Mayan history refer essentially to the amount of labor being expended on public works, rather than to any cataclysms which affected the lives of the bulk of the population. As the Classic Period approached its zenith in the central area, more and more elaborate ceremonial or civic centers of pyramids, temples, and ball courts were being built. The so-called decline of the area means only that no new centers were being built, and old ones were increasingly neglected. In other words, no public labor was being mobilized by a political authority. Thus the rise and fall of the Classic and the later northern Maya may have been merely an alteration in the strength of large-scale political authority. This is

radiocarbon dates tend to support this correlation. See L. Satterthwaite and E. K. Ralph, "New Radiocarbon Dates and the Maya Correlation Problem," *American Antiquity,* Vol. 26, No. 2, 1960.

a minimal conclusion; if other matters, such as pestilence, soil exhaustion, peasant revolts, failure of leadership, or other things which affected the population as a whole, occurred, they are unknown to us.

The life of the ordinary family in Yucatán in late Mayan times was probably the same as it had been for more than a thousand years. The highly civilized aspects of Mayan culture which have attracted attention—the architecture, calendar, writing, sculpture and painting—were the products of specialists who were supported by the upper class members of the bureaucratic government. The arts, therefore, could flourish or decline in a particular place, depending on the political history of that place. But with respect to the habits of the ordinary Mayan people, it would seem that we deal with a more basic aspect of Mayan culture, certainly in the sense of its being the more durable.

The main focus of interest of the Maya peasant was the cornfield. About 80 percent of the diet of the modern Maya of Yucatán is maize, and it probably was at least that in pre-Spanish times when there was an even smaller variety of cultivated foods. The agricultural practices were similar to those in many other tropic zones. The essentials consisted of felling a section of forest, burning the wood and brush after it had dried, planting and harvesting for two or three years, and then leaving it to fallow for a decade or so. The trees were ringed or cut during the rainy season and were burned near the end of the dry season. The day for the burning was determined by the priests and was apparently of considerable ritual importance. Each year every family cleared and burned a new cornfield to go along with the other two or three remaining from the previous years' burnings. According to Morley's calculation, the average family head worked at his own clearing and farming only about 48 days a year. "With so much free time, the Maya Indian for the last two thousand years has been exploited —first by his native rulers and priests, next by his Spanish conquerors, and more recently by private owners in the hemp fields."[8]

The Mayan house was a simple pole-and-thatch edifice of one room, a considerable contrast to the brilliant temples which these simple farmers had to help construct. The Mayan houses were widely scattered, or at best nucleated into small hamlets. There

[8] Morley, *op. cit.,* p. 140.

was no true urban settlement, such as that found at Teotihuacan and other Meso-American sites, probably because of the nature of the agricultural system and its fallowing problems. The so-called Mayan cities were largely civic centers only, containing the temples, pyramids, ball courts, and perhaps the homes of some of the higher dignitaries.

Not much is known of the domestic life which went on in the relatively unfurnished huts. The people sat on little stools and slept on a low platform. Corn-grinding was done on the stone *metate* still in use, and cooking was done on a small stone hearth and round clay griddle. A sixteenth-century source describes Mayan eating customs as follows:

As to the meals which they ate in the time of their antiquity, they eat the same today. This is corn boiled in water and crushed. When made into dough, they dissolve it in water for a drink [*pozole*], and this is what they ordinarily drink and eat. An hour before sunset it was their custom to make certain *tortillas* of the said dough. On these they supped, dipping them into certain dishes of crushed peppers, diluted with a little water and salt. Alternately with this they ate certain boiled beans of the land, which are black. They call them *buul,* and the Spanish, *frijoles.* This was the only time they ate during the day, for at other times they drank the dissolved dough mentioned above.[9]

Everyday dress of the common people was simple. Men wore a cotton breechclout and sometimes a large square cloth knotted around the shoulders. Women wore a tubular cotton dress, with holes for the head and arms. Men left their hair long and arranged it in braids. A bare spot was burned on the top of the head, and the braids were wound around like a coronet with a queue left to dangle behind. Women's hair styles varied a great deal, with the greatest difference being between styles for girls as contrasted with those for married women. Tattooing and body painting were used in personal decoration. The clothing of the nobility and priesthood was essentially of the same style, but much more splendidly and intricately decorated. As among the Aztecs and others, the ceremonial shoulder robe was sometimes made of brilliantly colored feathers, and a great ceremonial headdress, often made to represent the head of a jaguar, bird, or snake, was the most striking part of the costume. Accessory decorations consisted of various ear, nose, and lip ornaments.

[9] Quoted in Morley, *op. cit.,* p. 176.

Head deformation was common among the Maya; at least it appears to have been universal among the people depicted in Mayan art. The desired head shape was achieved by binding the heads of babies for several days between two flat boards, one in front and the other in back. Another desired physical attribute was to be cross-eyed. Parents tried to cause this condition by tying a tiny ball of resin to the baby's hair so that it would dangle between the eyes and cause the child to focus on it a great deal. When a child became 4 or 5 years old, a new status was symbolized by further decoration. A small white bead was fastened to the top of a boy's head, and in the case of girls a string was tied around the waist with a red shell suspended from it as a symbol of virginity. Both boys and girls were required to wear these objects until they went through their puberty ceremonies.

The major event in the puberty ceremony, which boys and girls attended together, was the ritual removal of the symbols of childhood by a priest, after which a feast was held and gifts distributed. Following this occasion, girls were considered marriageable. Boys, meanwhile, lived together in a communal bachelors' hut until marriage. Marriage sometimes took place not long after the puberty ceremony, because families frequently had arranged the alliance while the couple were young children. Little is known of the marriage rules beyond the fact that a person could not marry anyone of his own patrilineal surname. The boy's family bore the expenses of the wedding celebration as well as contributing a substantial gift to the bride's father, and for a few years after the marriage the couple lived with or near the bride's family before setting up their own household. In other respects, the society was patrilineal; the surname descended from father to son, and land inheritance was also from father to son.

Illness was believed to be caused by spirits who became displaced by some wrongdoing on the part of the ill person. Shamans tried to cure the sickness by prayers and rituals and by administering infusions of herbs. Death was greatly feared, and the grief demonstrated by the surviving relatives of a dead person was very great and lasted for days. Burial customs among the common people were simple, however; the body was wrapped in a cloth, its mouth filled with ground maize and a valuable bead or two, and then it was interred under the house. The most important of the rulers, on the other hand, were buried in stone vaults under pyramids and temples, and great amounts of valuables were placed with them.

The supernaturalism of the common people—the folk religion— probably consisted largely of various beliefs about nature gods, particularly, if we may judge from accounts of the modern Maya, those having to do with rain and fertility. The cosmology also included creation and evolution myths. The world creator was Hunab Ku, who, according to the *Popol Vuh,* one of the surviving sacred books of the Maya, molded man out of corn. Hunab Ku seems to have remained remote from everyday affairs, and it was his son, Itzamna, who functioned much more as a Zeus. Landa records the Maya belief in a number of world-destroying floods (which is confirmed by a Mayan picture) of the sort found in so many other religions of the world. Maya Indians today in northern Yucatán believe that there have been three worlds prior to this one and that this, too, will someday be destroyed by a flood.

Mayan religion exhibited a good-and-evil dualism, also reminiscent of other religions of civilization. Benevolent gods bring rain, fertility, and good fortune; malevolent gods cause death, sickness, famine, drought, and so on. All of nature, as well as the soul of man, is always dependent on the outcome of the struggle between these two forces. In Landa's description, the Maya seem to have a concept of paradise and hell, but we cannot be sure this was not due to Christian influence in his time.

Certain principal gods presided over separate heavens, which were arranged in layers. Thirteen layers constituted the Upper World, of which the lowest was the earth surface itself, and nine layers made up the Underworld, of which the lowest, *Metnal,* was ruled by Ah Puch, the Lord of Death. Any or all of the gods were worshiped and placated by fasts and ritual taboos and several common ritual practices. Bloodletting by piercing the ears, cheeks, lips, and tongue in order to sprinkle blood over the gods' images was one of the most common practices. The burning of incense made from the resin of the copal tree was also an important ritual act, as it is today among many Maya. Fasts, offerings of various valuables, and blood sacrifices of animals and even human beings were given to the gods depending on the gravity of the situation.

Human sacrifice, as depicted by Mayan paintings, was performed similarly to the well-known Aztec formula[10] and was a feature of great public ceremonies performed by the priesthood. The victim, often a captive of war, was stripped, painted blue, and a special headdress was put on him. Four helpers of the priest, each taking an arm or leg, stretched the victim backward over the altar, and the priest cut open his breast and took out the heart. The blood was then smeared over the idol of the god for whom the sacrifice was made. The skin of the victim was removed, and the priest arrayed himself in it and performed a ritual dance. If the victim had been a valiant warrior, the populace was given the body to eat, presumably as a form of communion in order to acquire some of his valuable spiritual qualities. Another form of sacrifice, again similar to that of the Aztecs, was to array the victim as described above and tie him to a stake, where he became a target for arrows.

One striking form of sacrifice was that performed at the famous Well of Sacrifice, a deep *cenote* at the site of Chichen Itza, so well known to modern tourists. Living victims, including women and children as well as men, were bound and thrown into the deep hole along with great numbers of ornaments, pottery, incense, and other valuables. Harvard's Peabody Museum dredged the Well of Sacrifice in 1905–1908 and recovered gold and copper objects which had been brought from the south as far as Colombia and from the north as far as the present site of Mexico City.

Probably the religion of the common people in their everyday life turned mostly to Chac, the rain god, and to the practice of only the simplest version of the Mayan rituals and sacrifices. But Mayan society was a great theocracy, and the specialized priest-rulers maintained a complex body of doctrine, gods, and ceremonies additional to the religion of the folk. Of particular interest is the unusual unity of gods as parts or aspects of time cycles and astronomical phenomena. Associated with these was the use of hieroglyphic writing, all of which together were specialized as esoteric knowledge of the priestcraft and government.

---

[10] Most of the scholars of the Maya interpret Mayan sacrifices as due to influence from the Mexican (Toltec) region. There seems to be a general disinclination to blame things like this on the Maya; on the other hand, such wonders as astronomical calculations, mathematics, and hieroglyphic writings—equally general in Meso-America—seem to be regarded as Mayan achievements. There is as little reason for the one interpretation as for the other.

The calendar, which in many ways was complicated and cumbersome, was nevertheless more accurate than ours in making adjustments to the exact length of the solar year. Along with the mechanical aspects of counting, an unusual philosophy of time and its involvement with gods and rituals suggests time consciousness as a central theme in Mayan intellectual life. One of the striking features of the Mayan remains are the steles—upright stone monuments with hieroglyphic texts carved on them. The carvings denoted the date of the monument and various additional matters of calendrical importance, such as data on the state of the moon, the position of the planet Venus, and so on. More than a thousand of these hieroglyphic steles have been found to date.

The Maya allied the divisions of time with anthropomorphic gods, something after the manner of the ancient concept behind our own days of the week—Woden's day, Thor's day, and so on—but all of their divisions of time, not merely the days, were thus conceived. Pictorially, a division of time was considered to be a burden which a god carried until its end, when he was relieved by the next god. Apparently, the complex thought of the priests on this matter carried down to the peasantry, for even in some Mayan villages today the days are considered divine and are referred to anthropomorphically as *He*. All of these gods had certain attributes or aspects which could affect the fortunes of the people during a particular cycle of time. This was an idea similar, apparently, to the astrology of the ancient Mediterranean world.

The Mayan conception of time and the place of the people in it was not evolutionary or even essentially historical. Time apparently went back to infinity (and forward, as well), but the cycles were repetitive—former times were different only as fortune differed under particular gods. In other words, whenever the gods of a period were in the same order as some other time, the combinations of evil and beneficent influences were in the same balance; hence, conditions could be predicted.

The computations required to calculate just which gods would be together at any given time were very complex, because the astronomical phenomena used by all calendars in time-reckoning are not related, nor do they come out in round numbers. A *day* is one obvious time unit, but the tropical solar year is approximately 365.2422 days, and the sidereal year is 365.2564 days; the synodi-

cal revolution of Venus is 583.92 days, and the lunar month is
about 29.53 days. All of the cycles had to be related to one another
and to the divine almanac of 260 days, and this relationship had
to be accurate over enormous spans of time. The Mayan achievement in accomplishing this has been one of their most intriguing.
The Aztec calendar, and others similar to it in Meso-America, was
like the Mayan calendar in many respects, but did not carry the
problem beyond 52-year cycles, and apparently did not correct for
the fractional discrepancies in the solar and Venus years. The
Maya, however, calculated so accurately that the fractional error
in their calendar amounts to only one day in 6000 years. But, as
in all of the primitive civilizations of the world, the mathematics
and fine empirical observation which made this result possible served
occult rather than scientific purposes; this was astrology rather
than astronomy.

The Maya, like the Aztecs, actually had two almanacs in con-
current everyday use. One almanac, the *haab,* approximated our
year of 365 days. It consisted of 18 months of 20 days each (360
days), plus a final period of five days that were considered so unlucky that all unnecessary activity was tabooed. No leap-year day
was added, but the deviation of the year from the actual solar
year was carefully calculated in order to keep the long calendar
corrected. A *tzolkin* ("count of days") almanac of a 260-day year
corresponded to the pattern of ceremonial life. Twenty names of
days (also gods) were adjusted in order with 13 numbers. The
name of the fourteenth day-name began with 1 again. The permutation of these cycles of 13 numbers and 20 names took 260 days
before the number one and the first day-name occurred together
again. A permutation of the two calendars was also made, so that
the first day of the *haab,* the 365-day year, and the first day of the
tzolkin 260-day almanac would appear together every 52 years.
When this happened, a great celebration was held, beginning with
the five unlucky days at the end of the last *haab* year. We know
nothing of the rituals performed at this time, but may presume that
it was one of the most important Mayan ceremonial occasions. We
know that the Aztec believed that the world might come to an end
at the close of a 52-year period. On the last night of the five-day
tabooed period at the close of the cycle, the population retired from
the city to wait to see what the dawn would bring. After the sun
rose, the people rejoiced and the priests rekindled the Sacred Fire,

from which the family hearths were lighted, and another 52-year life was resumed. It seems likely that the Maya had a similar concept.

Mayan mathematics was closely related to their astronomical observations; we have no record of a Mayan enumeration of people or currency. The units were ones, fives, and twenties, designated by dots for ones, bars for fives, and positions for twenty and multiples of twenty. Positional numeration and the sign for zero, which is a necessary aspect of positional numeration, have been considered the greatest intellectual achievement in the New World. In only one other place, India (whence the Arabs and finally the Europeans acquired it), has this ever been invented.[11] The achievement, of course, as in so many other important inventions, is based on a simplifying principle. All other of the world's arithmetical systems, such as the familiar Roman numeration, merely made up distinct symbols for each higher unit, so that large numbers became very long and cumbersome in notation and difficult to manipulate. The concept of "place" and zero is essential even in the simplification of ordinary arithmetical addition and subtraction.

The peoples of the Meso-American region were the only ones in the New World to have achieved writing. The hieroglyphic writing, like the mathematics and astronomy, seems to have been used mostly by the priesthood in the context of religion rather than in mundane or civil affairs; the books were sacred, as was so frequently the case in the ancient Mediterranean world. About four hundred native manuscripts from central Mexico are available to us today, but only three Mayan books have survived, because of the moist climate in the Mayan habitat. The Maya took their sacred books seriously, as Landa attests:

> These people also made use of certain characters or letters, with which they wrote in their books their ancient affairs and their sciences, and with these and drawings and with certain signs in these drawings, they understood their affairs and made others understand them and taught them. We found a great number of books in these characters, and, as they contained nothing in which there was not to be seen superstition and lies of the devil, we burned them all, which they regretted to an amazing degree and caused them affliction.[12]

[11] Unless one includes the Inca use of positions on their mnemonic device, the *quipu.*
[12] Quoted in Morley, *op. cit.,* p. 249.

Mayan writing is not truly alphabetic, but ideographic; the characters represent ideas and things rather than sounds. It is thought by some scholars that some of the Mayan glyphs are phonetic of syllables, but this cannot be established until a more complete deciphering of Mayan writing can be made. At present, about one-third of the Mayan hieroglyphs can be read, and most of these refer to calendrical information. Bishop de Landa furnished a key to these particular Mayan writings by drawing the Mayan signs for different aspects of the Mayan calendar and attempting a phonetic transliteration of them. The work of deciphering continues very slowly, because there is no key to ideographic writing; it is not like breaking a code or puzzle. Knowing one glyph is of little help in discovering the meaning of the next one, because there is no relationship among the elements in words, as there would be if they were spelled with an alphabet.

Mayan songs, myths, and poetry were entirely oral. One of their characteristics is a high literary quality and a tendency toward antiphony of the sort commonly found in the Old Testament. For example: "The fan of heaven shall descend; the wrath of heaven, the bouquet of heaven, shall descend. The drum of the Lord 11 Ahau shall resound; his rattle shall resound." But apparently the hieroglyphic writing was not used to record literature, nor was it used to recount deeds of rulers or the history of cities.

The Maya seem to have been somewhat distinctive in the New World in certain kinds of artistic achievement. They shared a roughly similar art and architecture with other Meso-American peoples, to be sure, but scholars agree that the delicacy of their carvings, paintings, and even the otherwise massive stone buildings is greater than elsewhere. The most peculiarly Mayan architectural trait was the use of the corbeled vault. Other Meso-American peoples made stone buildings with horizontal wooden beams supporting roofs and bridging entrances. This creates a massive and squarish appearance, but the Mayan buildings make quite a different impression because of the vaults. These were not true arches locked together at the apex with a keystone, but false arches, with the two lateral sides inclining toward one another and bridged at the narrow apex by a capstone. Possibly related to the problems of stress involved in this kind of arch is the Mayan use of lime concrete as mortar, as veneer, and as solid mass. Pyramids and temples elsewhere in Meso-America, as at Teotihuacan, were often much larger than their Mayan counterparts; yet the greater grace and subtlety of Mayan building have made for much more modern interest.

Mayan pictorial art was highly conventionalized, and yet the style itself is much more animated, lifelike, and varied than that of the Aztec or Toltec. Nevertheless, design and symbolism were the important aspects of art rather than any attempt at representation; hence to modern eyes the Mayan art, while obviously skillful, does

A MODERN MAYAN WOMAN WEAVING. *Courtesy, The American Museum of Natural History*

not seem *artistic* in the usual sense of the word. Its purposes, certainly, were not akin to modern notions of the function of art. Mayan art was sacred art—hence its conventionalization—and it was ornamental rather than didactic. And perhaps most important of all, it was not only occult but also esoteric; it was not for the people but for the gods, and possibly no one even saw most of it except the artist himself and the high priests who alone were allowed in the temples.

One of the impressions of Mayan life and character that has been formed by practically all students of Mayan culture seems to be manifest in their art, a deeply spiritual or mystical mood at all times, coupled with moderation and orderliness. Interestingly, it appears that while most of these impressions have been formed in the process of studying Mayan archaeological remains, those who have known the modern survivors of the Maya, particularly the Maya in out-of-the-way places, are struck by the same personal qualities. One ethnologist, Karl Sapper, felt that the qualities most esteemed by the Maya (with whom he lived for 12 years) were moderation, self-control, and personal subordination. Alfred Tozzer, writing of the Lacondones, the most isolated and unacculturated of modern Mayan groups, indicates that mildness of temperament, honesty, and generosity were not only the most important ideals, but characteristic of their behavior. Even in the period of their earliest distress under the Spanish yoke, Bishop de Landa, in some ways one of their worst persecutors, said this:

The Yucatecans are very generous and hospitable; since no one may enter their houses without being offered food and drink, of what they may have had during the day, or in the evening. And if they have none, they seek it from a neighbor; and if they come together on the roads, all join in sharing, even if little remains for themselves.[13]

It is apparent from the study of the archaeology of Yucatán, and from the early observations of the Maya left by the Spaniards, that any strong Mayan empire, if there ever was one, had disintegrated before the arrival of the Spaniards. In 1527, when Spanish forces under Francisco de Montejo invaded Yucatán, a rather different task awaited them than what the Cortez party faced in the Aztec empire. There the conquest was accomplished politically as well as militarily. The coming of the Spaniards was a spark which touched off a revolt of the many native states that were already restive under Aztec domination; the Spaniards adroitly provided the leadership to these peoples and the huge and populous area fell to them in a very short period. There were no such political opportunities in Yucatán.

The first Spanish expedition into Yucatán frequently met with local opposition, which it was able to overcome, but it never encountered any Indian groups that made dependable allies. More significantly, the Indians of the Yucatán area were so scattered in

[13] Quoted in Morley, *op. cit.,* p. 33.

locally autonomous units that no defeat inflicted on one group had any affect on the next. And once the Spaniards left an area of defeated natives, they found they had to conquer them all over again on returning. Not until 1542, fifteen years after the original attempt at conquest, did the Spaniards truly have a foothold in Yucatán. This was at Mérida, the present-day capital of the state. The conquered Indians who could be controlled were divided among the Spaniards as *encomiendas,* and as such owed tribute and various services to their masters, who in turn were supposed to protect them and teach them the elements of Catholicism and citizenship.

The Spaniards never were able to exploit the agricultural potential of Yucatán with the *encomienda* system. The economic basis for the first Spanish settlements was cattle ranching, but no great prosperity and no large Spanish population resulted from this. The scattered Indians were barely controlled; even as late as 1847 a revolt against the white man's rule, the War of the Castes, nearly succeeded. It was not until the beginnings of the present century that a plantation system began, and Yucatán, or at least Mérida and the region around it, became part of the world of modern commerce. These plantations grow a species of yucca called *henequen,* which yields a coarse fiber used in spinning twine or rope. In recent years Yucatán has become the world's largest producer of cheap twine.

The acculturation of the Maya Indians who did not flee to other regions was a slow process of blending Spanish with Mayan culture. But in modern times the development of henequen plantations has sparked a general population growth and economic advance that have gradually spread from Mérida farther and farther into the hinterlands. The general trend resulting from these changes has been to alter isolated Mayan peasant villages in the direction of modern towns.[14]

FURTHER READINGS

Gann, T. W. F., *Maya Cities. A Record of Exploration and Adventure in Middle America,* London, 1927.

[14] See Chapter 18 for a description of a modern Mayan village and some further discussion of modern cultural changes.

Gann, T. W. F., and Thompson, J. E., *History of the Mayas,* New York, 1931.

Hay, C. L., *et al., The Maya and Their Neighbors,* New York, 1940.

LaFarge, O., and Byers, D., *The Year Bearer's People,* Middle American Research Series, Pub. 3, Tulane University, New Orleans, 1931.

Maudslay, A. C. and A. P., *A Glimpse at Guatemala,* London, 1899.

Miles, S. W., *The Sixteenth-Century Pokam-Maya: A Documentary Analysis of Social Structure and Archaeological Setting,* Transactions of the American Philosophical Society, Philadelphia, 1957.

Morley, S. G., *The Ancient Maya,* 3rd ed. (rev. G. W. Brainerd), Stanford, 1956.

Proskouriakoff, T., *An Album of Maya Architecture,* Carnegie Institution of Washington, Pub. 558, Washington, 1946.

Redfield, R., and Villa Rojas, A., *Chan Kom, A Maya Village,* Carnegie Institution of Washington, Pub. 448, Washington, 1934.

Spinden, H. J., *Ancient Civilizations of Mexico and Central America,* New York, 1928.

Stephens, J. L., *Incidents of Travel in Central America, Chiapas and Yucatan,* New York, 1841, 2 vols.

Stephens, J. L., *Incidents of Travel in Yucatan,* New York, 1843, 2 vols.

Tax, S. (ed.), *Heritage of Conquest: The Ethnology of Middle America,* Glencoe, Ill., 1952.

Thompson, J. E., *The Rise and Fall of Maya Civilization,* Norman, Okla., 1954.

Tozzer, A. M., *Landa's "Relación de las Cosas de Yucatán,"* Papers of the Peabody Museum of American Archaeology and Ethnology, Vol. 18, Cambridge, Mass., 1941.

Villa Rojas, A., *The Maya of East Central Quintana Roo,* Carnegie Institution of Washington, Pub. 559, Washington, 1945.

Vogt, E. Z. (ed.), *Handbook of Middle American Indians,* Vol. 7, Austin, Texas, 1969.

Willey, G. R., "Problems Concerning Prehistoric Settlement Patterns in the Maya Lowlands," in G. R. Willey (ed.), *Prehistoric Settlement Patterns in the New World,* Viking Fund Publications in Anthropology, No. 23, New York, 1956.

Wolf, E. R., *Sons of the Shaking Earth,* Chicago, 1959.

The Inca
of Peru

The lofty, rugged Andes of western South America today contain the largest Indian population on the continent. Ecuador, Peru, and Bolivia are composed mostly of people descended in large part from the citizens of the great civilizations which had existed there for many centuries before the arrival of Europeans. The final flower of the primitive civilization, the empire of the Inca dynasty, was a complex state and a very rich one. It was rich in the precious metals which first fired the invaders to their headlong conquest, but also rich in men—men who were already submissive to alien rule and skilled in agriculture and handicrafts. This second wealth became the real basis of the Spanish empire's greatest colony.

A great deal of interest was aroused in Europe after the details of the conquest of Peru became known. Various writers found in the Inca empire a beautiful example for the planned economy, the benevolent state, or socialism or communism, or whatever the utopian scheme being promulgated. In that state there were no unemployed, no usurers, no destitute aged, no debtors' prisons, little crime—in short, few of the ills that were plaguing Europe as she emerged from feudalism into the age of cities and modern bureaucratic states. To many Europeans it seemed that the lives of all citizens must have been closely, though benevolently, regulated in the Inca state. Here was a triumph of planning, astonishing to find among illiterate American Indians.

The Inca state has become, through the ages, one of the most discussed and most analyzed of the primitive cultures which have so often been used as an argument to justify one or another political scheme. The Inca were misrepresented on a grand scale, partly because of ethnocentrism—the Inca were always judged in terms of the European concepts of politics, economics, and statecraft—and partly because of the delight the intellectuals took in dissecting a utopia so mathematically planned that everything numbered in decimal units. The near-myth of the Inca welfare state has become standardized by repetition through the centuries. We have good reason to mistrust this interpretation today, and considerable progress has been made toward a realistic and more plausible reconstruction of the Inca state.[1]

A MODERN PERUVIAN INDIAN. *Courtesy, Grace Line*

The physical geography of the region occupied by the Inca has highly unusual and greatly varied features. The narrow coastal zone from southern Ecuador to northern Chile is a true desert. The Humboldt current running north along the coast from the Antarctic makes the ocean much colder than the land; therefore the rains fall at sea. The sandy wastes are without significant vegetation or animal life, but the monotony of the land is relieved about every 25 miles by rivers which make their precipitous way down mountain canyons and valleys from the high snow fields. The isolated valleys of these rivers are extremely fertile under irrigation and were the sites of some of the earliest civilizations in South America.

The Andean cordillera which towers over the coastal strip is, next to the Himalayas, the highest range in the world. Below the peaks and perpetual snow fields lies an extensive highland surface

---

[1] A thorough reappraisal of the nature of the Inca state and its economy, and the relation of the state to the local peasant society, has recently been made by John V. Murra in *The Economic Organization of the Inca State,* unpublished Ph.D. dissertation, University of Chicago, 1956.

of level land and gentle slopes, one of the most distinctive features of the Andes. This bleak plateau, called the *puna,* lies between 10,000 and 15,000 feet in altitude—so high and so near the equator that the temperature varies much more from day to night than it does from season to season. The autumnal chill of daytime (the yearly average is about 50° F.) yields to such a truly penetrating cold at night that it is no wonder the natives were sun worshipers. The altitude definitely limits the output of human energy. Mountain sickness (*soroche*), compounded of nausea and dizziness, is frequent among visitors from lower altitudes, and people with weak hearts or respiratory diseases cannot survive there. Rainfall is light and confined to the period from October to April, so that crops are limited unless they can be put under irrigation. The altitude also restricts the distribution of farming and the type of food grown. The upper limit for potatoes, the crop best adapted to the highlands, is about 14,000 feet in the central Andes, and for maize about 11,000 feet. Above the agricultural zone, the *puna* provides sparse fodder for the hardy llamas and alpacas.

Another outstanding feature of the Andes, commensurate with the great altitudes, is the depth of the canyons cut into the western edges of the highland plateau. Some of them are nearly twice as deep as Arizona's Grand Canyon. The rivers are so fast that they cannot be followed either up- or downstream, and the canyon walls are so difficult to scale that the groups of people who live on the tiny river bottoms and terraces are among the most isolated in the world. This side of the mountains is the driest, but also the most habitable, once irrigation is established and the slopes terraced.

The eastern slope of the Andes is completely different. Heavy moisture-laden winds come from the Atlantic Ocean all the way across the Amazon River basin until they are pushed upward by the rising mountains to the cooler upper atmosphere, where the moisture condenses and keeps the eastern slope nearly continuously drenched. This upland is covered with dense forest and dissected by a maze of swift streams which combine to form the headwaters of the tributaries of the mighty Amazon. The highland empires penetrated this difficult terrain but never conquered the forest tribes.[2]

Such an environment as the highlands, the lower western slope,

[2] The *montaña* region, as the lower eastern slope of the Andes is called, is described in Chapter 9.

and the coastal desert would seem to present insuperable handicaps to the development of a civilization. The lack of navigable rivers, the poverty of both coast and highland in edible flora and fauna, and the difficulty of transportation would certainly offer little to hunters and gatherers. But given a knowledge of agriculture and the appropriate crops and, above all, irrigation, it seems that the most unpromising wastelands become the richest of habitats. Peru has several advantages for agriculturalists. The lack of rainfall has preserved the great natural richness of the soil in minerals, which in areas of heavier rainfall are leached away. The great extremes of altitude produce tiers of widely varying ecological zones that are relatively short distances apart; the opportunity for exchange of products between these adjacent zones permits both specialization and great variation in food supplies. Add to this the products of the prolific ocean and the millions of tons of guano (dried bird droppings) available for fertilizer, and the basis is laid, potentially at least, for great production and dense populations.

There are two aspects of the technology which make possible an effective exploitation of these potentialities: tools and techniques appropriate to the task and, no less important, an organization of people to wield the tools, command the labor necessary to build irrigation canals and terraces, manage the exchange of products, and defend the region against aggressors. This organization was, of course, the state, and this state may be thought of as an aspect of technology and economics as well as a social, political, or religious structure.

How the Inca empire came about is an interesting story and one which is relatively complete inasmuch as a considerable amount of archaeological work has been done in Peru, particularly in the coastal valleys where presumably many of the early stages of the cultural advance occurred. In contrast to the evidence in the regions of the Aztec and Mayan empires of Mexico and Guatemala, where no underlying developmental stages have yet been uncovered, several sites in coastal Peru reveal preagricultural, preceramic cultures which were followed by the beginnings of agriculture, pottery, weaving, and finally by the stages of development leading to the great cities and empires of later periods.

The beginnings of agriculture in coastal Peru occurred some undetermined number of years before the Christian era. This Formative Period, as archaeologists call it, was the time when all of the basic technological elements of Andean civilization were being elaborated and diffused along the coast. Soon a distinctive style in buildings, art work, ceramics, and weaving became crystallized and widely distributed, even into the highlands. This style is known as *Chavín*. Following the Formative Period came a period of regional developments and local specialization and differentiation which was probably paralleled—perhaps even created—by the rise of petty political principalities. A similarity in basic elements is manifest throughout, but the distinctive styles suggest that separate ethnic groups were involved in the respective regional developments.

Along the coast and highlands of southern Peru a culture now known as *Nazca* developed and began to replace the Chavín. Nazca pottery was particularly noteworthy for its brilliantly polished and painted decorations. Sometimes as many as 11 different colors were employed on a single pot. Textile arts were developed which used both wool from the alpaca, vicuña, and llama and domestic cotton, and embroidery was a characteristic technique. Metallurgy was undeveloped, however; gold was the only metal known, and the technique of working it was simple hammering and incising.

The florescence of a culture in northern Peru, that of the *Mochica,* was equally spectacular. Large pyramids and temples, elaborate tombs which by their splendor tell that kings and courts existed, and irrigation, roads, and other evidence demonstrate that there was a widespread political system. Copper, silver, and gold were used in ornaments, and the textiles were excellent, but the best evidence of artistic specialization was the elaborate red and white pottery. The pottery was frequently decorated with realistic paintings of scenes from daily life, including much which in our day would be judged obscene. From the depictions in many of the paintings, it can be seen that theocracy was already the mode of government and that wars of conquest were being undertaken. The Mochica were themselves finally conquered, however, and apparently a period of confusion and political breakdown, a Dark Ages, descended upon northern Peru.

Meanwhile, in the Bolivian highlands near Lake Titicaca, a new empire, called *Tiahuanaco* by archaeologists, expanded its influence and briefly extended its power up the coast even as far as the ravaged lands of the Mochica. But it too, after a few centuries of dominance, came to the typical close of the cycle for these empires, which was anarchy. Each of the successive empires used the same basic elements: irrigation, similar kinds of crops and domestic animals, common pottery and weaving techniques. The death of an empire was merely the disintegration of a political system; the life of the people went on.

By the time a new empire again extended a hold over coastal Peru, about A.D. 1000, all of the culture traits characteristic of the later Inca phase were well established. This new empire, the *Chimu,* differed from the earlier ones mostly in size. The net of irrigation works now extended over wider areas, suggesting a more complex and perhaps better integrated governmental system. True urban developments also appeared for the first time. Houses made of great molded adobe blocks were set into large units, or compounds.

But the fate of all the would-be coastal empires was being decided on the great highland plateau where more anarchical conditions prevailed than on the coast. The whole Andean highland area was composed of a great number of separate groups, each with its own dialect or language. One of these groups—speakers of the Quechua language, and today, usually called the Inca after their own name for the ruling lineage—lived near the present city of Cuzco in Peru, whence they began, sometime after A.D. 1200, to establish their hegemony over the locality. Inca traditions concerning the royal dynasty are shadowy and mythical until the time of these first conquests.

The first leader to rule over conquered groups as well as his own people was Pachacuti Inca, who was crowned in 1438.[3] It was during his reign that defeated neighbors were made into permanent subjects of the state rather than merely being looted. Pachacuti's son, Tupa Inca, acting as military commander for his father, aided in extending the power of their state north to Quito, Ecuador; south as far as Chile; and finally even to the coast, where the great Chimu empire put up a final spasm of resistance. The subsequent reign of Tupa Inca was one of great success in consolidating the

---

[3] The chronology and history used here are from J. H. Rowe, "Inca Culture at the Time of the Spanish Conquest," in J. H. Steward (ed.), *Handbook of South American Indians,* Smithsonian Institution, Bureau of American Ethnology, Bull. 143, Vol. 2, Washington, 1946, pp. 183–330. Rowe's interpretation differs from that of previous works, but it is the most plausible and thorough reconstruction available.

huge holdings. His reign lasted for 22 years, until his death in 1493, after which he was succeeded by his son, Huayna Capac. The work of building the empire's holdings went on smoothly; probably the most noteworthy event, and the most astonishing to the emperor, was the news he received in 1527, the year of his death, of the first exploratory ex-pedition of Pizarro, which had touched briefly at Tumbez.

Four years elapsed between Huayna Capac's death and Pi-zarro's conquest of the empire. Most fortunately for Pizarro, those years were a period of in-tense civil war. Huascar, the son of Huayna Capac, was the obvi-ous candidate for the emperor's mantle, and he was so installed by the High Priest in Cuzco. Atahuallpa, another son, who had become governor of Quito, revolted, claiming that Huayna Capac had divided the empire and that he was to have the northern half. The civil war was eventually won by Atahuallpa, and, coincidentally, the news of the final battle in which Huascar was captured was brought to him in Cajamarca at about the same time that Pizarro again arrived in Peru.

DETAIL OF INCAN STONEWORK. *Courtesy, The American Museum of Natural History*

The great empire of the Inca consisted of more than 6,000,000 subjects, and included peoples of distinct languages and cultures. Subsistence varied from region to region, but the form of distribu-tion maintained by the state somewhat equalized the resources. Potatoes were the mainstay in the highlands, and they could be grown at much higher altitudes than grains. Maize was the most important crop on the coast and in the lower highlands. Potatoes were probably more important in the average family's daily fare, but maize, because it stores well, was the crop emphasized by the state, and consequently it had more prestige associated with it. On the *puna,* above the limits of maize, another grain, quinoa, was grown. These two grains, and potatoes as well, were usually eaten as a sort of gruel or porridge, although maize was sometimes used in other ways: ground into bread flour, eaten off the cob, or made into beer. A greater variety of plants was cultivated on the coast: beans of several kinds, manioc, squash, sweet potatoes, tomatoes, and many fruits. Cotton and agave for textile fibers were also grown on the coast.

The Andean peoples used wild tobacco, but only for medicinal and magical purposes, mostly in the form of snuff. A common drink was *chicha,* a brew of naturally fermented maize or other starchy food. Most distinctive of the Andean intoxicants, however, was coca, the dried leaves of a shrub imported from the eastern forests. When these leaves are chewed with lime, a small amount of cocaine is released. The Indians used this drug when they were faced with excessive work, hardship, or inadequate food, as it is used to this day in the Andes.

Meat was not a frequent item in the Indians' diet. There were few animals to hunt: birds, rodents, and at higher altitudes occasionally a guanaco and less often a deer. The coastal peoples caught fish and turtles, and the highland peoples raised small numbers of guinea pigs, dogs, and Muscovy ducks, but their use as food was largely on fiesta occasions. The llama and alpaca, the only burden-bearing animals ever domesticated in the Americas, were much too valuable to be used frequently as food. When large animals were butchered, their flesh was usually cut into thin strips and dried into *charqui* (from which the English term *jerky,* or jerked meat, is derived). The llama, the largest of the domesticated camels, served as a pack animal, although it was not ridden or harnessed. Its wool was also used, but the smaller alpaca and vicuña provided the finest wool, and they were kept almost exclusively for this product.

Great irrigation canals and aqueducts diverted the water which made the otherwise barren land fertile. These were, of course, products of a great deal of continuous labor by thousands of citizens over many hundreds of years. It should be possible to measure

the gradual increase in population and community size, the extension and developing complexity of labor and of political systems—
the growth of the civilization, in short—by charting the irrigation
improvements which succeeded one another century after century.
By the time of the Inca empire, the original coastal irrigation
systems had been extended over all feasible areas in both coast
and highland. Terracing was also a product of public labor over
many generations. Much of the land in both the highlands and
the coastal valleys would have been completely useless had the
slopes not been terraced and leveled. Some areas were terraced
even where irrigation was impossible for the purpose of obtaining
a last extra increment from the unfriendly land. Altogether, this
is a type of agriculture so *in*tensive, rather than *ex*tensive, that it is
more foreign to a North American than to an Oriental. Even fertilizer, rarely used by primitive agriculturalists, was fully known to
the Inca. Guano from the great deposits laid by the Pacific Ocean
coastal birds—deposits so rich and extensive that they are still
being exploited for the world market—was distributed by the state
over a wide area of the coast. Both human and animal excrement,
ashes, and even fish when available were also used, but on a more
local basis. The potato-growing peasants of the highlands depended
more largely on fallowing.

State-controlled labor was responsible for many other impressive
characteristics of the Inca civilization and its predecessors. Great
fortresses, palaces, and temples were built of huge stone blocks,
delicately fitted without the use of mortar. The size and massive-
ness of the architecture, with some walls hundreds of feet in length,
were its outstanding feature. There were no artistic embellishments
of any kind. A complex network of roads united the empire, most
of them the products of a great deal of labor. Many were paved;
some were cut into solid rock; others passed over causeways if the
land was marshy, or over suspension bridges which spanned the
highland chasms.

Such features of Inca civilization as those mentioned above were
the products of the state's organization of labor. But the less
spectacular household and village economy lay at the basis of the
civilization. Had it not been productive enough for a numerous
population and for a surplus to be at the disposal of the state, the
Andean peoples would have remained merely an aggregation of

TERRACES AND ARCHITECTURAL RUINS OF MACHU PICCHU. *Courtesy, The American Museum of Natural History*

PERUVIAN INDIANS ATTEND COMMUNITY DEVELOPMENT MEETING. *Courtesy, United Nations*

primitive tribes or small chiefdoms. And at this local level, it is true, much of the daily life of the people was not qualitatively distinct from other less distinguished cultures. It was at the intervals when the state intervened in their lives that something new was added. Life in a primitive tribe is essentially family life, and a boundary is drawn at the village level. Civilized people, on the other hand, lead lives that are not thus circumscribed.

A typical Andean village consisted of a small number of lineages called *ayllu*. The community as a whole held ultimate jurisdiction over the land, but it was divided among the several ayllu, who administered it directly. Each individual household held portions of the ayllu land and passed them on to their male descendants. At any given time it would appear that the individual family owned the land it tilled, but the ayllu could reallot parts of its fallowed or idle lands among individual families in order to keep a balanced distribution. Land could not be sold or otherwise disposed of by the individual families. The products of the soil belonged outright to the family which occupied the plot. Most of the day-to-day agricultural labor was also individualized, but much of the infrequent and more difficult labor of planting, harvesting, housebuilding, repair of irrigation ditches and roads, and the like was done by a cooperative work group called the *minga*.

The system of land tenure at the local level is rather typical of primitive agricultural villages. In the Andes, however, there were also agricultural plots which were not under the jurisdiction of the community. In some areas, particularly in the conquered lands along the Pacific coast, land was taken from the villages in the name of the Inca state and for the state church. In the highlands, the state, using the traditional minga as a prototype, taxed the communities a certain amount of labor every year. This corvée labor among its several tasks created new land by leveling and terracing slopes. This land then belonged to the state. The state sometimes turned over lands of this sort to individuals as estates when the individuals had performed some special service to the state. Such people were local chieftains (*Curaca*), or members of the Inca dynasty and military leaders.

The laborers who worked all these lands, however, were not permanently resident serfs. The residents of the locality worked the lands on regularly appointed shifts just as they worked the corvée on state-owned roads, canals, and fortresses. As a system, this is distinct from socialism. The significant characteristic of the Inca rule is that the state clearly did not assume any responsibility for the subsistence or well-being of the ordinary citizen. It was not a welfare state. The village, like any primitive village, took care of its own. The "socialism" or "communism" was the normal communalism of all primitive villages and was based on family and lineage corporateness. The state interceded in this existence only to the extent that it was able to drain off surplus labor in the corvée. All the state did was to tax (in the form of labor and military conscription); its responsibilities to the citizenry were few.

In one important respect, trade, the action of the state was such that European observers were led to attribute a fully developed rational socialism to the regime. This was largely because there was no free trade by individuals in important goods and because there was no medium of exchange or market place of any consequence. But the way in which the Inca state handled goods was still on the primitive model, on a larger scale but essentially similar to the way in which Nootkan, Melanesian, and Polynesian chiefs, for example, collect and redistribute goods in their petty principalities. The Inca state functioned in trade, then, largely as a *redistributive* organ.[4]

At the village level, storehouses or granaries were filled with supplies of maize and cloth primarily, which the community had access to in times of need. Individuals or families who were incapacitated were also allowed to draw upon them. These stores have been attributed to the foresight of the benevolent state by many commentators, but actually is was an ayllu and village function in no way unusual in intent among primitive chiefdoms. The state, in superimposing itself over the villages, merely extended the already existing principle by putting up storehouses for the grain and other products which the labor levies had created by working on state and church lands. These were used to feed the army and the specialists and officials who lived in the larger cities.

Probably the most important economic consequence of the state's redistribution of goods was its control of the circulation of products from one distinct ecological zone to another, sending grain to a potato-growing area, alpaca and vicuña wool from the highlands to the coast, and so on. This kind of redistribution handled the most important functions of what earlier had been merely local trade. But this function of the state is socialism only if the word is so loosely used that primitive tribes are to be seen as socialistic states. The analogy is to the primitive system except in one matter, but even this is of degree rather than kind. A Polynesian chief, for example, accepts gifts of the surplus production of all the families who are lucky enough to have a surplus at that particular time. Later he gives most of it away again, and those who need the most are given the most. It is phrased as the *generosity* of the chief, but economically it is merely redistribution. It is not clearly exploitative —not tribute—except to the extent that some small proportion of it is held back for the chief and his family and perhaps a few hangers-on. When a similar thing was done by the Inca, it differed in scale—many thousands more workers contributed, and the total

[4] See Chapters 10, 11, and 12 for discussions of this form of exchange.

SILVER FIGURINES CHARACTERIZE INCAN ARTISTRY. *Courtesy, The American Museum of Natural History*

amount withheld was greater in order to feed the enlarged group of members of the royal lineage, specialists, army, and priests. The Inca state at its height of splendor was becoming increasingly exploitative. There were finally 12 lineages of Inca in the leisure class and a great horde of retainers, artisans who made elaborate ornaments and garments for the rulers, dancers, musicians, along with priests, acolytes, and lesser servants of the church.

Labor time was, then, largely an aspect of the primitive redistribution system and partly a form of tax which did not directly benefit the laborers. In one other matter the state exacted a tax which was a product of labor rather than labor itself. Cloth, both of wool and cotton or mixtures of these, seems to have been of prime interest to the state. As in other parts of the economy, there were two aspects to the weaving industry: the local subsistence activity and the national or state activity. Women in the village households were constantly at work spinning and weaving, primarily to provide the fabric for their own families and secondarily to produce specified quantities for the state to use in clothing its soldiers and retainers. Also, as in the case of nearly all handicrafts,

MODERN INDIANS DRESSED IN INCA STYLE. *Courtesy, Grace Line*

certain particularly skilled male specialists were maintained by the state to make fine textiles for the ruling class. At the climax of Inca civilization, the more important members of the hierarchy were so prodigal with clothing (so fine it has never been surpassed for its quality) that they never wore the same garment twice.

The peasants wore cloth of much ruder homespun, but in the rigorous climate of the highlands it was necessary that the people be well clothed. Men usually wore a cotton breechclout, a sleeveless tunic, and a shoulder mantle drawn over the back and secured by a knot at the chest. Women wore a wrap-around cloth which extended from beneath the arms to the ankles, with the top edges drawn over the shoulders and fastened with straight pins. A sash around the waist and a shoulder mantle completed this usual ensemble. Both sexes wore sandals when out-of-doors. Ornamentation was restricted in large part to members of the upper class, who adorned themselves richly with gold and silver bracelets, rings, armbands, and breastplates. Members of the Inca lineages were allowed to pierce their ears and distend the lobes with large spools and other ornaments. The Spaniards, noting the distinctiveness of this sumptuary law, called the Inca kinsmen *Orejones* (Big Ears).

The Orejones, most of whom resided at the capital city, Cuzco, were exempted from labor and military services, as were certain other special classes of the society. The Curaca were a sort of provincial nobility who had once been chieftains over their own regions. The Inca fitted them into the state bureaucracy as a means of ruling indirectly through them. As time went on the descendants of the original Curaca were educated in Cuzco in Inca customs, and they became relatively indistinguishable from the original Inca caste. The *Yana,* also privileged with respect to conscription, spent full time at their various specialties as servants and retainers, musicians and dancers, and as professional handicraft specialists, all of these activities being of service to the rulers. The *Aclla,* miscalled in some accounts "Virgins of the Sun," were the female counterparts of the Yana. Some served the church—hence the analogy to Roman vestal virgins—but the majority were servants and skilled weavers.

One kind of professional who deserves special mention is the *quipu* keeper, the recorder of the census and tribute records. The Inca lacked writing and mathematical notation, and so only a trained person was able to manage the recording. This specialist was practiced in the use of a mnemonic device called the quiqu, a stick or cord with a number of knotted strings tied to it. The strings themselves were frequently colored to represent distinct articles, people, or districts, while the knots tied in them ascended in units representing ones, tens, hundreds, thousands, and so on.[5] Some of the early Spanish commentators believed that the whole Inca society was divided into units of population from groups of tens to units of hundreds, then thousands, and so on, but we see now that

AN INDIAN WOMAN SPINS WOOL. *Courtesy, United Nations*

this was a census convention caused by the simplicity of the counting device rather than a functional organization of the society. Furthermore, the census took account only of households, rather than individuals. An unmarried man, for example, owed no labor service to the state.

The skill of the Yana metallurgists and weavers was of a very high order. The tapestries surpassed anything known in Europe.

---

[5] The concept of *place* is essential for the concept *zero,* empty place. It seems clear that empty places were employed numerically in the *quipu*; hence the Inca should be included with the Maya and Hindus as societies which had acquired this important form of numerical notation.

True smelting of copper and silver was a known technique, and even the making of bronze was practiced, though the Inca culture cannot be considered a true Bronze Age culture because the metal was not used for tools and weapons. The plenitude of the precious metals, particularly gold, excited the Spaniards greatly, but to the Inca the value of gold lay in the properties which facilitated the making of finely hammered ornaments and even threads for the ornamentation of textiles. Cuzco was virtually a golden city; the palace had golden friezes and panels of gold and silver, and the famous Temple of the Sun had a garden full of lifelike plants and animals all made of hammered gold.

Courtesy, Museum of the American Indian, Heye Foundation

Music was one of the fine arts of the Inca, again more complex and developed than in most primitive societies. Among their most characteristic instruments were reed panpipes, each reed of graduated length and pitch; flutes, trumpets, and whistles; gongs, bells, and rattles; and several kinds of skin drums and tambourines. The musical scale was the five-toned, or pentatonic, which they used to sing the hymns, epics, and the plaintive love songs still heard in some Andean villages. Music was frequently accompanied by dances, and some of the dances also were a simple form of drama.

The elaboration of custom, the wealth, and the size of the court in Cuzco apparently misled the Spaniards, who assumed that government by these rulers was equally elaborate. Actually the Inca rulers at Cuzco governed very little. The extent of territory and numbers of people incorporated in the region were very great for a primitive state, and this sheer size increased the income and made possible the sumptuousness of the capital city. But the local customs of the conquered regions were not fundamentally altered. Their

352

local rulers were merely subverted, so to speak, and life went on as before.

The Inca indirect rule did not even alter the varying forms of customary law found in different parts of the empire. Nearly all disputes and crimes were settled by custom in the community where they occurred. There was no independent or state judiciary. The imperial law was essentially one designed to prevent disorders which would threaten the established order, and the majority of the few crimes punished by the state were those committed by actual members of the state bureaucracy. Treason, of course, was the most heinous, followed by lese majesty, official misconduct, evasion of tribute, and murder. Fines were unknown, and no elaborate prisons were built; forced labor in the mines for lesser crimes and death for all others were the modes of punishment. Some people, called the *Mitma*, were engaged or forced to serve as a sort of part-time occupation army in a newly conquered province, but another important aspect of this resettlement was to extend the maize-growing area which was the basis of the state's subsistence.[6]

The daily life of the peasantry was divided between work in the fields and in the home, the routine broken up frequently by village celebrations and rituals. The average home in the Peruvian highlands was small and square or rectangular, the walls laid up of fieldstone and mud or of adobe bricks, with the gabled roof thatched with grass. There were no chimneys and often not even a window; consequently the interior was dark and smoky. Furnishings were sparse, consisting of a slightly raised sleeping platform and sometimes a sitting bench, a low clay stove, and a few clay pots, dishes, and pitchers. Food and spare clothing were stored in large jars. The houses of several close patrilineal relatives were usually grouped together, surrounded by a wall. These compounds were built on hillsides so as not to occupy valuable agricultural land. Therefore, a village was an irregularly shaped agglomeration with the various compounds often a considerable distance apart. Such an open village could not be defended easily, of course, but the inhabitants had ready a fort, or refuge, on a nearby hilltop where they could retreat to defend themselves.

The Andean extended family as a unit was associated with others into the larger ayllu, a local kin grouping. A person was allowed

[6] J. V. Murra, *op. cit.,* Chapter 7.

to marry a fellow ayllu member; hence the children's membership in the ayllu was sometimes simultaneously through the mother and the father, although it was normally considered patrilineal, possibly because it was through males that most property was inherited by primogeniture. The ayllu was not a clan of the sort possessed by so many American Indian tribes; it was not unilateral or exogamous or totemic. It was probably much like the genealogical, corporate kinship group of the Polynesians, although specific and conclusive information is lacking.

The pattern of kinship nomenclature was consistent with the bilateral, nonexogamous character of the ayllu. The terms *brother* and *sister* were extended to include all cousins—the distinction between cross cousins and parallel cousins, which would be expected if the ayllu were an exogamous clan, was not made. Father's brother was called *father* and mother's sister was called *mother*, for, of course, in the close confines of the ayllu society these relatives came close to playing these roles; but father's sister and mother's brother were distinguished from them. The system of address heavily emphasized sex difference; distinct terms were used according to the sex of the speaker and of the person addressed. An emphasis on generational differences was also reflected in the terms.

The individual households considered children an important economic asset and undoubtedly, as in nearly every primitive society, a large number of children was desired if they came at suitable intervals. Chroniclers give little information about the particulars of practices during pregnancy and childbirth. It appears that there was some fasting and that sometimes midwives were called to assist in the delivery. After the birth, the mother took the child to a stream and washed herself and the baby. After four days the child was swaddled voluminously and tied into a cradle board which the mother could carry about on her back. Here the baby remained until it was old enough to walk. When the child was about 2 years old, it was weaned, and its hair was cut at an elaborate ceremony attended by relatives and family friends, who brought gifts for the occasion. The child's oldest uncle cut its hair and nails, which were thereafter carefully preserved, and he gave it a name which would be retained until another naming ceremony at its maturity. Throughout the rest of childhood, the children played together and helped their parents. Formal instruction was reserved for children of the Inca and Curaca and for girls selected to go into convents or to become Aclla in Cuzco.

At the age of about 14, boys were given a puberty ceremony which involved donning the breechclout and receiving a new name. This was probably a simple matter in the villages, where it was held once a year for the youths who were ready, but the sons of the Inca were put through ceremonies lasting for several weeks. Great *chicha*-drinking celebrations were held, llamas were sacrificed in great numbers, and the boys were subjected to ordeals and tests of strength and endurance. Several long pilgrimages were made to sacred shrines. After one of these the boys were given their breechclouts, after another their weapons, and finally the candidates' ears were pierced for the Inca earplugs which signified a new status as warrior. They were thereafter addressed by their new names. Titles of rank were also assumed at this time.

The girls' puberty ceremonies were held immediately after the first menstruation and were individual rather than collective affairs. The girl fasted for three days in seclusion, after which her mother bathed her, braided her hair, and dressed her in fine new clothes. Then she came out to address the relatives assembled for the feast. The mother's elder brother gave her a new name, and other relatives gave gifts.

Among the peasants, marriage was prohibited between relatives closer than first cousin, and first cousins could marry only if the wife was to become the principle wife. To marry closer was incest, a terrible crime. The later Inca emperors, however, made one of their sisters the principal wife, or empress. This exception to the rule has been explained as an attempt by the Inca to demonstrate how they were set above ordinary human beings and ordinary law. The same custom prevailed in similarly organized societies, such as the Hawaiian and Egyptian, however, and may well be related to the great significance of inheritance at the apex of the society. A consolidation and perpetuation of total power are accomplished by the closer marriages.[7]

Secondary wives or concubines were common among the nobility

[7] Rostworowski de Diez Canseco argues convincingly that Inca royal incest was a way of strengthening the succession rights of one particular son, and thus helping to avoid the anarchy and civil war that results from the claims to succession of sons of other royal wives. ("Succession, Coöption to Kingship, and Royal Incest among the Inca," *Southwestern Journal of Anthropology,* Vol. 16, No. 4, 1960.)

and other important people, but the agriculturalists could rarely afford them. All people of mature age were supposed to marry, and a person was not considered a true adult until installed in his or her own household. Within the range of choice allowed by the various restrictions on marriage in the villages, individual preference seems to have played a part in the selection of a marriage partner, but the parents had the power to make the ultimate choice. Marriages were ceremonialized in two distinct ways. One was a sort of civil ceremony in which the local state representative, or governor, publicly in the name of the emperor legitimized the weddings of a group of couples, perhaps as a function of census-keeping. The other was a traditional wedding arranged by the two families in accordance with local custom, which included exchange of presents and a feast. Divorce was prohibited because the emperor had sanctioned the wedding. A widow could not remarry anyone except her husband's brother (the levirate). Men presumably had more freedom, but the sororate was common in the event of a wife's death.

The Andean peoples believed that disease was caused by supernatural powers. Moral misconduct and neglect of religious duties might anger the gods, supernatural beings might be manipulated by sorcerers, or certain supernatural forces resident in particular springs or winds might cause illness, usually by causing a foreign object to enter the body or by displacing one of the body's vital organs. One particular belief held by the Inca is still found in many Andean villages. This is the idea that a sudden fright can cause the soul to fly out of the body, leaving the person in a slowly weakening condition unless the soul can be restored.

Curers, or shamans, were local folk practitioners who were believed to have special knowledge and skills which enabled them to influence the supernaturals. By this token, they also functioned as diviners and could become sorcerers as well, should they decide to use their powers for harmful purposes. The typical American Indian cures were used. The shaman first made sacrifices and undertook to divine the cause of the illness; then, if he discovered that organs had been displaced, he rubbed and massaged the patient until the organs were urged back to their proper position. If he divined that a foreign object was present, he extracted it by the sucking method, after which he produced some small object by sleight of hand and displayed it to the patient. Trepanation may have been practiced at the time of the conquest as a cure for headaches or perhaps insanity. Archaeological deposits in Peru frequently contain skulls which had small holes bored into them or small sections sawed out. Some of them were healed, and a few even had been subjected to more than one operation.

Sorcerers were greatly feared by the Andean villagers. They were believed to cause death by practicing sympathetic and contagious magic, which is to say that they might make an image of the victim and then burn it or otherwise torture or kill it, or they might acquire a bit of the intended victim's hair or nail clippings to use in devising a spell. Sorcerers practiced their magic in utter secrecy, of course, or they would have been put to death. As a consequence, no one ever knew for sure who was actually a sorcerer, and a person who accused another of sorcery was more easily able to do harm to him than a true sorcerer could.

The death of a family member was ceremonialized immediately by a gathering of friends and relatives who, all dressed in black, performed a dirgelike dance to the accompaniment of drums and singing. The female relatives cut their hair and wore their cloaks over their heads. Mourning was maintained by the relatives for as long as a full year if the deceased had been an important personage. The corpse was wrapped in cloth and buried with his most cherished personal possessions, and the rest of his property was burned. The death of an Inca was ritualized similarly, but the arrangements were more elaborate, lasted longer, and concubines and servants were sacrificed and buried with him. The tombs for ordinary people were simple stone crypts into which the body was placed in a sitting position. Sometimes the viscera were removed in an attempt at mummification. Kings were given elaborate burials in the coastal regions in pre-Inca times and their tombs are well known to archaeology. The attempt at mummification was more thorough and, aided by the extreme dryness of the coastal atmosphere, was rather successful. The tombs of the later Inca at Cuzco have been looted and defiled, but some evidence exists that the Inca followed the practices of previous regimes.

It was believed that the soul of a dead person would take up residence in some object of nature, either a landscape feature or a plant or animal. Particularly prominent gods, nature spirits, and souls of important ancestors were worshiped at their residing

357

places, *huacas,* which thus were something like Roman shrines. These huacas could be almost anything, a whole city like Cuzco, a stone, a spring, or a mountain. The Indians also believed in a variety of more portable objects which contained supernatural power. These amulets were usually pebbles, animal stomach stones, or crystals of such unusual shape or color that they had struck the fancy of the owner. They were carried about as good luck charms, often as a permanent component of a little handbag, like the medicine bundles of the North American Plains Indians. But it was the souls of particular ancestors which were revered most; and the more distant the ancestors, the more generalized, remote, and godlike they became.

Each ayllu was also a cult group, worshiping its mythical ancestor by various private rituals and formulas. All of the individual villages in the Andean region probably had somewhat similar general notions of ancestors, nature spirits, and generalized, remote celestial beings, as well as particular specific gods of individual households, ayllus, and villages. The Inca rulers superimposed on these local folk religions a national church, which in one sense was merely an imposition of some of their own particular folk beliefs as an overlay, but more importantly was the basis for a systematic hierarchy of official priests. This priesthood involved the very nature of the government itself, for like most primitive states the Inca government was a theocratic organization.

The Inca beliefs which were the basis of the state religion began with the notion of the Creator, the ruler of the supernatural populace in the same sense that the Inca emperor ruled the earth. The Creator had no name, but was addressed by a long series of titles, one of which, Viracocha (Lord), the Spaniards learned to use in reference to him, and which, interestingly enough, the Indians also used in addressing the early Spaniards, so awed were they by the bearded, pale, strange-looking newcomers. Viracocha was a sort of culture hero; after he created the universe and mankind, he traveled around among the people teaching them the right way to do things. After this, he retired and allowed lesser divinities to look after the administration of his domain. The Sun was the most important of these more active gods and was the ancestor of the Inca dynasty. As in many other societies, he was a sort of male principle as well, and responsible for the growth of crops. Thunder was perhaps the next most important god, and to him prayers for rain were addressed. Moon was a female principle ("Mother Moon") and wife of the Sun; she was also significant because her cyclical appearances were the basis of the yearly time count and festival calendar. Earth and Sea were also viewed as female. Particular stars, planets, and constellations were patrons of certain activities. Unlike most primitive peoples, the Inca addressed prayers to these divinities and made offerings. A common prayer for water runs as follows:

> To thee, Lord, who nourishest all things and among them wast pleased to nourish me and the water of this spring for my support, I pray that thou wilt not permit it to dry up, but rather make it flow forth as it has done in other years, so that we may harvest the crop we have sown.
>
> O fountain of water which for so many years has watered my field, through which blessing I gather my food, do thou the same this year and even give more water, that the harvest may be more abundant.[8]

Sacrificial offerings were part of most ceremonial occasions as well as accompaniments of individual prayers at shrines. The usual sacrifices were llamas and guinea pigs, but food and chicha and, in almost every case, some fine clothing were also offered. Human beings were the most valuable sacrifices and the rarest, being offered only for the most solemn state rituals, such as those designed to end a pestilence or famine, at the time of a military defeat, at the installation of a new emperor, or when the emperor was in danger from sickness or in battle.[9]

The periods of great public ceremonials were perfectly appropriate to an agricultural sun-worshiping society. The solar year was marked by the great festivals to the sun at the winter solstice (June 21) and to the moon at the spring equinox (September 21) and by the summer solstice festival (December 21), when initiation rites for noble youths were held. All of these ceremonies were performed in the Great Square in Cuzco, and attended by the emperor and his court. Other ceremonies were held at frequent intervals specified by the calendar. Certain ceremonies, the most

---

[8] Rowe, *op. cit.*, p. 301.

[9] As late as the year 1903, a case of human sacrifice was reported. Villagers in the Urubamba Valley decided to make a sacrifice to end a drought that year, and the shaman selected a subject and persuaded him to offer himself. This man was honored with a festival, at which he got drunk and threw himself into the river. *Ibid.*, p. 306.

important being the *Itu,* could be held at any time the Inca needed the gods' help, as during a pestilence, drought, or war. Central features of the Itu were similar to those of most of the others: the people fasted for two days beforehand, and then all provincials and dogs were banished from Cuzco while the images of the gods were brought to the Great Square and solemn processions, prayers, and sacrifices were made. This restrained and orderly day was followed by two days of joyous feasting, dancing, and drinking.

The religious customs of the disparate groups composing the empire were not fundamentally altered by the Inca. As in other aspects of culture, the rulers added an overlay at certain points, allowing local cultural autonomy most of the time. So effective was the Inca policy of indirect rule that the Europeans were content at first to continue the Inca formula, even to the point of leaving the native incumbents in many of the administrative posts. But oppression by the Spaniards tended to create a defensive unity among the Indians which finally became so complete that most of the separate languages were lost in time, along with many distinctive local customs. Since the nineteenth century the Indians of Peru have thought of themselves as an ethnic unity, a kind of nation.

The Spanish force under Pizarro, which, after the brief reconnaissance in 1527, returned to conquer the populous Inca empire, was composed of only 200 men equipped with 27 horses. Fortunately for Pizarro, the empire was torn by civil war, and his meager but intrepid company was able to complete the overthrow of the empire in the brief period between January, 1531, and November, 1533. Resistance to the invaders was made particularly feeble and disorganized because Pizarro captured and executed the emperor, Atahuallpa, who had won the civil war. This technique of capturing the head of the organized resistance, incidentally, had been used with great success in the earlier conquest of Mexico.

The natives of Peru easily accepted the new rulers for a time, for the relation of the rural villages to the local authority was relatively undisturbed. In certain key areas, such as the valley of Cuzco, however, the invaders pre-empted the best land, and the coastal region also was a focus of their interest. Lima, the Spanish capital, and its port, Callao, were founded in 1535. Lima quickly became a fabulously rich city and the seat of Spanish culture and

THE INCA OF PERU

social life, as well as of government. Many of the highland areas populated by the agricultural villages were apportioned among the conquerors as *encomiendas,* as in other parts of Spanish America.This institution was based on what was in theory a two-way set of obligations. The Indians were expected to pay their *encomendero* an annual tribute in food or other goods in return for his obligation to protect the Indians, judge disputes among them, and teach them the Christian faith. The Spaniards held no rights whatever to the land. The jurisdiction over the Indians was to last only for the life of the encomendero and one heir, after which time the Spanish Crown felt the Indians would be fully educated and able to look out for themselves. Association between the encomendero and his Indians was hedged by many restrictions designed to protect the Indians from exploitation by acquisitive masters.

These intentions of the Crown, however, were not acceptable to many of the conquerors, most of whom aspired to become aristocratic landholders and were particularly avid for this status because they were of humble origin; Pizarro himself, it may be noted, had once been a mere swineherd on an estate in Spain. In time, by varying means, private estates, *latifundios,* some of them thousands of square miles in area with supplies of Indian labor to work them, were acquired, and the outlines of the modern hacienda system of the highlands began to take form. In a few areas true plantations developed, specializing in a particular crop for the commercial market, and in others cattle ranges of huge dimensions were taken from the Indians. In time, however, the characteristic highland institution became the hacienda. In these regions, the Indian villages continued to use their land in the traditional communalistic way, paying a tribute to the owner, often in a European crop, such as wheat, which they did not use themselves. But the owner was no longer the encomendero with only a very few legal privileges; he was in business. The Indian communities were effectively held to the land, partly because of traditional ties to their villages, but also often because they were legally bound to remain because they had gotten into debt to the owner. When the hacienda was sold, the villages were included in the transfer as though they were a fixed part of the resources.

Two great scourges decimated the native population of Peru during the early colonial period. The Inca labor draft, the *mita,* was revived to provide men for the great silver mines, and so un-healthful were the working conditions and so arduous the labor that great numbers of Indians died or ran away to escape conscription. The other menace was the death-dealing diseases, particularly smallpox and measles, which the Europeans brought. It has been estimated that the native population was halved within two cen-turies of Spanish rule. The disorder in the social and economic life was matched by conflict and disturbance of another sort. The colonial government, which originally had intended to teach Chris-tianity to the heathens, was not able to accomplish the conversion as easily as had been believed possible, and soon instituted great destructive campaigns against idolatry, as though it had finally lost patience with mere education. The practitioners of the native re-ligion were isolated, and in some regions burned; the cult objects were destroyed and burned; and everywhere persecution was prac-ticed in some form or other.

Finally, after about 150 years, considerable adjustment was made between the indigenous and the colonial cultures. Hacienda peonage had endured to the point where the Indians were finally no longer aware of any alternative, so that an illusion of normality or in-evitability existed to a degree that kept the peasant villages polit-ically inert. Any rebellion from then on had to be caused by an intolerable worsening of conditions. Many of the villages had been grouped by the government into larger units (*reducciones*), and the reconstitution usually resulted in the Spanish town plan, with rectangular street grids, central plaza, and large church. Native administrative officers of the towns were also created after the Spanish pattern. A modified Christianity which manifested a loyalty to the Church and sufficient orthodox ritual elements to be satis-factory to the rulers had been incorporated gradually with old pagan elements. Some villages even began to hold Spanish bull-fights at their fiestas.

The degree of dominance of the colonists over the natives, both politically and generally in culture, was demonstrated by the re-bellions led by José Gabriel Tupac Amaru in the 1780s. The peas-ants were apparently intent on ameliorating an economic situation which was rapidly deteriorating as Spain and Peru became poorer. The leaders were descendants of the Inca and Curaca who hoped to regain their ancient power and prestige. But remarkably, the rebels manifested their loyalty to both Church and Crown, and at no point seemed to wish to do other than to redress certain wrongs perpetrated by Crown officials. Even during the later War of Independence (1821–1824), the Indians maintained a loyalty, however passive, to the Crown rather than to the Republicans. The consequences of the defeat of the rebellions were of some importance. A number of administrative reforms were made in favor of the Indians, but other laws further suppressed several survivals of Inca culture. More significantly, the dwindling mines were then largely abandoned, and the onerous mita labor ended as Spain's economy worsened. The final amalgam of colonial and native culture became stabilized, and in some areas remains relatively unchanged to the present day.

It is only since World War II that portents of change in the centuries-old pattern of life have become apparent. The political stirrings of the small, sleepy agricultural nations has been accompanied by an increasing participation in the world's economic affairs and frequently also by the beginning of local industries, however petty in size and importance compared to those of other nations. This means that wage work is increasingly available to the villagers, education becomes useful, and population movements, particularly toward cities or other seats of industry, widen the horizons of the villager, constituting an awakening from the stolid, ingrown, backward-looking character of the Peruvian peasants' ethos.

In the past and to the present, the most usual and expectable aspect of social change from a peasant status to that of greater participation in the modern world has been through race mixture. The term *mestizo,* which means literally a mixture of Indian and white, means also, by extension, an Indian who is *of* the white world. Gradually this second, derivative meaning has become the usual meaning; and since more Indians have moved into the economic orbit of the modern world and have followed this by giving up traditional peasant dress, speech, and other customs and habits, the term now refers primarily to a social and cultural condition rather than to a purely genetic one. And correspondingly, the term *Indian* has come to mean *peasant.* In the Peruvian census of 1876, Indians were put at 57.6 percent of the total population of Peru. In 1940, the census classified only 40 percent of the population as Indian. As in other parts of Spanish America, Indians are becoming mestizos, and presumably at a faster rate today than ever before. Of course, a part of the phenomenon is associated with race mixture, but the significant aspect is the reduction in the proportion of peasants, Indians who are relatively inert politically and economically in Peru's modern national life, and the increase in numbers of *citizens* of the modern world. People who think of themselves as Inca or Quechua or Indians are becoming fewer, while *Peruvians* are increasing. If trends of the present continue, if prosperity and industrialization advance and the correlated development of education and general modernity continues, Peru should become a nation whose population will not be composed of castes whose social and economic position are seen as immutable, but a modern nation of classes—social, occupational, and economic distinctions, to be sure, but not distinctions based on fixed criteria assumed to be biological. No one can be sure, of course, whether the world economy and Peru's place in it will continue in the present direction. Peru has no inner dynamic peculiar to itself; all of the significant changes have occurred as an indirect consequence of trends which have been worldwide.

FURTHER READINGS

Bennett, W. C., "The Archeology of the Central Andes," in J. H. Steward (ed.), *Handbook of South American Indians,* Smithsonian Institution, Bureau of American Ethnology, Bull. 143, Vol. 2, Washington, 1946.

Bennett, W. C. (ed.), *A Reappraisal of Peruvian Aachaeology,* Memoirs of the Society for American Archaeology, Vol. 13, No. 4, Pt. 2, 1948.

Bennett, W. C., and Bird, J. *Andean Culture History,* American Museum of Natural History, Handbook No. 5, New York, 1949.

Cobo, B., *Historia del Nuevo Mundo . . . ,* Seville, 1890–1895, 4 vols.

Cunow, H., *La Organización Social del Imperio de las Incas,* Paris, 1933.

James, P. E., *Latin America,* New York, 1942.

Karsten, R., *A Totalitarian State of the Past,* Societas Scientiarum Fennica, Commentationes Humanarum Litterarum, Vol. 16, No. 1, Helsinki, 1949.

Kirchoff, P., "The Social and Political Organization of the Andean Peoples," in J. H. Steward (ed.), *Handbook of South American Indians,* Smithsonian Institution, Bureau of American Ethnology, Bull. 143, Vol. 5, Washington, 1949.

Kosok, P., "The Role of Irrigation in Ancient Peru," *Proceedings, Eighth American Science Congress,* Washington, 1940.

Kubler, G., "The Quechua in the Colonial World," in J. H. Steward (ed.), *Handbook of South American Indians,* Smithsonian Institution, Bureau of American Ethnology, Bull. 143, Vol. 2, Washington, 1946.

Markham, C. R., *The Incas of Peru,* London, 1912.

Means, P. A., *Ancient Civilizations of the Andes,* New York, 1931.

Moore, S. F., *Power and Property in Inca Peru,* New York, 1958.

Murra, J. V., *The Economic Organization of the Inca State,* unpublished Ph.D. dissertation, University of Chicago, 1956.

Murra, J. V., "On Inca Political Structure," in V. F. Ray (ed.), *Systems of Political Control and Bureaucracy in Human Societies,* Proceedings of the 1958 Annual Spring Meeting of the American Ethnological Society, Seattle, 1958.

Murra, J. V., "Rite and Crop in the Inca State," in S. Diamond (ed.), *Culture in History,* New York, 1960.

Murra, J. V., "Social Structural and Economic Themes in Andean Ethnohistory," *Anthropological Quarterly,* Vol. 34, No. 2, 1961.

Prescott, W. H., *History of the Conquest of Peru,* New York, 1847, 2 vols.

Rostworowski de Diez Canseco, M., "Succession, Coöption to Kingship, and Royal Incest among the Inca," *Southwestern Journal of Anthropology,* Vol. 16, No. 4, 1960.

Rowe, J. H., "Inca Culture at the Time of the Spanish Conquest," in J. H. Steward (ed.), *Handbook of South American Indians,* Smithsonian Institution, Bureau of American Ethnology, Bull. 143, Vol. 2, Washington, 1946.

Sofuier, E. G., *Peru,* New York, 1877.

Strong, W. D., and Evans, C., Jr., *Cultural Stratigraphy in the Virú Valley,* Columbia University Studies in Archaeology and Ethnology, Vol. 4, New York, 1952.

Trimborn, H., "Der Kollektivismus der Inkas in Peru," *Anthropos,* Vols. 18–20, Vienna, 1923–1925.

Valcarcel, L. E., "Cuzco Archaeology," in J. H. Steward (ed.), *Handbook of South American Indians,* Smithsonian Institution, Bureau of American Ethnology, Bull. 143, Vol. 2, Washington, 1946.

Willey, G. R., *Prehistoric Settlement Patterns in the Virú Valley, Peru,* Smithsonian Institution, Bureau of American Ethnology, Bull. 155, Washington, 1953.

17

The Ashanti
of West Africa

The great Negro African kingdoms are among the most interesting and complex civilizations ever attained by nonliterate peoples. Particularly along the west coast, militaristic monarchies with large capital cities grew to dominate trade and industry over wide dependent areas. All of the essential characteristics of government are present in these states: they collect taxes, make censuses, conscript armies; they even have constitutions and courts of law. The history of the relations of these states with the modern nations of Europe shows the strength of their native institutions; for they have stood the test of conquest, colonization, and acculturation without loss of national unity, and today some are entering the world stage as independent nation-states with modernized political institutions.

The former British Crown Colony of the Gold Coast contained as its most centrally located and most powerful native kingdom the proud Ashanti people. The history of the course of empire in this region makes particularly inspiring reading to Negro nationalists in other parts of Africa today; for despite the surrender of Ashanti sovereignty to the British after the Ashanti War of 1873–1874

A NEWLY INSTALLED CHIEF IS SURROUNDED BY HIS FAMILY AND TRIBE. *Courtesy, United Nations*

ASHANTI WOMEN ENTERTAIN AT INSTALLATION OF CHIEF. *Courtesy, United Nations*

and the final incorporation of the Ashanti into the British colonial system after the so-called War of the Golden Stool in 1900–1901, the Ashanti nation and most of its governmental institutions remained intact. Finally in 1957, in confederation with the neighboring Fanti peoples, the Gold Coast nation now called Ghana was formed as a modern sovereign state.

In common with other West African kingdoms, the Ashanti state was established in its historically known location shortly after the Europeans were first encountered. Some of the militaristic and economic features of the state were directly related to the wars and dislocations caused by the Europeans, who avidly sought the famous gold deposits which gave that portion of the coast its name, and later by the competitions involved in the slave trade. During the sixteenth century, when the Portuguese were the most active Europeans in West Africa, the Ashanti were a series of small independent chiefdoms, each with its own capital town and inchoate political institutions. By the early part of the eighteenth century, the general pressure and competition along the Gold Coast had caused a series of wars which finally unified the several independent Ashanti divisions. The leader who accomplished this, Osai Tutu, and his head priest and adviser, Komfo Anokye, are now revered heroes of the Ashanti. One of the political inventions of this period was a symbol of nationalism which was needed to help unify the various Ashanti groups and to demonstrate the divine right by which the new dynasty was to rule over them all. This was the Golden Stool which Komfo Anokye is said to have brought down from the sky. It represented the ancestors of *all* the Ashanti. This state grew in power, territory, and internal strength until it was defeated by the British in 1874. But by then the Ashanti as a whole were consolidated as a people and have remained firmly united to this day.[1]

The Gold Coast consists of a highly variable terrain; there are coasts and mountains, forests and grasslands, fertile agricultural areas and near-deserts. The territory of the Ashanti, inland and centrally located in the Gold Coast, is mostly fertile and partly mountainous. Rainfall is plentiful during the rainy season from

---

[1] The following account of the Ashanti refers to the culture prior to 1875 as it existed before the influence of the British. This is the period described by R. S. Rattray, the primary authority.

April to November, and the land is well drained by many streams. The dry season, however, is very dry. It is depressingly hot all the year. It is probably a somewhat more healthful area than the coastal strip, but, like the west coast in general, it apparently deserves its reputation as an unhealthy climate. Malaria is the greatest scourge, but there are also many other kinds of fevers: blackwater, yellow, relapsing, typhoid, typhus, cholera, and others. Leprosy, elephantiasis, and sleeping sickness are some of the more spectacular diseases, but intestinal and skin parasites are a greater problem because of their higher frequency.

The Ashanti number more than 200,000 people, all speaking a single language, Twi, one of the members of the widely distributed Niger-Congo family. They live in a number of scattered villages and some larger towns, of which a few number more than 1000 inhabitants. The houses of the poorer people are of plastered wattle-and-daub construction surmounted with a domed grass-thatched roof, often in the form of compounds—connected buildings arranged around a court. Some of the larger towns have veritable palaces for the families of important chiefs. The walls of the larger houses are of sun-baked clay, enclosing many rooms. Complicated scroll designs adorn the walls and posts, and a sort of wide veranda runs all along the sides of the house. Clay walls are not suitable for such a rainy climate, but the overhanging thatch roof protects them from being washed away. Sometimes leaves are sewn together, shingle fashion, to roof important houses.

Hunting is not an important economic activity of the Ashanti, for the country has been farmed so intensively that large game has become scarce, but fish are frequently obtained by trade from the coastal groups, some of which are highly specialized as fishermen. Domestic animals include the inevitable dogs and goats and great numbers of fowl, especially chickens, which are used for sacrifices and divination as well as for food. A few sheep, pigs, and cattle are kept in some districts.

Horticulture is the basic economic activity of the Ashanti. The most important staple plants are plaintains, yams, and manioc. Manioc, incidentally, originated in the New World and was introduced, along with maize, into Africa early in the period of white colonization. Other plants cultivated by the Ashanti are sweet potatoes, millet, beans, onions, peanuts, tomatoes, and many fruits.

The oil palm is of great importance. Palm wine, along with maize or millet beer, is a favorite drink, and the oil has many culinary and domestic uses. Many of the vegetable crops can be harvested twice a year, and the manioc, or cassava, plant, a very starchy root, can be harvested daily in whatever quantity is needed for the day's use, after it has been allowed about two years of growth. Fields are prepared by burning shortly before the onset of the rainy season and cultivated with an iron hoe. Since fertilizers and crop rotation are unknown, fields must be fallowed for several years after two to four years of continuous cultivation. Most of the villages and towns, however, are permanently located, for the fields are used again after fallowing.

Like other West Africans, the Ashanti are experts at many handicrafts and have a number of professional specialists. Ironworking by bellows and charcoal fire after the fashion of the village blacksmith is one of the most specialized crafts. Ax and hoe blades, knives, daggers, projectile points, nails, hammers, and many ornaments, bells, and fine chains are made by the smith. Hand-modeling of pottery is also a specialized craft, as is woodcarving. Great attention is lavished on the carving of wooden stools, and beautiful wooden figurines of human beings are also made, so fancifully symbolic and abstract that they have become collectors' items for many Europeans.

The Ashanti formerly made bark cloth for clothing, but some time in the seventeenth century the art of weaving was learned. Women grow and pick the cotton and spin it into thread, but the weaving of the cloth is man's work alone and is specialized in family lines. A small horizontal loom is used, from which results a narrow bolt. Complicated designs are woven into the fabric, or are made by stamp dyeing. Particular care is lavished on the cloth used on the great umbrellas which shelter chiefs on state occasions. One famous umbrella, that pertaining to the Golden Stool, and known as *Katamanso*, "The Covering of the Nation," is made of camels' hair and wool. All important umbrellas have an ornamental figurine on top, plated with gold or silver.

One of the most interesting of Ashanti technological items is the talking-drum. Messages can be drummed across Ashanti, about 200 miles, as rapidly as a telegraphic communication. The drums very nearly do talk the language. The drummers are very proficient, and the people have cultivated a fine ear for the nuances of sound, but the high development of the drum language is made possible because of the nature of the Ashanti language. It, like many other African languages, is tonal; a much greater amount of meaning in a word or phrase is conveyed by its tone than is true of English, for example. Drums can reproduce these tones, punctuation, and the accents of a phrase so that it is nearly like hearing the phrase itself. The kinds of messages sent by drumming are set holophrases, so conventionally known that the receiver can instantly perceive the message and grasp its entirety. The repertory of the drummers includes stock phrases which call particular chiefs to meetings, give notice of danger, call to arms, give notice of the death of an important individual, and so on. Some drums are used only to drum proverbs—a ritual performance rather than a broadcast of messages.

The household, which is often polygynous, is the basis of day-to-day economic and social life. The matrilineal lineage, however, is the unit of society of greatest significance in Ashanti ideology and in all practical economic, social, political, and religious matters which are above the level of domestic household affairs. A person, male or female, is seen as related by blood to others only through his mother. Descent along the female line is the principle which determines land rights, inheritance of other property, and offices and titles. Social and political status is also derived from this line, and it is the focus of the ancestor cult, the basis of much of the religious activity. Emotional ties between individuals are thought to be created by the blood they share, and it is mother's blood which creates the child's body.

The father is regarded as the catalyst of the conception and the provider of the spirit (*ntoro*) to the infant. A child receives from his father his life force, "a small bit of the creator," and also his distinctive personality and disposition. The male lineage is a relatively clear-cut one, even though it is not considered so important as the matrilineal line, because males often continue to live in their place of birth after marriage—the wives go to their husbands' homes. There is a strong tendency, therefore, for many of the members of a patrilineal lineage to live adjacent to one another in a sort of village precinct.[2] Any person, therefore, is in some measure

[2] M. Fortes has shown that in modern times the residence pattern, though ideally patrilocal, is frequently of other types, ("Time and Social Structure: An Ashanti Case Study," in M. Fortes (ed.), *Social Structure: Studies Presented to A. R. Radcliffe-Brown,* London, 1949.)

a member of two lineages: one is the line of males who provide his spirit; the other is the female line, which is given greater significance by being the line of inheritance of land and other goods, offices, and status. This matrilineal line is seen also as a lineage which is a part of a much larger clan, *abusua,* the component lineages of which all descended from a common ancestress. Both the male ntoro line and the abusua line are totemic (some particular plant or animal aided or collaborated with the ancestors), practice the appropriate food taboos, and prohibit marriage with any fellow member.

The land belongs to the abusua ancestors who are buried in it. No individual Ashanti owns land; he only occupies a portion of it which has come from his clan ancestors. He does own the products of his labor on the land and can dispose of them as he pleases, but he may not be removed from the land, nor has he any right to sell it or to determine which of his descendants should get the major share. All this is prescribed by rigid traditional rules of inheritance. Because the abusua is matrilineal, a man's goods are passed on to his brother, if the incumbent dies fairly young, or to his sister's sons. In rare cases particular kinds of personal property can be passed on from father to son, and such a testament must be agreed on by the members of the abusua. As in the case of the Trobriand Islanders and the Navaho,[3] certain conflicts are created in this system, for it appears that a father often desires to pass on his wealth to his son.

Both men and women possess individual property that they have made or acquired by their own efforts. All other possessions are family and lineage property, consisting chiefly of carved stools which symbolize the kindred household and lineage gods and fetishes, and various heirlooms, none of which can be disposed of by individuals. Trade in Ashanti is of two kinds, an import-export business which is run bureaucratically as a state enterprise and the more petty local trade which takes place in town markets. Various handicrafts and food products are exchanged there. This minor trade is conducted individually by women, but usually in the interests of the household. Some things are bartered directly, with much haggling, but frequently a sort of money of cowrie shells intermediates in the exchange. Local representatives of the state regu-

[3] See Chapters 11 and 8.

late the market, settle disputes about prices and quality of goods, and exact a transaction tax.

Slaves are also bought and sold, but this occurs as a personal transaction rather than in the market. Usually these unfortunates are prisoners of war, but sometimes they are actually sold by their own people as punishment for some criminal action. Sometimes natives of Ashanti are placed in a condition of servitude because their relatives pawn them to secure a debt. The work done by a pawn is considered interest on the loan. Pawns are usually redeemed, and in any case retain their clan affiliation, and their offspring suffer no stigma. Slaves are not cruelly used; in the opinion of the public, a person who mistreats a slave is contemptible. Slaves are allowed to marry, and their children belong to the master. Frequently, the master takes a female slave as a wife, in preference to a usual marriage, and often enough her children inherit some of the father's property and status. This preference is a result of the conflict between the matrilineal system and the desires of a husband and father. In a normal marriage, the wife has considerable status, but many husbands prefer a slave or pawn wife who has no powerful abusua to intercede on her behalf every time the married couple have an argument. A husband also has more control over his children if the mother is thus isolated from her own kin, and he can pass some of his property to his own sons.

The pattern of kinship terminology among the Ashanti kindred is a variation of a common type which has been called *Crow* by anthropologists, after the Crow Indians of the American Great Plains. All the members of the matrilineal lineage are given the same kinship terms as the relatives of a single matrilineal compound. Thus, people of the same generation are all siblings. A woman calls all members of the children's generation *child,* and a man calls them all *sister's child.* In parents' generation, all women are *mother,* and men are *mother's brother* (the actual father, of course, is not a member of the lineage). Grandparents and grandchild terms are self-reciprocal—that is, they are undifferentiated. Members of the father's lineage are undifferentiated except by sex; it is as though all male members of that lineage were called *father,* and females *female father.*

Status differentiation among families is largely a political matter. The most important of all is the royal family. Next in importance are those families whose heads are chiefs of territorial subdivisions of the kingdom. In each of the chiefdoms, a particular matrilineal lineage provides the chief, but he is chosen by the lineage from among several men who are eligible for the post.

Elections take place in the following manner. The senior female of the chiefly lineage is asked to nominate a chief from among the eligible males of the lineage. She, in turn, consults all of the elders (male and female) of the lineage, and together they make the selection. This nomination is sent to a council of elders, who represent other lineages in the town or district. They in turn present the nomination, with appropriate arguments, to an assemblage of the people. If they do not approve, the whole process is begun again to nominate a different man. The new chief is enstooled by the elders, who admonish him with the list of expectations they have of him. He, in turn, takes a solemn oath to the Earth Goddess and to his ancestors to fulfill his duties.

The chief is surrounded by a great deal of pomp and ceremony, and theoretically he has considerable despotic power, including the ability to make judgments of life or death on his subjects. When he sits upon the stool, he is sacred, as the holy intermediary between his people and the ancestors. But his power is more apparent than real. He must listen to the Council of the Elders, govern justly and bravely, and behave circumspectly. Should the Elders and public opinion turn against him, he can be impeached—destooled—and then he becomes merely another ordinary man, except that he is derided for his failure.

The chiefs of the district divisions, as well as village and subdivisional chiefs, are elected in the same way, and each swears fealty to the one above him. The *Ashantihene* (King of all Ashanti) is chief of the division of Kumasi, the nation's capital, and is appointed in the same way as the others, but the other local chiefs are subject to him. His power, too, is circumscribed by the elders and by public opinion in his own division, and the chiefs of the other areas have a considerable constitutional check on him. As a symbol of the nation, his importance is testified to by the extraordinary deference ritually accorded to him, but the context is religious —he sits for the sacred ancestors. The land, for example, is said to belong to the king, but the phrase means actually that it belongs to the tribal ancestors whom he represents. He cannot alienate land or, in fact, indulge in any act of arbitrary power not agreed upon by the people.

The presence of aristocratic clans and the power of elders would seem to be evidence of a sort of oligarchical tendency in Ashanti political life. But there is an additional feature of the society which in considerable measure assures a kind of democratization of the governmental process. In modern urban civilization, it tends to be the poor and the illiterate who need special machinery or organization in order to have a hearing, but in primitive life older men typically monopolize political power and young men are relatively helpless. The Ashanti have elaborated a peculiar institution called the *mmerante,* an organization of young men. At their meetings they select a representative to argue their views, and he adds his opinion at all meetings of the Council of Elders and chiefs. No action can be undertaken without consulting the representative of the Young Men.

The Ashanti state addresses itself to the problems of internal order by evoking religious rather than secular-legal postulates. The state is, after all, a theocracy; hence crimes are viewed as sins. Acts which are antisocial with respect to the body politic are seen as offenses against the ancestors first, and only derivatively and secondarily are they defined as harmful to the community. If the chief or king failed to punish a crime, the ancestors would be angry with the whole Ashanti people. The penalty for all crimes is death. Only the king has the power to exact this penalty. But the king also has the power to commute the sentence, which lays the way open for bribes and ransom. These are not so regulated as to be considered fines, properly speaking, but they are a considerable source of revenue to the state, which consequently welcomes quarrels and litigation. Such commutations are actually more frequent than execution.

The most abhorred crime is murder. Suicide, curiously, is considered murder, and the miscreant, though already a corpse by his own hand, is subjected to decapitation, the standard punishment for murder. In a sense a suicide is also guilty of "contempt of court," because of the rule that only the king can kill an Ashanti. Hence, he is not only decapitated but all of his property is forfeited to the king. The Ashanti feel that intent must be established in a murder trial; if the homicide is judged accidental, the murderer pays a heavy compensation to the lineage of the deceased. On the other hand, certain actions which can be interpreted as an intent or threat to kill are punished just as if an actual homicide were committed. A person judged insane would not be executed for murder because of the absence of responsible intent. And drunkenness, except for the extreme crimes of murder and cursing the king, is considered a valid defense. Several kinds of sex offenses, such as incest within either the matrilineal or patrilineal lineage, intercourse with a menstruating woman,[4] rape of a married woman, adultery with any of the wives of a chief,[5] are all capital crimes. Other assaults or even insults against a chief or a member of his court, or for a woman to call a man a fool, also are considered crimes punishable by death.

Cursing the king—that is, calling upon a supernatural power to cause the death of the king—is such a horrible crime that the Ashanti do not speak of it as such; they call it *blessing the king*. A man who angers another man to the point that the latter is driven to curse the king is considered also to be at fault, and he must pay a heavy indemnity. Sorcery and witchcraft are special crimes, and are not punished by decapitation but by strangling, clubbing, burning, or drowning, for a witch's blood must not be shed.

Ordinarily disputes between individuals are settled by the families or lineages concerned, but it is possible to bring disputes to a trial if one of the disputants utters a tabooed oath of a chief or of the king. The case is then tried in the court of the district chief whose oath has been used. In the end, the king's court is the sentencing court, however, for only the king can order the death penalty. In the trial, the two litigants state their cases in long orations directed to the chief and his court and the Council of the Elders. Cross-examination of the testimony can be made by anyone present, but eventually, if the proceedings do not lead to a verdict, a special witness is called, and his testimony decides the case. Strangely, there is only one witness; the two litigants do not each have their own witnesses. It is assumed by everyone that the oaths the witness must swear insure his telling the truth. The idea that he might be friendly or hostile to one of the disputants is un-

[4] The supernatural danger of menstrual blood is a common, if not universal, theme among primitive cultures.

[5] This is an offense against the royal ancestors, inasmuch as a chief's wives are *Stool* wives. The punishment is not simple decapitation; the condemned man is sliced to death with such fine surgery that he may live during two or three days of the torture.

thinkable, even if he is a kinsman. Sometimes, particularly in cases such as witchcraft or adultery, which would have no witnesses, questions of fact are decided by ordeals. The ordeal is requested by the accused, rather than imposed by the court, and frequently takes the form of drinking poison.

The character of the judicial system emphasizes that the Ashanti concept of rectitude and good behavior favors harmony among the people. One must act always in terms of the rules made by the gods and the ancestors. Ancestor worship is fundamental to the Ashanti moral system, and lies at the base of the governmental sanctions. The link between mother and child is the relationship that is the basis of the whole network, which includes ancestors and fellow men as well. The rituals and beliefs associated with conception, pregnancy, and birth reflect the main assumptions on which the unity of the kingdom is founded.

Conception is believed to be caused by the mingling during intercourse of the male spirit, ntoro, with the female blood. When pregnancy reaches the eighth month, the woman goes to her own mother's home. Males are not permitted to attend parturition. The woman is placed in a sitting position and assisted by four midwives. As soon as the baby is born, it is given its name, which is the particular day of the week upon which it is born. The umbilical cord is cut against a piece of wood, and the infant is then bathed. The afterbirth is merely thrown away rather than given the ritual burial so common among other primitive cultures.

During the first eight days after birth the baby is known as a *ghost child,* and the period is considered one in which it is not certain whether the child will remain alive or die. It is believed that a ghost mother in the spirit world has lost this child and will make an effort to get it back. After the eighth day a ceremony is held to acknowledge that the baby is a true human baby, and a patronym is given it. This is the name of the paternal grandfather or grandmother, and it is one of the ties which bind the child to the members of the patrilineal lineage, the ntoro. The original *day name* remains important, however, and is more frequently used.

Twins are not killed unless they are born in the royal family. Ordinarily, boy twins become fly switchers in the court, and twin girls are potential wives of the king. Presumably, if the twins are a boy and girl, no particular career awaits them. A woman who bears triplets is greatly honored. This is because three is regarded as a lucky number. The birth of a third, sixth, or ninth child is attended by special rituals, for they are to be held in esteem all their lives. Five is an unlucky number, and the fifth child in a family will always be plagued with misfortune. Parents of large families are greatly respected, while childless couples are derided.

Childhood is a happy time, a play time, and Ashanti parents are very indulgent. A child is not considered responsible for any of its actions, for it has no power to do good or evil until after puberty. The death of a child does not require funeral rites; the body is merely buried in the refuse dump. Such children are called *pot children,* after the receptacle in which the body is placed for burial. The absence of funeral rites is not caused by lack of sentiment, but because a child is harmless; hence there is no worry about controlling the soul, which is the original purpose of all funeral rites.

Puberty rituals are held only for girls. Boys are given instruction by their fathers, but no public observance of the change in state from child to man is made. As a girl nears the time when her first menstruation is expected, she goes to her mother's home. When she discloses the fact of her menstruation, the mother goes into the village beating an iron hoe with a stone to arouse the populace and make known the good news. All of the old women come out and sing *bara* (menstrual) songs. The mother spills a libation of palm wine on the earth and recites the following prayer:

Supreme Sky God, who is alone great, upon whom men lean and do not fall, receive this wine and drink.

Earth Goddess, whose day of worship is a Thursday, receive this wine and drink.

Spirit of our ancestors, receive this wine and drink.

This girl child whom God has given to me, today the *bara* state has come upon her.

O mother who dwells in the land of ghosts, do not come and take her away and do not have permitted her to menstruate only to die.

Five days after the onset of menstruation, the girl is bedecked with finery and displayed publicly. At this time she also engages in ritual bathing and eating, which lift the taboos she has observed. After the ceremony a girl is addressed as *mother* by younger children. Old women regard this change in state with sadness, for they believe that it will cause the death of one of them. Just as each birth in this world is a death in the spirit world, the "birth" of a girl into full womanhood takes one away from the living group.

There are many restrictions and taboos placed on menstruating women, for they are regarded as ritually unclean. They may not cook food for any adult male, nor can they eat of any food cooked for a man. If an unclean woman enters the ancestral stool house, she will be killed instantly, for "if this were not done the ghosts of his ancestors would strangle the reigning chief." She may not cross the threshold of any man's house (she lives in a special hut during these periods), and she may not swear an oath, nor may one be sworn against her, and all sacred places are forbidden to her.

If a girl has not been betrothed in childhood, she is expected to become so immediately after her puberty ceremony. Marriage itself is not regarded as an important ritual event, but rather as a state which follows soon and normally after the puberty ritual. A man is expected to marry a cross cousin, i.e., either his father's sister's daughter or his mother's brother's daughter. Parallel cousins, of course, are members of the same abusua group and hence prohibited as marriage partners. Frequently the marriage has been promised even before the couple are born. If not, a boy is sometimes allowed some initiative, but always the consent of both households is necessary. The only formalities required to make a marriage legal are these consents and an appropriate payment of bride price, various goods given by the boy's family to the girl's.

A girl is required to be virginal on her marriage, and after marriage adultery is punished severely. If a wife is caught in adultery, or confesses it, her parents must make the husband a compensatory payment, and the seducer is also required to pay an amount which is commensurate with his social status. Adultery with any of the innumerable king's wives was punished in the old days by a horrible torture of the seducer and the death penalty for the guilty wife and the close relatives of both. A man may divorce a wife for adultery, as he may for barrenness, drunkenness, quarrelsomeness, mother-in-law trouble, and witchcraft. A wife may divorce a husband for impotence, adultery, laziness, witchcraft, desertion, or for taking another wife without asking her permission, if she is his senior wife.

Polygyny is legal and very common, but, as indicated above, the senior wife must be consulted. Jealousy is apparently not frequent, and a woman likes to have a co-wife, if she is compatible, added to the household—it lightens the work and adds to her husband's prestige.

A major event in the lives of the Ashanti people is the sickness and death of a close relative. In case of illness, there are two possible causes, and two kinds of practitioners who may be called. One is the ordinary herbalist who by means of divination finds the supernatural cause of the illness and treats it with herbal concoctions. But if pure witchcraft is the cause of the illness, a specialist is called. This specialist, or witch doctor, is a person possessed by a spirit and is able, by the use of the spirit, to combat witchcraft. A witch, as usual, is one who has this same power, but uses it as black magic, that is, for antisocial or malevolent purposes.

If efforts to cure a person are unavailing, the last rites are performed. These consist of pouring a little water down the throat of the dying person when it is believed the soul is leaving the body and of saying the following prayer: "Your clansmen [naming them] say: Receive this water and drink, and do not permit any evil thing to come whence you are setting out, and permit all the women of the household to bear children." This rite is considered so important that old people are loath to be alone for long without someone available to perform it for them in case of a collapse. After death, the corpse is washed, and the body is dressed in its best clothes and adorned with packets of gold dust (soul money), ornaments, and food for the journey "up the hill." The body is generally buried within 24 hours. Until that time a riotous wake is held consisting of dancing, drumming, shooting of guns, and much drunkenness, all accompanied by the wailing of the relatives.

The sixth day after death is the Day of Rising, when the soul is finally dispatched from the vicinity. The central ritual of this day consists of all the blood relatives' shaving their heads and putting the hair into a large pot. A sheep is sacrificed and cooked, and this food, utensils, and the pot of hair are taken to a special part of the cemetery where the ghost will find them and take them for his journey. After these rites, normal life is resumed except for mourning on the eighth, fifteenth, fortieth, and eightieth days, and at one year.

Funeral rites for kings are much more elaborate affairs and involve the whole kingdom, of course, and they deserve special mention because the west coast kingdoms have been famous for the human sacrifices made at the king's funeral. A number of the king's wives are strangled, which in Ashanti is the aristocratic method of being put to death, in order to accompany him to the afterworld, along with representatives of the palace staff. These victims are supposed to be joyful at their opportunity, and sometimes volunteer for duty in the afterworld. In all the districts, towns, and villages of the kingdom, sacrifices of slaves, criminals, and waylaid strangers go on while the king lies in state.

The greatest and most frequent religious ceremonies of the Ashanti are those whose purpose is to recall the spirits of the departed rulers, offer them food and drink, and ask their favor for the good of all the people. These ceremonies, called the *Adae,* occur every 21 days. On the day before an Adae ceremony, the talking-drums announce it to the people, and the stool treasurer gathers together the sheep and liquor which will be offered. On the day of the Adae, the priest-chief officiates in the stool house where the ancestors come, and offers each stool food and drink. The public ceremony occurs outdoors, where everyone is free to join the dancing. Minstrels chant the tribal traditions, and the talking drums keep extolling the chief and the ancestors in traditional phrases.

The other large ceremony is an annual event which lasts for a week or two in September. The *Odwera,* as it is called, is the time for cleansing the society of sin and defilement and for the purification of the shrines of the ancestors and gods. After a sacrifice of a black hen and a ritual feast in which both the living and dead are believed to share, a new year begins, and everyone begins it clean, strong, and healthy.

In all ceremonies, the strongest motif is the ever-present concern with the ancestors. But Ashanti religion and cosmology are not simply ancestor worship, for the universe is peopled with many other kinds of spirits as well. The greatest, the Supreme One, is the creator of all things and head of a pantheon of lesser gods, each of whom is in some way a part of or a descendant of the creator. These act as intermediaries between the people and the creator; hence many of them are local patrons of a village, district, or household. Others are gods of a place or geographic feature, the most sacred of these being the gods of rivers. All of these gods, including the Supreme One, are subjects of a great number of myths which explain how they acquired their characteristics.

Each of the important gods has a temporary abode on earth.

This shrine may be almost any material object, from a simple stone to an elaborate image. Specially trained priests look after these objects, and part of their knowledge consists of knowing how to call the god to come and to speak, using the priest himself as a medium. There are a great many minor spirits who abide in tiny beads and other small objects which are carried by ordinary people as supernatural charms and fetishes. In addition, all animals and plants are believed to have souls which can be prayed to or otherwise moved to action, and even earth is seen as a powerful female principle from which plants grow. The Earth Goddess has no priest or fetishes, but important offerings and prayers are made to her. Some spirits are hostile and are found in the forests, and from them black magic and witchcraft may be learned. Nevertheless, all are related; the hostile spirits, the souls of man and his ancestors, of animals and plants, the earth, and all of the ranks of gods are descended from the remote Supreme One.

There are both Christian and Moslem converts in Ashanti in modern times, and in principle it would seem there would be no intellectual or logical conflicts. All three are hierarchical and involve the conception of a supreme being. There has been a conflict, nevertheless, particularly between Christian converts and the older Ashanti. The Ashanti government is theocratic; at every point religion is an aspect of the king's and chiefs' rule as well as being the rationale of all traditional ethical and moral conduct. Some Christians alienate themselves from their communities because they refuse to participate in fetish observances, even when these are a part of ordinary obedience to their chiefs. The Christians' attempt to resolve this conflict by separating ceremonial (religious) observances from secular government—the chief as ruler from the chief as sacred head—has, of course, weakened the position of the chief.

Christianity has been described as a thin veneer, however, over the fundamental world view of the Ashanti. Particularly, the ancestors are still important to them, and elders are still greatly respected. Matrilineal descent, as opposed to the Christian emphasis on the patriarchal family, is still important, and bride price and the concept of the spirit descending from the Supreme One through males are still fundamental in defining the nature of group relations.

It is amazing that the Ashanti have been able to accommodate so much of their traditional institutions to modern social changes.

Europeans never actually colonized the Gold Coast except for a handful of Danes about 1820; one great source of conflict was therefore absent, and the British were able to inaugurate their famed system of indirect rule because of this absence of conflict and because of the cohesiveness of the Ashanti society.

The first Europeans to visit the Gold Coast were the Portuguese in 1471. They were interested in gold and spices, and by a papal order were given monopoly rights over this part of western Africa. Subsequently, the development of plantation systems in the Americas created a great and continuing demand for slaves, and the British, Dutch, Danes, French, and others began to compete with the Portuguese and in 1642 dislodged them from the Gold Coast. The coastal groups provided the market with slaves and acquired most of the wealth, initially at least. But this period of trade in slaves from far inland, the subsequent dispersion of European goods, and the great competition stimulated the militaristic phase of the increasingly larger Ashanti state, although it was itself not directly under the domination of any European power at the time.

From 1750 until 1821 British trading companies held a monopoly over the Gold Coast until the British government, having become committed to free trade as a political doctrine, gradually took over more and more of the Gold Coast administration. But, nearly from the first, the British used the existing Gold Coast political institutions to maintain their control. The Ashanti, living inland, never were as affected by the presence of the foreigners as the coastal peoples. The Ashanti even frequently raided them, which led to several skirmishes with the British. Once, in 1824, the Ashanti defeated the British and killed the governor. In 1874 the Ashanti area was successfully invaded by the British, and the kingdom was held in subjugation until 1900. In that year the Ashanti revolted in the famous War of the Golden Stool,[6] and the British annexed Ashantiland as a crown colony and deported the king, Prempeh I, an enduring humiliation for the Ashanti.

Nationalistic pressures began to build up in western Africa in the present century, as they have in many other colonial areas. Still predominantly agricultural, the Ashanti nevertheless have made many

[6] Rattray, in *Ashanti,* Oxford, 1923, pp. 287–293, says that the bloody revolt would not have occurred had the British respected the Ashanti valuation of the Golden Stool, which the Ashanti feared the British would take away; and particularly had not Sir Frederic Hodgson demanded that the Stool, which was hidden, be produced for him to sit upon.

modern advances. Some important Ashanti have been educated in the United States, England, and other European countries, and a school system has been built up on the Gold Coast. An increase in trade and cash cropping rather than subsistence agriculture, particularly noteworthy in the cocoa trade, and developments in modern small-scale manufacturing are transforming Ashanti life.

In 1951 Kwame Nkrumah became Prime Minister of the colony and under his leadership the Gold Coast became the independent state of Ghana in 1957. Political stability was threatened, however, by the fact that Ghana was composed of large rival linguistic groups, notably the Fanti, Ashanti, and Akan (Twispeakers). In 1966 Nkrumah and his Convention People's Party, largely of Fanti membership, were overthrown by a military group who ruled until 1969 as the National Liberation Council. Elections were finally held in 1969 and Dr. K. A. Busia, an Ashanti (and an anthropologist) became President.

Ethic and kinship loyalties therefore exert powerful centrifugal forces against the newer political loyalties demanded by the state. For example, Brong-Ahafo, which had been a part of the Ashanti confederacy, became a separately administered region in 1959. Despite considerable modernization it is rare for an Ashanti to marry an outsider, and it would appear that the internal homogenization so necessary for national stability is still not proceeding rapidly because of the considerable tribalistic loyalties.

The state's economy faces the same problems that afflict all nonindustrial states. Ghana is largely an agricultural society, and the agriculture has two facets, its subsistence value and its commercial value. Ghana supplies one-third of the world's cocoa, and most of the state's revenue derives from this sale. Inasmuch as cocoa prices are determined outside Ghana, such dependence on one crop is very dangerous. It is, in any such nation, natural to want to diversify the commercial products and, above all, to attempt industrialization. The Volta River hydroelectric scheme is what the present government of Ghana hopes will finally insure the nation's economic independence.

As of 1970 industrial progress has not been rapid. The major cash crop is still cocoa, and the present government favors private enterprise and has rather withdrawn from the former close links with Easten Europe. Ashanti art has become prosperous, especially

384

through sale of gold-weights and Kente weaving, both of which have come to be of symbolic value for a growing pan-African culture.

Community development projects have become very important among the Ashanti. The government Department of Community Development has successfully encouraged many Ashanti villages to complete such self-help projects as improving roads and water supplies, street lighting, and especially school building to the point where almost every community has a school. The community projects use communal labor, which is a continuation of a long established tradition of voluntary communal labor on the neighborhood level. Wealthier communities engaged more fully in cash cropping of cocoa usually tax themselves in money rather than labor.

FURTHER READINGS

Apter, D. E., *Ghana in Transition,* New York, 1963.
Arhin, Kwame, "The Structure of Greater Ashanti (1700-1924)," *Journal of African History,* Vol. 8, No. 1, 1907.
Basehart, Harry W., "Ashanti," in D. M. Schneider and K. Gough (eds.), *Matrilineal Kinship,* Berkeley, 1961.
Bowdich, T. E., *Mission to Ashantee,* London, 1819.
Brokensha, D. W., *Social Change at Larteh, Ghana,* Oxford, 1966.
Busia, K. A., *The Position of the Chief in the Modern Political System of Ashanti: A Study of the Influence of Contemporary Social Changes on Ashanti Political Institutions,* Oxford, 1951.
Busia, K. A. "The Ashanti," in *African Worlds,* London, New York, Toronto, 1954.
Christensen, J. B., *Double Descent Among the Fanti,* Human Relations Area Files, New Haven, 1954.
Dupuis, J., *Journal of a Residence in Ashantee,* London, 1824.
Forde, C. D., *African Worlds,* Oxford, 1954.
Fortes, M., "Time and Social Structure: An Ashanti Case Study," in M. Fortes (ed.), *Social Structure: Studies Presented to A. R. Radcliffe-Brown,* London, 1949.
Fortes, M., "Kinship and Marriage among the Ashanti," in A. R. Radcliffe-Brown and C. D. Forde (eds.), *African Systems of Kinship and Marriage,* London, 1950.

Herskovits, M. J., "The Ashanti Ntoro: a Re-examination," *Journal of the Royal Anthropological Institute,* Vol. 67, 1937.

Hoebel, E. A., "The Ashanti: Constitutional Monarchy and the Triumph of Public Law," in E. A. Hoebel, *The Law of Primitive Man,* Cambridge, 1954.

Lystad, Robert A., *The Ashanti: A Proud People,* New Brunswick, N.J., 1958.

Plass, Margaret Webster, *African Miniatures: The Goldweights of the Ashanti,* London, 1967.

Rattray, R. S., *Ashanti,* Oxford, 1923.

Rattray, R. S., *Religion and Art in Ashanti,* Oxford, 1927.

Rattray, R. S., *Ashanti Law and Constitution,* Oxford, 1929.

Tordoff, W., *Ashanti under the Prempehs,* London, 1966.

Ward, W. E. F., *A History of the Gold Coast,* London, 1948.

PART V

MODERN
FOLK
SOCIETIES

Chan Kom:
A Village in Yucatán

Like many other villages in the world today, Chan Kom is neither an isolated primitive society nor yet a town typifying modern civilization; it is rather, in some way and somehow, a little of both. Ethnologists have long concerned themselves with describing and analyzing primitive *cultures,* relatively self-contained societies which were characterized by distinctive modes of life and conduct. Western civilization is less easy to describe, not only because of its complexity as a culture, but perhaps also because the societies and the culture are not coterminous. The culture embraces a great number of communities and many kinds of communities, some of them partaking of civilization only in part and in various degrees.

The fullest and most complex manifestation of Western civilization is always in the great urban centers, and most analytic studies by economists, historians, and the like have been concerned, therefore, with these centers. Until recently, the more isolated villages of the less-industrialized countries have been ignored almost entirely. Robert Redfield, more than anyone else, helped to direct the attention of ethnologists to this untended field. These villages, being relatively self-contained and largely based on subsistence activities

389

rather than being commercial and industrial economies, are in many ways analogous to primitive communities and thus lend themselves to study by the traditional ethnological techniques of description and interpretation.

But the *folk societies*[1] posed a problem the ethnologist had not previously faced. These villages are functional parts of modern nations, however unchanging and separated they may appear. And nations have cultural and economic relations with other nations. A certain measure of the village culture is merely a local manifestation of something which has its source and dynamic outside the village. An ethnographic study of a village, therefore, cannot be as complete an analysis as a similar study of a self-sufficient, isolated primitive tribe.

Redfield faced this analytic problem squarely in his studies in Yucatán. His attempt to formulate a scheme by which the culture of such a village as Chan Kom could be dissected and understood aroused a good deal of interest in the fields of anthropology and sociology and has led many of the younger anthropologists to make studies of similar communities. The basis of Redfield's approach was to posit an *urban* culture type at one pole of a continuum and a standard, or ideal, primitive culture (*folk culture* in his use of the term) at the other. A village like Chan Kom could be described as existing at a point along this continuum at a particular time. Its various cultural components and aspects could be judged as primitive to a degree and in particular respects and urban (modern, Western) in others.

This approach also includes a theory of culture change: Primitive tribes manifest preurban forms of society and culture; under influence from civilization they move historically toward the urban type. Many particular premises of this view, such as its emphasis on communication rather than economic development, have been criticized and rejected; some anthropologists have ignored the scheme in its entirety. It is not in keeping with our descriptive purpose to attempt an evaluation of the method here. The significant fact is

[1] Redfield's book, *The Folk Culture of Yucatan,* Chicago, 1941, stimulated the use of this term, now common in anthropology. In current usage, Chan Kom is a *folk society,* as opposed to a primitive tribe on the one hand and modern civilization on the other. Redfield meant the term to refer to primitive communities, with villages such as Chan Kom, primitive in only some ways, being therefore partly folk, but usage has changed its meaning. There had been no term so appropriate for communities such as Chan Kom until Redfield supplied it.

that anthropology now considers folk cultures such as that of Chan Kom a legitimate subject of interest, and progress has been made toward refining methods by which such cultures may be examined and described and the results made useful to social science.

Yucatán is one of the states of modern Mexico, a short rectangular peninsula projecting northward into the Gulf of Mexico. The basic population consists of descendants of the Maya Indians, who, before the Spanish conquest, were the aboriginal population of the area. The Mayan language is still spoken by most of the rural population, and certain everyday habits and traditions of their aboriginal forebears still exist. Most of the Yucatecan population has been heavily influenced by the 300 years of Spanish colonial rule, however, so that in the great majority of communities it is an old, or rural-colonial, variant of Spanish culture which is manifested, rather than something purely aboriginal.

A MODERN MAYAN PEASANT OF YUCATÁN. *Courtesy, Museum of Anthropology, University of Michigan*

The peninsula of Yucatán, while a part of Mexico, is in some respects a quite backward area, and its cultural ties with Mexico are considerably hindered by geographic isolation. Dense tropical forests and mountain ranges have slowed the building of road and railroad communication with Mexico. There is only one port, Progreso, and one real city, Mérida, and cultural influences from the outside world are therefore funneled through these two, where communication is concentrated.

Yucatán is a subtropical country. The air is warm and rather moist all the year. The total amount of rainfall averages about 48 inches annually in the region of Chan Kom, but nearly all of it is concentrated in the summer months. The fluctuations from year to year are considerable however; hence the agriculturalists are understandably preoccupied with rainfall even though it would seem that in an average summer they might have sufficient.

The topography of most of Yucatán is simple and monotonous, being composed of a great, very flat stratum of porous limestone, rising above the sea only a few feet. The interior of the country is entirely without rivers, streams, and springs, because it is so level and because the limestone absorbs so much of the rainfall. The nature of this land and rainfall relationship has created an unusual and useful feature very typical of Yucatán. This is the *cenote,* a deep, circular hole eroded into the limestone in which ground water accumulates well below the surface of the land. Most of the settlements have depended on this source of water so fully and for so long that its importance is symbolized in religious myth and thought.

Like many other backward or underdeveloped parts of the modern world, Yucatán has two economies. One is the economy which creates goods, or often simply *a* good, to export to the rest of the world. From the proceeds of exports, things from the outer world are imported into the country. The other is the local, or subsistence, economy of the region. In Yucatán, the first consists almost entirely of the production of henequen, from which sisal fiber is drawn to be made into twine and bags. It is grown on large estates which are heavily capitalized and employ a wage labor force. This is an industry, in a very real sense. The basis of the subsistence economy is maize, which is grown by the independent peasants by primitive methods, in small plots carved out of the forests.

Mérida, and its port, Progreso, are the centers of the export-import economy. And Mérida has been, since its founding in early colonial times, the center of Spanish economic, political, and cultural influence. The outstanding cultural contrast to it is found in the remote tropical forest on the other side of the peninsula, where live some scattered, still primitive Indians, refugees from progress. Except for the workers on the henequen plantations around Mérida, a large part of the remaining population of Yucatán consists of independent peasant agriculturalists living in small villages.

Chan Kom, a fairly typical peasant village, contained 251 people in 1930. The village itself is not an ancient one. The War of the Castes, a series of peasant revolts which began in the 1840s, resulted in the depopulation of the area, and the people did not resettle it for several generations. Chan Kom was finally colonized little by little by people from other similar villages, and about the turn of the century it came to be an independent entity rather than an outlying area of one of the nearby villages.

In one sense, this very newness of Chan Kom represents something typical of the Yucatecan peninsula. A habit of migration has been forced on the Maya by the nature of the soil and rainfall. After a few generations, the arable land around a village becomes depleted, some fields more than others, so that a few of the families begin to move away to cut and burn new fields out of the wilderness of scrub and bush grown up in the years since it was last used. They usually retain their ties to the home village for a generation or two. It remains their "civic center", to which they return for market days and religious celebrations, but often the new town eventually becomes large enough and well enough established to serve its own people as ties to the parent villages weaken through time.

In 1925 Chan Kom came to be a *pueblo,* a village formally recognized by the government of Mexico and the State of Yucatán as an administrative entity with certain rights and responsibilities. This meant relations with the outside: a school, taxes, voting, and local connections to national political parties. Chan Kom became, then, similar to many villages in much of the modern world. The people lived a life ancient in many respects, corresponding to a long-established unwritten tradition, yet beginning a partial dependence upon money and markets and outside authority.

Life in Chan Kom in 1930–1931, when Redfield first studied it, was quite isolated, so far as modern avenues of communication were concerned. The village was a day's walk from the railroad connection with Mérida. People frequently visited other villages and towns, but all transportation was on foot or by horse or mule. People from the outside occasionally passed through Chan Kom, most of them traveling merchants and peddlers. Now and then a schoolteacher or governmental official arrived, or a North American visitor to the nearby Mayan ruins of Chichen Itza. But except for the schoolteacher, no outsiders lived in Chan Kom. The *Comisario,* the representative of the government, was elected from among the villagers.

There had been a school in Chan Kom since 1910, but much of the instruction was in Mayan. About one of five men and one of twelve women could speak Spanish, the national language. About five people in the whole population could read a Spanish-language newspaper with comprehension. Nobody in the village had ever been outside Yucatán, but most of the men had traveled to Mérida at one time or another. A few of them had seen a movie.

All men were agriculturalists. Those few people who had some specialized occupation—a carpenter, a barber, a baker, a mason, two storekeepers—all subordinated these tasks to their main concern with farming. This was also true of the more important religious and curing specialists, such as the shamans, the midwife, the bone-setter, and the marriage negotiator. The crops were grown always by independent farmers, by their own hands, for their own benefit; there were no plantations or full-time hired hands. The amount of wealth which a man acquired was largely proportionate to his own efforts.

Maize was the true wealth, for on it everything else depended. Usually a man planted about twice what his family would consume in order to convert the surplus into cloth, salt, sugar, lard, and other necessities which he could not manufacture himself. A few pigs and some poultry, and sometimes cattle, were raised for profit. These surplus items, along with the staple maize, were sold to traveling buyers, or carried to a larger town's market. Other crops, such as chili, beans, fruit, a little tobacco, and sugar, were normally consumed locally.

After the early period of haphazard settlement around the cenote, the village steadily altered its physical outlines toward the typical Spanish-American town plan. The center of everything was the plaza, a square of about 100 yards on a side. The cenote was there, as was the rude church which housed the image of the village saint, the municipal building, the store, the school, and a few masonry houses. The other houses, of rude thatch and mud, were built outside the plaza. All of these buildings, despite the differences in outside appearance, had much the same simple furnishings. The people slept in hammocks, and used little wooden benches to sit on. Cooking fires were built directly on the floor, and the cooking was done either by boiling the food in a clay pot or by baking it on a clay griddle supported over the fire by three stones.

Typical foods eaten by all the families nearly every day were flat, unleavened, baked cakes of ground maize and a sort of gruel or mush, also of maize. Both of these dishes, called respectively *tortillas* and *atole,* are very common in the rest of Mexico. Boiled beans were the next most frequent dish. Chili peppers were eaten at every meal; other garden products, such as tomatoes, cabbages, onions, were used frequently but in small quantities. Meat was esteemed but eaten only about once a week, and was usually game. Domestic fowl and beef were used primarily for fiesta dinners. Chocolate was the common drink, but a few people were beginning to use coffee. These foods were prepared in ways which are typical of most of rural Mexico.

The usual everyday dress was of factory-made cotton fabrics, nearly always home sewn, though a few articles were bought ready-

A MODERN MAYAN HOUSE NEAR CHICHEN ITZA, YUCATÁN. *Courtesy, Museum of Anthropology, University of Michigan*

made. The men wore short white trousers, sandals, blouse, and straw hat; a rectangle of cotton cloth was tucked in the waist of the trousers and hung loose to the knees in front like an apron. Women wore skirts and a long, loose, sleeveless blouse (*huipil*); the common Latin-American *rebozo* (large scarf) was worn to cover the head and shoulders; no sandals or shoes were worn ordinarily. On fiesta days women wore gayer colors, earrings, rings, and necklaces, while the men usually dressed up in the well-known South Mexican *guayabera* (a loose blouse), a red silk neckerchief, and long white trousers (*calzones*).

This is the folk costume of the peasantry and, as in many parts of Mexico, it is clearly distinguished from the modern city style of dress (*catrín*) as symbolic of peasant, or lower-class, status. To dress in modern style would be to put on airs in the local community. Redfield reports that in 1948, however, many younger people had begun to abandon the folk costume, at least on some occasions. This apparently simple change was symptomatic of a new perspective on the part of the people; in effect it amounted to a turning away from the traditional folk culture in general.

Chan Kom was not a town divided into classes of agriculturalists and businessmen, poor and rich, illiterate and educated, although there were minor individual differences in all these matters. In this regard, too, the folk of Chan Kom were reminiscent of a primitive community. Except for the few subsidiary specialties, all the families participated in the same economy, and in the whole culture. All of the individuals did not, however, for as in all societies, primitive or not, major subcultural differences obtained between the sexes and between different age groups.

A woman's world was the home, and her activities were typically individual rather than cooperative, except at fiesta time. Kitchen gardens were cared for by women, though sometimes planted by men. Midwives were about the only women who had a specialty which took them out of their own domestic routines. Drawing water at the public cenote was one of the few opportunities for an ordinary girl or woman to get out of the house and converse with other people. Everything that is public, as opposed to domestic, was the province of the men. This rule applied to officeholding, political meetings, and even entertainment. Age divisions of the population were not so clearly defined. The most specialized activities, especially those involving esoteric knowledge, such as shamanism, midwifery, and marriage negotiation, were the province of the older people. Children very gradually began to assume adult tasks, and, by the time of puberty, most of them were working quite responsibly.

The major activity of all men was concerned with the *milpa* (a maize field). There was almost no part of the year when some kind of milpa work was not being done: clearing brush and burning over a new plot, planting, weeding, or harvesting. Much of the land produced two harvests a year for about two successive years, after which its productivity fell off rapidly. After about seven to ten years of fallowing, it could be cleared and planted again. Men tried to keep at least two milpas going at the same time, one old one and one new one.

A new milpa was cleared with a small steel ax, leaving a few of the largest trees for shade. This clearing process took place in autumn or early winter so that there would be a dry period of at least three months before the field was burned over. After the burning, in the latter part of May or early June, just before the rainy season, the maize was planted together with beans and squash in a row of small holes made by a digging stick. No care was taken thereafter until harvest time, except that the new wild growth, which comes up before the crop has gotten a good start, was cut over once. The harvest began in late fall, but was not completed all at once. The farmer brought a load home as convenience dictated. When only stalks were left, the brush fences were let down so that cattle could get in to feed.

Everyone grew maize, beans, and squash, the classic horticultural trinity of aboriginal America. Root crops, such as yams and sweet potatoes, were planted separately. Many people also raised fruit trees, most commonly papaya, orange, lime, and grapefruit. The kitchen gardens were planted to onions, coriander, cabbages, *Chenopodium,* tomatoes, and mint. Hogs and cattle were grown almost entirely for sale. The people did not like pork, and cattle were rarely butchered and almost never milked. These animals were allowed to roam at will; as in the rest of rural Latin America, people fenced their fields rather than confine the hogs, cattle, horses, or burros. Most of the men of the village kept bees. Honey was primarily used as a sweetener, but, as in Latin belief elsewhere, it also was believed to have medicinal qualities, especially as a strengthening agent.

Concepts of land rights in Chan Kom held a kind of middle ground between individual and communal ownership. The *ejidos* were communal lands granted to villages by the Mexican government, but they were neither fertile nor extensive. The other land plots, though cultivated by individuals, were not felt to be individual property. They were, in fact, owned by the government, as is all land not in title to individuals or communities. Though one could purchase a plot, the necessity of abandoning a plot to fallow it led the *milpero* ordinarily to relinquish his interest in it. The work a man had expended on a milpa in clearing, burning, and sowing it was what was valuable; if he were to sell the land he had occupied, this labor would have been what he was really selling. Villages as a whole had a tendency to regard the land within their orbit as theirs, in a sense, for they resisted the encroachment of any milpero from another village.

Labor was often pooled in various ways. One form of communal labor was compulsory, as a form of taxation. All men between youth and about 45 years of age had to take their turn at being one of the four members of the *guardia,* a sort of police squad. Sometimes a special communal work drive was held to make a street or to clean the town. All males served this duty whenever the village decided upon it. Men also cooperated with friends or relatives in building a private house, or in lime burning, and received an equivalent amount of work from the recipient of the favor at another time.

Social organization in the village began with the family system. The small monogamous nuclear family comprised both the individual household and the basic economic producing and consuming unit. Polygyny was rare and disapproved, and there were only a few cases of two or more closely related married couples living under the same roof. Family ties among several households were frequently very important, however. Two of the family lineages in the village were very large and the households of each tended to stand together on many issues, often opposing the other lineage. But some married couples had no close relatives in the village, and a few others paid no great attention to the families related to them.

Family lines were essentially bilateral; that is, a person frequently had as much concern for his mother's relatives as for his father's, although, much as in North America, there was a tendency for paternal relationship ties to dominate. The fact that the surname was passed on by the father created some emphasis toward his line. Men were the heads of families, and so there was also a likelihood that family bonds between males would dominate those between females. This was manifested in a bias toward patrilocality; many newly married couples set up a household independently of their parents; but if they first had to live with someone until they could take care of themselves, they went to live with the boy's parents. The equating of the maternal and paternal lines was again evident, however, in the rule which prohibited marriage with any first cousin, whether it be from the father's or the mother's line of relatives.

The pattern of kinship nomenclature was no longer of the aboriginal Mayan sort, but essentially old Spanish, although many of the kinship terms were in the Mayan language. In two instances, departures were made from modern European and North American forms: older siblings were called by a different term from younger siblings, and these same terms were extended to first cousins and sometimes to brothers- and sisters-in-law.

The people of Chan Kom supplemented the social ties of descent and marriage with an important institution of fictional relationship, godparenthood (*padrinazgo*). This form of relationship, once found all over Europe, was brought to the Indians by the Spaniards, and today in nearly all of rural Latin America in flourishes more hardily than in the Iberian Peninsula itself. The tie was formed when a family selected a godfather (*padrino*) and a godmother (*madrina*) for a child's ritual ceremony, such as baptism. Thereafter, these godparents were to be prepared to aid the child and even to act as substitute parents in any emergency. The child's parents also entered into a close, but highly formalized, relationship with the godparents. This was called *compadradazgo*, coparenthood. These adults addressed one another as *compadre* (*comadre* if a woman was addressed), unless their relationship had been previously so intimate and constant that these terms of address seemed too formal.

It would appear that the coparent relationship was of more consequence than the godparent tie of adults to a child, for the godparents were chosen chiefly to insure the formalization of regard and intimacy between the coparents. The responsibilities and the degree of respect were not symmetrical, however. The godparents had the most responsibility, for they were the ones who had promised to undertake obligations, while the actual father and mother of the child owed gratitude and great respect to the godparents. The creation of ritual kinship of this kind had the function of extending kinship ties to individuals who were not kin. Coparenthood also could be created between kinsmen, thus further intensifying the ties which already existed.

The most important ritual occasion which created godparenthood in Chan Kom was baptism. The godparent of baptism was the one who became a substitute parent in time of need and the one to whom the child showed the greatest respect and obedience. A married couple was often selected, but on occasion only one god-parent was chosen, a man if the child was male, a woman if the child was female. Godparents were also selected for a wedding ceremony, but their responsibilities were not great. The godfather of the wedding instructed the groom in the ritual of the ceremony and was supposed to counsel him then, as well as thereafter, in his responsibilities as a husband. A godmother acted as a similar sponsor for the bride.

There was one other important ritual involving the acquisition of godparents. A pagan and domestic custom rather than an official Catholic one, this ritual occurred when a child was three months old if a girl, four months if a boy, and marked the transition from the carrying of the infant in the mother's arms to the position astride her hip. When the baby was judged old enough to assume this latter position, an intimate family ceremony was held with the parents and godparents of the *hetzmek,* as this manner of carrying the child was called. Just as for baptism, a couple, or a single person of the same sex as the child, were chosen as godparents. Families tried to choose godparents for their children from among the most honest, hard-working, respected villagers.

There were no economic classes in Chan Kom. All the people had the same basic occupation—farming—and nearly equal opportunities to acquire wealth. All status and prestige were relative, from individual to individual, and were acquired by behaving intelligently and circumspectly and by working hard.

The position of the people of Chan Kom with respect to Yucatecan society at large, however, was fixed and inherited. Yucatán as a whole had classes of people which reflected racial, economic, social, and educational differences, all of which largely coincided. Essentially there were two classes, Indians (*mazehualob*) and whites (*dzulob*), with the latter somewhat subdivided, from their own perspective, especially in the city, where there were considerable differences in wealth, occupation, and social status. Indians, such as the people of Chan Kom, were poor peasants; they looked like Indians, they wore a folk costume, spoke Mayan and were illiterate. In some of the larger towns there were *mestizos*, half-Indians, who had a higher social status. A true *dzul* had a much lighter skin and was assumed to have greater intellectual powers than an Indian, and he was urbanized in the sense that he was literate, wore city clothes, and spoke Spanish. Actual skin color and racial physiognomy, however, were less important criteria of status as a dzul than were the cultural attributes of literacy, education, and kind of profession.

Government in Yucatán as a state was solely in the hands of the upper class. The local government of Chan Kom, however, while it conformed to the governmental statutes of Mexico and of the state, was entirely in the hands of the local population. Before the Mexican Revolution (1910–1921), Indian villages had their own officers exercising traditional authority. One local chief was the village leader, a respected man who served for life. All village disputes were brought to him, and he settled them with the advice of older men. From 1925 on, the leader was the Comisario, who was elected for one year only. The election was informal; all adult males participated, but it was always understood beforehand who should take the office, and so no actual ballot was taken.

The Comisario served a village which was well united and homogeneous; therefore his judgments tended to reflect public opinion. He was not the ultimate repository of power, for everyone understood that there was an outside government which could take certain kinds of action. A person who had been judged in Chan Kom in a way which he felt was unfair could appeal his case to the authorities in the town which were the seats of the larger administrative units of the state, the *municipio* and the *partido*.

Political ties with the state and nation also were maintained by two organizations, the Local Agrarian Committee and the *Liga Local*. Both institutions were created by the Mexican Revolution and therefore were quite new to the village. The Agrarian Committee collected taxes for public improvements, and it was the body which received petitions from villages for allocations of ejidos. The Liga Local was a political organization affiliated to the Socialist Party, which governed Yucatán. All adult males were supposed to belong to it and provide the local support for the state government. There were no other political parties in these rural areas; democracy was not seen as a two- or multi-party system, but rather as full participation by all males in the functioning of *the* party. Therefore, the final voting in the election of deputies did not excite the people of Chan Kom. There was only one candidate, that of the government party, and he was usually a person unknown to them.

Although Chan Kom was not a primitive village existing in isolation, there were, nevertheless, a great many aspects of its day-to-day culture which resembled those of preliterate tribes. Especially notable was the pervasiveness of supernaturalism, the ceremonies and rituals associated with it, and the great assortment of traditional folk beliefs. The major aspects of religion were codified in ritual. Some of these pertained to the collectivity—public festivals which promoted social cohesion. A great many, on the other hand, were concerned with the individual's relation to nature and the cosmos. These individual rites took their most notable and most public form at the life crises: birth, baptism, hetzmek, marriage, illness, and death.

Pregnancy and birth were phenomena surrounded by a good many superstitions and rituals. At the time of delivery a mother was secluded from everyone except the midwife and her husband. It was believed that cold was very dangerous at this time, as during pregnancy. The mother was warmed by a fire and was given drinks which were considered hot or warming. Delivery was made with the mother either kneeling or standing, supported by a rope under her armpits, or by her husband. The new baby was washed in warm water, bundled in warm cloths, and given directly to the mother's breast. The afterbirth was either burned or buried under a hearth; in both cases its warmth was assured so that the mother would not get cold.

Both mother and child were protected carefully during the first week against "winds" which might bear sickness, and from strangers who might have the evil eye. The first seven days, called the *Seven Sacraments,* were considered the most dangerous period of the child's life.

Children were nursed for about two years or longer, and often children were not weaned until lactation was terminated by another pregnancy. Babies were not raised by any schedule, but were fed whenever they seemed hungry and put to bed when they were sleepy.

A baby was named for one of the saints associated with the day of its birth. If the child was born after noontime, it was given the name of a saint associated with the following day. This was done because a calendrical day was thought to go from noon to noon, rather than from midnight to midnight. These given names, being taken from the church calendar, were all Spanish. Nicknames and abbreviations were in such common use, however, that most people forgot the full baptismal names of their fellow villagers.

Surnames, however, were all in the Mayan, rather than the Spanish, language. There was often some confusion about surnames, because a great many couples were not officially married. The children were illegitimate from a legal point of view, and they sometimes were called by the mother's surname, sometimes by the father's. As in most of the rural and primitive world, with its daily face-to-face association among members of the community, formal, legal names were really unnecessary. Nicknames and kinship terms were adequate.

A child was baptized as soon as possible, for it was a great calamity if a child died before this ritual had taken place. A very important part of the baptism was the prior selection of godparents, which was done with a good deal of ceremony and prayer. The godparents then prepared the baby for the anointing, having bought for it the proper clothing, arranged the occasion with a priest, and paid the fee. The parents held a ceremony called the *handwashing* about a year after the birth of the child in order to show gratitude to their compadres, the child's godparents. The native pagan ceremony, the hetzmek, was like baptism in that it ritually marked a change in the child's relations to society and involved the aquisition of new godparents.

The rearing of children was marked by patience and tolerance, although children were given small responsibilities at an early age and obedience to orders was expected. Older children, especially girls, were given considerable custody over their younger siblings. Respect for parents and all people of older generations was inculcated at an early age, so that, despite a seeming lack of rigor in the disciplining of children, deference was a noteworthy aspect of children's behavior, at least from the point of view of a North American.

Education in sex and the facts of procreation was not given to youngsters. It was felt to be improper to impart such knowledge until some measure of maturity was reached. As has been noted in other rural areas in Latin America, children were often wise about certain aspects of sex, for they had discovered elders in the sexual act and, of course, had watched farm animals with interest.

Other events, such as menstruation and childbirth, were not observed, however, and often a girl's first menses came as a complete and shocking surprise to her. And sometimes a newly married couple were unaware of the first stages of pregnancy at a time when older relatives had already made arrangements for the birth.

Marriage, as in primitive society, was essentially a contract between two families. Both boys and girls married soon after puberty. By the time a boy had achieved this physiological change, his parents had begun to consider the families of various eligible girls. The wishes of the boy or girl were not considered in this matter; they did not fall in love and plan a marriage themselves. There were no conventional patterns of courtship, such as serenades or clandestine meetings. Even romantic love stories were not known. The boy's parents, who were the initiators, tried to make a good marriage for him by selecting a girl who was healthy and hardworking and whose family would make a welcome set of in-laws. They were restricted somewhat in their choice by the fact that relatives as close as first cousins should not marry, and also by the necessity of selecting a family which would be likely to accept the proposal.

A boy's parents, usually accompanied by his godfather, visited the girl's parents with gifts of rum, cigarettes, bread, and chocolate as a way of initiating the marriage proposal. This visit always took place late at night to keep it secret from the boy and the girl. If the visit went well, the food was served, and the callers were asked to come again. Three such visits were made before the marriage offer was finally accepted. A professional marriage-arranger usually acted as intermediary in arranging the details of the marriage gift from the boy's family. This consisted, in varying amounts and quality, of the girl's wedding outfit of clothing, rings, and a gold chain, and of food for the fiesta. The actual act of betrothal was signified by the delivery of the gifts. The two families presided but, significantly, the bride- and groom-to-be did not meet on this occasion; the contract was between the families.

The wedding itself occurred after the civil ceremony which was required by law. Sometimes a family might further solemnize the union with a church ceremony, but this was expensive as they had to go to a larger town where there was a priest. More often a traditional ceremony was held at the home of the groom's parents.

The central ritual consisted of the usual offerings of rum and cigarettes, and a dinner. Two turkeys were given by the boy's father, one to the bride's father and one to the padrino of the marriage. Finally, the padrino explained the duties of a husband and wife.

As people grew older, the most recurrent crises were those of sickness. The concepts of sickness in Chan Kom, and even many of the cures, were those of primitive cultures. Evil supernaturalistic forces were always at work, sometimes wholly impersonally, but sometimes at the desire of a human malefactor. The most prominent concepts were those of the sickening winds, the evil eye, witchcraft, spirits, and disease-bearing birds.

One very prominent concept of disease and treatment was not exactly supernaturalistic, however. This was the idea of a kind of physical and physiological principle, common in much of rural Latin America, that things and people were dichotomized into hot and cold types. People varied temporarily between hot and cold states; a feverish person was hot and a chilled person was cold, obviously. But some people were permanently different from others in these regards, and many times the physiological state of affairs could not be discerned by mere temperature.

Foods and drinks were also classed as hot or cold. Exceptionally hot foods were, for example, honey, beef, coffee, and *pinole* (a beverage made of seasoned ground maize and water). Some exceptionally cold foods were peccary, turkey, pork, rice, limes, squash, lard, and all foods baked in an earth oven. Other foods were intermediate. It is apparent that these foods were not hot or cold of themselves—temperature was not the criterion. They were classified, rather, in terms of their presumed effect on the human body. A normal person would want to keep to a diet fairly well balanced between the two kinds of foods. Too much hot food would cause a fever; too much cold food would lead to general debility. A sick person either has, or is verging toward, a fever or a chill. Medicines and diet were prescribed to bring back a balance, a hot infusion for a cold illness, and vice versa. If a person was actually *hot*, however, as from hard exercise, it would be very dangerous to take something cold. This was the most common concept of illness, and an imbalance was believed to be the cause of such things as weakness, anemia, loss of appetite, and sterility.

Evil winds were another common cause of illness. Winds were distinguished from one another partly by their source—winds from the water were very dangerous—and partly in terms of the illnesses they were supposed to cause. The various contagious diseases were products of the evil winds, but so were rheumatism, asthma, and even headache. Somehow the winds were personified, for they were viewed as having taken possession of the sufferer. The medicine man cured the illness by identifying the wind which caused it, and then by magical means getting it to leave the patient's body.

The evil eye was something like the winds in that it seemed to be an emanation and a form of contagious illness-producing evil. Persons born on Tuesday or Friday were likely to have this evil power, as were people who were drunk or crazy. Some people who had this evil eye were not aware of it, or might have it only intermittently. Usually, too, they were not thought to be guilty of wishing to do harm. The cure of sickness caused in this way was by means of counterinoculation. There were many different private remedies, but they all typically attempted to counterbalance the evil influence, and some even involved the cooperation of the evil-eyed person himself.

Witchcraft and black magic were believed to be causes of death, but not common ones. Failure to take proper precautions against wind, cold, and evil eye was more usually blamed. To some extent a lapse from piety and ritual, or a failure to observe right conduct, also contributed to illness. A prolonged debility which could not be accounted for otherwise might finally suggest to the sick man that he was being bewitched, however, especially if he was already suspicious that he had malicious enemies. Witches, in Chan Kom as elsewhere, caused the illness by magically introducing foreign objects, such as certain insects or winds, into the person, or they made a small wax image of the victim and buried it or wounded it. Witches could transform themselves into animals and steal valuables, or commit sexual acts on sleeping persons. The concept of how a person could become a witch was typically European; the witch acquired supernatural power by making a pact with the devil.

Beliefs and practices that attended the dying were also strongly influenced by old Catholic-European concepts. Prayers were said over the dying person in order to secure the release of the soul from the body and to prevent demons from the underworld from getting control of it. Small children and people who had lived a good life would go to the heavens beyond the clouds, *Gloria,* but the souls of less upright people passed a time in purgatory, where they were burned white before passing to Gloria. Souls of very bad people went directly to *Metnal,* beneath the earth, as did all witches and suicides. After long periods the souls of the good dead were reincarnated in newborn infants, because "God has not enough souls to keep forever repopulating the earth." If a baby showed signs of being precocious it was said that its soul had been on earth before.

It was felt desirable that the soul of a dead man be speeded on its way. The members of the family could not weep, because the soul might be constrained to stay near them. A small round hole in the roof was made above the hammock of a dying person so that his soul could fly up unimpeded. Sometimes, if it was felt that the soul was having difficulty getting free of the body, the slowly dying person might be whipped with a rope. Interment took place 24 hours after death. During the night the friends and relatives kept a vigil, or wake, in the room where the corpse reposed on a table. Thereafter, prayers were recited at the home of the deceased for nine evenings and on All Souls' Day each year.

Despite the striking presence of so many elements of Christian ritual and belief in the life-crisis activities, the people of Chan Kom were not monotheistic; rather, they had an astonishing multitude of gods and spirits in their cosmology. The bush was full of supernatural beings. All aspects of nature had spirits which must be placated, cajoled, and rewarded by offerings if one was to make use of them. The most important natural feature was the cenote, the source of all water. When the shaman-priest made his prayers in the agricultural ceremonies, he cited the spirits of all the cenotes in the region, for they could withhold rain from the maize on which human life depends. Cenotes were also the sources of the winds, both evil and beneficent, and were openings to the underworld. A suicide, the most sinful of all people, would drown himself by diving into the cenote to pass to Metnal. Four rain gods occupied the cardinal directions of the universe, and a fifth, the most powerful, occupied the central position, just as the cenote held the central position in a village, with the four entrances to the village leading to it.

All of the gods and spirits were not equal to one another. The greatest was *Hahal Dios* (Great God), who sat in Gloria. Saints were arranged below him in order of their importance, and finally the souls of virtuous, baptized dead completed the hierarchy. Many of the saints were of the usual Roman Catholic sort, patrons of various places, professions, and arts. Each family had a patron saint, as did the village as a whole, to serve as intermediaries to the Great God. The other god-spirits, which were patrons, in a sense, of the various aspects of nature, were not in the sky but all around, mostly residing in their appropriate cenote, tree, animal, or stone, but also sometimes moving around and ever watchful. More time in ritual on the part of individuals actually seems to have been given over to these beings than to the sky gods. The most important ritual involving the whole community, however, was the village fiesta held on the name day of the patron saint. This was much like village fiestas in all of Latin America.

The ceremonial core of the fiesta was a *novenario,* a sequence of nine prayers, given to honor the saint, who was represented by an image. This was serious worship, but it was merely the occasion for the fiesta, not the fiesta itself. A true fiesta was made by its secular aspects, the dances, fireworks, bullbaiting, feasts, drinking, gambling, music, and noise and excitement. For southern Mexico and Yucatán one of the most typical and perhaps the most important of the secular activities was the dance. The music was of a particular style, called the *jarana.* The dance, also called jarana, had to take place where the *santo* could see it, for it was an offering to the saint. The jarana was a social dance, exceedingly rhythmic, though danced in a rigidly stylized way. It was very popular with the young people, and they often danced until dawn, for it was one of the few public occasions when the two sexes ever mingled in play. No fiesta, or any other kind of celebration, was complete without a jarana.

A fiesta cost a good deal of community labor, money, and planning. It was regarded as an obligation of the community as a whole to renew each year its offering to the name saint, and also to act as hosts to the many visitors from neighboring communities who came to partake of the hospitality. These expensive communal functions were traditional in Yucatán, but they seem to be incompatible with modern life and individualistic aspirations. They survive today in full form only in the most backward parts of the country, most notably in the Indian communities of Quintana Roo. Chan Kom, a forward-looking, progressive village, has lately turned its collective energies toward building roads and public schools, practical secular moves toward participation in the modern world. The truly religious aspects of all its public festivals and private or domestic supernatural observances are being displaced by secular, utilitarian interests.

The rapid series of changes in Chan Kom, both in practice and in ideology, since 1930–1931 (the perspective from which this account was written) have probably been nearly duplicated in thousands of folk villages over the world during the past 20 or 30 years, for the influences of urban-industrial civilization have become increasingly pervasive and have accelerated in tempo during that time. The history of Chan Kom is unique, however, because Redfield, a fine ethnographer, has recorded the details of these changes. He has described them not only in terms of the economic and technological basis of change with which most readers are now quite familiar, but he also has analyzed the alterations in cosmology, ritual, attitude, emotion, and sentiment which accompany these changes.[2]

The natives of Chan Kom were largely illiterate in 1930, and their world view was restricted by the temporal limits of their experience. Because they were illiterate, their history was merely an oral tradition, and increasingly mythlike as it extended further and further back from the memories of living men. The relics of the past which surrounded them, especially the great Mayan archaeological ruins at Chichen Itza, were attributed to the age of a mysterious race of men, the *Itza,* and not to their own actual history. This mythical past was considered the *Good Times,* when there were no evil or stupid men and nature was cooperative. But the Itza were finally banished for an impiety, and this Eden came to an end. The source of secret wisdom was lost. Present-day man lived in *Bad Times.*

So far, these traditions appear to be typically primitive. But what of the future? Will the millennium be a return to the ancient Good Times? The answer to this is interesting, for it shows how these

[2] Especially in *A Village That Chose Progress: Chan Kom Revisited,* Chicago, 1950; but see also the interesting chapter V, "'Man Makes Himself,'" in *The Primitive World and Its Transformations,* Ithaca, 1953.

Maya now have a link to modern civilization which is not only economic and political but ideological. There is a Good Times already in existence, and they have seen it; what remains is to acquire it. This contemporaneous Eden is seen as a community of masonry houses, whose inhabitants own cattle and phonographs, and are prosperous because of good roads and better marketing conditions. Here is one of the striking differences between many peasant villages which are linked to the modern world and most truly primitive tribes; the changing peasantry are inclined to be *prospective,* the primitives *retrospective.*

In a primitive culture the people do not conceive of seeking their own salvation. People are a part of nature; they are *in* nature as individuals and so is their society. The idea of making over society or even their own selves by practical measures seems to be a concept peculiar to modern civilized men. Perhaps the most striking aspect of modern influence on a folk community occurs when slow, crescive changes are finally felt, and the people, now looking ahead rather than back, acquire the idea of reform—change by intention and design. The consequences are sometimes explosive, as witness the cases of peasant villagers that broke out of the crust of their traditions with their discovery, and with an astonishing wholeheartedness and determination formed the core of the Red armies of Trotsky and Mao Tse-tung, and the guerrilla bands of Zapata.

The change from an orientation toward tradition to one of conscious progress needs proper conditions. Some people are carried forward willy-nilly under new forces before it occurs to others to accept change and perhaps to push it. But then the attitude can become contagious. The great wave-force of the Mexican Revolution which began in 1910 has not yet spent itself, and the social and economic concomitants of it are just beginning to reach such backwaters as central Yucatán. The *idea* of progress, however, apparently got there much earlier.

As early as 1917 the people of Chan Kom were faced with a decision which they resolved in favor of progress. The settlement could have remained isolated and unrecognized politically, but it was decided to accept the offer of the Mexican government to become a pueblo, which meant the beginnings of political dependence, the payment of taxes, and, importantly, the development of public schooling. In 1925 the government got around to surveying the lands and conferring title to the ejidos, and the formal ceremony of Chan Kom's new status was held. National and state political figures attended, and there was a great fiesta with flags, music, dancing, and speeches. From that time, the orientation toward the city and modernism in general has accelerated.

In certain striking ways the transformation of the village was a tiny-scaled reproduction of the transformation of northern Europe from medievalism to the commercial-industrial society. For example, in the early 1930s first one family and then others turned from the tradition-oriented, highly ritualized folk-Catholicism to Protestant-ism. As in Europe, the new allegiance signalized a clean break with the past. The virtues taught by the Protestant missionaries—sobriety, industry, austerity, individual self-help—seemed to fit the notion of progress and the new cult gained ground. Finally, the village was split, as France and Germany were split, into two religious camps. At first the dissension was marked by considerable bitterness and occasional violence, but gradually the fundamental alikeness of the members of the two groups and sheer passage of time tended to modify the hostility and suspicion. Actually the partisans were neither sophisticated Protestants nor proper Catholics; much of the religious ceremony and ritual practiced by the community remains folklike and essentially pagan. The partial adoption of Protestantism coincided with the period of greatest enthusiasm for change. It took the form essentially of an emotional embrace by the most radical part of the population and was dis-proportionate to the actual rate of change.

The struggle between science and supernaturalism which occurred in Europe was also repeated in Chan Kom, but, unlike the Protestant Revolution, it did not finally result in open conflict between two groups. The younger people doubt the efficacy of magical cures more than oldsters, and modern scientific techniques are often used in illness, but they have not displaced the old folk remedies com-pletely. They are only added to them. Perhaps if a fuller division of labor and a social class system had developed, there might have been a true schism.

In certain of their attitudes and perspectives, the people of Chan Kom seem to be changing more toward an Anglo-American than a Latin ideal. There is a tendency toward less formality, so far mani-fested largely by the younger people. There is increasingly a greater familiarity between the sexes and an added ease of manner. Practicality, prudence, acquisitiveness, and respect for private property are cultivated ideals. Even baseball, the North American national game, is becoming popular.

The younger generation which will soon rule the village has little interest in the older traditional standards of life. Its orientation is toward the city, and it likes the *things* of the city as well as its values and pleasures.

The people of Chan Kom are, then, a people who have no choice but to go forward with technology, with a declining religious faith and moral conviction, into a dangerous world. They are a people who must and will come to identify their interests with those of people far away, outside the traditional circle of their loyalties and political responsibilities.[3]

FURTHER READINGS

Chamberlain, R. S., *The Conquest and Colonization of Yucatan:1517–1550,* Carnegie Institution of Washington, Pub. 582, Washington, 1948.

Hay, C. L., *et al. The Maya and Their Neighbors,* New York, 1940.

Redfield, R., *The Folk Culture of Yucatan,* Chicago, 1941.

Redfield, R., *A Village That Chose Progress: Chan Kom Revisited,* Chicago, 1950.

Redfield, R., *The Primitive World and Its Transformations,* Ithaca, 1953.

Redfield, R., *The Little Community,* Chicago, 1955.

Redfield, R., *Peasant Society and Culture,* Chicago, 1956.

Redfield, R., and Villa Rojas, A., *Chan Kom, A Maya Village,* Carnegie Institution of Washington, Pub. 448, Washington, 1934.

[3] Redfield, *A Village That Chose Progress,* p. 178.

A Moroccan Village

The part of the Arab World distinguished geographically as North Africa stretches along the southern border of the Mediterranean Sea from the Atlantic Ocean on the west to the Egyptian frontier on the east. It is essentially a fertile strip which separates the great Sahara Desert from the sea, and includes Morocco, Tunisia, Algeria, and Tripoli. In general, it is a land of Mediterranean climate, divided into two distinct seasons: from October through March is winter, cool and rainy; and summer, the rest of the year, is hot and dry. The inhabitants are more or less typical Moslems, but in North Africa and the Middle East there has been a long history of conquests, an ebb and flow of migrations, and a blending of previously distinct populations. The apparently homogeneous Arab World has been created out of a truly complicated ethnic and cultural past.

Morocco, the westernmost area of North Africa, has been, until its recent liberation, nominally under the rule of a sultan, but he functioned largely as the religious leader of the Moslem population. In administration, the sultanate was divided into three territories: French Morocco was a state of the French Union, and the largest of the three; Spanish Morocco was a protectorate of Spain; the third division was the smaller International Zone of Tangier. The recent European rulers were merely the latest of many, however.

Even in Pleistocene times, North Africa was apparently marginal to higher cultures which were developing elsewhere. The first civilizing influence was of agriculturalists of Mediterranean physical type who entered from the direction of the Fertile Crescent about 3000 B.C., bringing wheat, barley, and legumes and pigs, sheep, goats, and cattle. It has been presumed that these invaders were the ancestors of the modern Berber population.

By about 850 B.C., the Phoenicians established their colony of Carthage in present-day Tunisia. They probably had trade relations with the local populations, but established no permanent colonies there. Roman expansion finally destroyed the power of Carthage in the Punic Wars, and after 146 B.C. Rome became the master of North Africa. In A.D. 42, Mauretania (Morocco) was established as a province, colonies were formed, and many new culture traits were introduced. Probably, because of the great stimulus to commerce that the Mediterranean-wide control of Rome provided, the number of cities was greatly increased. During the fourth century A.D., however, the Empire had run its course, and North Africa lapsed into relative anarchy.

The political and commercial vacuum was suddenly filled in the latter part of the seventh century with the first great expansion of Islam. The Moslem Arabs came from the east and quickly invested the cities and commercial centers. The natives of Morocco, even the simple country folk, apparently found the doctrine of Mohammed congenial and made at least a nominal capitulation to it. The second invasion of Arabs, which occurred in the eleventh century, was a greater migration of peoples. Many of them were tribal bedouin from Arabia, and in North Africa they settled in rural areas and mixed to some extent with the native Berbers. Their descendants are the modern Arab population of rural North Africa. Some of the Berbers, however, never accepted the newcomers and retreated to mountainous areas and out-of-the-way upland valleys which they continue to occupy today. Many of them are sedentary, practicing a rather primitive dry farming; others are primarily herdsmen. Their major divisions include the Shawia, Kabyle, Shluh, Riff, and Berber. In the Sahara Desert, the Berbers became the camel-breeding nomads and predators now known as the Tuareg.

The expansion of Islam had reached Spain in A.D. 711, and

during the period until the Christian reconquest of Spain in the fifteenth century, a great civilization, comparable to other centers of the Arab World, came into being. The Arabs in Spain, incidentally, were called *Moros*—from Mauretania in North Africa— hence the English word *Moors* and the name of the modern sultanate, Morocco. Many of the Moors and Jews expelled from Spain after 1492 settled in Morocco, and some of the Spanish Moors now form distinctive colonies there, as do many of the Spanish Jews, who still speak an old-fashioned Andalusian Spanish.

The beginning of modern European control over North Africa was initiated by the French in Algeria in 1830 and continued to Tunisia in 1881. In 1907, the French began to invade Morocco, and simultaneously the Spaniards began to extend their control beyond their several colonial towns. Morocco was thus one of the last of the countries of the world colonized by European powers. The Moroccans fought both Spaniards and French in a series of guerrilla wars under the famous Riff leader, Abd-el Krim, and it was not until the mid-1930s that the whole territory could finally be considered conquered.

After World War II, however, the movement for independence gathered momentum again. In 1956 Morocco attained its freedom, incorporating the former French and Spanish holdings as well as the International Zone of Tangier under the rule of King Muhammad V, formerly the Sultan of Morocco. Despite independence, all Moors are conscious of the recent history of their conquest. Men who fought against the French and Spanish are still living honored lives in communities all across the land. The influences of modern Europe in North Africa are pervasive and varied, and they are not merely political. All of the invaders prior to the recent Europeans were roughly of the same level of technology; the differences lay largely in political, commercial, and military organization. But the latest invaders represented European industrial technology and were therefore capable of introducing materials which can truly revolutionize the conditions of life and engender political movements of a magnitude and fervor which have not been seen before in North Africa.

Mediouna, a village of 315 persons (in 1948) in the former International Zone of Tangier, reflects all of the major cultural consequences of the varied history of Morocco. Berbers and Arabs have mixed there, with Arabic speech and Moslem religion and culture predominating as in many other Moroccan settlements. The physical type more closely resembles the Berber, typified by a short, heavy body structure, square face, and strong musculature. Hair is usually dark brown—lighter among infants—and the beard and mustache are heavy. The skin is brunet-white and sun-tans to a deep brown. The language is Arabic of the western type. None of the Berber dialects is known any longer. Mediouna was studied in 1948–1949 by William D. Schorger, and the following description refers to that period of its history.

Courtesy, United Nations

The village lies about a mile from the Atlantic coast, separated from it by a rolling alluvial plain used for fields and pasture. The general aspect of the terrain is reminiscent of southern California and parts of Spain's Mediterranean coast; it is a warm and rather arid climate, and the flora are thorny drought-resistant plants, including prominently the palmetto and prickly pear, which were brought by Spaniards from the Americas. The important resources are the fertile soil, and, special to the region, a conglomerate rock outcrop from which the villagers manufacture stones for hand grinding mills. This artifact—*quern* in British usage—is sold for sale to the outside market.

One special characteristic of the climate deserves further description—the winds. The direction of the wind is a major concern in Morocco and most of the western Mediterranean region. Westerly winds are typically benign, and are the rain-bearing winds. The east wind, known to Europeans as the *sirocco,* is a menace in the dry season because it has traveled such great distances over parched, hot land that it brings greater heat and drier weather than the normal. The sirocco blows strongly and sometimes for days on end, creating high temperatures, drying up standing water, burning grass

and crops, and, above all, creating great tension and nervous ir-
ritability among the people. The Moors remain indoors and inactive
during such a blow, if they can.

Agriculture and animal husbandry are the major occupations of
the residents of Mediouna. Stonecutting is a subsidiary specialization which provides most of the cash income with which the inhabitants buy necessities from outside the village. The villagers are,
therefore, similar to peasants anywhere, largely self-sufficient, with
only tenuous economic and political ties with the nation-state of
which they are a part. Despite the proximity of the sea, the villagers
have no economic orientation toward it; they own no boats, and
their whole tradition is an inland one.

The political organization of Mediouna is, like the economy,
characterized by considerable local autonomy. Under the district
head, or Sheikh, who is responsible for 11 villages, a *Muqaddem*
serves as village headman. He is traditionally chosen by the village
council made up of the heads of all the households. There is only
one other functionary, the Warden of the Mosque, detailed by the
council to act as caretaker of mosque property. No vote is taken
by the council for any of its decisions; the principle of consensus
rather than majority rule is followed. By law, council meetings are
open to the public and are usually held out-of-doors. Legislation is
very rare; the meetings are usually held to judge cases of theft or
injury at the request of a plaintiff. There is no concept of a crime
against society for which there is no individual plaintiff. If one of
the Islamic injunctions is broken, and there is no plaintiff, it is assumed that God will punish the offender on Judgment Day.

Land ownership is individualized. A considerable proportion of
arable fields are owned by the people who work them. In some cases,
people work another's land on a share-cropping basis, or for a cash
rental. This is as close as good Moslems are allowed to approach
the taking of interest, which is forbidden by the laws of the Koran.
A small amount of land owned by the mosque is worked in this way.
Outsiders from the city own about one-third of the land around
the village. Much of the pasture land is commons, owned by the
village as a whole and free grazing land for anyone. It is marginal
land, not as good as that already under cultivation, but it is capable
of production and can be used for crops by anyone who has no
other land. After 10 years of use, an occupant may assume title to

the plot. There are, therefore, no families denied land in Mediouna. Water resources are also common property. Anyone may use water from any of the village springs, and anyone may use the overflow for garden irrigation.

The major field crops are millet and wheat; lesser crops are chick-peas, barley, beans, and maize. A kind of crop rotation is followed, but no fertilizer is used on the fields. The value of manure is recognized, and it is used on gardens, but apparently it is not plentiful enough for use on the larger fields. The field crops are planted before the winter rains and are harvested in spring; they yield, therefore, but once a year. Garden plots, on the other hand, are irrigated and yield continuously. They are all located in areas where underground seepage or the overflow from springs can be used to irrigate them; consequently they are limited, and all possible sites are occupied. The most common garden products are Irish and sweet potatoes, tomatoes, eggplants, onions, squash, garlic, red peppers, carrots, and watermelon. Figs and prickly pears are the most important of the fruits grown. Apples, plums, and grapes are also known, but none of the fruits are tended with particular care.

The labor of plowing and sowing is considerable; but once the crops are in, little care is needed until harvest time. Reaping the harvest is woman's work. In true Biblical fashion the work parties of women and girls go together cutting the grain with sickles and carrying the sheaves to the communal threshing floors. Here the grain is scattered over the floor in a thick mass, and domestic animals are driven around and around to thresh the seeds from the stalks. After about three hours of this trampling, the men go to work at the arduous winnowing, which is accomplished by tossing the threshed mixture repeatedly into the air with pitchforks. Some of the chaff is blown away in the breeze, but essentially the process consists of allowing the heavier grain kernels to get to the bottom of the pile. The chaff and straw are saved as animal fodder, and the grain is removed to the houses, where it is picked over and cleaned again by the women before it is stored.

The most important domestic animals are cattle. Cows are milked, and oxen are used in plowing the fields. Horses, mules, or burros may be used in threshing, but never in plowing. Sheep, goats, chickens, and dogs are the other animals. Swine, of course, are tabooed throughout the Moslem world. Dogs are considered unclean by Moslems, and they are not treated affectionately or allowed in the house. Goats are milked, and sheep are important for wool; either may be used for meat on important occasions, although sheep are preferred. The ubiquitous burro of the Mediterranean world is of great economic importance, as it is the only form of transportation the majority of the families have. It is cheap to maintain and hardy. A horse, of course, is expensive to buy and to feed, and only a few of the wealthier families own one. It is more of a prestige

MOROCCAN FARMER PREPARES HIS LAND FOR THE FALL SEASON. *Courtesy, United Nations*

item than a practical matter. Mules are much more useful and hardy, but are taken more for granted.

Quern manufacture is the one local specialization of Mediouna, and apparently most of northwestern Morocco is supplied from this single source of stone. The great majority of the population of Morocco still grind their grain in 2000-year-old fitted millstones of this kind. Mediouna has been an important producer of querns at least since Roman times. Nearly all grown males in the village know the techniques of stonecutting and engage in it when they need some cash and are not otherwise occupied. It is, therefore, only a sporadic employment, not fully professionalized.

There is only very limited economic opportunity in Mediouna outside the traditional agriculture and stonecutting. The villagers' economic connections to the outside world are in the market of the nearby city of Tangier. The village itself has no shops or market, or even a coffeehouse. The villagers can produce the bulk of their own subsistence in staple foodstuffs, their own shelter, and the raw wool for clothing. Other cloth, metal tools, kitchen and dining equipment, and such desired food supplements as spices, tea, sugar, fish, and olive oil must all be purchased. Needless to say, no one has many, or as much as he might wish, of the products of the city market and shops.

The costume and ornamentation of the villages are all set by outside—Arabic—standards and are all purchased from the city except for the homemade knitted skullcap and a broad-brimmed palmetto-leaf hat. The male costume consists of loose pantaloons of dark-colored cotton cloth gathered at the knee and with such a baggy seat that the crotch is sometimes nearly as low as the knees. The shirt is cut with full sleeves, a tight Russian collar fastened at the left shoulder, and a long shirttail which is tucked into the pants. A vest of brightly colored cloth, embroidered with numerous buttons down its front, is worn over the shirt. Sometimes another shirt of white cotton is worn over all this. The second shirt has no sleeves or collar, and the head slit is drawn together at the neck by drawstrings. If the homemade skullcap or palm-leaf sun hat is not worn, the head is wrapped in a turban of 18 to 20 feet of cotton cloth. Goathide slippers are the ordinary footgear. Surmounting all this, for outdoor wear, is a voluminous woolen robe with short sleeves and a parkalike hood. This robe, the *jelaba,* is worn all the year; in winter it protects the wearer from rain and cold and in summer from the heat of the sun. The hood serves to protect the wearer and also, when hanging, as a great receptacle which takes the place of pockets and handbags. In some respects this outer garment is like an academic robe in that its color is an indication of status. Manual workers and farmers, for example, wear brown robes which do not show dirt, while schoolboys and elderly men of property wear white. Most men, particularly when traveling, carry a large leather envelope under the robe suspended by a cord from the shoulder for the transportation of valuables, papers, and the inevitable snuffbox or hashish pipe.

Women's costume is, as in other countries, more elaborate and variable than men's, but in Morocco most of the basic elements are similar to men's. The loose pantaloons, blouse, and vest are usual, and a few distinctive feminine items are added. A large square of striped cotton is wrapped around the waist as a skirt, and another is draped over the head like the Spanish *rebozo*. It serves as protection from the elements, and for purposes of modesty, and it can be used as a backsling to carry a baby. Women use cosmetics for special

A MOROCCAN SALESMAN DISPLAYS HIS WARES. *Courtesy, United Nations*

occasions. Henna is used to tint the palms of the hands and soles of the feet a pale orange, and antimony (kohl) is used as an eye-shadow.

Men's hair is worn short, but mustaches are grown at as early an age as possible. A full beard is a sign of adult status. Women's coiffure is of little outward significance, for Islam decrees that once a girl approaches puberty, her head should always be covered. Jewelry is worn by women only. It is of gold, principally heavy, simple bracelets, but sometimes earrings and necklaces. This jewelry is largely the sum of the household's cash assets and serves as an indicator of the wealth of the family. The price of the gold—which is sold by weight, no matter the ornamentation—is fairly constant, and the jewelry is often a rather liquid asset, sold and bought again, depending on the economic vicissitudes of the family.

A family, in Mediouna a husband, wife, offspring, and sometimes aged close relatives, is the basic economic unit. Each household is so self-sufficient that, except for the community government and religious observance, it could subsist independently of the rest of the village. The village itself is merely an irregular collection of

Courtesy, United Nations

family homes, each fenced as a compound which comprises the home, animal barn, cookshed, chicken roost, and outdoor oven. The fence itself is of cane, brush, or hedge, so high that it is difficult to see inside. The impression gained from the appearance of a village composed of such private compounds is that this is not a planned community so much as a mere agglomeration.

The house itself is designed for protection from the weather rather than as a pleasing social environment. It is usually a cavelike rectangular structure with a gabled thatched roof, solid-looking walls, and only two small windows in the front wall. Many of the homes are simply a single room, about 10 by 15 feet in size, made of irregular stone blocks set in a clay mortar. A ceiling of planks creates an attic space. Some houses are of two such rooms, one in front of the other. A few houses, belonging to larger or wealthier families, are of four rooms. Houses of well-to-do families are plastered and whitewashed inside, and outside walls are plastered if they face the prevailing wind.

Moslem custom emphasizes sexual dichotomy in all affairs, and in house arrangements this necessitates separate areas for male gatherings; women must be particularly sequestered when visiting men are present. If the house is of only a single room, there must be another hut in the compound where the women can carry on their work in such an event. If the house is of two or more units, half is reserved for male pursuits and half for women.

Houses are quite permanent, and the population does not fluctuate much; consequently, new houses are built but rarely. When one is constructed, its completion is ritualized rather fully. A sheep is sacrificed, and some of its blood is thrown through the door in order to drive off evil spirits. On moving into a new house, the owner entertains friends and relatives with a dinner which is preceded by a ritual libation of milk and also of a mixture of henna and olive oil, both sprinkled in the corners of the rooms to insure that evil spirits will not disturb the repose of the occupants.

Household furnishings are meager. People sit on the floor on straw-filled cushions or sheepskins, and the floor itself is sometimes covered with a reed mat. Beds are made of straw-filled burlap bags, sometimes elevated from the floor on planks, sometimes not. Much of the rather constricted living space is taken up by storage boxes and chests, tubs of stored grains—or sometimes mere piles of it—hanging garlic ropes and onions, and the few personal possessions. Cooking utensils are stored in the outside cookshack.

A family in Mediouna eats three times a day, lightly at dawn and noon, more heavily after sundown. Breads of various forms made from different mixtures of wheat, barley, and millet are the staple food. Meat is expensive and rarely used, but is highly esteemed. It is usually sautéed in olive oil and served in a stew, as are vegetables. Beverages used ordinarily are water and milk, but none is drunk with a meal, and tea is reserved almost entirely for social ceremonies. No intoxicating beverages are used, of course, for Islam prohibits their use.

A meal always begins with the diners exclaiming, "In the name of God," and ends with, "Thanks be to God." Each course of a meal is served in a single bowl set on the floor in the center of the diners, and the individual dips into the portion of the bowl nearest him with his fingers. It is polite to use only the right hand. If a guest is present, it is customary for the host to select particularly choice bits from the bowl and present them to the guest. Moors always wash the hands carefully before a meal, and consider eating with a European fork especially disgusting because it has been in other people's mouths.

The laws of hospitality, particularly with respect to the sharing of food and water, are perhaps the most important obligations in Arab custom. Most Moslems consider this one of the great contrasts between themselves and nonbelievers. A refusal, or even a stinginess, about sharing food with visitors or with the poor is damned by both men and God. Conversely, a refusal to accept the offer of food is a grave insult. When a guest is present for a meal, the grown males eat by themselves, served by the women. Women and children eat the leftovers later in seclusion.

Social relations of individuals with the village at large are determined primarily by the universal distinctions of age, sex, and kinship. Most of the villagers are related in complicated ways, because the preferred marriages in the Arab World are locally endogamous. Specifically preferred is the paternal parallel cousin—i.e., a boy should marry his father's brother's daughter. Marriages are not so severely restricted in Mediouna, perhaps because of the small size of the community and its proximity to others and to the city; but even so, 79 percent of the existing marriages have been within the village. The postmarital residence custom is neolocal, that is, the new couple set up a separate household wherever it is convenient; thus there is no particular alignment of relatives in adjacent houses or quarters of the village. If a man marries someone from outside the village, marriage is patrilocal; the children grow up in the father's village, but again the village itself is not caused to be more orderly in respect to coresidence of relatives. For this reason, cross cousins are not clearly separated from parallel cousins by residence.

The fact that heritable real property is individualized, and that nuclear families are separated in space as well, fits the pattern of kinship terminology. A person's father is termed separately from father's brother, and mother's brother has still another designation. Similarly, mother, mother's sister, and father's sister are each designated separately. In one's own generation, the children of these separated aunts and uncles each have separate terms. Another way of putting it is to say that one's siblings are distinguished from cousins, cross cousins are distinguished from parallel cousins, and all three are further distinguished according to whether they are on one's father's side of the family or one's mother's. This kind of isolation is continued in the children's generation as well. Only in the grandparents' and grandchildren's generation are the relatives left undiscriminated.

Despite the fact that most of the villagers are related, social behavior and etiquette are not primarily determined by degrees of relationship so much as by age and sex. Among relatives, there is a tendency for a young person to have more of a joking or permissive relationship with his mother's brother than with his paternal uncle, who stands more as a second father; but avoidances or exceptional social distance are not observed between any categories of relatives to any degree comparable to the usual practice among primitive tribes. Between the sexes, particularly when unrelated or distantly related, however, avoidance is more extreme and more regulated than in any other culture in the world. The Arab view seems to be that sexual desires cannot be sublimated; women naturally attract men, and men cannot resist. The only recourse to prevent unrestrained adultery is nearly absolute physical separation. It is a culture dominated by males, however (as are all others in varying degrees); hence it is women who are separated from men, rather than vice versa. The women's area of the house is for them to retire to if a male chances to visit. If a woman has to go into the street, she must cover herself from the eyes of passing men. In Mediouna, the long veil of some Moslem regions is not worn, but the head shawl can be drawn across the face to serve as well.

The life of an individual in Mediouna is demarked by the usual times of ceremonialized crises found in any society—birth, marriage, illness, and death—as well as one other, circumcision, which has its counterpart in some parts of the primitive world. Birth is regarded as the province of females only; men not only never attend, but are quite ignorant of the details of the process. Women are stoical about the possibility of pain and the actual dangers involved in the rather unsanitary methods. Pregnant women remain active at their household tasks until the pains of contraction begin, and when labor is imminent, a woman retires to the female quarter, accompanied by female relatives or friends and the village midwife. Delivery takes place with the woman seated on the edge of a seat or box, while the other women stand at her sides to support her. The midwife receives the baby, cuts the umbilical cord, and swabs the baby, after which it is given to the mother, who has been put to bed. In contrast to many peoples the world over, no special ritual is concerned with the disposal of either the umbilical cord or the afterbirth.

The idea of scheduled feeding seems inhumane to the villagers. A baby should be fed when it desires. Another abhorrent idea is that a wet nurse, even if a close relative, should suckle another's child. "It is not good for the child to get milk from another woman."

Seven days after its birth, a baby is given its name. It can be any name; the common Arab practice of naming a first-born boy Mohammed is not always followed here, nor is there any custom of naming children after particular relatives. The ceremony itself is simple. A feast is given for relatives and close friends, and the name is announced by the family. The same celebration is held for both boys and girls, but in some respects it is clear that male children are preferred. Even at the naming feast, the pitch of the festivity is higher if the child honored is a boy. The rate of infant deaths is high, and the people are aware of the poor expectation of survival of a baby. The death of a baby is not ceremonialized to any extent, and the people pass over the occurrence rather easily. A baby is not named until seven days have passed because the people do not allow themselves to accept the baby as a close part of the family until the days of greatest danger are over.

The ritual of circumcision is made for all boys; it is necessary in order to make a boy into a proper Moslem. The operation is performed between the ages of 3 and 7—never after 7—thus it is not, properly speaking, a puberty or initiation rite. A specialist is paid to perform the operation, and a feast is held for relatives and friends.

Marriage is regarded as the natural state for all adults. A boy should marry as soon as he is capable of supporting a household.

The marriage is a contract between families; in theory, neither the bride nor groom has a choice in the matter. Although the preferred Islamic marriage is between a boy and his paternal parallel cousin (father's brother's daughter), in Mediouna the actual selection of mates depends more on the possible economic advantages of a particular marriage alliance between families. Paternal-parallel-cousin marriage, of course, has a stabilizing effect on a society. Patrilineal lineages tend to maintain their original economic resources and social status by following this custom, which appears to be the reason for its being the official ideal; but, as might be expected in modern times when societies are increasingly less stable, families who can see an advantage in a particular marriage are likely to violate the custom.

The arrangements for the marriage are made primarily on the initiative of the boy's father. Ideally, the father locates a prospect, the rest of the family judge her, and the arrangements are carried out without consulting the boy or girl at all. Before the wedding, the boy calls on the girl's family, but he is not supposed to see his prospective bride. A significant part of the arrangement is the transfer of cash, foodstuffs, and a pair of slippers from the groom's family to the bride's. The cash is used for the bride's gold jewelry, which remains her personal property as a form of insurance against desertion or divorce. The food is used for the wedding feast held at the bride's family home, and the slippers are symbolic of the girl's journey to the groom's home.

The marriage ceremony itself takes three days. The legal aspect is taken care of first by the groom, his father, and the bride's father before a legal clerk. During the first two days, the bride and groom each remain in their own familys' homes, entertaining their friends with small feasts. On the third day, the groom is barbered, shaved, and dressed in his new clothes. Then he is entertained by his male friends at a sort of bachelor dinner, while the bride is cloistered at a neutral house with her female relatives. Late at night, the groom steals away from the party and joins the bride.

In Islamic law, a husband can divorce his wife for any reason whatsoever, and the wife has no opportunity to contest it. On the other hand, it is nearly impossible for a wife to initiate a divorce. In actual practice, the wife's relatives may be powerful enough to protect her, and public opinion itself may modify the stringency of law.

Adultery on the part of the wife is considered a heinous crime and is the most acceptable grounds for divorce. Infertility is also an acceptable reason, even to the wife's own family, for the purpose of marriage is to beget children. Only one man in Mediouna has attempted, however, to increase the size of the family by having two wives at the same time. It is legally and morally permissible to have as many as four, but apparently no one in Mediouna can afford to think in such grandoise terms.

Illness in the village is treated by both materialistic and spiritualistic methods. Cuts, bruises, broken bones, and the like are, of course, taken care of in a practical way. Illness by unseen and unknown causes is treated by infusions of various herbs and by bloodletting—both are techniques of local specialists—and also by religious specialists, who by drumming and chanting exorcise the evil spirits from the patient.

Death is spoken of as a passage from a difficult world to a blissful peace with God. In other respects, too, the quality of funeral belief and practice is not greatly different from that of Christianity. A corpse is washed with soap and water and dressed in new white cotton clothing and covered with a shroud of the same material. On the day following the death, the burial takes place. Bread and figs, purchased especially for the funeral, are distributed to all the people who have gathered for the burial rite. The body is then put on a litter and carried to the cemetery, followed by the procession of mourners. The body is placed in a shallow grave, passages are recited from the Koran, and the grave is then filled. The grave itself is marked by an oval ring of stones laid around it. No more formal observances of the death are made, but for three nights friends and neighbors visit the bereaved family, offering food and companionship to help divert them from their sorrow.

The rituals, beliefs, and ethics of the inhabitants of Mediouna, as well as of the other natives of Morocco, are all formally those of the orthodox (Sunni) Islamic teachings. Islam has, of course, spread itself widely, and through time a number of local adaptations have occurred. This is particularly true with respect to the development of mystic cults of particular local saints. Consequently, not all of the actual behavior and ritual found in a particular village conform exactly to the theoretical or ideal expectations of Islam. Nevertheless, no Moslem village, however isolated, has merely a folk religion. Its most striking and important tenets derive from the urban, literary, and scholarly teachings of the prophet Mohammed, and cannot be understood without reference to them.

Islam, like Christianity, is a revealed religion. Moslems believe that God (Allah) revealed it to Mohammed (ca. A.D. 571–632) through the angel Gabriel. Much of the content of the religion is based on the Judaic tradition and, to a less extent, on Christianity. Educated Moslems themselves regard Islam as the third and final phase of a religious evolution which commenced with Abraham and passed through Judaism and Christianity. The others are therefore not irreligious, but Islam is the highest (and the correct) phase of religion. Mohammed himself is considered a prophet, not a god, and he is not worshiped to the extent that Jesus is by most Catholics. In fact, it is felt to be wrong to refer to the religion as *Mohammedanism,* for there should be no implication that Mohammed was other than a prophet and teacher. Such was also the position of Jesus with the early Christians, but Moslems feel that Christianity is now a gross polytheism, particularly because of the emphasis on Jesus or the Holy Trinity. A Moslem is confident that he has the final truth in religion, but he recognizes the religious kinship of Jews and Christians. All are "people of the Book," as opposed to pagans.

As a faith, Islam stresses three basic principles. The most important is the faith in God, and in His *oneness* and uniqueness. The second principle is that of divine revelation; God can communicate with human beings. This belief is particularly relevant to the faith in regard to the divine origin of the Koran. It also allows and acknowledges that earlier prophets such as Moses and Jesus had had knowledge revealed to them by God. The third article of faith is in the future life. Incorporated in this principle is the idea of the final judgment which holds a person responsible for his actions on earth. Less significant, but related, are the beliefs in angels as messengers and influences for good and in Satan as the power of evil.

Like Judaism and early Christianity, Islam is the ideology of theocracy. The Koran, supplemented by the *Hadith* (the sayings of the Prophet) and learned interpretation, is a guide to conduct in all aspects of life and also relates the usual origin myths and careers of early prophets. The population of the Islamic world, when it is

429

not dominated by European governmental institutions, regards the Koran as the final authority on all legal problems. In fact, whole schools of legal theory are founded upon various interpretations of passages in the Koran.

The ritual practice of Islam, as distinguished from belief, is based upon the Five Pillars, which are kinds of observances. The first consists of the ritualized public declaration of faith, "There is no god but God, and Mohammed is the messenger of God." Theoretically, this is the minimum ritual requirement for a Moslem. He is a member of the faith if he states his adherence in this form.

The second pillar is the five prayers made during each day. They must be made after dawn but before sunup, just after the sun passes is midday zenith, when it is halfway between its zenith and its setting, immediately after sundown, and before going to bed, which must be sometime between the onset of night and midnight. In all cases, the prayers are directed toward Mecca, in the east. These prayers may be said wherever the person finds himself, privately or in company, at work or at home. Before each prayer a person must ritually purify himself by washing the exposed parts of the body (ordinarily the hands, face, and feet) with soap and water if possible, but at least with clean earth or sand. The prayers themselves are not personal and extemporaneous petitions to God, but are formal thanks for favors already granted.

The third pillar is the observation of the Sacred Fast. During all of the ninth lunar month, which is called *Ramadan*,[1] there must be complete abstention during all the daylight hours from food, drink, smoking, and sexual intercourse. Only young children, soldiers in war, sick people, or travelers are exempted, and these latter three must make up the days of fasting later as soon as conditions permit. The fast often imposes considerable hardship; the death rate actually rises considerably in this month. It is felt that the discomfort helps produce the proper disdain for the fleshly pleasures of this world. In cities and larger towns, a cannon is fired to signal the official fall of night, and the faithful, poised to break their fast, fall to. A frequent consequence of the succession of days which seemingly grow longer and longer is that tempers become

---

[1] The twelve months, being a strictly lunar calendar, do not correspond to the solar year, and therefore creep around the seasons. Ramadan therefore has no constant date in the European calendar.

shorter. Partly, too, the frazzled nerves are caused by lack of sleep, for there is a tendency to stay up later and later to eat, drink, and visit, in spite of the necessity of getting up very early in time to eat heartily before dawn.

Speaking of city life in North Africa, Carleton Coon observed:

Ramadhan is a very critical time in Moslem-Christian relations. Not only does it produce physiological effects on the Moslems which make them more sensitive than usual to criticism and injustice, but it serves as a symbol to reinforce their mutual relations in a common front against outsiders. To a hungry, thirsty man driving a recalcitrant donkey into the market about four o'clock on a hot afternoon, the sight of a sleek Christian sitting in a sidewalk cafe sucking at a long, ice-cooled drink is infuriating. If ever there is to be trouble, that is the time.[2]

The fourth pillar is the requirement of charity, called *zakat*. In theory, zakat involves not only the giving of alms to the poor but also a form of tithing by which a specified portion of a person's income is collected by officials for a sort of community chest. This latter practice is not found in Morocco today, but private charity remains a very important consideration among all Moslems.

The fifth pillar concerns the pilgrimage (or *hadj*), to Mecca. Not many people can go from as far as Morocco, of course, but those who have done so are extraordinarily honored.

The peasants of a community such as Mediouna typically add peculiarly local traits to the formal, universal practice and modify or ignore others. For instance, one seldom sees anyone in Mediouna praying in a public place. A person prays at home or in the mosque; if he is at work in the open he might not pray at all. Adherence to such rituals as prayer varies with age. Old people stick close to the prescriptions, while young people find little interest in theological discussions and sometimes neglect prayers entirely.

The mosque in Mediouna is the center for formal religious observances and contains also the village school. The *Fqih,* a religious teacher or learned man, is the only official paid by the villagers. His primary duty is to teach the young, but he also officiates in many religious activities. Islam has no true priesthood. Rituals are led by whoever is considered the most learned person, and it often happens that the person paid to teach children is also considered the most learned, but he is not paid as a religious leader. Probably the most

[2] "North Africa," in R. Linton (ed.), *Most of the World,* New York, 1949, p. 428.

frequent formal occasion at which he officiates is the Meeting on Friday (the Moslem Sabbath), when he conducts prayers and delivers a sermon in the mosque. Friday, incidentally, is not a day of rest or abstention, but merely the occasion of the weekly congregation.

To modern-day urban European or American Christians the rural Moslems seem to be an extraordinarily pious people, even in ordinary daily life. The frequency of prayer is, of course, a notable phenomenon, as is the rigidity with which ritual prescriptions and taboos, such as the Ramadan fast, the ritual butchering, and the prohibition against graven images, alcoholic drinks, the eating of pork, and so on, are upheld. Europeans are also impressed by the great amount of pious exclamations, invocations of the word God and Mohammed, and quotations from the Koran in ordinary speech. One is reminded of the ascetic Puritans of an earlier America.

Feast days, the times of greatest conviviality and celebration in the community, are also religious. One of the most important is *el Moulud,* which celebrates the birthday of the Prophet on the twelfth day of the third month. Seven days of community festivities follow the birth date. Another important feast is held during the month of the pilgrimages to Mecca. On the tenth day of the twelfth month, every family that can afford it ritually sacrifices a sheep for the feast. Two other feasts are held just before Ramadan and just after. Another feast is *el Ashur,* which celebrates the beginning of the new year. It is particularly marked by general hilarity, dancing, and clowning, though not, of course, by drunkenness. A small village such as Mediouna does not have the population or the wealth to make much of a public occasion of these feasts, compared to what goes on in the city. Many of the younger villagers prefer to dress up in their best clothes and mingle with the crowds in Tangier rather than participate in the festivities in their own village.

Other feasts and religious observances are frequent in Islam, but are variable from locality to locality. These are related to brotherhoods or cults of saints. In Morocco there are several major cults and many minor ones. The main feature of this aspect of religion is the concept of *baraka,* spiritual power that varies from person to person. A descendant of the Prophet, a *Shereef,* is likely to inherit more of this power than anyone else, but he may lose or increase the power during his lifetime by his behavior. A Shereef who is assumed to be spiritually powerful and who is a wise and pious teacher of the Koran collects a body of disciples who eventually promulgate his views more widely. If he has been successful, after his death he becomes regarded as a saint. Saints are honored with annual feasts by their adherents. This process is obviously similar in spirit, however smaller in scale, to the rise of Mohammed himself and the many other teachers before him.

A MUSICIAN ENTERTAINS HIS FRIENDS. *Courtesy, United Nations*

In 1970, Morocco had been an independent kingdom for 14 years. But the recent experience of European colonization, which was similar, if shorter, than that of the rest of North Africa, continues to affect its relations with the Western powers. In most of North Africa, European colonists came to control the best land and became by far the wealthiest people, with absolute control of government and all but the pettiest parts of the economy. The resulting social relations between the natives and the Europeans became castelike, with the proud Moslems occupying the place of degraded, poverty-ridden serfs, a cataclysmic decline from the status Islam once had as the largest empire and the most brilliant civilization of the Mediterranean and European world.

Such a situation is serious. The Europeans, and particularly the French government, in North Africa had attempted to allay the dangers with measures which only aggravated the situation. The measures, which are of the same kind which have characterized colonialism elsewhere and failed, were essentially three: (1) to prevent the natives from developing a competing technology, and thus to keep the area as a source of raw materials and a market for processed goods; (2) to restrict increasingly the political liberties of the natives, and to increase police surveillance and size of army garrisons; (3) to increase the restrictions on *social* liberty, which is to say, to widen the social chasm between the conquerors and the conquered (frequently the most galling restriction of all, particularly to the wealthiest and most educated Moslems).

The strained relations of Europeans and Moslems were greatest at the points where the two economies met and where the social encounters were most frequent—in the cities. A small peasant community such as Mediouna reflects the national situation only indirectly. There has been only one foreigner (the anthropologist) residing in the village, but 870 acres of agricultural land in Mediouna have been sold to outsiders, who were Europeans or their clients. This process of alienation was not forced on the villagers; quite to the contrary, they eagerly sought buyers for their land. It appears that the new orientation, perhaps itself an indirect consequence of European influence, was toward cash in hand. Fewer people today think in the age-old typical peasant terms of the security of land-holding for themselves or their heirs. The eagerness for money is such that the seller makes no discrimination in terms of the nationality or religion of the purchaser.

Since independence the International Zone of Tangier has been abolished to become a province within the normal administrative divisions of the central government. The International Zone had been a free port until 1956, with a co-called Mixed Court which protected foreigners. With the ending of the Zone's favored status, the city's economy collapsed. The most immediate effect on Mediouna and other nearby peasant villages was that the city no longer could provide wage work for the surplus rural population.

Nowadays a few young men sell manufactured "native crafts"

to tourists visiting Tangier and the nearby Caves of Hercules. Five young men have gone to Europe as laborers, but the basic problem of rural underemployment remains in Mediouna. As elsewhere in the rural world in modern times the generation gap has widened into a gulf, as the "wisdom of the elders" has become nearly irrelevant to the new political and economic problems.

FURTHER READINGS

Barbour, N. *A Survey of North West Africa,* London and New York, 1962.

Coon, C. S. *Tribes of the Rif,* Cambridge (Mass.), 1931.

Coon, C. S. *Caravan: the Story of the Middle East,* New York, 1958.

Geertz, C. *Islam Observed: Religious Development in Morocco and Indonesia,* New Haven, 1968.

Gellner, E. *Saints of the Atlas,* London and Chicago, 1969.

Gibb, H. A. R. *Mohammedanism,* London, 1962.

Meakin, B. *The Moors,* London and New York, 1902.

Schorger, W. D. *The Stonecutters of Mediouna: Resistance to Acculturation in a Moroccan Village,* Unpublished Ph.D. dissertation, Harvard University, 1952.

Schorger, W. D. "The Evolution of Political Forms in a North Moroccan Village," *Anthropological Quarterly,* 42:263–286 (1969).

Westermarck, E. A. *Ritual and Belief in Morocco,* London, 1926.

A Chinese Peasant Village

To the average Westerner three facts predominate among the many which characterize his sense of China's exoticism. First, perhaps, is that Chinese culture is very ancient as civilizations go; many distinctive customs are survivals from a misty past. Second, China is huge. Not only is the land area extensive, but it is swarming with human beings. Its population of more than half a billion makes it the largest nation in the world. Third, he thinks of China as pre-eminently a peasant society, massive and immobilized by the strength of the tie to the soil.

These aspects of China's distinctiveness are in some measure true, but China is a very complex nation, and any generalization about it requires modification. China does have one of the oldest of surviving civilizations. But we must remember that changes have also occurred in China, that it has great cities within which dwell classes of people who are modern in culture, and that—and we need no reminder for this—a great revolution is going on today which is not merely political, but economic, social, and even religious.

The Chinese do constitute nearly one-fourth of all mankind, and some of the provinces have a congestion of population equal to any in the world. But there are also parts of China with very sparse population. Huge areas in the north are occupied by widely scattered Mongol herders, and in Sinkiang, a northwestern province, there are other areas populated only by herders and hunters. Some parts of Manchuria and north and central China are fertile and well cultivated, but in general it is the delta of the Yangtse and Yellow rivers and southern China, particularly along the coast, where the agriculture is so productive and the population so dense.

The stereotype of China as a land of peasants is largely true. About 80 percent of the population are full-time, and another 11 percent are part-time, agriculturalists. The agriculture is of an especially intensive kind; in the rice region the average size of the family farm is only about three acres, as opposed to about 150 acres in the United States. China's farms are carefully tended and very fertile, but the average family is also miserably poor by Western standards. The obvious richness of the soil, as manifested by the small plots, is not a sign that the productivity of labor is high. In the United States (in 1947), only 2.2 man-hours of agricultural labor were required to produce 1 million calories of food, approximately the yearly requirement for one person. The average Chinese peasant works 186 man-hours to obtain the same amount of calories.

The great majority of Chinese live in villages of 1000 people or less. Peasant villages, a kind of folk society, have many of the social characteristics of primitive tribes: they are largely illiterate, family and extended kinship ties are very strong, the people feel a close attachment to the soil and the locality, and a considerable self-sufficiency in subsistence is maintained. Yet the peasant culture is a part of the nation's culture, in this case a *class* within Chinese society with a distinctive subculture of its own, but related to the whole civilization.

The largest of the intensively farmed areas of China is the China Plain, the delta made by the confluent mouths of China's two greatest rivers, the Yangtse and the Yellow. This is classical China and approximates, as a region, the stereotype of China as ancient in culture and densely populated. The valley plains of each of the two rivers carry this intensively cultivated part of China inland in two narrowing bands of essentially similar topography and culture.

The Yangtse plain, the region of the village described in the following pages, has the highest population density in China—897 people to the square mile. The principal produce is rice, with wheat, beans, cotton, and oil seeds following. Two crops a year are usual, because the climate is mild and the rainfall is supplemented with extensive irrigation. As in most of the peasant world, the rural Chinese regard the land and their labor on it as essential to

Young Chinese share the commune work. *Eastfoto*

sustenance, but they are also tied in some measure to the economy of the nation by the small-scale export of a regionally specialized product. On much of the Yangtse plain the supplementary economic activity is the production of silk, a domestic industry.

The dense population of the Yangtse plain is mostly nucleated into small villages, which in turn lie scattered around a larger town which serves as a market for the peasants' sale of rice and silk and the distributing point of goods manufactured elsewhere. Kaihsienkung, a representative peasant village in this region, was studied in 1936 by a famous Chinese anthropologist, Fei Hsiaotung, in one of the earliest and best known of the attempts anthropologists have made to analyze the communities of the great civilized nations.[1] The description which follows treats this village as it was seen by Fei in 1936.

Kaihsienkung is composed of 1400 people, but it controls only 461 acres of land, and a part of this is taken up by the dwellings of the village proper. All of the agricultural land, however, is irrigated river mud and therefore highly productive. The region is a complex network of interlaced streams, canals, and lakes; and because the waterways are the primary avenues of transport, all the villages of the region are located along the streams. Kaihsienkung itself is actually divided into four parts by the waterways which flow through it. Each house is very close to the next and all hug the riverbank closely. More than two-thirds of the households of the village are engaged mainly in agriculture. The farming is 90 percent devoted to the cultivation of paddy rice, and thus depends on complete water control. The term *water control* is used advisedly, for not only is it necessary to irrigate the rice fields, but it is equally important to drain them properly.

The land cultivated by the village is divided by streams and irrigation canals into segments called *yu*. In order to irrigate all parts of the yu, it is carefully graded and the flow of water regulated by a system of dikes. To drain the same area in wet periods, a deeper ditch and dike system must also be created. The maintenance of all this requires constant attention, which together with the complexity of wet rice culture and the absence of machines and draft animals means that the amount of human labor over a year is very great compared to that expended on fields of equivalent size in many other agriculture zones of the world. The crops are tended as carefully as so many house plants.

Rice culture begins in June, when a small nursery plot is prepared for seeding. For about a month the tender young shoots require very little space, but the utmost care. Meanwhile, the main field is meticulously prepared for the transplanting by breaking up the soil, manuring it, and leveling it for irrigation. No plows are used; all of this work is done by human labor with hand implements. The water is finally introduced into the fields by a homemade water lift operated by man power. All in all, preparation of an average

---

[1] Fei Hsiao-tung, *Peasant Life in China*, New York, 1939.

family-sized rice plot takes more than a month of arduous labor. But this is preparation—only the beginning.

The hardest work is transplanting the young shoots from the nursery to the irrigated plots. Children and men are mobilized for the work-torture of stooping from dawn to sunset to plant the delicate seedlings. Unremitting toil will finish the planting of an average plot in about two weeks, after which great care is taken with the water regulation, weeding, and fertilizing with dried human and animal dung and oil-bean residue. If seeding began in June, the rice harvest is ready in November. Reaping is done with a simple long sickle, and afterwards the sheaves are taken to an open space at the front of the house or even into the front room. Threshing consists merely of switching the ears of grain against the inner sides of the storage bag where the dislodged grains collect. The hulling of the grains is a laborious process, but the still greater labor of the second hulling and polishing is now taken over by modern mechanical devices.

The fact that men only, and children at emergency times, work in the fields, while the women remain always at home, is a special characteristic of the silk-producing regions of China. Women spend their available time reeling silk, and before the competition of the factory system hurt the Chinese market for family-produced silk, the women often attained an economic rank equal to men. Marginal (higher) land near the houses is given over to mulberry trees, the leaves of which are the food of the family's silkworms.

An average of about 10 percent of the land is used for wheat, oil seeds, and the various garden vegetables which supplement the rice fare of the average household. The abundant watercourses are the source of minor protein foods, such as fish, shrimps, and crabs, as well as several wild water plants. The rights to the wild products of the watercourses are communal, as is the water used in irrigation.

The rights to agricultural land are individualized, but complicated by the local theory of land tenure. Land is thought of as two layers, the surface and the subsoil. The titleholder and taxpayer of the land is the possessor of the *subsoil* rights. Frequently, he also controls the *surface* rights in the name of his household; that is, he and his family cultivate their own land. Absentee owners may lease or rent cultivation rights to others. A cultivator who has surface rights but no subsoil rights is termed a tenant. Sometimes the tenant sublets the cultivation rights or hires laborers to do the actual tilling. If the rights to a plot are thus distributed among three different persons, all have certain claims on the produce. The subsoil owner expects rent from the tenant; the tenant or surface owner gets a portion of rent from the lessee. Any given plot of land might have one, two, or three persons involved in its tenure rights, therefore, and any given person could work one plot in which he owns both subsoil and surface rights, another with surface rights alone, as well as working on another as a paid laborer. This complex of roles exists because the men attempt to keep their time as fully employed as possible.

The curious-seeming division of land into subsoil and surface rights apparently is related to the customs which have grown up around absentee ownership. About two-thirds of the subsoil of the village is owned by people from the neighboring market town. The alienation of land from original peasant owners typically begins because the peasant needs money desperately to meet some emergency, and he then mortgages his land. Typically, also, he cannot pay back the loan and the land title which was the security finally goes to the moneylender. But the peasant cannot be dispossessed of the cultivation rights so long as he pays the interest, which is stabilized as rent; hence the phrasing, subsoil rights and surface rights. Both are forms of differential ownership, differing from the usual notion of renting or tenancy because the renter cannot be removed or interfered with in any way. Even should the cultivator fail to pay his rent for a long period, the subsoil owner usually finds it impossible to remove him because of the difficulty of finding a substitute; the villagers defend the rights of the tenant by refusing to collaborate with the subsoil owner. There are expensive legal sanctions which the subsoil owner can apply, but he usually waits for the peasant to pay.

This local land situation has become an aspect of the relationship between market town and peasant village; the moneylenders and absentee landlords are townsmen, the peasants are villagers. The moneylender cannot come to the village and cultivate the land himself; he owns no surface rights. It makes little difference to the villagers, therefore, which townsman owns the subsoil. The "ownership" is really only a claim to the rent agreed upon and is even sold on the market among city people much as stocks and bonds might be. So formalized becomes the institution, finally, that the absentee owners of village subsoil typically have never seen their tenants and turn over the job of collecting the rents to professional bureaus. Here, then, is one version of the landlord-peasant problem which is so frequently cited as the cause of rural unrest. Usually the institution has been seen as a personal relationship; hence *bad* or *grasping* landlords are cited as the cause of peasant revolts. But it seems more fruitful to regard the relationship as one between town and country, or as the influence of a financial system on a subsistence system, in the light of the facts mentioned. Greater understanding of China's difficulties, which are, of course, frequently manifested as struggles between persons, can result if they are seen as the clash of economic and related sociopolitical institutions.

There is no class distinction in Kaihsienkung itself which conforms to the distinction between landlord and tenant. The landlords are not found in the village, and the villagers themselves usually hold two or three kinds of land rights simultaneously. Furthermore, the kinds of holdings vary greatly from generation to generation in the same family, depending on the amount of male labor available to the household. In general, too, there is a surplus of human labor, and the households try to earn money by means other than agriculture, even though the emotional tie and concept of true security lie in agriculture.

The domestic silk industry is the most important subsidiary enterprise of the villages in the region of Kaihsienkung, as it has been for more than 1000 years. But because the factory system in Japan, and later in some other parts of China, has caused a general decline in the domestic industry, a recent (early 1930s) attempt has been made by outside teachers from a technical school to reform the silk industry of the village in line with modern methods. This meant essentially a change from individual hand-winding of silk to a village factory using mechanical power. The factory was planned as a cooperative village venture, and as such reveals matters of interest which will be related to the discussion of culture change and future trends in the final paragraphs of this chapter.

The decline in silk prices caused the villagers to seek out all possible means of enlarging their subsistence base. The two most important in recent years have been sheep-raising and trade ventures. Inasmuch as pasture is lacking, no family keeps herds of sheep.

Instead, some families build a small hut and pen which confine from one to five sheep. They are fed dried mulberry leaves in winter; in summer grass and other forage are collected for them by children. About 500 sheep are kept in the village in this fashion. The sheep

PEASANT WOMAN WORKING STONE RICE MILL. *Ewing Galloway*

dung is used for fertilizer, and the new-born young of the sheep are sold in town for their skins. Needless to say, no one becomes rich from raising sheep. In a year, the sale of new lambs from one ewe earns a family only a tiny fraction of its subsistence.

Trade transport is undertaken by many villagers during the slack periods in the agricultural year. The trader takes his boat to a neighboring province and buys on credit a load of local produce which he then undertakes to sell in one of the coastal towns. In effect, the margin of profit is merely a wage received for acting as a trade agent and transport worker. Not much money is made at this work at any given time, but such a large number of villagers engage in it that it must be considered an important activity.

The houses of the village usually consist of three connected rooms of mud walls and tiled roofs. The front room, which opens to the pathway and stream, is used for household work, such as reeling silk

A TYPICAL SCENE IN KAIHSIENKUNG, 1956. *Courtesy, W. R. Geddes*

and threshing rice, for worship at the ancestral shrine, and for receiving guests. Directly behind the front room is the kitchen, a smaller room containing the stove and the shrine of the kitchen god. Another large room is the bedroom, which is divided by wooden partitions into separate sleeping places for as many married couples as inhabit the house. Sometimes grown unmarried boys sleep in the front room, but girls remain in their parents' room because of the belief that women must not sleep in the presence of the ancestral shrine. Behind the house are the latrine and the earthenware pits where human excrement is preserved for use as a fertilizer.

The clothing worn by the villagers varies according to the season.

In summer, men wear only cotton shorts, putting on a shirt for formal occasions. Distinguished elders, such as village headmen, must have long silk gowns, and when the weather is hot, they carry them on their arms when they are not at home. Women wear long skirts and sleeveless blouses. Heavier skirts and jackets are worn by both men and women in cold weather, and the long gown of distinction may be padded. The clothing is made by the women, but the cloth—cotton and linen—is purchased. A tailor is hired to make wedding clothes and other items of higher quality for formal use.

The largest item of expenditure in a household is food. In a year, food requires about 40 percent of the budget. The staple is rice, which the village produces in surplus. Garden vegetables are next in importance, but gardens are so small that some of this food is purchased from other villages that specialize in truck gardening. Fish are caught locally, but pork, the only meat eaten, is purchased by retailers from the market town. Sugar, salt, and most spices are also purchased from the town.

Breakfast is a light meal, consisting usually only of rice porridge and salty preserved cabbage. The noon meal is the heaviest, but the evening meal is the important social occasion. The whole family, except for the woman who is serving, sits in an arrangement following the kinship order. The male family head sits facing the front of the house, the oldest son sits on the left side, the next on the right side, while the women take the "lower" side, facing the family head. The evening meal is eaten in the front room, or if the weather is warm, the table is set outside. On a summer evening the street is lined with a row of tables, with the families eating and at the same time chatting with their neighbors.

The family, called *chia,* is the basic social and economic unit of the village. The chia is patrilocal, that is, wives come from outside; hence children grow up in a household and neighborhood dominated by their father's male relatives. The chia in ideal form consists of aged parents and all their sons, sons' wives, and sons' children. Such a large household is considered a traditional characteristic of Chinese society and is often rationalized as being a reflection of filial devotion—a reluctance of the sons to separate from their parents even after they are married and have their own children.

In actuality, the size of the chia varies with economic conditions. The largest chia are found among townsmen and reflect the advantages of pooling resources in a financial economy. In the villages of rural China the chia consists typically of four to six persons, the smaller size being related to the amount of land which can be advantageously worked on a communal basis. If a family has several sons, therefore, the household will subdivide on their marriage in ways depending on the economic situation. This does not mean that the ties of relationship are severed or become nonfunctional, but merely that the group members are not all coresident participants in a single household economy. Population control is also a means of regulating the size of the chia. Infanticide, particularly of girl children, occurs in poorer households. Wealthier families are proud to have a large number of children—a sign of wealth. The fact that the amount of land a family controls tends to correlate directly with the number of sons works in the long run as a wealth equalizer; a larger amount of land becomes subdivided into small parts among a larger number of sons.

The greatest emphasis in Chinese ideology is on the continuity of *incense and fire,* the term designating the patrilineal descent line. Another way of describing this emphasis is to say that parent-child relationships dominate husband-wife relationships. Married sons retain close ties, if not actual coresidence, with their parents. The sons' wives are outsiders, selected by the sons' parents for the purpose of begetting children to carry on the paternal line. The wife has little status as a member of the family until she has children, and through fulfilling this role, she becomes considered more a family member as time passes. But her status and significance are not regarded as due to a role as companion or mate of her husband; the couple's affection for one another may grow into love, but this fact is not given the significance that it receives in the United States.

An emphasis on sons in a family is created by the consideration of incense and fire. A daughter leaves the home on marriage to assume her husband's surname and by custom has no claim on her parents' heritable property except for the dowry which she takes to her husband's family. Sons have the duty of caring for their parents as they become old and helpless; the daughters have no such obligation. Related to this total situation is an ancient and traditional social derogation of women which is reflected even in forms of etiquette, behavior, and attitudes which reduce them to a status very inferior to men. In modern times one of the most striking of the changes occurring in China is the greater freedom and higher status of women.

The mode of inheritance is at once a reflection of the traditional Chinese social organization and one of the causes of its perpetuation. A chia consisting of a father, mother, and two sons may be taken as a simple example. When the older son is married, the chia property is divided into four shares. The first is reserved for the parents in order to provide for their subsistence. Each of the sons receives a share, and the older is given an extra share. This fourth part is smaller than the other three, usually, and varies depending on the economic contribution the older son has made to the chia, which ordinarily would be greater than that of the younger. It is also felt that the older should receive a larger share because of his future ceremonial obligation to his parents after their deaths.

The second son's share is actually not given outright, but is held until he marries. If, as sometimes happens, the older son sets up a separate household, leaving the younger as support of the parents and as future head of that chia, then the younger can expect to receive the parents' part of the land undivided after their deaths. Should the older and younger sons both remain in the chia, they share the parents' land after their deaths.

The house also is subject to division. If none of the sons has moved out of the household, the death of the father leaves the older son in charge of the house and his younger brother support of the mother. The house itself is divided into two parts; the right half belongs to the elder, the left to the younger. As sons get married, they always have the possibility of setting up a new household if economic conditions are such that the parents agree to it. In such a case, the older son ordinarily has first chance to do this because he is the first to marry. But no matter what the conditions, at least one of the brothers, usually the younger, must remain in the parents' household to care for them and their property. In a sense, the two apparently opposite principles, primogeniture and ultimogeniture, are both operative in this situation. The older son has more privileges and more responsibility than the other, and usually gets a larger share of the land, but in the end it is often the younger brother who inherits the family house after fulfilling his duty of staying with the parents in their old age. Thus the continuity of the parental line in the original ancestral home could as well be a

447

succession of younger brothers as older brothers.

The daughter traditionally has no share whatsoever in the division of land or household. The dowry she takes to her new home consists of furniture, ornaments, clothing, and the like, and money if possible, but none of the resources important in inheritance. When a woman marries and leaves the chia, her economic dependence on her family ends. But a son, even if he sets up his own chia, sees his parents frequently, contributes to their well-being in various ways, and even is limited in his own economic freedom because his father's

Courtesy, Ewing Galloway

decisions must be heeded. The only time a daughter may participate in carrying on the family line and use its property occurs when the parents have no son. In such a case they try to find a husband for her whose family "gives him up" to them. He moves into the girl's chia and is, in effect, adopted by her family so that the family name, as well as property, will be continued through him and their daughter.

As indicated earlier, the chia frequently becomes too large and unwieldy, and then one or more of the sons establishes his own separate chia. Because social relations remain strong among the related chia, however, through time the village becomes a complicated network of kinship ties. And in addition to the actuality of kin relationship, there are strong ideological reinforcements. The generally understood principle of lineage membership in Kaihsien-kung is that all patrilineal descendants who can trace relationship to a common male ancestor within five generations constitute a *tsu*. Whether the chia that are members of a tsu associate with one another frequently and cooperate in various matters, however, depends much more on propinquity and mutual liking than on the degree of consanguinity. Essentially, the function of the tsu as a unit is of significance largely in that it comes together on ceremonial occasions, such as weddings, funerals, and offerings to the ancestors. In China as a whole, it was a classical rule that all persons with the same surname could be considered members of a great patrilineal descent group (clan). In Kaihsienkung, as in most other parts of modern China, this assumption of relationship no longer exists, nor do those of a common surname carry on any ceremonial activities together, although there remains a feeling against intermarriage. The tsu is the largest functional kinship group.

The affinal family, the wife's paternal chia, has some functions in the extension of kin relationships beyond the man's patrilineal relatives, but they are particularized rather than extensive. The most important relationship stemming from marriage is that between a woman's child and her brother, the child's maternal uncle. This uncle is usually the one of the mother's brothers who has remained in her chia to become its head or potential head. The uncle has many special obligations to the child: he is the guest of honor at the several ceremonies held for the child; he selects the child's name; he gives a special gift when the child finally marries; and, most important, he stands as mediator in all disputes or conflicts between father and son. The last role, which is formally recognized and considered very important, is of special interest as an indicator of the dependent status of women. In many crises between father and son, the mother could be expected to intervene, but in rural China it is felt that only men may dispute. The mother's marriage was arranged by the two chia and any crisis which might involve *her* interests should be handled by a man, normally her brother. Other maternal kin of importance are the wife's mother, who comes to supervise at childbirth, and any of the wife's sisters who might have married into the neighborhood. On no occasion, however, do any of the wife's relatives other than those of her immediate family participate in any formalities with her husband's kin.

Status terms which denote categories within the genealogy are widely used as forms of address among villagers, whether or not they are related. The terms for father, mother, or grandparents are not thus extended, but a person frequently addresses any senior male in his village by the term for paternal uncle, which carries with it a connotation of obedience and respect; one of his own generation as *elder brother* or *younger brother,* particularly as close friendships are formed; and a youngster as *son.* Similarly, nonrelatives of one's mother's or wife's village may be addressed by the terms used for the affinal or maternal relatives. The kinship term for maternal uncle, in particular, if addressed to senior males of the mother's village, conveys the expectation of friendly indulgence. Personal names, on the other hand, may be used only by seniors in addressing juniors with whom they are closely associated in village life.

The pattern of kinship terminology used in rural China is a modification of an ancient and widespread type found among many primitive peoples. Originally, it appears, cross cousins were separated from parallel cousins and the kinship terms for these latter were the same as sibling terms. Commensurately, mother's sister and father's brother were called *mother* and *father,* respectively, while the cross aunts and uncles (mother's brother and father's sister) were given separate terms.[2] Descriptive additives have been used for a long time, however, so that although terms used in address are sometimes applied widely to nonrelatives, as indicated above, the terms of reference have become individualized—that is, collateral lines of descent are no longer merged.[3] It seems probable that the earlier system was a reflection of the importance of the extended family—the chia—of brothers living together with their families, whereas the modern pattern reflects an increase in the importance of the nuclear family so that father's brothers and mother's sisters are clearly differentiated from father and mother.

[2] This system, usually called *bifurcate-merging,* or *Dakota,* by anthropologists, is the kind described in the classical literature of China (Marcel Granet, *Chinese Civilization,* New York, 1950).

[3] Han-yi Fêng, "The Chinese Kinship System," *Harvard Journal of Asiatic Studies,* Vol. 2, 1937. The Chinese descriptive kinship terms now resemble the pattern used by the Nuer and Moroccans. (See Chapters 7 and 18.)

In modern patterns of nomenclature, however, one significant trait is retained—the distinction between younger and older siblings and younger and older of the father's brothers. Relative age remains one of the most important determinants of status.

In a village as large as Kaihseinkung, not all of the social relations can be on the basis of kinship, even though kinship terms are frequently used in address. And because the villagers have economic relations with other parts of the nation, both as individuals and collectively as a village unit, there must be organizational forms which are suprafamilial—governmental or political, in the broad sense of the terms.

The local government of the villagers consists of a headman. A village head is always a respected and literate elder who holds office because of the confidence the other villagers repose in him. Typical among the multifarious tasks of the headman are to help the villagers write letters or interpret documents, to aid in the calculations involved in the local credit system, to manage marriage ceremonies, to arbitrate disputes, and to care for public property. He is, of course, also the man charged with executing administrative orders coming from the outside government. (At the time of Fei's study, Kaihsienkung had two headmen. The elder of the two did not deal with the higher government, having allowed a younger man to fill the official post.) Neither of these men is a member of any privileged class, nor do they receive any direct pay. Presents are sometimes given them for some personal service, but apparently the high prestige the position carries is the greatest reward.

From the point of view of national adminstration, the village is subdivided in four parts—*pao,* or neighborhoods. These are united into a *hsiang,* which includes a few neighboring hamlets. Above this is the *chu,* corresponding roughly to the functional marketing area of the town; then the district; and finally the province of Kiangsu. All of these are based on the principles of Sun Yat-sen, that the people should be self-governed by elected headmen and councils. The system was introduced in 1935 and was so new at the time of Fei's study that he could not properly assess its functions. Since the civil war, the new regime has abolished this organization and created great changes in the function and form of local aspects of the national government.

Despite the ancient complexity of Chinese government and economics, the villagers still regard the male lineage as the primary social unit within which most of the significant occurrences of an individual's life take place, whether social, economic, or religious. The interest in posterity remains the main ideological theme, and the production of sons the most important focus. The major ceremonial occasions of an individual's life cycle all reflect the concern with the continuity of incense and fire from father to son.

During a woman's pregnancy, particularly if it is her first, the whole household, and her own parents as well, are in a general state of fearful emotion. The woman, as a consequence of this tension, is exempted from her usual household duties and expected to observe a large number of taboos. She must abstain from excess of temper and be on her best behavior because the fetus "needs education." The personality of the child may be warped if she misbehaves, looks at abhorrent objects, or eats certain foods. The father has no special obligations during the pregnancy except to observe the taboo on sexual intercourse.

The delivery is made under the supervision of the woman's mother, who remains with her for several days. No one else pays much attention to the child for about a month, believing that the child will have a better chance for survival if the sadistic devil-spirits who have the power to cause its death are led to believe that no one is particularly interested in it. After the danger is over, the ceremony of *menyu*—"child-reaching-full-month"—is performed. At this time, the household and other paternal relatives foregather, and the maternal uncle shaves the baby's head and gives it its personal name.

Because the women of Kaihsienkung do not do outdoor work, the babies are close to their mothers almost uninterruptedly. The period of suckling may last as long as three or more years, and the mother gives the breast to the child any time it cries. Fathers see much less of their children because they are away almost every day. Later, as the child is growing up, the father's influence increases, but he becomes increasingly the source of discipline, and a respectful social distance is thereby created. The child, if a boy, is considered the father's replacement, and he is continually encouraged to model his behavior after his father's.

A child's education takes place almost entirely in the home. There is a village school, but the child's ever-growing participation in the economy of the chia comes into conflict with the school's demands, and very few of the village children attend school long enough to become literate. Literacy, to the peasants, is an attainment useful for a headman or for the gentry of the town and is, therefore, prestigeful, but it is of little value to the average peasant; and parents, therefore, do not encourage their children to go to school when their help is urgently needed in the fields or at home. It may be supposed that a youth's attainment of literacy is considered a long step away from the parents' status and could lead to his leaving the homestead for wider opportunities rather than maintaining his filial obligations. The more urban Chinese families, on the contrary, frequently devote a large share of the household's capital to the educational training of one of the sons. This may result in direct advantage to the household of a townsman, but not ordinarily to the average peasant family.

Filial obligation and the associated inheritance problems come to a head at the time of the marriage of a son. There is no such thing as courtship; the parents are in complete charge of the choice of partner and the marriage arrangements. The couple to be married are usually from different villages and are not acquainted with one another. Even after the engagement is fixed, they must avoid social contact. The marriage arrangements are made long in advance, sometimes when the children are only 6 or 7 years old. Commonly, a girl's parents hire a professional matchmaker who seeks out eligible families in the neighboring villages. The matchmaker carries a piece of red paper on which are written the characters describing the year, month, day, and hour of the girl's birth. This broker initiates the proposal by placing the paper before the kitchen god in the home of an eligible boy, and then explains to his parents the circumstances of the girl's family. Often a boy's family receives several red papers and is thus able to make a choice. The red papers are finally taken to a fortuneteller, who makes calculations from the papers' dates and suggests a decision. Cross-cousin marriage is a preferred type, particularly that of a boy with his father's sister's daughter, but such possibilities exist only infrequently.

When a boy's family has informed the matchmaker of its choice, the girl's parents must be persuaded to accept the proposal. The custom is for them to refuse at first; but finally they agree, and lengthy negotiations are begun to determine the marriage settlement. The boy's parents must make a gift of money, clothing, and ornaments to the girl's family on three separate occasions, and the amount is decided upon only after heated argumentation. All of these gifts actually are brought with the girl to her new husband as part of her dowry, and so it is not truly bride payment or purchase which recompenses the girl's family.

The wedding is one of the high spots in the life of the chia. The bridegroom first goes to his bride's chia, where a complicated night-long ceremony is held. The culminating scene occurs when the bride finally is to be taken from her father's house. She puts on a partly ritualized and frequently entirely sincere show of resistance and breaks down in tears at the prospect. The bridegroom's friends and family also assemble at a great feast at his house, and the bride is recommended to them. She formally becomes an appended part of the new chia by worshiping at the ancestral shrine.

The first year or so of married life is sometimes a miserable one for the girl. She is watched continually for signs of laxness in her duties. She must work very hard at the household drudgery and treat her husband and new relatives with great respect. Meanwhile she begins to raise her own silkworms and prove that she is an economic asset. During this time, and until the birth of a child, husband and wife show only indifference to one another before other members of the household. They do not sit near one another, and most public conversation takes place through a third person. They have no special terms of address or reference for one another until a child is born; after that the husband refers to his wife as *mother of*——— (the child's name)[4] After the birth of a child, the whole family integrates more closely around the new mother, and her own behavior becomes freer and more natural. Nevertheless, the wife never has the freedom to request a divorce, while the husband, or his parents, can repudiate the marriage should they choose.

If the new couple continue to live in the husband's chia and are fortunate in begetting a male child, the man's father and mother gradually begin a withdrawal from economic activity and household responsibility. In time, the husband does most of the work in the fields while his father retains an advisory position, and the wife comes to take a more important position in the house while her

---

[4] This custom of *teknonymy*, to use the anthropological term, is also frequent in primitive societies.

mother-in-law retreats to the status of a lovable and respected person rather than that of the domineering boss of the house that she appeared to be when the marriage took place. The older the parents become, the greater the overt respect and love shown for them.

The funeral of a parent, particularly if it is for the father, is a ceremonial event of great importance in China because, as in birth and marriage, the important concept of filial succession is clearly dramatized. A death is symbolized to the community at large by burning a package of the deceased's clothing and a paper chair before the front door. Neighbors then gather to assist in making the funeral arrangements, cooking food, cleaning, and so on, because the chia members are in such a state of mourning that they cannot take care of normal responsibilities. One of the first things to be done is to engage a priest to recite Buddhist sutras at the head of the dead man.

Two or three days after death, the corpse is put in a coffin and taken to the cemetery. In Kaihsienkung, coffins are not buried underground as they are in the towns, but are set among the mulberry trees and covered with a shelter of brick and tiles. The spirit has, by this time, left the corpse and gone to join the other ancestral spirits. On the seventeenth or eighteenth day after death the spirit will come back to the chia. Its advent is prepared for by building a small wooden pavilion in the front room which will hold a tablet inscribed with the name of the deceased. For 49 days heavy daily mourning, marked by wailing of the women, must continue. All of the close relatives wear sackcloth and white headcloths to symbolize the mourning state.

At the end of two years and two months, the pavilion is burned, the tablet is placed in the ancestral shrine, and mourning is officially at an end. From then on, the deceased is an ancestor and is worshiped in the regular way. Special sacrifices of food and paper money are made on the anniversaries of his birth and death to symbolize the economic obligation of each generation to the previous one. Additionally, the lineal ancestors are collectively worshiped five times a year. The ancestor spirits seem to be considered to be benign in their influence, but sometimes they may cause illness or misfortune as a warning of some lapse of piety, such as selling the land and thus breaking the continuity of landholding.

As is apparent, the most frequent and omnipresent aspect of religion is the worship of ancestors. In addition to these there are certain special gods who are the object of more sporadic veneration. The most important god is the Kitchen Inspector who is sent by the Emperor of Heaven. He is charged with the duty of watching over the behavior of the members of the chia and reporting to the Emperor at the end of each year. He is represented by a paper inscription placed in a small shrine over the kitchen stove. Sacrifices are made to him on the first and fifteenth of each month; a first-fruits sacrifice is made at the beginning of the season of each food; and at the end of the year when he is ready to leave with his report a sacrifice is made. The food sacrifices are made by laying a dish of the food before the shrine, lighting two candles, and burning a bundle of incense. The year-end feast is made in the front room. After the meal, the paper inscription is burned along with incense and a paper chair. It is hoped that the Inspector will make a favorable report so that the chia will have good fortune the next year.

Most of the concern of the kitchen god is with the observance of a number of taboos. Many of the taboos have to do with the proper handling of rice; certain others are concerned with ritual uncleanliness caused by sexual intercourse or women's menstruation; another category is connected with a veneration of learning manifested by prescriptions for the care of paper with written characters of any kind on it. The kitchen god, like other supernaturals, is anthropomorphic and somewhat childish; he can be cheated, bribed, and bullied, and many taboos are broken behind his back when he is distracted. Even the Emperor of Heaven is not all-seeing and omnipresent; he is served by a supernatural administrative organization of agents, and if the machinery breaks down he is left unaware of what is happening to his mortals—in heaven as it is on earth.

Another god, Luiwan, is the protector against locusts and is sometimes thought of, vaguely, as a god of harvests. He is worshiped twice a year at feasts given in his honor. Other gods vary from neighborhood to neighborhood; one may be the object of special veneration in one locality and ignored in another. In earlier years all of these gods were brought together after the autumn harvest at a sort of thanksgiving celebration. This was the nearest thing the villagers had to a community fiesta combining religion with recreation. The high point was the presentation of an opera by a traveling company.

There are two temples in the village, each owned by Buddhist priests. The priests keep ancestor records for their parishioners and participate in the funeral ceremonies as described above. The feeling of the people toward their temple or priest has nothing to do with sectarian loyalties, or with other religious attitudes, such as faith or belief, so familiar to Christians. The priest does not preach religious doctrines to the people or regard them as a pastor does his flock; he is merely a sort of custodian of the temple and of the altars and images of the gods contained there. Even his reciting of Buddhist scripture over the dead is merely formula, for the language used is foreign to the people and not meant for their comprehension; apparently the more esoteric the reading, the more potent the magic is thought to be.

The cosmological ideas held by the people are bewilderingly complicated. Concepts of local gods and legends are blended with vague ethical precepts relating to familial behavior, probably stemming from Confucius, along with ideas of transmigration and Western Heaven from Buddhism, and magical aspects from Taoism. The average Chinese peasant is not interested in theology and has no feelings of religious exclusiveness or of monotheism. Francis L. K. Hsu discovered in a village in southwest China that at one single religious meeting the names or titles of 608 gods and spirits were invoked. Interestingly, the names of Jesus Christ and Mohammed were included among them. Clearly, as Professor Hsu points out, the spirit world and the human world are counterparts of one another.

In the popular mind the spiritual hierarchy is a part of the social order just as much as the bureaucratic and political hierarchy is. That is why it is irrelevant or even erroneous to speak of different religions in China. . . . As there is no question of a community living under two social orders, so it is inconceivable that there should be two spiritual orders. If two religions are both true, they must find their place in the existing hierarchy.[5]

The Chinese villages, such as Kaihsienkung, have long been politically and economically dependent on factors outside their own immediate areas. But always their relation to the outside world

[5] "China," in R. Linton (ed.), *Most of the World,* New York, 1949, p. 779.

Chinese children attend a market during spring festival. *Ewing Galloway*

Young and old attend the People's Court. *Ewing Galloway*

has been dependent and passive. Subsistence farming, reverence for the land, security through familial ties, a world view dominated by the succession of father by son, have been the most significant parts of their circumscribed world. But during the past 50 years or so the balance has been slowly shifting toward national participation, and even a sort of consciousness of international affairs.

Even by the time of Fei's visit to Kaihsienkung in 1936 certain alterations in economy were evident, with concomitant changes being felt in many other aspects of life. Most significant was the depression in the domestic silk industry caused by the superiority of the factory system developed elsewhere. This led to attempts at such marginal enterprises as sheep raising and transport trade of vegetables. Meanwhile, the costs of weddings, funerals, cloth, and other necessities continued high, and the villagers resorted to moneylenders until they had lost subsoil rights to two-thirds of the village land. The logical question became whether to give up silk raising altogether or to introduce the factory system. Here is the problem confronting most of the nonindustrialized areas of the world today, no matter what the product. To compete they must industrialize; not to compete is unthinkable because it means only a steadily increasing poverty for the people and a loss of power and independence by the nation.

At the time of Fei's visit to the village, an attempt had recently been made to set up a local cooperative silk factory, initiated and guided by volunteers from a city technical school. Nearly all the village chia bought shares in the enterprise, but the bulk of the capital was borrowed. No large profit was ever made from its operation because silk prices remained low and interest on the debt had to be paid, but nevertheless many changes in village life were felt. More than 350 women had worked in family silk raising, but the factory needed only 70 employees to produce the same amount of silk. This is a saving to the community, in a sense, but to nearly 300 households it means nothing more than unemployment of the women. Family life was altered, but, more important, there came to be an increasing movement of unmarried girls to the city to become wage earners in the factories there.

The increase in the amount of wage working, and the realization by nonwage workers that such work might become possible, have been among the most noticeable consequences of this relatively small bit of industrialization. Husband and wife, under the circumstances, come to have a geographic and financial mobility, even if only potential, which does not leave them so utterly dependent on the husband's parents. Lapses in filial piety are, in recent times, the most frequently decried aspect of modernism. Associated with this is an increasing independence of women. Along with the sporadic, but nevertheless real, wage-working opportunities is a vision of further change along these lines, particularly as increasing freedom is seen to be related to an increase in prosperity, itself a desirable state.

The prosperity has not come, however, except to rare individuals. The bulk of the population remains caught in the so-called agrarian problem of increasing attrition of population upon the land, which the slow and small-scale introduction of factories could not alleviate. The vision of greater prosperity and independence, for China as a nation as well as for small localities such as Kaihsienkung, has now become translated into terms of political revolt. Can China ever match the industrial expansion of the West? A grave disadvantage is the lack of capital and raw materials; a possible advantage is that she may avoid errors or bypass stages of development which the West passed through.

It is certain that for some time to come the costs of industrialization must be borne by the peasants. The poverty of the peasant masses for this reason will probably not be alleviated soon, any more than it was in Russia. But perhaps, as in Russia, the fervor for change, particularly toward the ideals of social and economic equality, will sustain the new regime through a long period of economic crisis. Clearly, the Communist government of China is determined to try. It is unfortunate that at this writing there is no reliable information available to us which would permit a further description of changes undertaken by the present People's Republic which have affected villages such as Kaihsienkung.

The above paragraphs stand as they were written for the original edition in order to emphasize an astounding piece of good fortune: as the second edition was being prepared, a manuscript became available that does in fact provide reliable information about recent changes in Kaihsienkung under the People's Republic.

This restudy should be of great interest, and several pages will be devoted to a summary of it.

In 1956, the anthropologist W. R. Geddes joined a New Zealand cultural group for a visit to China that was sponsored by the Chinese People's Association for Cultural Relations with Foreign Countries. In Peking he was given permission to visit Kaihsienkung for four days. He made the most of this opportunity by using local volunteer helpers to make a census and collect information by means of questionnaires prepared in advance, while he and his interpreter visited, observed, questioned, "spending all the days and most of the nights in unremitting investigations." The hospitable villagers seemed pleased with this attention, and no difficulty was encountered in getting information from them. Cross-checking techniques were used to ensure reliability of all data, however, in accordance with modern field methods.

Economic changes in the village have been considerable. The silk factory was destroyed during the Japanese occupation and was not re-established. The seasonal migration in search of odd jobs in other areas or in the city has ended. On the other hand, real household income achieved in the local agricultural system has risen more than 60 percent. This amelioration of the previous peasant distress was accomplished by the cooperative system. Production is now augmented by the use of animal labor in the fields, water control by machinery, and better manuring, all of which require such capital as to have been beyond the means of the individual farmers. The cooperative also plans differential utilization of the total planting area and efficient deployment of the labor force, which also has resulted in increased total production. The rice yield has increased by at least 100 percent (the figures showed 120 percent), and more diversified kinds of vegetables also augment the diet.

It is apparent that there is widespread support for the cooperative system and that this support is largely due to its actual economic success. Peasants are hardheaded and cautious, particularly in Kaihsienkung, and they continually balance what is promised against what is achieved. This careful attitude is manifested by the fact that the same rigid population control practiced in 1936 has continued and the population in 1956 was nearly the same as it was before. But considering the traditionalism of peasants anywhere and the deep feeling of attachment to family land in China particularly—or what Mao Tse Tung called "the natural tendency of the peasant toward capitalism"—it does seem remarkable that individual rights to land were given up in the first place, apparently willingly, *before* the economic benefits were demonstrated.

The development of the peasant cooperatives in China was planned to progress gradually through four phases, and this was the key to its success. The first phase was the abolition of land-lordism and the redistribution of land. This of course is only a temporary palliative, for it does not ensure a continual rise in production. But, needless to say, it was a development most welcome to the villagers, for in 1936 the peasants were already losing control of their land to absentee landlords and brokers, so that many had only a tenant's status.

The second phase of the program was the voluntary formation of mutual-aid teams of villagers. These teams worked together on the land of the members, while the produce of each field still belonged to the owner. The advantages of planning at this stage resulted in some increase in production.

The third phase involved the cooperative working of all the fields according to a master plan. Each owner received a share of the total produce in proportion to the amount of land owned. A further rise in production occurred because of the planning of the whole enterprise.

The fourth phase was to complete the collectivization of the land. Produce was no longer to be allocated by amount of land owned but in accordance with the amount and value of the work contributed. Interestingly, former landlords were allowed to participate. This phase has been completed in Kaihsienkung, with the exception of one peasant who continues to work his own land. He is regarded as a "negative force" but not as a "counter-revolutionary."

Each phase resulted in an alleviation of previous hardships for the peasants; presumably this was the main reason they joined the cooperative movement. But there were other reasons as well. Once on its way, the cooperative benefited from governmental aid that could only be granted in terms of large-scale work. Pumps for irrigation, chemical fertilizers, campaigns against insects, and so on became investments of the community as a whole. Once on its way, too, the pressure of the cooperative as a majority of the community against its delinquent members must have been considerable.

Governmental and Party propaganda also probably played some part in inducing people to join the cooperative, but one may suspect that this factor was not strong at first. Most of the peasants were illiterate and like other peasants in the world they were ingrown, tradition-bound, and suspicious of outsiders. But with the success of the cooperative this situation has been changing, and it will continue to change, probably quite rapidly, as the younger, now-literate, generation becomes fully adult.

Geddes recounts that on entering the village one is struck by the number of huge posters exhorting the people to "Get Educated! Wipe out Illiteracy!" The practical means of education are much improved over those of 1936. There are classes for adults at the school as well as informal teaching volunteered by educated persons. The cooperative itself has a library. The people are eager to learn, and literacy is spreading rapidly. The majority of adults (as of 1956) can now read and write at least simply. The education of children is much more intense than formerly. The present school has four teachers, three classrooms, and 116 pupils. Attendance is consistent, although it is not compulsory.

An interesting matter is the enthusiasm of the children for membership in the Chinese Pioneers, an organization for boys of 9 to 15 years. The Pioneers are sponsored by the Communist Party and have ideals, something like Boy Scouts, of service to the nation and to the local public. The Five Loves—for the Motherland, the People, Science, Labor, and Public Property—are fostered.

So far as adults are concerned, the changeover to a Communist-directed state is largely to be judged as an economic benefit. On the political-ideological side there has been less effect, for it must be remembered that arguments pro and con about liberal democracy *vs.* Marxism-Leninism and policy about international affairs are remote from the present understanding of the Chinese peasants. Particularly, it should be remembered that they have never known democracy at first hand. In fact, today the people of Kaihsienkung participate much more in the political organization than ever before.

There are now equal voting rights for women. There is also much freer eligibility for administrative office because of the removal of the status barriers which before had kept the majority of peasants from holding any sort of office. The village of Kaihsien-kung has 30 elective administrative sections. The village itself has a headman who is elected every two years. Elections above the county level are indirect; the voting is by the lower administrative officers.

Many of the changes since 1936 are those described in Fei's study as beginnings, but now they are further advanced. There is now a much higher status for women, an increased decline in the authority and status of the aged, and a lessening of the importance of kinship ties beyond the household. These are in a sense negative alterations in that they represent a continued breakdown of the old order.

But sometimes the changes would seem to be related to, or at least encouraged by, communist ideology. The increased freedom for women is related to freer choice in marriage; the matchmaker is no longer used, and there is no bargaining. Similarly, the ancestor cult of the continuity of fire and incense is in eclipse. The representation of the kitchen god is still kept above the stove, but the people profess little interest in it. The government tolerates religious beliefs of any kind but does not encourage them. Atheism, however, is freely promulgated where it had not been before, although probably not as forcefully as in Russia. It should be mentioned in this regard that there was a very powerful state-church monopoly on religion in pre-Revolutionary Russia, and it strongly opposed the revolution. There was nothing like this in China, for China has long had numerous religious sects with a long tradition of tolerance among them, and with no governmental influence by any of them except in the most philosophical sense.

The direction of cultural changes in such Chinese rural areas as Kaihsienkung seems to be largely toward modernity. Many of the changes are even quite familiar to the Western World, with the exception of the new form of land tenure. And so far as the evidence goes, this latter change seems likely to succeed simply because of its superiority to the previous system of absentee land-lordism and extreme fragmentation of holdings. Geddes ends his manuscript fittingly on this note:

. . . it does seem that the people of Kaihsienkung are today very much better off materially than they were twenty years ago and they have much greater security. This situation reduplicated thousands of times over China constitutes the greatest strength of the Communists and their greatest achievement. They have brought succor to the countryside. I hope it will also eventually constitute their greatest memorial."[6]

FURTHER READINGS

Buck, J. L., *Chinese Farm Economy,* Chicago, 1930.
Buck, J. L., *Land Utilization in China,* Chicago, 1937.
Cressey, G. B., *Land of 500 Million,* New York, 1955.
Fei, H. T., *Peasant Life in China: A Field Study of Country Life in the Yangtze Valley,* New York, 1946.
Fei, H. T., and Chang, C. I., *Earthbound China,* Chicago, 1945.
Fried, M. H., *Fabric of Chinese Society,* New York, 1953.
Geddes, W. R., *Peasant Life in Communist China,* Society for Applied Anthropology, Monograph No. 6, Ithaca, N.Y., 1963.
Hsu, F. L. K., *Under the Ancestor's Shadow,* New York, 1948.
Hsu, F. L. K., "China," in R. Linton (ed.), *Most of the World,* New York, 1949.
Latourette, K. S., *The Chinese, Their History and Culture,* New York, 1946.
Levy, M. J., *The Family Revolution in Modern China,* Cambridge, 1949.
Lin, Y. H., *The Golden Wing,* London, 1948.
Tawney, R. H., *Land and Labor in China,* London, 1932.
Yang, M. C., *A Chinese Village,* New York, 1945.

[6] The manuscript by Geddes has been published since the above passages were written. The quoted section is from p. 56 of W. R. Geddes (see *Further Readings*).

21

A Village in India

The attempt to describe an Indian village points up one of the major difficulties faced by the ethnologist in investigating a social group which is a part of an old, great, and complicated civilization rather than the self-contained, relatively homogeneous society of most primitive tribes. Even a single village in such a nation as India is extremely complex. The village itself has a unity, to be sure, but many of the women are from other communities; every individual in the village belongs to a caste, and with several castes represented in a village there are a great many variations in custom which are determined outside the village; and finally, in many Hindu villages there is a body of Moslem adherents, so that two quite distinct religious systems exist side by side in the same village.[2]

Shamirpet is a village of about 2500 people, centrally located on the Deccan plateau about 25 miles from the city of Hyderabad. The language spoken over most of the region is Telugu, but many also speak Urdu, in north India spoken chiefly by Moslems, as a second language. Otherwise, Shamirpet has most of the usual characteristics of rural communities in central and peninsular India. The village social structure is made up of typical occupational

[1] Most of the data in this chapter are taken from S. C. Dube, *Indian Village*, London, 1955.

[2] The emphasis in this chapter is on the Hindu community. The small group of Moslems is mentioned at times, but only in order to point up some aspect of their relations with the Hindus.

castes. Among the Hindu population, about 1400 people belong to the *clean castes,* and about 680 are *untouchables.* The castleless Moslems number about 340. Two of the lowest of the clean castes are people recently assimilated from tribal societies. This agglomeration of varying peoples into the caste system is one of the ways by which the complex ethnic and cultural melange of India has been formed.

Shamirpet is not an ancient village, though its ways are ancient. According to legend, it was founded about 350 years ago when the Moslem ruler of Hyderabad caused a large irrigation reservoir to be constructed. Many of the people who had worked on the project built homes near it and were joined by other settlers who were attracted by the irrigation facilities. The village remained a feudal estate belonging to a noble Moslem family until 1948, when Hyderabad was incorporated into the Republic of India. Since then Shamirpet has had no hereditary ruler, but is under the jurisdiction of the modern district administration.

The countryside is characteristic of the Deccan plateau. Fertile green fields, barren rocks, clumps of tall palmira trees and evergreen shrubs, and the great numbers of lakes and reservoirs which dot the region make a varied and picturesque sight. The rainfall averages about 25 inches annually, and the climate is warm all the year, though not usually uncomfortably so.

The closest ethnic ties of the people of Shamirpet are to the other Dravidian-speaking peoples of India whose ancient kingdoms contributed much to the complex of Indian civilization. Racially, the people of the region represent a rather homogenized mixture of many elements. The Moslems of the region are descended mostly from local converts rather than from the northern immigrants, and so they do not differ greatly from the local Hindus in appearance.

In dress and ornamentation the Hindus and Moslems differ a good deal. The Hindu mode is variable according to wealth. All but the wealthiest men wear the standard long Hindu loincloth, or *dhoti,* and a vest or shirt. Girls wear a plain skirt and blouse. The wealthier families wear clothes of better quality and the mode differs particularly on dress-up occasions. Then the man is likely to wear a coat, and sometimes may change his dhoti for the *pyjama,* the thin pants from which the Western pajama style is derived.

The women of the wealthier families wrap themselves in the grace-ful, colorful *sari*. The Hindus ornament themselves heavily with gold and the less-expensive silver products of the local craftsmen. Earplugs and earrings, nose pins and rings, as well as bracelets, anklets, rings for both fingers and toes, heavy necklaces, and belts are worn, particularly by the women.

The Moslem population dresses without much variation within the group. Men wear loose pyjama trousers and a vest or shirt. Out of the intimacy of the home, the men also wear a long coat buttoned up to the neck and a round red fez or a black sheepskin cap. Girls wear tight pyjamas and a tunic which falls to the knees, and around the shoulders a thin scarf. Married women usually wear a sari and blouse, and because they must veil themselves in the presence of all but the closest relatives—observe *purdah*—they always wear out-of-doors a long garment which veils them from the crown of the head to the ground.

The village is not laid out in a definite plan. The wide main street is lined by the whitewashed stone buildings which house the various government offices, school building, post office, and constabulary, as well as the numerous small shops. In narrow, crooked lanes branch-ing from the main street are the residences of the people of the clean castes and of the Moslems. The two untouchable castes and a group of specialized hunters live in communities somewhat sepa-rated from the rest of the village. The narrow lanes of the town are frequently quite dirty because the householders often throw their refuse into them and use them as latrines as well. One of the untouchable castes has the duty of sweeping the streets and, aided by scavenging pigs and dogs, does fairly well, considering the circumstances.

The houses of the village are of three main types. The largest, a style known as *bhawanti,* usually is occupied by the well-to-do farmers and the more successful of the professional specialists. Most of the Moslem houses are of this kind. Frequently of as many as five or six rooms, the bhawanti stands inside a walled compound. Inside the compound, a courtyard contains a cattleshed, a toolshed, and the house itself. About a half-dozen of the finer homes have a pit latrine in the court. The house itself is of stone, with a tiled roof and a long veranda facing the courtyard. The rooms are so arranged that they enclose an inner patio on three sides. The furnishings of the rooms appear meager and comfortless. A few hard wooden chairs, stools, and benches suffice for seating. The most ornate item is usually the bedstead. The furniture, the doors, and frequently even the walls are embellished with carvings and paintings.

The common house type of people of average income is also of stone and has a tiled roof, but it is much smaller and less ostentatious than the bhawanti. The courtyard plan is followed, but the property itself is only about half the size of the bhawanti. The usual house of the poor is the *gudse,* a one-room mud hut with a thatched roof. It contains little or no furniture and only a few household utensils.

Shamirpet is a larger and more complex village than Chan Kom. Agriculture is by far the most usual occupation, but many professional specializations exist. Pottery manufacture, stoneworking, barbering, trading, weaving, laundering, and herding are the principal nonagricultural tasks. Each of them pertains to a particular caste of the village, though many members of these castes do in fact sometimes cultivate varying amounts of land.

Rice and millet are the principal crops of the region. Maize, peanuts and other oil seeds, tobacco, and a large variety of vegetables and condiments are also grown. The villagers are sophisticated about fertilization and the use of irrigation, and the small plots of land have a high yield. Bullock-drawn wooden plows of the ancient style are still used by the villagers, and to a limited extent male water buffaloes are also used as draft animals. Cows and female buffaloes are milked and could provide an important protein element in the diet, but the cattle are in poor condition due to lack of good fodder and thus produce very little milk. Herds of goats and sheep are kept by the shepherd caste, and pigs are raised by *Erkalas,* a caste otherwise devoted to hunting and mat making. Many chickens are kept, and dogs are popular pets. The cat population of the village is large, but cats are not treated as pets.

The people of Shamirpet are not adequately nourished by modern scientific standards. Even the well-to-do suffer from subnutrition, and the rest of the population is in a state of mild malnutrition as well. Certain vitamins are in deficient supply, and both protein and fat intake is inadequate, particularly among the lower income brackets. Food habits and taboos, like other customs, are variable in the village. The *Brahmins* (priestly caste) and *Komtis* (trader caste) are complete vegetarians; they are forbidden even fish and eggs. All the Hindu population abstains from beef. The Moslems, on the other hand, eat beef but must not use pork. Fish and meat are very expensive, and many of those allowed to eat them seldom are able to. Milk and clarified butter (*ghee*) are prized by the whole population, but are so scarce and expensive that very few people can make them a part of the daily fare. Cheap vegetables, when in season, and lentil curries are the usual supplement to the predominantly rice diet of the bulk of the population.

The economic system of the village as a whole is closely related to the caste system. Most of the castes hold traditional monopolies over a major craft or occupation, although the members have some freedom to undertake certain subsidiary tasks, such as agricultural or wage work. All of the castes are intricately bound together in the functioning of the village economy. The measure, as well as the feeling, of reciprocity among them is very great—each has a role to play which is essential to the others. Each caste is endogamous, and because the village is small, it is frequent that a man must get his wife from another village. Ties of kinship, therefore, as well as the brotherhood of craft specialization, unite the members of castes between villages; but within the village itself, functional unity is created by an organic division of labor among castes. The behavior of members of one caste in a village to those of another is regulated by ancient traditions, most of which prescribe a considerable social distance nearly as rigid as the rule against intermarriage. A prominent feature of the relationship of castes is their hierarchical order.

Hindus believe that their ancient society was originally divided into five groups called *varnas* ("colors"). The first three of these, and the most important as well, were the Brahmins (priests and learned men), Kshatriyas (warriors and rulers), and Vaishyas (traders). These were considered the *twice-born* castes. The fourth group was of occupational castes or subcastes, lower than the above, but not classed as untouchables. In the fifth group were all the unclean, or untouchable, castes. In Shamirpet, the present system is more complex. The modern castes are arranged in the following order of superiority:

Twice-Born Castes
Brahmin (priests)
Komti (traders)

Occupational Castes

Kapu-Reddi (agriculturalists)	*Kummari* (potters)	*Golla* (shepherds)

Kapu-Mattarasi
(agriculturalists)

Sale (weavers)	*Gaondla* (toddy-tappers)
Sakali (washermen)	*Mangali* (barbers)

Vaddar (stoneworkers)	*Erkala* (hunters and mat makers)	*Pichha-Kuntla* (minstrels and storytellers)

Untouchable Castes

Mala (farm laborers)	*Madiga* (farm laborers, beggars)

All of the castes enumerated recognize the above order of superiority-inferiority. One of the most usual forms of recognition of this hierarchy is the refusal of a person to accept food from the hands of anyone of an inferior caste. The position of an individual is permanent; he is born into his caste and his status can never change, either upward or downward. Frequently, the castes have become subdivided in the past, so that most of the castes have endogamous divisions or subcastes, and sometimes they too are felt to be inferior or superior to other divisions of the same caste. Each of the castes and endogamous subdivisions is usually composed of exogamous groups of lineages which function as clans do in many primitive societies. The groups are named and members must marry into a different name group from their own.

Many of the services of members of the various castes are rendered without any immediate return. They represent an obligation of that caste and carry the expectation of reciprocal services from

471

other castes. An agriculturalist, for example, will get new implements periodically from the carpenter, pots from the potter, hair-
cuts from the barber, and so on; and later, after the twice-yearly
harvests, he gives appropriate shares to those who served him.
The affiliations between individuals become fixed and traditionalized and even descend in family lines through many generations.
Casual visitors who wish to engage a specialist for some piece of
work, however, must pay cash in advance; they will find that the
moneyless economy of reciprocity in which the villagers operate
does not mean they are not sharp dealers.

The small Moslem enclave is casteless and, within itself, even
relatively classless. The Moslems are generally in the higher-income
level of the village and, because the rulers of Hyderabad were
Moslems until recently, their self-view is a proud one. Many Moslems are traders, and others are among the more well-to-do agriculturalists. The Hindus have a much older religion and have a
feeling of superiority over the Moslems. Until 1948, the Moslems
had the political backing of the state, but after Hyderabad ceased
to be ruled by Moslems, the Hindus began freely to show scorn.
After a few years, however, the attitudes became less passionate,
although both groups remain convinced of their own inherent superiority. So far as the village social economy is concerned, the
Moslems are regarded as a kind of caste, roughly equivalent in
status to the Hindu agricultural castes. Moslem customs, such as
their disregard of caste traditions and their custom of parallel-
cousin marriage (Hindus prefer cross-cousin marriage), are ridiculed by the Hindus. Moslems are also regarded as ostentatious:
"A Muslim will eat stale rice inside his house, but when coming out
he will apply some clarified butter to his lips. Then he will belch
loudly and say, 'How much fried rice and meat have I eaten
today!'" Moslems, on the other hand, consider the Hindus cow-
ardly and mean.

The political organization of the village is composed of two
completely distinct sets of functionaries. One organization is that
which grows out of the village itself and which decides most normal
village affairs, social as well as ritual. The other is a group of six
representatives of the Indian government who are responsible for
tax collecting, official census records, and police functions. The
most important of these from the villagers' point of view is the

patwari, because he is the revenue and land-records official. Also appointed by the government is a group of 14 low-caste laborers who perform various menial tasks for the village.

The more purely local organization of functionaries begins with the office of village headman. This person is the richest in the village and has inherited his position from a long line of ancestors who held the office before him. His word is not law any longer, but he still enjoys a position of great influence in arbitrating village disputes. Usually, he does not make decisions of importance arbitrarily, however, but consults the village council, in which he plays the major role. The council, or *panchayat,* is composed of the richest and most influential persons in the town and the headmen of the various castes and religious cult groups—27 in all. The panchayat's functions are several: it helps the headman decide disputes which do not go to the government courts (and villagers try to avoid this last resort), it arranges the details of the village ceremonies, and it frequently takes the initiative in arranging for community-improvement projects. Although there are often several opposing factions contesting any decision, the minority nearly always yields, finally, in the interests of community cohesion. A good deal of social control is exercised also by the castes. Each caste is linked to its equivalent caste in other areas in the maintenance of the caste traditions, and each caste in the village has its hereditary headman who leads in the enforcement of these traditional rules of behavior. A breach of behavior by a person is often treated first by the caste headman; only the more serious cases go to the village council.

The social position of individuals is, of course, largely determined by caste membership. Nevertheless, it is possible to rise in status in the village by the acquisition of wealth. An untouchable Mala peasant who rose to become a prosperous agriculturalist is one of the most influential men in the village. He continues to observe all of the traditional forms of deference to those of higher castes—he is still an untouchable—but his voice in village deliberations is an effective one. Status differentiation also occurs with age. Elderly people are respected and are granted more authority than younger people. In general, too, a higher status within the caste system is achievable by the possession or refinement of certain highly regarded skills and personality traits. An ability to talk well is an asset, and a sense of humor is much appreciated. Education is coming more and more to be considered important, particularly because an educated man has an opportunity to rise to influence in government jobs, and also to assert his rights better in the modern world. In 1951–1952, however, the educated people in the village had had no more than four years of schooling in the village school.

At any given level, men normally have a higher status than women, particularly in public affairs. All political offices are held by men, and nearly all of the occupational activities which are public are carried out by men. Woman's work consists of household tasks, and any part she takes in the larger economy is typically indirect and secondary. The sexual division of labor is quite rigid; a man seen sweeping, drawing water, or cooking, for example, would be mercilessly ridiculed. It is equally unthinkable that a woman should handle a plow or appear in public selling something, although widowed or middle-aged women have freedom to do certain of man's tasks without censure when it is necessary.

Patterns of land ownership reveal considerable differentiation. Of the approximately 3000 acres pertaining to the village, more than one-fourth is owned by one family. Eight families own about 100 acres each, 20 families average 40 acres each, and 160 families own only five acres each. About 110 families are completely landless, and an equal number have less than five acres. Someone from nearly all of these latter families must work as an agricultural laborer or on shares with an owner, even though some other economic specialty is practiced. There are no absentee landowners in Shamirpet, however.

While the father is alive, land is owned and worked jointly by him and his sons. On the death of the father, however, the land, livestock, and implements are distributed equally among the sons, a practice which probably accounts in part for the large number of very small holdings. Land is sold only for the direst reasons, and when this is done, the whole household mourns. To the Indian peasant, earth is the mother and parting with a fragment of it is like a familial loss. Cattle, too, are treated almost like family members, and the death or sale of one can be the cause of real sorrow.

The normal family unit in Shamirpet, as in much of rural India, is patrilineal and patrilocal; the continuity of residence and land control is through the line of sons. In theory, the sons should remain living in the family compound to raise their own families in turn, even should there be several of them. This ideal joint household is not always found, however, particularly among the average and poorer families, inasmuch as the small packet of land and the meager village lot may not be able to contain them all. Frequently, too, domestic quarrels result in the breakup of the joint household. But estrangement does not last long, for the component units of the joint family, for whatever reason they separated, find it necessary to engage in a number of common enterprises. Feasts, festivals, and particularly rituals concerned with the major life crises of the birth, marriage, or death of one of the members bring them together frequently.

The birth of a child is celebrated with considerable ritual as well as elation, particularly if it is the first child born to a couple. Traditionally, boys are preferred. A daughter is considered less of an asset to the family because she will go to some other family on her marriage. In actual behavior, however, families do not seem to give more affection to boys than to girls. When a child is newly born, the mother and other members of the immediate family are considered to be ritually impure. On the third or fifth day after the birth, certain rites are performed which cleanse all the members of the family except the mother. On the twenty-first day (or the thirtieth in some castes), the child is given its name, its head is shaved, and it is installed in its new cradle. The mother is bathed ceremonially and becomes ritually pure again. The ceremony also involves a feast and singing by the assembly of friends and relatives. Several of the occupational castes participate as a matter of tradition: the Brahmin gives his astrological predictions for the future of the child; women of the barbers' caste act as midwives to the women of the clean castes; a barber shaves the child's head; Madigas play music; washermen take care of the linen and clothes.

Children are treated with great affection. The mother nurses the child whenever it shows the desire, and in general the infant is the focus of attentive delight of all the family. Sometimes a child is breast-fed until it is 4 or 5 years old. The indulgences come to a rather abrupt end at about 5 years of age, however. By then the child's mother may be occupied with another baby, and at any rate a 5-year-old is supposed to learn to get along with age mates, with whom he begins to play, and his family's emphasis shifts to teaching him to discriminate between proper and bad behavior. The father, particularly, becomes more authoritarian, and the child's attitude toward him becomes increasingly respectful as he grows older. The mother is primarily concerned with the training of daughters, particularly emphasizing the problems which will arise when they are married and must go to live among critical in-laws.

The onset of physiological puberty marks a significant change. A girl's first menstruation is signalized by elaborate ceremonies. First she is secluded for the duration of the period, after which she is bathed and dressed in new clothes. For several days the family worships its household gods, and finally the girl is taken with a procession of women to complete the ceremonies at the family shrine. The ceremony marks her attainment of womanhood, and she is considered ready for marriage. For boys the actual physiological signs of puberty are less noticeable and come more gradually, and their change in status is not ceremonialized so clearly as in the case of girls.

Adult status is the same as the married state—all full adults should be married. Most of the marriages among the Hindus are negotiated by the families concerned; ordinarily the young people have little choice. There have been a few cases of elopements, but they are always regarded as breaches of the established rules. The preferred marriage is of cross cousins, particularly with the mother's brother's daughter, but only about one-fifth of the recent marriages were with cross cousins—most of them were between unrelated or more distantly related families. In all cases, a boy should marry a girl from a different village. In nearly all marriages, but particularly among the agriculturalists, the bride's family must furnish a dowry.

The ritual of Hindu marriage is somewhat variable from caste to caste, but among them all the general influence of old Sanscritic belief is apparent. The boy's parents usually begin the negotiations, and the ceremony itself is held in the bride's family home. Inasmuch as the boy's relatives often are not in their home village during the ceremony, the bride's family provides a house for them to live in. On the first day, a large dinner of welcome is served to the visitors, and the next day the rites begin. The first ritual is the worship of the bride's family patron-god, in which both bride and groom participate. The most important rite is the *lagnam,* during which the Brahmin chants religious verses and the groom ties a necklace of black beads, the symbol of married status, around the bride's neck and puts rings on the second toes of her feet. The final seal of religious authority takes place with the couple seated before a fire while the priest reads sacred verses amid burning incense. Several minor rites follow, and finally the bride is "given away" to her husband and his family to the accompaniment of sad leave-taking songs.

According to tradition, the husband's will should always be obeyed. He is the wife's master, and she is the faithful, submissive servant. Anyone in Shamirpet would say that this should be so; yet in actual behavior the husband is not nearly so authoritarian or the wife so docile. During the first few years of married life, the wife's independence is, of course, less than it is later when she has proved herself, has trained several children, and has grown to take an increasingly indispensable role in the household. If she is living in a joint household with her in-laws, her position is particularly delicate at first, but not so much because her husband is hard on her as because her mother-in-law is apt to be critically insistent on the traditional submissiveness of the young wife. Frequently, however, a married couple spend only the first few years in the joint household, preferring to set up an establishment of their own as soon as finances permit. Then, of course, the wife's greater independence is assured.

Both the Hindus and Moslems understand that death has physiological causes. It is only when the circumstances of a death are unusual that it is attributed to supernatural causes such as witchcraft or to the anger of gods. In the Hindu community, both cremation and burial of the dead are practiced. Children are always buried, but in the Brahmin and Komti castes the adult dead are usually cremated. In general, aged or rich and respected persons are cremated, but the untouchables and other lower castes commonly practice burial.

When a person dies, the news is sent to friends and relatives, and the corpse is washed, dressed in finery, and tied to a wooden or bamboo bier, covered with a new cloth, and decorated with flowers. A procession accompanied by musicians, if these can be afforded, takes the bier to the graveyard or cremation ground. Before the bier is placed on the pyre or in the grave, the male heir of the deceased sprinkles water around the pit or pyre three times. A near kinsman sets fire to the pyre, or if it is a burial, all the relatives help fill the grave. As the people return home, they stop for a purificatory bath on the way. If the death occurred at an auspicious date and time of day, it is believed that the soul goes directly to the Supreme Being; otherwise it hovers around the roof of the house for 11 to 13 days.

On the third day after the death, the house is ritually purified by cleaning it, washing all linens and clothes, and disposing of all the kitchen pots. On the eleventh or thirteenth day, depending on the day the soul is to leave the vicinity of the house, food and water are offered the soul, and the near relatives cut their hair and bathe, and a final feast is held. Among the higher castes, the relatives collect the deceased's bones from the cremation grounds and immerse them in a holy river. In some cases a wealthy family takes the bones all the way to the Ganges, the holiest river in India. During the next village *petramasa* festival, a day dedicated to ceremonies in honor of the ancestors, the members of the deceased's family put on an elaborate ritual to call the spirit to take up its abode in the household shrine along with the other ancestors.

An unusual form of death, or any other inexplicable calamity or repeated bad luck, is taken to be the work of supernaturals. Ancestor spirits may become hostile to the living relatives if they are not honored properly; village goddesses may retaliate against offenses; unfavorable stars may be the cause of bad luck. The Brahmin is the person who can divine the cause and prescribe the action to be taken. Usually the remedy is simple. Ancestor spirits are easily placated by an apology followed by worship. Village goddesses usually require the sacrifice of a sheep or goat before their anger is appeased. If unfavorable stars were the cause of the misfortunes, fasting and specific rituals recommended by the Brahmin are followed. Ordinarily, the Brahmin is consulted before a person plants crops or begins any important undertaking to insure that the stars will be in auspicious order.

Witchcraft and the action of malevolent ghosts require more drastic steps. As in the concept of witchcraft in so many other parts of the world, the witch or sorcerer is possessed of secret formulas and endeavors to remain unknown, though people may suspect who is the malefactor. Ghosts are more difficult to handle; the usual technique is simply to avoid them, but some of them have been tamed and are thus in the service of some persons. The ghosts are thought of as the vengeful spirits of dead people who were dissatisfied at the time of death. Pregnant women, suicides, persons who died hating someone, and those cut down in the prime of life by murder, drowning, or lightning are apt to become ghosts.

Many difficulties of daily life that lead people to request supernatural help are met by private or family rituals of prayer and small sacrifices to ancestors or gods. Often people fast, or vow to fast, if a specific wish is fulfilled or difficulty overcome.

Hindu religion is a great and variable congeries of disparate elements. To the usual folk beliefs in ghosts, demons, and ancestor spirits has been added a great nationwide overlay of Hindu national gods and goddesses, festivals, scriptures, prayers, and ceremonies. Additionally, many castes, localities, and families form unique cult groups in any given community. The Islamic religion contrasts sharply with this loose and heterogeneous complex. The Moslems of Shamirpet belong to the Sunni sect and are to follow their sect's interpretations of religion as explained in the Koran.

Except for the Brahmins, the Hindus have no fixed time of worship, and only a few people visit the village temple for daily devotions. The gods are appealed to only at times of difficulties and during the village festivals. As practiced in a village such as Shamirpet, Hinduism is not the classic metaphysical system, but a rather mechanical religion of fasts, feasts, festivals, and prescribed rituals which cover critical periods of life. Spiritualism is not the keynote so much as practicality.

The religious festivals are of three major types: family ceremonies, caste ceremonies, and village ceremonies. Family and caste festivals are too numerous and variable in content for adequate description here. Village festivals are much less frequent, but more significant in community life, inasmuch as everyone participates, including the Moslems. Perhaps the most important of the three large yearly village festivals is that devoted to *Pochamma,* the goddess of smallpox. The Moslems, not supposed to believe in Hindu gods, are as fearful as the other villagers of the local gods and goddesses; therefore they participate in this festival.

479

Preparations begin early on the day chosen for the festival. Each family takes a new clay pot, colors it with fanciful decorations, and fills it with rice as an offering to the goddess. A special priest, meanwhile, goes around the village collecting rice for a common village offering and oil for burning the lamps near the shrine. Before the time chosen for the worship itself, the drummers of the Madiga caste begin beating their drums to call the people to a central place in the village. When all have arrived carrying their pots of rice (*bonam*), a procession is formed to follow the drummers through the village. As they near the shrine, some of the people become possessed of the spirit and fall into a trance. At the shrine itself, the presiding priest offers the goddess the common bonam of rice collected earlier. The bonams of individual families are then presented by the priest, one at a time in the hierarchical order of the castes, and within each caste in the order of descending status of the individual families. The priest's choices in this precedence frequently create difficulties and even enmities between families. Sheep and goats are sacrificed by the shepherd caste on behalf of the entire village, and individuals do the same for their families. The heads and forelimbs of the animals are left at the shrine, but the rest of the meat, as well as the rice, is taken home by each family for a feast.

The India-wide Hindu belief in the three manifestations of divinity is present in Shamirpet: Brahma is the creator; Vishnu, the sustainer; and Shiva, the destroyer. Rama and Krishna are the principal incarnations of Vishnu worshiped. The most important Hindu philosophical concepts are also found in the villagers' ethos. One of the most prominent of these is the doctrine of *karma,* the notion that one's destiny in the next life depends on one's actions in the present life. On the face of it, this would seem to direct one's attention to his choices and invoke a strong conception of free will. Yet coupled with this aspect of karma is the companion idea that actions in a past life govern one's character in the present. Frequent remarks are: "If it is written in our fate, we must submit to it. Human effort cannot alter the will of God. What is predestined must have its course." Such conceptions do not, of course, prevent the people from trying to solve their problems, but it does rationalize the spirit of resignation which overtakes them when they fail to overcome their difficulties.

Transmigration and multiple rebirth are firm beliefs among the Hindus—life is a never-ending process of linked existences. A person who behaves ethically will go to heaven or become reborn into a family of high caste. Persons who behave badly will go to hell or be reborn into a lower caste, or, if their actions were quite reprehensible, into one of the lower animal species.

WINNOWING GRAIN. *Courtesy, United Nations*

The villagers' concepts of heaven and hell are vivid. Heaven is a happy place. "In heaven you have only to desire a thing and the next moment you find it there. All people in heaven live in luxurious palaces where an army of countless servants looks after all their comforts. There you have the choicest foods, and the best of everything." A person of an untouchable caste believed that "You can get all the rice that you want to eat, and all the sweets. And you can do what you like for there are no officials to curse you and abuse you." Hell, on the contrary, is a horrible place. It is not the abode of a devil, however, who captures or entices souls away from God. Hell is composed of hundreds of compartments, each more dramatically fearful than the next, but a sinner is consigned there by God, and His merciless wardens move the unfortunate sinner from one torture to another.

Hinduism differs in one particularly salient respect from Islam and Christianity. As noted, the Hindus of Shamirpet live in surprising amiability in the same village with the Moslems. Despite their conviction of superiority, they do not crusade or proselytize, send missionaries, or otherwise attempt to convert unbelievers. The religion is an extremely elastic amalgam of many kinds of gods and demons, local rituals and customs. Were the small Moslem group less independent-minded, it seems likely that they and most of their special rituals and beliefs could be absorbed into Hinduism to become merely one more of the great number of special sets of customs.

Hinduism does have a consistent emphasis on moral and ethical behavior, however, despite the willingness to accept strange new gods and rituals. The correct action which will insure a fortunate afterlife is called *dharma*. Dharma counsels such meritorious behavior as following the caste traditions; pious observance of fasts, festivals, pilgrimages, and ritual bathing; and avoidance of ritual pollutions, such as dining with a person of a lower caste. Some taboos are peculiar to particular castes, but some are village-wide prohibitions of such crimes against society as murder, violence, and incest. In general, dharma may be said to prescribe the *right way* and to prohibit sin.

India had frequently been stereotyped as a timeless land with its fatalistic people embedded in an unyielding crust of ancient custom. But today the new position of the Hindu nation in world affairs, independently following its difficult neutralist policy, is one evidence of modern changes in India of which everyone is aware. But what is happening in the Indian microcosm, a village like Shamirpet?

First, it must be recognized that many of the changes involved in the recent and dramatic emergence of India as a nation had their beginnings long before the present epoch of post-World War II colonial upheavals. India had been a crossroads of momentous cultural influences and commerce and conquests for centuries. In prehistory, it is likely that the great civilizations of the Indus River, such as Mohenjo-Daro, were the work of immigrants. The Vedic invasions were the most influential later, but probably were only some among many. Of the historically known invasions, Alexander the Great's conquest in 326 B.C. had only a few permanent effects; but after the twelfth century A.D., when the Moslem penetration finally resulted in the dominion of Islam over nearly all of India under the so-called

Mogul Empire, a considerable cultural, as well as political, influence was felt which has lasted until the present day, even in such small communities as Shamirpet.

A second wave of very different influence, this time from western Europe, began with the Portuguese conquest of Goa in 1510. British, Dutch, and French commercial interests soon joined in competition for India's commerce, and finally the British East India Company became dominant. The British Empire in India followed in 1757. The long rule of the British has, in one way or another, affected many aspects of Hindu national culture, particularly law, government, and economics. Since the withdrawal of the British and the 1947 division of India into Moslem Pakistan and Hindu India, the stresses and strains have been numerous, partly because of the new problems of relations between Hindus and Moslems in many parts of the peninsula, and partly because of the economic and social changes of the sort which are now occurring in all of the formerly dependent areas of the world.

Shamirpet itself, a part of the semiautonomous independent state of Hyderabad, was not so much affected by British rule as some other parts of India, and the rise of the national independence movement, particularly the influence of Gandhi and the Congress Party, had less immediate effect there than in the rest of India. The most important political event was the abolition of feudal landlordism in 1948, when Hyderabad became a part of the India Union and the privileged position of the Moslems was ended. Welfare activities, governmental and police jurisdiction, and even agricultural development programs became acceptable in Shamirpet. In 1951 the villagers voted for the first time in history, in this case to elect their representatives to the Union Parliament and to the state legislature.

Communication with the city has improved in recent years. In addition to the age-old bullock carts, which are still widely used, there are a 1928-model Ford belonging to the village headman, 10 bicycles, and a bus service. People have seen the circus and the cinema in the city. The village has three phonographs, and in one of the tea shops there is now a crystal radio. Modern Western dress is frequently worn by younger members of the higher castes. Here and there one may see sun glasses and fountain pens; even safety razors and flashlights are owned by a few people.

Some purely economic innovations are accompanying these more visible changes. Mill-made cloth from the city is gradually replacing the local weaving. One rarely finds the natives engaged in spinning, which used to be the nearly incessant leisure-time activity. Barbers, carpenters, blacksmiths, and goldsmiths now use more factory-made tools and instruments. More money must circulate to sustain these changes. Consequently, a greater percentage of cultivators now grow crops for cash, and they try to increase production through the use of improved seeds and various chemical fertilizers. No significant change is noted in agricultural tools, but this may be because a much greater capital outlay would be required.

Modern scientific concepts of diseases and their treatment are making some headway against the folk medical superstitions. To be sure, most people still believe that smallpox and cholera are the result of the wrath of the two goddesses, but people no longer run and hide on the arrival of a government vaccinator. Injections, in fact, are eagerly sought as quick and sure relief for any and all ailments. This rapid acceptance of, and even enthusiasm for, injections has been noted, incidentally, in many other peasant communities all over the world. The folk remedies, chants, fasting, protective magic, and so on are still being used against disease as well; peasant people do not usually regard science and magic as two different philosophies in conflict, but, rather, modern medicine is merely newer than the other. Frequently, the age-old remedies are tried first, but a sick person who takes a turn for the worse will accept scientific medicine or even go to the city hospital when the other remedies have failed.

The social organization of the village as represented in family and caste relations is changing slightly, mostly by a sort of loosening of principles; but the caste system is not broken down yet. A few new occupations, which cannot be fitted into the castes, and a slightly increased economic and geographic mobility have made it possible for some people to ignore the more rigid aspects of caste. The Constitution of the Republic of India has legally abolished untouchability, and although it is still in evidence in Shamirpet, it is sure to become a less effective taboo in the near future.

The isolated bits of modernity now creeping into the daily lives of the people of Shamirpet have not as yet been sufficient in number, weight, and momentum to alter the structure of the rural ethos. The boundaries of the universe, temporal as well as spatial, remain close to Shamirpet for the bulk of the people. Caste mythology is the nearest thing to history, and the traditions and social institutions are thought to have originated when humankind itself first appeared on the earth. National consciousness is still vague; there are people in the village who do not know the names Mahatma Gandhi and Jawaharlal Nehru.

Courtesy, United Nations

In contrast to the modern ethos of the Western world, which seeks to control nature, the fundamental element in the thought of the villagers is the aim of adjustment of the individual to the universe and to the society which is a part of it—the notion of dharma.

485

When something radically disruptive happens, it is usually attributed to fate rather than some positive volition. All forms of relationship between things, individuals, or groups of people are fitted into a hierarchical structure. The most obvious sign of this is, of course, the caste system, but the same view is extended to gods, animals, even foods. Even though recent changes modify some of the harshness in the treatment of an untouchable by a person of high caste, the idea of dominance and submission remains essentially the same.

Such fundamental Western concepts as the "rights of man," or "All men are created equal," are still incomprehensible to the villagers. The traditional way is the right way; any deviation from it is into a blind alley. But this is the ethos, and human beings have always found it possible to maintain a world view and rationale of existence at the same time that acts contradictory to them are performed. Individuals in Shamirpet now readily adopt items of modern civilization, and as the changes in urban and national India increase, so too will the effects on Shamirpet become more apparent.

FURTHER READINGS

Dube, S. C., *Indian Village*, London, 1955.

Dube, S. C., *India's Changing Villages*, Ithaca, 1958.

Gough, E. K., *The Social Structure of a Tanjore Village*, in McK. Marriot (ed.), *Village India: Studies in the Little Community*, Chicago, 1955.

Hutton, J. H., *Caste in India*, Cambridge, 1946.

Marriott, McK. (ed.), *Village India: Studies in the Little Community*, Chicago, 1955.

Radhakrishnan, Sir S., *The Hindu View of Life*, New York, 1927.

Rawlinson, H. G., *India: A Short Cultural History*, New York, 1938.

Thorner, D. and A., "India and Pakistan," in R. Linton (ed.), *Most of the World*, New York, 1949.

Conclusion
Contemporary Ancestors and Primitive Contemporaries

It should be repeated that the societies chosen for this book were intended to represent a good sample of standard well-known ethnological materials. This attempt included a range of societies from simple to complex, and with ecological and culture-area diversity as well. But a warning should now be posted that these criteria of diversity are somewhat at cross-purposes with another implied use of the book: that is, the sample of societies is not ideal for the comparative method. In fact, the problem of sampling is at present the single most imposing methodological problem in the study of cultural evolution. An obvious difficulty is that the descriptive literature at our disposal is uneven in quality and reliability and is not fully representative of all kinds of aboriginal societies; and of course our sample must be of the books that are, not the societies that might have been.

The comparative method was originally a product of evolutionary thought, with information about contemporary primitive peoples being used for creative thinking about past ages. Aristotle used this method consciously and carefully in his *Politics,* as did Thucydides in *The Peloponnesian War*. Later classic examples are Hobbes, Locke, Ferguson, Lafitau, Rousseau, and Turgot. In more modern times the French historian, Marc Bloch, was a foremost proponent of the technique, which he named the "regressive method." All of the above used incomplete and naive accounts by travelers, missionaries, soldiers, captives, and so on (although Bloch made his own observations as well) and were therefore liable to mistakes of fact. On the other hand, "scientific" ethnographies by trained observers describe mainly the remnants of societies that somehow survived and adapted themselves to the European colonial and imperial expansions. It is therefore impossible to make a fully satisfactory sample of kinds of aboriginal cultures from modern descriptions. But the fact that there are methodological dangers in the use of early accounts and inadequate numbers in modern accounts of relatively pristine aboriginal societies does not mean that we should give up; rather, caution and criticism should preempt mechanical statistics.

The original edition of this book did not explain the basis of the classification of the societies into evolutionary levels or stages. Its sole aim was to provide a sample of widely differing kinds of cultures for whatever purposes the instructor had in mind; it seemed undesirable as well as unnecessary to commit him to any particular theoretical point of view. Many teachers have since asked me to supply an explanation of the classification, however, and so it appears here for whatever uses it may have.

The theoretical basis of the classification is simple and involves but a few assumptions. The first human beings had a simple, rudimentary culture based on hunting, the collecting of wild vegetables, and perhaps fishing. This cultural economy spread over most of the globe, as attested by archaeology. It is assumed that the population must have been thin and the residential groups small, only a very few of such groups having been allied in any larger unity. Some technical improvements occurred throughout the Paleolithic era, but it was not until the ability to domesticate plants and animals was achieved—the so-called Neolithic revolution—that any substantial part of human society was enabled to transcend the social level of bands to form true tribal societies. Presumably a few areas of especially high natural productivity, such as the Northwest Coast of North America, were exceptions to this; but it was the Neolithic technology of plant and animal husbandry, nevertheless, which made a widespread transformation of society possible, and tribal societies then began to occupy space formerly used by hunters and gatherers. Large areas of the world remained, however, that were not productive under primitive plant or animal husbandry, and there the hunt-ing-gathering, Paleolithic-like culture persisted. Thus finally about 8,000–10,000 years ago two quite different kinds of societies, Paleo-lithic-like bands and Neolithic tribes, existed contemporaneously. Out of tribal society grew a new and different society, larger than the tribal, more complex, with its parts integrated in a new way. Presumably a higher productivity of labor became possible through centralized direction, specialization, and redistribution of products from the center. Being larger and more firmly integrated, these new societies, *chiefdoms,* rapidly displaced or transformed tribes, just as tribes had replaced bands in the areas adaptively favorable to the tribal form of production and organization.

From chiefdoms arose the state-organized societies, and after these came the great empires of archaic civilization. All these forms of society appeared successively and spread into areas occupied by some proportion of the previous kinds of societies. But it is evident that not all of the former societies were replaced. Today, some representatives of all these stages remain, and they can be so classified.

The latter assumption is undoubtedly one that will be the most difficult for some anthropologists to accept, because we are ac-customed to saying that "cultures are always changing" and, there-fore, that a modern primitive society cannot be taken as an example of an ancient type. But I do not think they are *always* changing in important respects. The notion of adaptation must be fundamental to any concept of evolution. Any society occupies an environment and tends to undergo its cultural changes in adjustment to that environment until it is successful (survives competition) in it, after which it resists change. And certainly ethnographic literature in-cludes remarkable examples of this cultural conservatism.

It is true, of course, that cultures have changed: evolution is itself a kind of change. But surely *all* cultures are not *always* changing; if they were, we could not account for the presence in modern times of bands, tribes, and so on, without assuming some sort of mental incapacity on the part of the people themselves. And we know from a great deal of evidence that this would be an unsound assumption. Hence, the evolutionary perspective is useful in suggesting a kind of classification of contemporaneous primitive cultures, which not only helps us to put them into an order based on significant similarities and differences, but also helps to account for the simultaneous presence of such disparate types of society. The theory of evolution in biology had a similar significance, suggesting a classification of extant forms of life at the same time as it helped to account for the differences that arose among them.

Although it would seem that the increasing productivity of labor via technological improvement accompanied the evolution of these successive levels, this greater harnessing of energy remains difficult to measure. What we are essentially interested in are the social *results* of the improvement. The results—or perhaps we should say the necessary concomitants—are the changes in the structural complexities of the societies. Such changes are readily apparent and make the best criteria for evolutionary status. All we need to grant now is that larger and more complex societies did in fact come about successively in certain areas at certain times, and that we can make a useful classification of them in the evolutionary terms suggested.

A further assumption is that a more complex structure has, almost by definition, greater specialization, differentiation, and integration in, for example, religion, art, and polity, as well as in the purely social realm. Naming the social structure of a culture—if the name is conceived broadly and definitively enough—can also serve to define its culture type in important respects.

The specific cultures described in this book were not chosen, it should be remembered, to be closely representative of the structural classification. Geographic and historical (or diffusional) determinants exist, and the examples contained herein were chosen purposely to show as wide a range as possible with regard to habitat, technological means of adaptation to habitat, and cultural traditions within each level. That is, the range of diversity at each level is as extreme as could be managed. If the classification still holds in the sense that there remain important cultural similarities among all of the examples within each level, in contrast to the adjacent levels, then it can be said that there is a "validity" to the classification, that it is intellectually useful.

Another source of cultural diversity hampers the present classification. All cultures in the modern world, primitive or not, are becoming increasingly affected by the expansion of modern industrial civilization. The adaptation of the more primitive cultures to this situation is exceedingly variable, because the industrial forces themselves are variable: some are commercial or otherwise indirect, and others are direct, as in the colonization or occupation of areas once controlled by indigenous populations.

Unfortunately the monographs available do not always describe a pristinely aboriginal culture, and in some cases the adaptation to civilization has progressed quite far. The chapters on the Arunta, Eskimo, Yahgan, Andamanese, Jivaro, Trobriand, Tahitian, Zulu, Maya, and Inca give quite good data on the aboriginal state of affairs, either because the societies were described at an early enough period, or because historical sources were used in the reconstruction of the culture. But other cultures—especially the Navaho, Kalinga, and Ashanti—are described in more recent times, and many of their cultural characteristics originated directly and indirectly in response to influences of civilization. The remainder of our examples lie somewhere between these extremes of aboriginality and acculturation. All are conventionally used in ethnological research and theory, however, and for that reason are presented in this book. But it should be recognized that the utility of the classification is not so great as it would be were all the societies equally representative of an aboriginal state of culture.

It was said that increasing structural complexity has been used as the main criterion of evolutionary classification. (This is also a frequent criterion of biological evolution. However, although this similarity is useful as an analogy, it is not a logical requirement that there be an identity in criteria of both biological and cultural evolution.) What do we mean by *structural complexity?* Simply stated, greater complexity implies more parts to the whole, more differentiation or specialization of these parts, and firmer integration of these parts within the whole. If it is true that more parts, and more differentiation of parts, ultimately evoke new forms or mechanisms of integration, then it may be that the forms of integration alone imply the levels of complexity.

It would seem that, in the course of cultural evolution, increasing size and density of the successively more evolved social bodies necessarily required increasing subdivision or segmentation—i.e., more parts—and increasing differentiation among them. This must have come about gradually, however variable the pace from one habitat to another. But the means by which the whole was integrated were, most likely, not as gradually evolved. In other words, the increased size, density, multiplication of parts, and so on probably went on under the same integrative means until those means failed to do the job. Kinship, for example, however extended via certain marriage rules or adoptions, can integrate a society only up to a certain point in its growth. After that, the society must fission into separate societies if growth continues. This kind of subdivision, more than likely, occurred many times throughout history. Only with the achievement of new integrative means can an increase in complexity keep pace with the growth. This is only a supposition; yet it would appear that qualitatively different means of integration have in fact been few in number in human society, and seem to compare well with the equal number of levels of societal complexity. Broadly, these appear to be five in number.[1] The *Band, Tribal, Chiefdom, Primitive State,* and *Archaic Civilization* or *Imperial* levels.

THE BAND LEVEL

Band society could be said to lie at the bottom of societal levels, as well as at the beginning, in the sense that it has no special integrative mechanisms except those common to all human societies. That is, the integration is primarily personal and largely familial, a characteristic of the sociality of all small groups of people, including those which are parts of a greater societal whole. Adopting a concept of J. H. Steward, we may call this the band level of socio-cultural integration.[2]

In all human social systems, some form of family raises children. But at any given time there are horizontal relationship ties between adults as well as vertical ties between adults and their children. Rules of exogamy and marital residence can extend, in time, the horizontal ties of kinship to include a relatively large number of people, or they can be so restrictive that kinship ties are intensified among a smaller group rather than dispersed and weakened. A residential group of cooperating families can establish ties, by means of intermarriage, with other residential groups so that amiable relations, consistent forms of etiquette, and perhaps co-

[1] Five, that is, prior to the present stage of national-industrial societies. These modern societies exhibit the previous forms of integration in various of their parts but also have powerful new integrative factors of the organismic kind, aspects of the extremely complex occupational network created by industrialization.

[2] Julian H. Steward, *Theory of Culture Change,* Urbana, Ill., 1955, chap. 3.

operation in economic endeavors and warfare is engendered. Thus kinship ties structured by various marriage rules are the integrating mechanism in band societies. The social bodies, the parts of the society, the differentiation of persons into statuses, and so on are all familial. There arise, of course, certain persons like curing shamans, "mighty hunters," and "dangerous men," but each one of these statuses is personal and idiosyncratic, disappearing when the person disappears. Social differentiation makes parts and statuses in the society that exist irrespective of the particular personnel who fill them. In band society these are familistic differentiations; every person is one or another kind of consanguinal or affinal relative.

The important characteristic of band society is its rudimentariness. In comparison with tribes, chiefdoms, and other successive levels, bands significantly lack other integrative means and are better understood once they are compared with the integrative means of higher levels of social structure.

THE TRIBAL LEVEL

Tribal society, unlike band society, has greater size, more subdivisions, and new forms of integration. Whereas band society is merely an association of familial residential units (themselves frequently called bands in anthropology), which ordinarily include only from 20 to 60 people loosely allied by marriage ties, a tribe consists of a much larger number of kinship and residential segments, each segment being composed of individual nuclear families. A tribe is in this way like a collection of a number of band societies. But, in another way, a tribe is not simply a collection of bands; it is a *supra*-band society. It is of a higher order because new forms of social differentiation have arisen, accompanied by new integrative means, that distinguish it as a tribe rather than as a number of bands. In the tribe, the band-like kinship segments of the society are only aspects of different *kind* of society; what was once the whole is now but a part of a new whole.

The new kinds of social ordering, which, in tribal society, perform integrative functions, are called *pantribal associations*. These organizations of people do not have a residential basis. Whereas residential groups, like households, patrilocal bands, neighborhoods, and villages, have as the primary basis of their organization the sheer physical fact of propinquity, associations do not. Residential groups such as households, for example, typically have some corporate functions like economic cooperation, childbearing, and so on; yet they are nevertheless formed in the first place by a complex congeries of determinants: biological needs, ecological and demographic necessities, technological manpower requirements, mutual defense, political dictation, and others. But obvious corporate functions do not single-handedly determine a household's structure. The residential basis, in other words, is influenced by several factors other than the explicit functions of the group. Associations, on the other hand, are organizations formed precisely to perform manifest functions: a sewing circle sews, a recreational club plays, and a volunteer fire brigade puts out fires. But for whatever purposes they are formed, they always have another latent or implicit function. Because they are made up of persons who are not organized due to mutual residence, they unify persons who belong to different residential groups.

Thus an important sociological significance of associations is that they always cross-cut some proportion of the society, allying persons from different groups who otherwise might not have any basis for sociability. Of course, some band societies also have associations— the Australian totemic ceremonial groups are a good example. But these are relatively limited in size and social significance; that is, they are not "pantribal." Societies above the tribal level may have an even greater number and variety of associations. But they are especially prominent at the tribal level because they are more numerous, larger, and more socially significant than among bands, and are not supplemented by other integrative means as they are in chiefdoms and states; they do the whole job in tribal society.

Pantribal associations are of such size that they are cut entirely across the tribe to its boundaries. Perhaps the most common example is the *clan*. A tribe may have a number of clans with every member of the tribe belonging to one clan or another. The clans have certain prescribed forms of interrelationships. Hence, all residential groups are cut across by clans, and all tribal members can be known to one another in terms of their clan relationships.

Not all tribes have clans, but all have some number of pantribal associations that serve a similar sociological function, for example, age-grades, kindreds, secret societies, and clubs for such single special purposes as the curing of illness or the performing of particular ceremonies. These all serve to unite persons who are members of different residential units.

Pantribal associations may or may not be based on concepts of kinship. Kinship associations are matrilineal or patrilineal clans, nonunilineal kindreds, and the more rare segmentary lineages (see "The Nuer of the Upper Nile River," Chapter 7). The others—those not based on kinship—are, typically, age-grade associations and the other special purpose clubs mentioned above.

The various rules of exogamy and marital residence which ally neighboring residential units in band society persist at the tribal level, but they alone cannot do the job of holding a larger society together, for the alliances formed by reciprocity become increasingly diffuse and attenuated as the number of residential groups is increased. Nor are tribes held together by the dominance of one group over another, and there are no permanent political-governmental institutions. The forms of leadership found at the tribal level are *charismatic,* based solely on the qualities of he who rises to lead some specific enterprise.

Pantribal associations are not only the sole means of uniting larger numbers of groups of people; they also serve to distinguish one tribe from another. This fact of social boundaries to the tribe is another point of differentiation of tribes from bands (the forms of alliance of groups in band society are so weak and personal that each society seems to shade off gradually to the next). It is hard to say, for example, just who the Arunta are, for they are merely a dialect division of a larger linguistic order. *The* Arunta are really a number of band societies united only by a vague sense of identity.

In contrast to higher social structures, a tribe is like a band in certain respects. A tribe is still largely familial; it remains egalitarian in that no one of the families or residential groups is politically superior or more powerful in hereditary rank than any other; and in neither tribes nor bands has differentiation of structure been carried to the point where there are separate bodies of political control, full economic specialization (other than that based on the universal age-sex differentiation), or even true religious professionals like members of a priesthood as distinguished from shamans. Tribes, like bands, are *segmental* in Durkheim's sense: the corporate residential units are alike, largely economically self-sufficient, gen-

495

erally equivalent in size and organization, and autonomous in large measure. In organization, tribes are advanced over bands in multiplication and integration of parts, but they are not strikingly advanced in specialization of parts.

THE CHIEFDOM LEVEL

The most obvious difference at the chiefdom level so interested Durkheim that he made a whole evolutionary scheme out of it. In contrast to the above-mentioned segmental types of primitive society, all higher forms are organismic. Differentiation and specialization, creations of functionally discrete rather than identical parts, have an enormously integrating effect because the various parts become interdependent. This differentiation exists at all higher levels —it is one thing that makes the United States today different from the United States of only a generation ago—but it first became important enough to have significant sociological effect with the advent of chiefdoms. Organismic solidarity, the interdependence of differing parts, cannot come about without some direction—a nerve center, so to speak—to coordinate the interaction, because otherwise interdependence is only symbiotic and weak. Chieftainship, and its direction of the activity of interdependent parts, is the form of integration of this new level.

The rise of centralized leadership involves a rise in the prestige of the person holding the office of chief. This prestige attaches to relatives of the chief, depending on genealogical nearness; and as time goes on, the status becomes hereditary. Thus, we find that not only unlike *parts* have arisen in the society but also unlike *persons*. This is to say that chiefdoms are typically nonegalitarian; they are characterized by differences in the hereditary rank, permanent higher and lower status of persons and their families, in addition to the universally human age-sex status differentiation.

The rise of the governing center, and of the specialized activity that makes chiefdoms out of tribes, appears to be closely related to redistribution as a mode of economic exchange. Exchange of goods in tribes and bands is typically reciprocal; gifts are given from person to person and group to group with the expectation of return gifts sooner or later. An important feature of this latter kind of exchange is its directness; there is no intermediary. In chiefdoms—

although reciprocity remains as a means of personal exchange—added to it is a kind of delayed, indirect movement of goods from producer to the redistributional center and later to the consumer.

One important aspect of such a system is labor specialization; producers were enabled to make or grow that product which their particular skill or terrain produces best. Specialization is encouraged in a chiefdom, and production can thus be enlarged. Another aspect is that people receive goods in proportion to their needs, depending on size of family, or because of a particular disaster, and so on. Thus contribution is not directly related to reward. (Such a system would approach the old socialist ideals: "From each according to his ability, to each according to his need.")

Centralized direction gives a society much greater military power than a tribe could have. The chiefdom promotes greater productivity with no change in technological methods; greater viability in withstanding famine, siege, and so on, by planned stockpiling of goods; and, obviously, greater size and density because of all these. These benefits provide the successful chief with some power, limited to be sure compared with that of a state government, but he tends to have a majority consensus in his favor simply because he successfully fulfills his duties; once functioning, chieftainship becomes a necessity to the society. A state, on the other hand, holds a monopoly of force and insists upon it, and it can manifest its power most strikingly. Yet a chiefdom controls people so much more successfully than a tribal body can be controlled that the word *anarchy* suggests itself as synonymous with band and tribal society, for they are forever threatened with feuds among the component groups.

Redistribution is not necessarily unfamiliar to most tribal and band societies. A coordinated game drive, for example, involves people who are assigned tasks under direction and requires that someone decide how to divide up the meat afterward. And a household itself typically has specialization (by age and sex), some direction of tasks by an adult, and distribution of food in proportion to need rather than in proportion to contribution. But a redistributional *society* does this with some consistency and with whole families or even districts themselves specialized. Redistribution is thus not a sudden invention that transforms society to the chiefdom level at a stroke. We cannot tell how chiefdoms arose in the first place, but it seems obvious that, considering the competitive advantages of centralization and specialization, those tribes who approached it most closely must have been selected for in contexts of competition.

Chiefdoms have never been demarked as a separate general class or level of society in other evolutionary schemes. L. H. Morgan and others in the nineteenth century and the modern evolutionists V. G. Childe and L. A. White have always thought of the major division in the evolution of culture as being between primitive culture and civilization—*societas* (kinship society) and *civitas* (civil or state society), in Morgan's terminology. Primitive societies, such as the tribes and bands described here, were thought to be essentially familial, egalitarian, classless, communalistic, and lacking in private property, entrepreneurs, markets, economic classes, and government. Civil society, on the other hand, was seen as the diametric opposite in each of these respects.

But if *societas* and *civitas* are the two major types of society, then where do the societies here called chiefdoms belong? Chiefdoms are familial, but not egalitarian; they have central direction and authority, but no true government; they have unequal control over goods and production, but no true private property, entrepreneurs, or markets; they have marked social stratification and ranks, but no true socioeconomic classes. Are they partly primitive and partly not? Are they in some sense transitional between *societas* and *civitas*?

Chiefdoms are so numerous and diffuse that it makes some sense to define them in their own terms, as a distinct level of society. They are not states. A primitive state may retain certain elements of the chiefdom stage—each successive stage normally incorporates elements of the previous stage—but a state has a new form of integration as an emergent feature, and it is definitive. A primitive state differs from a chiefdom most strikingly because it is integrated by a special mechanism involving a monopoly of force.

THE PRIMITIVE STATE LEVEL

States are characteristically distinguished from chiefdoms particularly, and from all the lower levels generally, by the constant threat of force from an institutionalized body of persons who wield it. A state constitutes itself *legally*: it makes explicit the manner and circumstances of its use of force, and it outlaws all other use of force as it intervenes in the disputes between individuals and groups.

States tend to become differentiated from chiefdoms in other ways as well. The most striking is the crosscutting of the society into political-economic classes. Chiefdoms have differences in individual rank, and sometimes the society is conceptually divided into two or three broad social ranks, like the Polynesian *Ari'i* (aristocrats) and *Manahune* (commoners), but these are merely social. This differentiation is fostered by sumptuary rules; certain items of dress and ornamentation and perhaps certain kinds of food are reserved for one stratum and tabooed to another. Sumptuary rules continue in primitive states, but the classes become an aspect of political and economic differentiation as well as social. Thus the aristocracy are the state bureaucrats, the military leaders, and the upper priesthood. Other people are the producers. Full-time professionalization in arts and crafts also develops, and the artisans can be regarded as still another socioeconomic group.

THE ARCHAIC CIVILIZATION OR IMPERIAL LEVEL

This level of archaic civilization is not included in the examples of whole societies in this book. Studies of particular small communities are all the ethnological field methods have been adapted to, so that only one aspect of the great civilization, the rural, or peasant, is represented. The words *civilization, civil, civilized, citizen, urbane,* and *urbanity* all suggest that it was from the cities, not from rural life, that civilization in the cultural sense arose. But it seems desirable to discuss briefly some of the characteristics of the civilizational level despite the absence of description of the urban aspect in this book.

The archaic or imperial civilizations seem to have originated in only a few places, China, India, and Mesopotamia.[3] And further, they may have influenced one another in some ways, so that conceivably there may have been a single origin. Later, others came about from their influence, as *secondary* or nonpristine civilizations— Egypt, Crete, Greece, and Rome are familiar examples in the Medi-

[3] Some anthropologists would add the Inca of Peru to these. But the Inca have been much exaggerated as a bureaucratic civilization, and the integration of their empire was so recent and fragile that it probably would have not have survived the civil war that was raging at the time of Pizarro's intervention.

terranean region. Although diverse in important respects, these had several common characteristics as preindustrial civilizations which may be cited as indicative.

The most usual distinction used to set off civilization from the more primitive stages of culture has been the presence of writing (and sometimes mathematical notation, which is closely allied to writing in its origin). V. Gordon Childe and others have emphasized the economic causes that were related to the growth of cities; and Karl Wittfogel has stressed in this respect the creation of autocratic bureaucracies as they were associated with the development of large-scale irrigation projects in the earliest empires.

To these should be added the possibility that the successful integration of an empire, a state which incorporates previously discrete cultural and/or ethnic and linguistic entities, presupposes a concomitant series of advances in jurisprudence, bureaucratic organization, military science, organized commerce, theocracy, communication, and so on. The problems of governance in empires were enormous because the societies were so much larger and more heterogeneous than the primitive states; thus, at first, they were solved successfully in only one or a few places. At any rate, such developments came about and spread widely, and some of the classical examples became huge and stable and have lasted nearly until modern times.

The important civilizational advances of the archaic empires were made in the urban centers. As time went on and the civilizations became more stabilized, the distinctions between the various ethnic components became modified and overridden by the increasing pervasiveness of the culture of the empire until the society became characterized more by rural and urban than by ethnic components. Two major classes of people were thus formed, and they tended eventually to form two subcultures, crosscutting to some extent the original ethnic or local cultural differences. One of these is the urban, or high, subculture (Redfield called it the *Great Tradition*) and the other is the peasant, or rural, subculture. The latter has lasted longer and is more visible to us today, for the great economic, political, and ideological changes of modern times necessarily have affected the cities first.

The primary original purpose of the book, to present a good sample of the kinds of societies known to ethnology, has conflicted with the present secondary aim, to give an example of the uses of evolutionary classification. In a sense this is not a flaw in logic, but a discrepancy in the ethnographic materials we own: primitive cultures are well represented, but archaic civilizations are not. Only certain peasant communities, which seem like primitive societies because they are small, have been made subjects of ethnological investigation, and these only recently.

The peasant (or "folk") villages of Part V are simply dependent parts of larger national states. It may be useful, of course, to extrapolate from them, as Bloch did among European villages for his reconstruction of feudal society, in order to think more clearly about structural characteristics of any small-scale, sedentary, subsistence-oriented society. This is simply a way of achieving greater ethnological sophistication, which is of course bound to be useful. But there is no true "peasant stage" in cultural evolution, nor, strictly speaking, is there a feudal stage.

Glossary

The use of technical terminology of professional anthropology has been held to a minimum in this book. Those few terms which were unavoidably used are defined here. Each one has also been explained and illustrated in the text on its first occurrence.

Acculturation. The process by which a culture is altered or new elements acquired during first hand continuing contact with another culture. The term is most often used to refer to the cultural changes in a dependent primitive society resulting from the influence of a highly developed and powerful civilization.

Affine. An affinal relative or *in-law*; one related through marriage.

Anthropomorphism. The ascription of manlike attributes to nonhuman phenomena. Most religions thus personify parts of nature such as Sun or Moon, or attribute wishes and desires and other human personality characteristics to animals and even to inanimate objects.

Avunculocal. See **Residence Rules.**

Couvade. A set of restrictions on the father's behavior during the period of gestation and birth of his child. At its most extreme, as among some South American tribes, the father actually has a long lying-in.

Cross Cousin. A child of a parent's sibling of the opposite sex; thus, one's maternal uncle's or paternal aunt's child. Maternal uncles and paternal aunts are sometimes also called cross uncles and aunts.

Diffusion. The spread of culture, or of particular culture traits and complexes, from one society to another. Unlike acculturation, diffusion does not require firsthand contact between the donor and recipient societies. A near synonym is *borrowing*. *Stimulus diffusion* refers to the spread of the idea of the trait, rather than the trait itself.

Endogamy. The restriction of marriage choice to members of the same locality (local endogamy) or group, class, or segment of the society.

Ethnocentrism. The view or attitude that the customs of one's own society are the superior, correct ones, and that, therefore, other customs are more and more inferior the further they deviate from them.

Exogamy. The restriction of marriage choice to persons who are not of the same locality (local exogamy), group, class, or segment of the society.

Folk Society. Originally, as used by Redfield, *folk society* was a polar, ideal construct having characteristics opposite to *urban society*. A folk society is small, isolated, homogeneous, and nonliterate, and behavior is highly conventionalized by coherent traditions which are prevailingly sacred rather than secular. In recent years, *folk* has been frequently used to characterize rural, backward, peasantlike villages which are subcultures of modern civilizations.

Levirate. The rule or custom that a widow marries a brother of her deceased husband. The junior levirate, which specifies that the remarriage be with a younger brother, is a frequent form. See also **Sororate.**

Local Group. In its broadest sense, local group could refer to any small social unit whose membership is definable in territorial terms. Usually, however, it refers to a small group of relatives in a hunting-gathering society who defend a common territory. In this case, *horde* and landholding *band* are synonyms.

Matrilineal. A line of descent, mode of inheritance or succession, or means of group affiliation which is traced exclusively through the mother.

Matrilocality. See **Residence Rules.**

Neolithic. The New Stone Age originally referred to the archeological periods in Europe characterized by ground and polished stone implements. It lay between the Paleolithic Age and the Metal Ages. Now more frequently used to refer to the period of early agriculture which grew out of the hunting-gathering stage.

Neolocality. See **Residence Rules.**

Parallel Cousin. A child of a parent's sibling of the same sex; thus, one's paternal uncle's or maternal aunt's child. Paternal uncles and maternal aunts may also be considered parallel relatives.

Patrilineal. A line of descent, mode of inheritance or succession, or means of group affiliation which is traced exclusively through the father.

Patrilocality. See **Residence Rules.**

Peasant Society. An agricultural community which produces crops largely for subsistence rather than for the market. Although existing as a rural subculture within a national society or state, peasant villages are typically nonliterate, tradition-oriented, and ingrown. See also **Folk Society.**

Relatives, Collateral. Relatives belonging to the same ancestral group, but not in a direct line of descent. Nephews, nieces, cousins, aunts and uncles are close collateral relatives.

Relatives, Lineal. Relatives in the direct line of descent, as parent to child.

Residence Rules, Avunculocal. A form of postnuptial residence whereby a couple lives with or near the husband's maternal uncle. This custom is often related to matrilineal inheritance of land.

Residence Rules, Matrilocal. A form of residence whereby a married couple live in the house, locality, or kinship group of the wife rather than of the husband. The children born of the union thus grow up among the mother's kindred. The term *uxorilocal* is sometimes used.

Residence Rules, Neolocal. A form of residence whereby a married couple live in a locality which is not significantly associated with or close to either the husband's or wife's kinship group. Postnuptial residence in the United States is characteristically, although not always, neolocal.

Residence Rules, Patrilocal. A form of residence whereby a married couple live in the house, locality, or kinship group of the husband. Their children thereby grow up among the father's kindred. The term *virilocal* is sometimes used.

Shaman. A medicine man, or curer, whose efficacy comes from his access to supernatural power. Usually the shaman is possessed by a spirit, but sometimes he ritually commands a spirit helper. The word *shaman* originally referred to Siberian medicine men, but is now a generic term.

Sororate. The rule or custom that a widower marries the sister of his deceased wife.

Teknonymy. The custom of calling a parent by the name of the child— *father (or mother) of John.*

Totemism. A mystical relationship between a human group and some class of natural phenomena, usually a plant or animal species. Frequently in primitive society, members of a particular lineage or clan consider themselves descendants of the totem and treat the totemic plants or animals ritually.

Index

Pentatonic scale, 352
Pérez, J., 226
Personal property, 372
Petramasa festival, 478
Pets, 255
Peyote eating, 135
Philippine Islands, 44
    See also Kalinga
Phoenicians, 414
Pictorial art, 331–332
Pipe smoking, 129
Pitcairn Island, 268
Pitchi, 7
Pituri, 8
Pizarro, F., 341, 360
Placenta, *see* Afterbirth
Plains Indians, horticulture, 114; language families and major tribal units, 115; social and political organization, 118
    See also Cheyenne
Planned economy, 335
Platypus, 3
Pleistocene era, 414
Pochamma, 479–480
Polar Eskimo, 66
Police squad, 398
Polo, Marco, 61
Polyandry, 221
Polygyny, 34, 105–106, 151, 175, 196, 221, 239, 300, 371, 379–380, 398, 428
Polynesia, 125, 207; geographic and climatic characteristics, 250–251
    See also Tahiti
Pomare, 268
Popol Vuh, 325
Postnuptial residence, 76, 78
Potlatches, 123, 215, 217, 218, 221, 227
Pottery, 339, 370
Pozole, 323
Prayer, 129, 267, 359, 378, 407, 430, 432, 479
Preservative techniques, 210–211
Prevention Detention Act, 384
Priesthood, 222
Primogeniture, 215, 231, 258, 278–279, 301, 354, 447
Progreso, 391, 392
Property concept, 277–278; Mediouna, 417–418; Navaho, 167, 168–169
Prophets, 147–148
    See also Shamans
Proto-Caucasoid race, 230
Puberty rituals and initiation, Andaman Islanders, 50–51, 54–55; Arunta, 20–22; Ashanti, 378; Chan Kom, 404;

Cheyenne, 127–128; Copper Eskimo, 77–78; Inca, 355, 359; Jivaro, 198; Maya, 324; Mediouna, 421, 426; Navaho, 173; Nootka, 219, 220; Shamirpet, 476; Tahiti, 265; Trobriand, 242; Tungus, 103; Yahgan, 37–38; Zulu, 306
Public opinion, force of, 49
Pueblo, 393, 410
Pueblo Bonito, 160
Puluga, 59
Pump drill, 255
Puna plateau, 337, 342
Punic Wars, 414
Punishment, *see* Crime and punishment
Purdah, 468
Puritans, 432
Pyjama, 467
Pyramids, 154, 317–318

Quern, 416, 419
Querquer, 197
Quinoa, 342
Quintana Roo, 319, 408
Quipu keeper, 350–351

Ra'atira, 259
Radcliffe-Brown, A. R., 15, 16, 45, 46
Rain makers, 155, 309
Rama, 480
Ramada, 166
Ramadan, 430–431, 432
Rape, 376
Rasmussen, K., 68
Rattles, 175
Rebozo, 395, 422
Redfield, R., 389–390, 396, 409, 412
Redistribution of goods, Inca, 346–347; Nootka, 217; Tahiti, 260; Trobriand, 232
Reducciones, 362
Reincarnation, 53–54, 199, 407, 481
Reindeer, 95–96
Reindeer-herding peoples, 92–93
    See also Tungus
Religion and cosmology, Andaman Islanders, 59; Arunta, 17–18; Ashanti, 381–382; Chan Kom, 402, 406–409; Cheyenne, 130–132, 134–135; Copper Eskimo, 80–81; Inca, 358–360; Jivaro, 199–201; Kaihsienkung, 456–457; Kalinga, 286–287; Maya, 325–326; Mediouna, 428–433; Navaho, 177–180; Nootka, 222–223; Nuer, 154, 157; Shamirpet, 479–482; Tahiti, 261–262, 264, 266–267; Trobriand, 247–248;

Religion and Cosmology (*Continued*)
Tungus, 108, 110; Yahgan, 39; Zulu, 308–310
Reservation system, Cheyenne, 133, 134; Navaho, 162–163
Revivalism, 134
Rinderpest, 156, 289
Rites of passage, 54
Ro'o, 266
Rome, 414
Royal Hunt, 301
Russia, and Tungus, 109–110
See also Cold war

Sacred fast (Islam), 430
Sacrifice, 149, 262, 325, 381, 423, 432, 455, 456, 479, 480
See also Human sacrifice
Sakali, 471
Sale, 471
Sand Hills, Battle of, 133
Sand paintings (Navaho), 176
Santa Fe Trail, 132
Santo, 408
Sapper, K., 332
Sari, 468
Scalps, 123
Scarification, 54
Schorger, W. D., 416
Sculpture (Maya), 322
Seal, 29, 68
Sedna myth, 81
Segal, Ronald, 313–314
Self-torture, 128
Seven Sacraments, 402
Sex, 22, 36; activity, 176, 242; customs, 53; education, 403–404; experimentation, 265; intercourse and pregnancy, 237, 240–241; license, 264
Sha hi' ye na, 116
Shaka, 293, 294, 295, 296, 299, 304, 306, 311
Shamans, 23–24, 39, 58, 75, 79–80, 106–108, 110, 129–130, 148, 154–155, 175–178, 198, 200–201, 218–219, 222–225, 286, 309, 324, 356–357, 394, 396, 407; dance, 218
See also Magic; Medicine men; Sorcery; Witchcraft
Shamirpet, birth, 475; caste system, 466–467, 470–472, 473–474, 484; ceremonies and rituals, 475, 476, 477, 478, 479; clothing and body decoration, 467–468; crime, 482; education, 474; food, 469–470; geographic and climatic characteristics, 467; illness

and death, 477–478, 484; labor, 470–471, 474; land ownership, 474; livestock and crops, 469; marriage, 476–477; nuclear family unit, 474; political organization, 472–473; present-day status, 482–485; puberty rituals and initiation, 476; religion and cosmology, 479–482; shelter, 468–469
Sheikh, 417
Shelter, Andaman Islanders, 47–48; Arunta, 10; Ashanti, 369; Chan Kom, 394; Copper Eskimo, 71–72; Inca, 353; Jivaro, 192; Kaihsienkung, 444; Kalinga, 275; Maya, 322–323; Mediouna, 422–423; Navaho, 166–167; Nootka, 212; Shamirpet, 468–469; Tahiti, 256; Trobriand, 232; Tungus, 98; Yahgan, 28, 33
Shereef, 432–433
Shilluk-speaking tribes, 140, 155, 156
Shiva, 480
Siberia, 65, 92
See also Tungus
Sickening Winds, 405
Sign language, 116
Sila, 81
Silk production, 440, 442, 459
Silver work (Navaho), 163–164
Singing duel, 82
Sinkiang, 437
Sit-down, 280
Sitting Bull, 134
Sky God, 154
Slaves, 215, 230, 373, 383
Sled dogs, 70
Social classes, 215
Socialism, 346
Society Islands, 253
Solar time, 327–328
Song and dance, 104–105, 180
See also Music and dance
Sorcery, 357, 376
See also Magic; Medicine men; Shamans; Supernatural; Witchcraft
Soroche (Mountain Sickness), 337
Sororate, 53, 78, 103, 126, 221, 227, 308, 356
Soul, concept of (Nootka), 222
Southern Tungus, *see* Tungus
Soyot, 93
Spain, 321
Spanish Colonial rule, *see* Inca
Spanish Morocco, 413
Spencer, Sir Baldwin, 5, 6–7, 25
Stealing, 35
Stefansson, V., 63, 73, 74, 84